*Prepared by* The Committee
on College Reading

J. SHERWOOD WEBER, *Editor*

Anna Rothe, Ruth Ulman, Arthur Waldhorn,
Olga Svatik Weber, Arthur Zeiger,
*Assistant Editors*

# Good Reading

A HELPFUL GUIDE FOR SERIOUS READERS

A MENTOR BOOK PUBLISHED BY
THE NEW AMERICAN LIBRARY

*Sponsored by*
College English Association

*Endorsed by*
Adult Education Association of the U.S.A.
American Library Association
National Council of Teachers of English

COPYRIGHT, 1935, 1937, 1938, 1941, 1946, 1947, 1948,
1951, 1952, 1954, BY THE COMMITTEE ON COLLEGE READING

© 1956, 1960, 1964 BY THE COMMITTEE ON COLLEGE READING

FIRST PRINTING, NOVEMBER, 1947
SECOND PRINTING, FEBRUARY, 1948
THIRD PRINTING (REVISED), SEPTEMBER, 1948
FOURTH PRINTING, SEPTEMBER, 1949
FIFTH PRINTING (REVISED), MAY, 1951
SIXTH PRINTING (REVISED), AUGUST, 1952
SEVENTH PRINTING, DECEMBER, 1952
EIGHTH PRINTING, JULY, 1953
NINTH PRINTING, NOVEMBER, 1954
TENTH PRINTING, APRIL, 1955
ELEVENTH PRINTING (REVISED), AUGUST, 1956
TWELFTH PRINTING, JANUARY, 1957
THIRTEENTH PRINTING, NOVEMBER, 1958
FOURTEENTH PRINTING, OCTOBER, 1959
FIFTEENTH PRINTING (REVISED), FEBRUARY, 1960
SIXTEENTH PRINTING, SEPTEMBER, 1960
SEVENTEENTH PRINTING, SEPTEMBER, 1961
EIGHTEENTH PRINTING, MAY, 1962
NINETEENTH PRINTING (REVISED), FEBRUARY, 1964

Library of Congress Catalog Card No. 33-10540

MENTOR TRADEMARK REG. U.S. PAT. OFF. AND FOREIGN COUNTRIES
REGISTERED TRADEMARK—MARCA REGISTRADA
HECHO EN CHICAGO, U.S.A.

*MENTOR BOOKS are published by*
*The New American Library of World Literature, Inc.*
*501 Madison Avenue, New York 10022, New York*

PRINTED IN THE UNITED STATES OF AMERICA

# The 19th Edition of *Good Reading*

For sheer entertainment, for general cultural enrichment, for learning what has happened or what is going on in the world, nothing surpasses the reading of good books. GOOD READING is dedicated to helping serious readers find their way through the huge maze of published volumes, both hardcover and paperbound. A handy, practical, inexpensive guide, it has demonstrated its value to several million readers since 1932. It is now offered in its 19th edition—reorganized, expanded, completely up to date.

GOOD READING contains descriptive book lists of about 2000 titles arranged in 28 conventional subject areas; besides author and title, each entry lists editions and prices, and describes succinctly the thesis or plot, special appeal, and level of difficulty of each book. Teachers, scholars, librarians, editors, have selected the most important and readable books from major regional and historical cultures, from all literary types, and from the humanities, social sciences, and sciences. Each chapter is introduced by an authority. And there are special features on how to use GOOD READING, on planning a total reading program, on reference books, on magazines, and on recordings of poetry and drama.

From its first edition in 1932, GOOD READING has been edited by the Committee on College Reading, which includes three dozen subject specialists working under the general editorship of J. Sherwood Weber of Pratt Institute. Through 18 previous editions GOOD READING has amply proved its worth as a helpful companion to the general reader, as a guide to supplementary reading for a large variety of college and high school courses, and as a reference book in libraries.

*Philip J. Polley*

## Endorsed by
## Leading Educational Organizations

Those of us who have long depended on GOOD READING to lead us to some of the great writing of all time will rejoice that a new edition has appeared. This valuable guide to worthwhile reading should be in every personal and public library.

> JAMES R. SQUIRE, *Executive Secretary*
> National Council of Teachers of English

GOOD READING makes a valuable contribution to the field of adult education by its excellent guidance to books in special fields of adult interests.

> GLENN S. JENSEN, *Executive Director*
> Adult Education Association of the U.S.A.

GOOD READING is a liberating force in the world, guiding readers and students with careful discrimination into a liberal self-education and to pleasures through good books. Each new edition more effectively fulfills its humane mission.

> DONALD A. SEARS, *Executive Secretary*
> College English Association

Good book lists make good reading themselves. GOOD READING will be of interest to all librarians and most helpful to them in encouraging reading. It should prove a substantial aid on college campuses and in the adult community as well.

> DAVID H. CLIFT, *Executive Director*
> American Library Association

# THE COMMITTEE ON COLLEGE READING

J. SHERWOOD WEBER, *Pratt Institute*
*Editor and Executive Secretary*

ATWOOD H. TOWNSEND, *New York University*
*Chairman and Editor Emeritus*

(Section or general editors for the 19th edition)

JOSEPH A. BYRNES,
City College of New York

JAMES T. CROWN,
New York University

DONALD DEMAREST,
Academy Library Guild

LOYD D. EASTON,
Ohio Wesleyan University

H. WENTWORTH ELDREDGE,
Dartmouth College

DANIEL GERZOG,
Pratt Institute

CHARLES B. GOODRICH,
University of Indiana

WILLIAM C. GREENE,
Massachusetts Institute of Technology

JOHN E. HANKINS,
University of Maine

EDWARD S. LE COMTE,
Columbia University

RICHARD LESTER,
Princeton University

HARRY T. MOORE,
Southern Illinois University

WAINO S. NYLAND,
University of Colorado

PAUL OBLER,
Orange State College

LESLIE M. OLIVER,
Lesley College

J. GREGORY OSWALD,
University of Arizona

WILLIAM PEDEN,
University of Missouri

ROBERT C. POOLEY,
University of Wisconsin

NORMAN T. PRATT, JR.
Indiana University

ANNA ROTHE,
Good Counsel College Library

DONALD A. SEARS,
Skidmore College, College English Assn.

PAUL SHEPARD,
Knox College

NORMAN C. STAGEBERG,
Iowa State College

NATHAN M. TALBOTT,
Iowa State College

TRUMAN M. TALLEY,
The New American Library

PALMER W. TOWNSEND,
Air Reduction Company

RUTH ULMAN,
H. W. Wilson Company

AUSTIN L. VENABLE,
University of Alabama

ARTHUR WALDHORN,
*City College of New York*

BERNERD WEBER,
*University of Alabama*

OLGA SVATIK WEBER,
*R. R. Bowker Company*

JULES ALAN WEIN,
*Pratt Institute*

ROBERT CLARKE WHITE,
*Castleton State College*

ARTHUR ZEIGER,
*City College of New York*

LOUIS C. ZUCKER,
*University of Utah*

## ADVISORY BOARD

CARL CARMER
STUART CLOETE
NORMAN CORWIN
THOMAS CRAVEN
ALDOUS HUXLEY

WILLY LEY
LIN YUTANG
CARL SANDBURG
CORNELIA OTIS SKINNER
JESSE STUART

# CONTENTS

| | |
|---|---:|
| TO THE READER: *J. Sherwood Weber* | 9 |
| ON READING: *Atwood H. Townsend* | 15 |
| 100 SIGNIFICANT BOOKS: *Committee on College Reading* | 19 |

## THE *GOOD READING* BOOK LISTS

| | |
|---|---:|
| KEY TO PAPERBOUND AND OTHER INEXPENSIVE EDITIONS | 21 |

### REGIONAL AND HISTORICAL CULTURES

| | |
|---|---:|
| 1. Greece: *John E. Hankins* | 29 |
| 2. Rome: *Norman T. Pratt, Jr.* | 37 |
| 3. India and the Far East: *Nathan M. Talbott* | 43 |
| 4. The Middle East and Africa: *J. Gregory Oswald* | 51 |
| 5. Latin America: *Donald Demarest* | 57 |
| 6. The Middle Ages: *Jules Alan Wein* | 63 |
| 7. The Renaissance: | |
|    On the Continent: *Louis C. Zucker* | 71 |
|    In Tudor England: *Leslie M. Oliver* | 77 |
| 8. The 17th Century: *Joseph A. Byrnes* | 83 |
| 9. The 18th Century: *William C. Greene* | 91 |

### LITERARY TYPES

| | |
|---|---:|
| 10. The Novel | |
|   A. 19th Century Continental: *Arthur Waldhorn* | 101 |
|   B. 20th Century Continental: *Robert Clarke White* | 108 |
|   C. 19th Century British: *Edward S. Le Comte* | 116 |
|   D. 20th Century British: *Arthur Zeiger* | 122 |
|   E. 19th Century American: *Daniel Gerzog* | 131 |
|   F. 20th Century American: *Harry T. Moore* | 138 |

| | | |
|---|---|---|
| 11. | The Short Story: *William Peden* | 148 |
| 12. | Poetry (including Poetry on Records): *Robert C. Pooley* | 154 |
| 13. | Drama (including Drama on Records): *J. Sherwood Weber* | 163 |
| 14. | Biography: *Waino S. Nyland* | 171 |
| 15. | Essays, Letters, and Criticism (including Magazines): *Charles B. Goodrich* | 177 |

### HUMANITIES, SOCIAL SCIENCES, SCIENCES

| | | |
|---|---|---|
| 16. | Fine Arts: *Atwood H. Townsend* | 191 |
| 17. | Philosophy: *Loyd D. Easton* | 203 |
| 18. | Religion: *Anna Rothe* | 211 |
| 19. | History: *Austen Venable* and *Bernerd Weber* | 216 |
| 20. | Politics: *James T. Crown* | 227 |
| 21. | Economics: *Richard A. Lester* | 234 |
| 22. | Geography: *Truman M. Talley* | 239 |
| 23. | Anthropology and Sociology: *H. Wentworth Eldredge* | 243 |
| 24. | Language: *Norman C. Stageberg* | 251 |
| 25. | Psychology: *Paul Obler* | 256 |
| 26. | Biological Sciences: *Paul Shepard* | 263 |
| 27. | Physical Sciences and Mathematics (with a supplementary list of Science Fiction): *Palmer W. Townsend* | 269 |

### SPECIAL SECTION

| | | |
|---|---|---|
| 28. | Reference Books: *Donald A. Sears* | 277 |
| | AUTHOR, TITLE, AND SUBJECT INDEX TO THE GOOD READING BOOK LISTS | 287 |

# To the Reader

## J. SHERWOOD WEBER

For more than three decades, GOOD READING has helped direct high school and college students—as well as adults pursuing their own courses of reading—to the books they ought to know. GOOD READING, of which more than a million and a half copies have been sold, began in 1932 with the organization, during the course of a conference of English teachers, of the Committee on College Reading under the chairmanship of Atwood H. Townsend, who served as editor of the successive editions until 1954. The prime objective was the pooling of resources to produce a guide to supplementary reading that could be used in colleges generally with convenience and profit. The first issues—quite modest pamphlets—were subsidized by the then-leading publishers of inexpensive series. Later editions, constantly expanded and broadened in scope, were distributed through the National Council of Teachers of English.

Since 1947—when it became a Mentor Book published by The New American Library—GOOD READING has been thoroughly revised and considerably expanded approximately every four years. Today it ambitiously endeavors to encompass most fields of knowledge to which the student and adult reader need guidance. This edition, the 19th, makes its predecessors obsolete in a variety of ways. Many of its chapters have new introductions; its annotated lists have been expanded; its data about editions is up to date; and two wholly new chapters appear ("India and the Far East" and "The Middle East and Africa"). But the editorial goal remains constant: to provide the general reader with a tactful and acute companion for his personal reading; the student with an experienced guide for his courses; the teacher with a knowing aide for preparing his reading lists and in advising students; and the librarian with an experienced consultant for shaping both general and reference collections.

## To the General Reader and Student

One excellent way to start using GOOD READING is to check through the whole list, or those sections of it that interest you, putting an "X" before the books you have already read and a "√" before those you want to read. By continually changing your "√'s" to "X's" you can keep a record of the progress of your own intellectual growth.

If you are seriously determined, you will set a standard for yourself and stick to it. A fair minimum is to read one book a week, but anyone who is really well read averages significantly more than this. No matter how busy you may think you are, you must find time for reading now, or surrender yourself to self-chosen ignorance.

Random reading is usually not as useful as organized reading. An easy way to plan the growth of your knowledge is to follow for a month or two an interesting trail that you happen to start on: perhaps European fiction, or Greek tragedy, or anthropology. If you like one novel by Balzac or Dostoevski or Steinbeck, or one play by Shakespeare or O'Neill, almost certainly you will want to read others by the same author.

But do not specialize too much. From time to time check the scope of your reading by turning the pages of GOOD READING to see where your large gaps appear. If you find that you know very little about painting, or Africa, or economics, you will know what to do.

Always read with a purpose, or rather a succession of purposes; follow a broad and flexible program, without binding yourself too rigidly to any scheme or system. Also take a chance once in a while: try a book you happen to see on a library shelf or that someone casually recommended. Give yourself the opportunity for intellectual lightning to spark your soul.

For those more systematically inclined, familiarity with the organizational pattern of GOOD READING will prove valuable. GOOD READING is a selective, annotated bibliog-

## TO THE READER

raphy ranging across the varieties of literature—"the literature of knowledge" as well as "the literature of power." Its 34 separate book lists (contained in 28 chapters) have been grouped into three parts: the first part has 10 sections, divided according to regional and historical significance; the second part has 11 sections, arranged by standard literary types; and the third part has 12 sections, devoted to the humanities, social sciences, and sciences; a special chapter at the end lists basic reference books essential for informed readers.

*The complete entry for any title, with rare exceptions, appears in the earliest chapter to which it logically belongs.* Although the title may reappear in subsequent chapters where relevant, it will only cross-refer to the original, fully detailed entry. For example, the complete entry for Plato's *Republic* appears in the section on "Greece." When Plato's *Republic* reappears in the chapters "Philosophy" and "Politics," it does so as follows: "PLATO *Republic.* See 'Greece,' page 34."

The brief essays that head each section outline the subject either historically, descriptively, or analytically. In addition, they often suggest authors or books the beginning student will find especially helpful.

The annotated book lists form the hard core of GOOD READING. Each book entry observes, with minor variations, the same general format: author, title, brief comment, editions in print. The reader ought to be aware of the conventions employed by the editors:

AUTHOR — Authors' names appear first (editors are noted as *ed.,* translators as *trans.*), except with some anthologies where title listing seems more appropriate. When known, authors' dates follow.

TITLE — Titles appear in English, not in the original language when the book is a translation. The date of original publication, when known, follows the title in parentheses. With revised editions of nonfiction, only the latest is cited. When a writer's short works (poems, essays, short stories, plays) exist in a variety of collections variously titled, no specific titles or publication dates are supplied. Multiple titles by the same author are ordered chronologically.

EDITIONS—Hardcover editions (except when in inexpensive series) are noted before paperbound, and the notations include publisher (in standard abbreviated form) and trade price (as of September 1963). Paperbound editions and inexpensive hardcover series bear the abbreviations explained on pages 21 to 26, where publishers' addresses and price ranges have also been supplied.

Among paperbound titles, we have generally listed only those most readily available in large bookstores. If not immediately in stock, these titles can be obtained by direct mail from the publishers.

Complete, up-to-date listings of all paperbound editions in print may be checked in *Paperbound Books in Print,* issued cumulatively three times a year and available for consultation at most bookstores or libraries.

The annotations have been carefully prepared to assist readers to determine, without excessive pain, the potential interest and value of each book listed. Each annotation succinctly indicates the general subject of the book, locates its thesis or capsules its plot, and distinguishes its special merit. When necessary, comments have been made about the level of difficulty and about the best available translations.

One further gloss on the organization of the book lists is relevant. In the first part, the lists have been divided into two groups, the first indicating *primary* sources (books written *during* a given period), the second indicating *secondary* sources (books written *about* the period). In parts two and three there are again generally subdivisions, but these arise as the need demands; the titles of the subdivisional headings will always clarify the reason for the breakdown. In each of the parts, whenever a subdivision occurs, entries continue to appear alphabetically by author or editor or, rarely, by title.

After you browse through GOOD READING for an hour, you will become adept at finding what you want. If, on occasion, you are seeking a book by a specific author or with a known title or on a general subject not explicit in the chapter headings, turn immediately to the "Author, Title, and Subject Index" at the back of the book.

## To the Teacher, Librarian, and Administrator

The uses which GOOD READING has found in schools, colleges, and libraries are legion. Teachers have been using its book lists for a variety of courses ever since 1932. It is particularly useful in comprehensive surveys variously labeled Humanities, General Studies, Western Civilization, Contemporary Civilization, Impact of Science, etc. Many teachers, finding that the selective lists in GOOD READING solve their problems of suggested outside reading, make the book a required reference text for their courses. Others have found this book invaluable in guiding students in their summer reading or in honors courses.

To make students aware of the primary use of GOOD READING, various devices have been employed. At some colleges, the introductory tour of the library concludes with a presentation to each student of a copy of GOOD READING. At others, it serves as the formal basis for the summer reading program. Many teachers informally recommend it when advising students on their self-directed postgraduate reading. Some teachers of Freshman English require students to check their reading background against one or more chapters of GOOD READING and then to write themes analyzing their own inadequacies and proposing a reading program to fill in the gaps.

Librarians have also found GOOD READING variously useful. Some keep a copy at the circulation desk, some next to the card catalog where it can be consulted by readers looking for the most useful books on a given topic, some in the general or special reference rooms, some in browsing rooms. Several large university libraries purchased a dozen or more copies of the 1960 edition for various locations. Finally, the book often serves as a key to book purchases for small high school, college, and public libraries.

* * *

Despite the occasional complexity of the explications above, GOOD READING is easy to use—and adaptable for numerous uses. The editors hope that it leads an increasing number of people to savor the great or significant books, both those that strive to light the dark places in man's understanding of his complex world and equally complex self, and those that intend simply to delight.

# On Reading

## ATWOOD H. TOWNSEND

Reading provides an endless opportunity, an ever-open door to ever-greater mental growth. All the wisdom our world has accumulated is to be found in books. No one could possibly read all the good books that have been written (even in one specialized subject), but the more of them you read, the richer you will be in true and useful wisdom.

If you determine to set out on the road toward continuous cultural enrichment, you will do well to fix a goal for yourself, and stick to it regardless of obstacles and distractions. A reasonable minimum would be one solid book a week, though people who are genuinely well read and informed average considerably more than this. If your determination is firm and enduring, you will find yourself embarked upon a lifetime program for unlimited self-education sure to yield lasting satisfactions.

Your choice of books to read will naturally vary with your changing needs and interests; yet it is well to have some sort of plan. Random reading is seldom as profitable as a purposeful program, though not too rigid a one. An easy, informal way to schedule the cultivation of your intellect is to follow for a month or more any subject that happens to appeal to you—perhaps politics, or archaeology, or Russian fiction.

Never force yourself to read a book that you do not enjoy. There are so many good books in the world that it is foolish to waste time on one that does not give you pleasure and profit. If you have chosen a book in good faith and have found it dull after an honest try, put it back on the shelf and devote your time instead to reading something else that will pay you richer immediate dividends.

However, if you find yourself bored by a book that many well-informed people regard as important and readable, be fair with yourself and confess that perhaps the shortcoming is not in the book but in you. Often a book which now seems dull or difficult will prove easy to grasp and fascinating to read when you are more mature intellectually. Sometimes young people, or those who read little, are puzzled or bored by certain great books because they lack the background and the maturity of mind necessary to meet the author of the book on his intellectual level. But this difficulty will correct itself, provided you go on reading and growing mentally.

Of course, not all the material worth reading is in books. Things move so swiftly these days that a consistent reading of a good newspaper such as *The New York Times* or a news magazine such as *Time* or *Newsweek* is essential. Concentrate on the important national and international news stories, the editorial columns, and letters from readers—not on crime, sports, and comics.

Most American magazines of large circulation are concerned primarily with entertaining their readers and so present few stories or articles of much value. Significant timely articles are found in such general literary monthlies as *Harper's Magazine* and *The Atlantic,* in such journals of opinion as *The Commonweal* and *The Reporter,* and in such organs of special interest as *Business Week, School and Society,* and *Scientific American.* Other good periodicals are listed on pages 187 to 188 of this book. To read only mass-circulation picture magazines and digests means that you have not grown mentally beyond the level of a high school sophomore.

Anyone who hopes to keep up with intellectual progress needs to read regularly a magazine of book reviews, such as the *Saturday Review* or the Sunday book section of *The New York Times.* By reading book reviews with some regularity you will discover what new books you want to read and you will have at least some idea about all important new publications, whether or not you have time to read them yourself.

A complete reading program, therefore, should include four factors: at least one good book each week, a newspaper or news magazine, magazines of comment and interpretation, and book reviews. If you keep feeding your intelligence with these four foods, you can be sure your brain cells will not be undernourished. To this must be added the digestive process that comes from your own thinking and from discussion with other informed, thoughtful people.

Try to do your reading in an attitude of easy relaxation combined with alert concentration. Too intent seriousness often undermines the pleasure of reading and leads to weariness. Too relaxed an attitude will permit things to slide past without registering. The ideal is to read easily, swiftly, skipping past greatly detailed passages but with attention alert to note and retain important points.

An important discovery of recent years is that, up to a point, the faster you read the better you remember, because your attention is concentrating on key ideas and not getting bogged down by details. If you know you are a slow reader, try pushing yourself to read faster by searching for key phrases and forcing yourself to skim past minor matters. Sometimes, however, it is well to go back and reread a passage, either because you did not quite grasp it, or because it said something so well that you want to enjoy it again and impress it on your memory.

It is often desirable to make books that you own part of your mind by underlining or by marking in the margin the more important statements or by writing down your thoughts. This will help you to understand the book as you first read it, because out of the mass of details you will have selected the essential ideas. It will help you to remember better the gist of the book, for the physical act of underlining, with your eyes on the page, tends to plant the thought firmly into your brain cells. And it will save time whenever you need to refer to the book.

Above all, never forget that creative intelligence is correlation of facts and ideas, not mere memorizing. What counts is what you can do with your new knowledge by linking it with other things you have read or experienced. If you read Plutarch's life of Julius Caesar, think how his rise to power paralleled the techniques of Hitler or Stalin or of your local political boss. If you read a play by Shakespeare or O'Neill or Edward Albee, think how the portrayal of one of the characters helps you to understand better someone you know. In everything you read, keep in the back of your mind what it means to your life here and now, how it reaffirms or challenges the things you were taught at home, in school, and in church, and how the wisdom you get from books can guide you in your thinking, in your career, in your duties as a citizen, and in your personal standards.

To sum up, what you read is both the measure of your intellectual level and the means of raising it to the utmost of your capacity.

# 100 Significant Books

This list is intended to present, not necessarily the best or greatest works of literature and thought, but simply a representative selection of books that many people have found rewarding to know. Originally prepared for the 1934 edition of GOOD READING, this list has been revised several times before this by the Committee on College Reading in consultation with the distinguished authors comprising the Advisory Board.

### Ancient Times

Aeschylus—*The Oresteia*
Aesop—*Fables*
Aristophanes—*Comedies*
Aristotle—*Nicomachean Ethics* and *Politics*
The Bible
Confucius—*The Analects*
Euripides—*Plays*
Herodotus—*History*
Homer—*Iliad* and *Odyssey*
Lao-Tsu—*The Way of Life*
Lucretius—*On the Nature of Things*
Marcus Aurelius—*Meditations*
Plato—*Republic* and *Symposium*
Plutarch—*Lives*
Sophocles—*Theban Plays*
Thucydides—*The Peloponnesian Wars*
Vergil—*Aeneid*

### Middle Ages and Renaissance

*The Arabian Nights*
Bacon—*Essays*
Boccaccio—*Decameron*
Cellini—*Autobiography*
Cervantes—*Don Quixote*
Chaucer—*Canterbury Tales*
Dante—*The Divine Comedy*
Machiavelli—*The Prince*
Malory—*Le Morte d'Arthur*
Mohammed—*Koran*
Montaigne—*Essays*
More—*Utopia*
Omar Khayyám—*The Rubáiyát*
Rabelais—*Gargantua and Pantagruel*
Shakespeare—*Tragedies, Comedies, and Histories*

## 17th and 18th Centuries

Boswell—*The Life of Samuel Johnson*
Bunyan—*Pilgrim's Progress*
Burns—*Poems*
Defoe—*Robinson Crusoe*
Descartes—*A Discourse on Method*
Donne—*Poems*
Fielding—*Tom Jones*
Franklin—*Autobiography*
Gibbon—*The Decline and Fall of the Roman Empire*
Hamilton et al.—*The Federalist*
Locke—*Essay Concerning Human Understanding*
Malthus—*Principles of Population*
Milton—*Paradise Lost*
Molière—*Comedies*
Paine—*The Rights of Man*
Pepys—*Diary*
Rousseau—*The Social Contract*
Smith—*The Wealth of Nations*
Sterne—*Tristram Shandy*
Swift—*Gulliver's Travels*
Voltaire—*Candide*

## 19th Century

Austen—*Pride and Prejudice*
Balzac—*Eugénie Grandet*
Browning (Robert)—*Poems*
Butler—*The Way of All Flesh*
Byron—*Poems*
Chekhov—*Plays*
Darwin—*The Origin of Species*
Dickens—*Great Expectations*
Dostoevski—*The Brothers Karamazov*
Emerson—*Essays*
Flaubert—*Madame Bovary*
Goethe—*Faust*
Hardy—*Tess of the D'Urbervilles*
Hawthorne—*The Scarlet Letter*
Hugo—*Les Misérables*
Ibsen—*Dramas*
Keats—*Poems*
Marx—*Capital*
Maupassant—*Short Stories*
Melville—*Moby Dick*
Poe—*Short Stories*
Shelley—*Poems*
Stendhal—*The Red and the Black*
Thackeray—*Vanity Fair*
Thoreau—*Walden*
Tolstoi—*War and Peace*
Twain—*Huckleberry Finn*
Whitman—*Leaves of Grass*

## 20th Century

Eliot—*Poems and Plays*
Faulkner—*The Sound and the Fury*
Frazer—*The Golden Bough*
Freud—*Introduction to Psychoanalysis*
Frost—*Poems*
Hemingway—*The Sun Also Rises*
Huxley—*Brave New World*
Joyce—*Ulysses*
Lawrence—*Sons and Lovers*
Lewis—*Arrowsmith*
Mann—*The Magic Mountain*
O'Neill—*Plays*
Sandburg—*Lincoln*
Shaw—*Plays*
Steinbeck—*The Grapes of Wrath*
Veblen—*The Theory of the Leisure Class*

# THE GOOD READING BOOK LISTS

## Key to Paperbound and Other Inexpensive Editions

The GOOD READING Book Lists use the following abbreviations to indicate titles available in paperbound editions and in the leading hardcover reprint series. Since prices of paperbounds increase frequently, we cite only the minimum price of a publisher's offerings; the exact price for any title can be checked in the most recent *Paperbound Books in Print*.

All normal trade edition book prices are indicated after the abbreviated publisher's name in the appropriate book list entries. If a book is published in both trade and text editions, only the trade price is cited. Some few titles marked "o.p." (out of print) are included because they are widely available in libraries and may soon be back in print.

| | |
|---|---|
| *AA* | *Ann Arbor Paperbacks:* University of Michigan Press, 615 East University, Ann Arbor, Mich. $1.35 up. |
| *AAS* | *Ann Arbor Science Paperbacks:* See above. $1.95 ea. |
| *Ace* | *Ace Books:* Ace Books, 1120 Ave. of the Americas, New York 36, N. Y. 35¢ up. |
| *AE* | *Apollo Editions:* Apollo Editions, Inc., 425 Park Ave. S., New York 16, N. Y. $1.25 up. |
| *AmCen* | *American Century Series:* Hill & Wang, Inc., 141 Fifth Ave., New York 10, N. Y. 50¢ up. |
| *Anch* | *Anchor Books:* Doubleday & Co., Inc., 575 Madison Ave., New York 22, N. Y. 95¢ up. |
| *Anv* | *Anvil Books:* D. Van Nostrand Co., Inc., 120 Alexander St., Princeton, N. J. $1.25 ea. |
| *Apex* | *Apex Books:* Abingdon Press, 201 8th Ave. S., Nashville 3, Tenn. 69¢ up. |
| *Appl* | Appleton-Century-Crofts, 34 W. 33rd St., New York 1, N. Y. 45¢ up. |
| *AS* | All Saints Press, 630 Fifth Ave., New York 20, N. Y. 50¢ up. |
| *Athen* | Atheneum Publishers, 162 E. 38th St., New York 16, N. Y. 95¢ up. |
| *Avon* | *Avon Books:* The Hearst Corp., 572 Madison Ave., New York 22, N. Y. 35¢ up. |
| *B&N* | Barnes & Noble, Inc., 105 Fifth Ave., New York 3, N. Y. 50¢ up. |
| *Bal* | *Ballantine Books:* Ballantine Books, Inc., 101 Fifth Ave., New York 3, N. Y. 35¢ up. |

| | |
|---|---|
| Ban | *Bantam Books:* Bantam Books, Inc., 271 Madison Ave., New York 16, N. Y. 35¢ up. |
| BC | *Black Cat Series:* Grove Press, Inc., 64 University Pl., New York 3, N. Y. 50¢ up. |
| Bea | *Beacon Press Paperbacks:* Beacon Press, 25 Beacon St., Boston 8, Mass. 95¢ up. |
| Berk | *Berkley Books:* Berkley Publishing Corp., 15 E. 26th St., New York 10, N. Y. 35¢ up. |
| BES | Barron's Educational Series, Inc., 343 Great Neck Rd., Great Neck, N. Y. 50¢ up. |
| BH | Bruce Humphries, 50 Melrose St., Boston 16, Mass. |
| Bison | *Bison Books:* University of Nebraska Press, Lincoln 8, Neb. $1.45 up. |
| Black | *Black and Gold Library:* Liveright Publishing Corp., 386 Park Ave. S., New York 16, N. Y. $3.95 up. |
| Bobbs | The Bobbs-Merrill Co., Inc., 4300 W. 62nd St., Indianapolis 6, Ind. $1.25 up. |
| Calif | University of California Press, Berkeley 4, Calif. $1.25 up. |
| Cap | *Capricorn Books:* G. P. Putnam's Sons, 210 Madison Ave., New York 16, N. Y. 95¢ up. |
| CCG | *College Course Guides:* Doubleday & Co., Inc., 575 Madison Ave., New York 22, N. Y. $1.45 up. |
| CGT | *Complete Greek Tragedies:* University of Chicago Press, 5750 Ellis Ave., Chicago 37, Ill. $1.25 up. |
| CHAC | *Chicago History of American Civilization Series.* Same as above. |
| Chart | *Charter Books:* Bobbs-Merrill Co., Inc., 3 W. 57th St., New York 19, N. Y. $1.25 up. |
| Chic | University of Chicago Press, 5750 Ellis Ave., Chicago 37, Ill. $1.25 up. See also *CGT, CHAC, Phoen.* |
| CN | *Harper Colophon Books:* Harper & Row, Inc., 49 E. 33rd St., New York 1, N. Y. $1.25 up. |
| Col | Columbia University Press, Columbia University, New York 27, N. Y. $1 up. |
| Collr | Collier Books, 60 Fifth Ave., New York 11, N. Y. 65¢ up. |
| Comp | *Compass Books:* The Viking Press, Inc., 625 Madison Ave., New York 22, N. Y. 95¢ up. |
| CoNC | *New Collins Classics:* W. W. Norton & Co., Inc., 55 Fifth Ave., New York 3, N. Y. $1.25 up. |
| Corn | Cornell University Press, 124 Roberts Pl., Ithaca, N. Y. 95¢ up. |
| Crest | *Crest Books:* Fawcett Publications, Inc., 67 W. 44th St., New York 36, N. Y. 35¢ up. |
| Crown | Crown Publishers, 419 Park Ave. S., New York 16, N. Y. 60¢ up. |
| Ctdl | The Citadel Press, 222 Park Ave. S., New York 3, N. Y. 95¢ up. |
| CUP | Cambridge University Press, 32 E. 57th St., New York 22, N. Y. 95¢ up. |
| Dday | Doubleday & Co., Inc., 575 Madison Ave., New York 22, N. Y. 50¢ up. |
| Dell | Dell Publishing Co., Inc., 750 Third Ave., New York 17, N. Y. 35¢ up. |
| Delta | *Delta Books:* Dell Publishing Co. See above. $1.45 up. |

## THE GOOD READING BOOK LISTS 23

*Dolp* — *Dolphin Books:* Doubleday & Co., Inc., 575 Madison Ave., New York 22, N. Y. 95¢ up.
*Dov* — *Dover Publications,* Inc., 180 Varick St., New York 14, N. Y. 60¢ up.
*Drama* — *Dramabooks* (paperbound): Hill & Wang, Inc., 141 Fifth Ave., New York 10, N. Y. 95¢ up.
*Drama-h* — *Dramabooks* (hardcover): See above. $2.25 up.
*Econ* — *Economica Books:* Smith, Keynes & Marshall, Inc., 4498 Main St., Buffalo 26, N. Y.
*Ever* — *Evergreen Books:* Grove Press, Inc., 64 University Pl., New York 3, N. Y. 75¢ up.
*Evman* — *Everyman Paperbacks:* E. P. Dutton & Co., Inc., 201 Park Ave. S., New York 3, N. Y. 95¢ up.
*Evman-h* — *Everyman's Library—Standard Edition.* See above. $1.95 ea.
*EvmanNA* — *Everyman's Library—New American Edition.* See above. $2.95 ea.
*FAP* — Frederick A. Praeger, Inc., 64 University Pl., New York 3, N. Y. 95¢ up.
*Gate* — *Gateway Editions:* Henry Regnery Co., 14 E. Jackson Blvd., Chicago 4, Ill. 65¢ up.
*GB* — *Galaxy Books:* Oxford University Press, Inc., 417 Fifth Ave., New York 16, N. Y. 95¢ up.
*GrDeb* — *Great Debate Series:* Henry Regnery Co., 14 E. Jackson Blvd., Chicago 4, Ill. $2 ea.
*H&W* — Hill & Wang, Inc., 141 Fifth Ave., New York 10, N. Y. $1.25 up.
*Haf* — *Hafner Library of World Classics:* Hafner Publishing Co., 31 E. 10th St., New York 3, N. Y. 95¢ up.
*HarB* — *Harbrace Modern Classics:* Harcourt, Brace & World, Inc., 750 Third Ave., New York 17, N. Y. $2.50 ea.
*Harp* — *Harper College Paperbacks:* Harper & Row, Inc., 49 E. 33rd St., New York 16, N. Y. $1 up.
*HarpMC* — *Harper's Modern Classics.* See above. $1.40 up.
*Harv* — *Harvest Books:* Harcourt, Brace & World, Inc., 750 Third Ave., New York 17, N. Y. 95¢ up.
*HB&W* — Harcourt, etc. See above. $1.45 up.
*HM* — Houghton Mifflin Co., 2 Park St., Boston 7, Mass. $1 up.
*HRW* — Holt, Rinehart & Winston, Inc., 383 Madison Ave., New York 17, N. Y. 65¢ up.
*HUP* — Harvard University Press, 79 Garden St., Cambridge 38, Mass. $1.25 up.
*IB* — *Insight Books:* D. Van Nostrand Co., Inc., 120 Alexander St., Princeton, N. J.
*Im* — *Doubleday Image Books:* Doubleday & Co., Inc., 575 Madison Ave., New York 22, N. Y. 65¢ up.
*Ind* — Indiana University Press, P. O. Box 367, Bloomington, Ind. $1.50 up.
*Key* — *Keystone Books:* J. B. Lippincott Co., East Washington Sq., Philadelphia 5, Pa. 95¢ up.
*Knopf* — Alfred A. Knopf, Inc., 501 Madison Ave., New York 22, N. Y.
*Lance* — Lancer Books, 26 W. 47th St., New York 36, N. Y. 35¢ up.
*Lib* — *Library of Liberal Arts:* Bobbs-Merrill Co., Inc., 4300 W. 62nd St., Indianapolis 6, Ind., 45¢ up.

| | |
|---|---|
| *Lita* | Littlefield, Adams & Co., 128 Oliver St., Paterson 1, N. J. 50¢ up. |
| *Little* | Little, Brown & Co., 34 Beacon St., Boston 6, Mass. $1.25 up. |
| *Loeb* | *Loeb Classical Library:* Harvard University Press, 79 Garden St., Cambridge 38, Mass. $3.50 ea. |
| *Macf* | *Macfadden Books:* Macfadden-Bartell Corp., 205 E. 42nd St,. New York 17, N. Y. 35¢ up. |
| *Macm* | The Macmillan Co., 60 Fifth Ave., New York 11, N. Y. 75¢ up. |
| *McGH* | *McGraw-Hill Paperback Series:* McGraw-Hill Book Co., Inc., 330 W. 42nd St., New York 36, N. Y. 95¢ up. |
| *Ment* | *Mentor Books:* New American Library of World Literature, Inc., 501 Madison Ave., New York 22, N. Y. 50¢ up. |
| *Mer* | *Meridian Books:* The World Publishing Co., 2231 W. 110th St., Cleveland 2, Ohio. $1.25 up. |
| *ML* | *Modern Library:* Modern Library, Inc., 457 Madison Ave., New York 22, N. Y. $1.95 ea. |
| *MLCE* | *Modern Library College Editions.* See above. 65¢ up. |
| *MLG* | *Modern Library Giants.* See above. $2.95 ea. |
| *ModSA* | *Modern Standard Authors:* Charles Scribner's Sons, 597 Fifth Ave., New York 17, N. Y. $2.25 up. |
| *ModSL* | *Modern Student's Library.* See above. $1.25 up. |
| *Nel* | *Nelson Classics:* Thomas Nelson & Sons, 18 E. 41st St., New York 17, N. Y. $1.50 ea. |
| *New* | New Directions, 333 Ave. of the Americas, New York 14, N.Y. $1 up. |
| *NHL* | *Natural History Library:* Doubleday & Co., Inc., 575 Madison Ave., New York 22, N. Y. 95¢ up. |
| *Noon* | The Noonday Press, 19 Union Square W., New York 3, N. Y. $1.25 up. |
| *Nort* | W. W. Norton & Co., 55 Fifth Ave., New York 3, N. Y. 85¢ up. |
| *NWP* | *New World Paperbacks:* International Publishers, 381 Park Ave. S., New York 16, N. Y. 75¢ up. |
| *NYU* | New York University Press, 32 Washington Sq., New York 3, N. Y. $1 up. |
| *Oce* | Oceana Publications, Inc., 40 Cedar St., Dobbs Ferry, N. Y. 50¢ up. |
| *Odys* | The Odyssey Press, Inc., 55 Fifth Ave., New York 3, N. Y. |
| *Open* | The Open Court Publishing Co., 1307 Seventh St., LaSalle, Ill. 60¢ up. |
| *Ox* | Oxford University Press, Inc., 417 Fifth Ave., New York 16, N. Y. $1 up. |
| *OxA* | *Oxford Standard Authors.* See above. $4.50 ea. |
| *PB* | Pocket Books, Inc., 630 Fifth Ave., New York 20, N. Y. 35¢ up. |
| *Pen* | *Penguin Books:* Penguin Books, Inc., 3300 Clipper Mill Rd., Baltimore 11, Md. 50¢ up. |
| *Perm* | *Permabooks:* Pocket Books, Inc., 630 Fifth Ave., New York 20, N. Y. 25¢ up. |
| *Phoen* | *Phoenix Books:* University of Chicago Press, 5750 Ellis Ave., Chicago 37, Ill. $1.75 ea. |

## THE GOOD READING BOOK LISTS

*PP*      *Papers in Psychology:* Random House, 457 Madison Ave., New York 22, N. Y. 85¢ up.

*Prem*    *Premier Books:* Fawcett Publications, Inc., 67 W. 44th St., New York 36, N. Y. 35¢ up.

*Ptmn*    Pitman Publishing Corp., 20 E. 46th St., New York 17, N. Y. $1.25 up.

*PUP*    Princeton University Press, Princeton, N. J. $1.45 up.

*Pyr*      *Pyramid Books:* Pyramid Publications, Inc., 444 Madison Ave., New York 22, N. Y. 35¢ up.

*Refl*     *Reflection Books:* Association Press, 291 Broadway, New York 7, N. Y. 50¢ up.

*RivEd*   *Riverside Editions:* Houghton Mifflin Co., 2 Park St., Boston 7, Mass. 75¢ up.

*RivLib*   *Riverside Library.* See above. $3 up.

*RivLit*    *Riverside Literature Series.* See above. 88¢ up.

*S&S*     Simon & Schuster, Inc., 630 Fifth Ave., New York 20, N. Y. $1 up.

*SA*      *Studies in Anthropology:* Random House, 457 Madison Ave., New York 22, N. Y. $1.25 up.

*SciEd*    Science Editions, Inc., 605 Third Ave., New York 16, N. Y. $1.45 up.

*Scrib*     *Scribner Library:* Charles Scribner's Sons, 597 Fifth Ave., New York 17, N. Y. $1.25 up.

*SenEd*   *Sentry Editions:* Houghton Mifflin Co., 2 Park St., Boston 7, Mass. $1.95 ea.

*Sig*       *Signet Books:* New American Library of World Literature, Inc., 501 Madison Ave., New York 22, N. Y. 35¢ up.

*SigC*     *Signet Classics.* See above. 50¢ up.

*SigK*    *Signet Key Books:* See above. 25¢ up.

*SigS*     *Signet Science Library.* See above. 60¢ up.

*SM*      *St Martin's Library:* St Martin's Press, Inc., 175 Fifth Ave., New York 10, N. Y. $1.25 up.

*Spec*     *Spectrum Books:* Prentice-Hall, Inc., Englewood Cliffs, N. J. $1.75 up.

*SS*       *Studies in Sociology:* Random House, 457 Madison Ave., New York 22, N. Y. 85¢ up.

*Torch*    *Harper Torchbooks:* Harper & Row, Inc., 49 E. 33rd St., New York 16, N. Y. 95¢ up.

*Tutle*     Charles E. Tuttle Co., 28 S. Main St., Rutland, Vt.

*TYC*     Thomas Y. Crowell Co., 201 Park Ave. S., New York 3, N. Y. $1.50 up.

*UL*       *Universal Library:* Grosset & Dunlap, Inc., 1107 Broadway, New York 10, N. Y. 95¢ up.

*Ungar*    Frederick Ungar Publishing Co., 131 E. 23rd St., New York 10, N. Y. 75¢ up.

*UWis*    University of Wisconsin Press, 430 Sterling Court, Madison 6, Wis. 75¢ up.

*Vik*       *Viking Paperbound Portables:* The Viking Press, Inc., 625 Madison Ave., New York 22, N. Y. $1.45 up.

*Vik-h*    *Viking Portables* (hardcover). See above. $2.95 ea.

*Vin*      *Vintage Books:* Random House, 457 Madison Ave., New York 22, N. Y. 95¢ up.

| | |
|---|---|
| *WL* | *Wisdom Library Paperbacks:* Philosophical Library, Inc. Distributed by Book Sales, Inc., 352 Park Ave. S., New York 10, N. Y. 95¢ up. |
| *Wmin* | The Westminster Press, Witherspoon Bldg., Philadelphia 7, Pa. |
| *WoC* | *World's Classics:* Oxford University Press, Inc., 417 Fifth Ave., New York 16, N. Y. $2.25 up. |
| *WSP* | Washington Square Press, Inc., 630 Fifth Ave., New York 20, N. Y. 45¢ up. |
| *Yale* | Yale University Press, 149 York St., New Haven, Conn. 95¢ up. |

---

NOTICE ON PRICES: All book prices quoted above and in the following book lists are correct as of September 1, 1963. Though publishers' prices are subject to change, most prices quoted here should not increase significantly during the four-year life of this 19th edition of GOOD READING.

# REGIONAL AND HISTORICAL CULTURES

# REGIONAL AND HISTORICAL CULTURES

## I. Greece

**JOHN E. HANKINS,** *University of Maine*

To know Greece and the Hellenic world is to know the springs of our own culture. In almost every significant activity of the human mind—in art, architecture, science, philosophy, politics, education, poetry, drama, even in athletics—we are greatly indebted to the ancient Greeks. Nor can we say with assurance that in any of these fields (except science) our modern culture has surpassed that of Greece.

The center of Greek intellectual life during the 5th century B.C. was the city-state of Athens. Athenian culture had a three-fold foundation: economic prosperity, democratic government, and freedom of thought. Athens' role as protector of other states in the Athenian confederacy brought her large sums of tribute money, sums expended on noble public buildings. Her government stimulated pride of citizenship but also had the faults of a democracy—indecisiveness, petty bickering, waste. Her devotion to intellectual freedom made her welcome ideas from the rest of the Mediterranean world, and her eminence as a maritime power kept her in constant touch with other peoples. Foreign scholars from far and wide flocked to Athens, where they found a willing audience.

Eventually Athens was conquered by Sparta, later by Philip of Macedon, and finally by Rome. Each conquest, paradoxically, resulted in the wider spread of her superior thought and culture. Philip's son Alexander conquered and Hellenized Egypt and the Near East. Rome adopted Greek culture as her own and spread its influence over Western Europe, North Africa, and the British Isles. Even during the centuries of the Roman Empire, Greek remained the first language of Eastern Mediterranean countries, and Alexandria in Egypt came to rival Athens as an intellectual center. Most cultivated Romans were bilingual: Vergil and Horace took their academic training at Athens. Nor should we forget that the original Greek of the New Testament and the Septuagint translation of the Old Testament made possible the rapid rise of Christianity from a Hebrew sect to an international religion.

Greek genius was assimilative, interpretive, and self-expressive. Numerous flourishing civilizations preceded that of Greece—Egyptian, Chaldean, Phoenician, Cretan, etc.—but of most of them only fragmentary records survive. The Greeks absorbed much from these earlier cultures as well as from the contemporary world, reinterpreting all that they learned in the clear light of unbiased intellect. In reading the Greek historians (Thucydides, for example), one marvels at their essential fairness and their patriotism without jingoism.

The Socratic dialogues of Plato draw upon a wide range of earlier philosophic theories, harmonizing them, arranging them, and charting a logical course through the intricate maze. Plato's pupil Aristotle was perhaps the greatest systematizer of all time, exercising his analytical genius upon physical and biological science, metaphysics, psychology, poetry, oratory, ethics, and government. His perception that every subject can be better understood through rational analysis, systematic arrangement, and reduction to first principles is probably the most influential concept in the history of human knowledge.

The same sense of fairness, of harmony, of proportion and balance is evident in the artistic and literary creations of the Greeks. The Parthenon, designed by Ictinus, is an architectural triumph of grace and symmetry. The Greek tragedians (Aeschylus, Sophocles, Euripides) saw life steadily and whole, portraying without rancor the tragedy of human fate. From an earlier period of Greek history, Homer's *Odyssey* is a model of a well-designed plot. Perhaps the Greek mind, unwarped by restraints, vigorous but open-minded, came nearer the perception of rational truth than any people before or since. This may account for its continued impact upon our modern world.

While Homer lived at least 300 years before the Age of Pericles (5th century B.C.), later Greeks probably knew less about his times than we do today. Except for his two monumental epics and the so-called *Homeric Hymns,* no written records of his period survive. But recent archaeological excavations of ancient Troy and Mycenae and other key places have taught us a great deal about Homer's world. Yet the *Iliad*—a stirring war epic, rich in descriptions of battle and of poignant sorrow for the dead —and the *Odyssey*—an exciting travel epic that encompasses the entire Greek world—tell their own stories in dramatic human terms which have enthralled readers throughout the ages.

Though the origins of Greek drama are obscure, it seems to have evolved from ritual, myth, and dance. In the form in which we know it, Greek drama began as entertainment for the annual festivals in honor of Dionysus, the fertility god. At first a single reader chanted epic verse from the stage, relieved at intervals by choral songs and dances. When Aeschylus added a second reader or actor, genuine drama began, but the chorus always remained a traditional feature of Greek drama. The plays were performed in outdoor semicircular amphitheaters, which to this day have acoustical qualities superior to those of most modern theaters.

Greek philosophy was at first in the hands of Sophists, itinerant scholars who accepted fees for discoursing to such students as were interested and willing to pay. Later Plato's Academy, "the world's first university," attracted the best minds in a systematic search for truth. This arrangement was later imitated by the Neoplatonists of Alexandria, who extended and refined upon Plato's more mystical theories almost to the point of incomprehensibility.

Later periods of Greek history, while not so creative, still made major contributions. The pastoral poem was developed by Theocritus, Moschus, and Bion; the pastoral prose romance by Heliodorus and Longus. In the early years of the Christian era, Plutarch developed biography and Lucian elevated satire to a high literary level.

To the student today, ancient Greece seems a beacon shining with a clear, steady flame, lighting the paths man can yet significantly pursue.

## A. Greek Literature

### Collections

***The Complete Greek Drama*** (1938). Ed. by W. J. Oates and Eugene O'Neill, Jr. Fair to good translations of 47 plays by Aeschylus, Sophocles, Euripides, and Menander, with useful notes. *Random House 2 vols $10.*

***Complete Greek Tragedies*** (1959). Ed. by David Grene and Richmond Lattimore. First-rate new translations, soundly edited and excellently introduced. *Chicago 4 vols $20, CGT 9 vols.*

***The Greek Anthology*** (1916–18). Ed. and trans. by various scholars. Extensive collection of short lyrics, epitaphs, epigrams, monument inscriptions, etc., drawn from many centuries. *Loeb 5 vols.*

***The Greek Historians*** (1942). Ed. by F. R. B. Godolphin. Complete histories by Herodotus, Thucydides, Xenophon, Arrian; other historical material. *Random House 2 vols $15.*

***Greek Literature in Translation*** (1944). Ed. by W. J. Oates and C. T. Murphy. Extensive and representative selection in modern translations. *McKay $6.95.*

***Greek Literature in Translation*** (rev ed 1948). Ed. by George Howe, G. A. Harrer, and P. H. Epps. Collection representing all stages of the cultural history of ancient Greece. *Harper $8.*

***Greek Poetry for Everyman*** (1951). Ed. and trans. by F. L. Lucas. An excellent selection of Greek verse, including work of minor authors. *Bea.*

***Poems from the Greek Anthology*** (1956). Ed. and trans. by Dudley Fitts. A good introduction to Greek literature. *New Directions $3, New.*

***The Portable Greek Reader*** (1948). Ed. by W. H. Auden. 726 pages bringing together the high spots of Greek literature and thought from Homer to Galen: 4 complete plays, poetry, philosophy, science, political writings. *Vik, Vik-h.*

***Ten Greek Plays in Contemporary Translations*** (1958). Ed. by L. R. Lind. A first-rate inexpensive collection of fresh translations of major plays presented with solid introductory material. *Houghton $4.50, RivEd.*

## Individual Authors

AESCHYLUS 525–456 B.C. **Tragedies.** Best known is *The Oresteia,* a trilogy comprising *Agamemnon, Choephoroe,* and *Eumenides,* three superb tragedies of bloodshed and revenge. The most readable translations are by Lattimore *(CGT),* Roche *(Ment),* and Vellacott *(Pen).* Other translations of plays: *CGT, Evman-h, Loeb, Ox, Phoen.*

AESOP *c.* 6th cent. B.C. **Fables.** Delightful animal stories illustrating folk morality with pointed, sometimes cynical, wit. *Lippincott $3.50, Evman-h, Pen.*

ARISTOPHANES *c.* 448–380 B.C. **Comedies.** Lyrical, topical burlesques, combining boisterous farce with poetic beauty: on Socrates, *The Clouds;* on politics, *The Knights;* on war and women, *Lysistrata;* on utopian schemes, *The Birds;* on literature, *The Frogs. Anch, Appl, Ban, Black, Evman-h, Harv, Loeb, Ox, WoC.*

ARISTOTLE 384–322 B.C. **Nicomachean Ethics.** A profound pioneer analysis of the modes, methods, and values of human conduct, informed by Aristotle's rational approach. *EvmanNA, Gate, Lib, Loeb, Pen, WoC.*

———— **Politics.** Influential analysis of the forms and functions of government, of man as a political animal. *Oxford $2.40, Comp, Evman-h, Gate, Loeb, ML, Pen.*

———— **Selections.** *Odyssey $2.50, Random House $7.50, Gate, Ment, Scrib, WSP.*

DEMOSTHENES 383–322 B.C. **Orations.** The best in oratory. *Loeb.*

DIOGENES LAERTIUS *c.* A.D. 150 **Lives of Eminent Philosophers.** Interesting basic biographical material. *Loeb.*

EURIPIDES *c.* 484–408 B.C. **Tragedies and Tragi-Comedies.** Realistic, very human dramas by the most modern of the great Greek playwrights. Best-known plays include *Alcestis, Hippolytus, Medea, The Trojan Women. Ban, CGT, Evman-h, Lib, Loeb, Ment, Ox, Pen.*

HERODOTUS *c.* 484–425 B.C. **History.** Shrewd analysis of geopolitics in the ancient world, and lively narrative of the crucial struggle between democratic Greece and totalitarian Persia. *Oxford 2 vols $4.80, Tudor $2.98, Loeb, ML, Pen.*

HESIOD *c.* 770 B.C. **Theogony. Works and Days.** Myths of the gods, fables, proverbs, social protest, moral advice, prayers, religious chants by a probable contemporary of Homer. The translations by Richmond Lattimore are recommended: *Michigan $3.95.* Others: *Lib, Loeb.*

HOMER *c.* 750 B.C. **Iliad.** This great epic about an episode during the siege of Troy is still the most universally admired poetry of action ever written. The verse translation by Richmond Lattimore *(Phoen)* is highly recommended. Other versions: *Van*

*Nostrand $1.75, Ban, BES, Evman-h, Loeb, Ment, ML, MLCE, MLG, Nort, Pen, SM, UL, WoC.*

———— *Odyssey.* Return of Odysseus (*Ulysses* in Latin) from the Trojan War to his home in Ithaca. Rousing adventure of individual exploits combined with great human interest. The verse translation by Robert Fitzgerald *(Anch)* and the prose versions by W. H. D. Rouse *(Ment)* and T. E. Shaw *(GB)* are particularly good. Others: *Houghton $5, Van Nostrand $1.75, Ban, Evman-h, Loeb, ML, MLCE, MG, Pen, SM.*

LUCIAN c. A.D. 125–210 **Dialogues of the Dead. Dialogues of the Gods.** Pungent and witty satires with philosophic implications. *Oxford 4 vols $6.75, Peter Smith $3, Anch, Lib, Loeb, Pen.*

PINDAR 522–443 B.C. **Odes.** Chief writer of choral or "Pindaric" odes celebrating Olympic triumphs and special events. Richmond Lattimore's translations are excellent: *Chicago $4.25, Phoen.* Other: *Loeb.*

PLATO c. 427–347 B.C. **Republic.** While describing in detail the nature of justice and the characteristics of an ideal state, Plato develops his Doctrine of Ideas, his theories of education, and other fundamental aspects of his influential philosophic world view. The skillfully annotated abridged translation by F. M. Cornford is preferred *(Ox)*. Others: *Evman, Pen, Scrib, Vin.*

———— **Other Dialogues.** Probing philosophical discussions, with Socrates usually the main speaker. Most interesting are the *Apology* (Socrates' trial), *Phaedo* (Socrates' death), *Symposium* (on love) *Gorgias* (on justice), and *The Laws* (on government). Some or all of these are contained in countless editions.

PLOTINUS A.D. 204–275 **Philosophy.** The thought of the best-known Neoplatonist, who studied at Alexandria and lectured at Rome. *Oxford $5, Appl, Collr.*

PLUTARCH c. A.D. 46–120 **Lives.** Short biographies, paralleling the lives of famous Greeks with the careers of famous Romans. Remarkable character interpretations. *Dell, Evman-h, HRW, Loeb, Ment, MLG, Pen.*

POLYBIUS 204–122 B.C. **Histories.** An outstanding interpretation of Rome's rise to power. *Indiana 2 vols $10, Loeb.*

SOPHOCLES 496–406 B.C. **Tragedies.** In the whole range of Greek tragedy, two of his **Theban Plays**—*Oedipus Rex* for plot, *Antigone* for wide-ranging moral significance—are perhaps the best plays. The best translations of *Theban Plays* are by Banks *(Ox)*, Fitts and Fitzgerald *(Harv)*, Roche *(Ment)*, and Watling *(Pen)*. Other translations and other plays: *Appl, CGT, Evman-h, Loeb, WoC, WSP.*

THUCYDIDES c. 470–400 B.C. **The Peloponnesian Wars.** A perceptively analytical yet stirring account of the fateful struggle between Athens and Sparta. A classic work of history. *Ban, Dolp, EvmanNA, GB, Loeb, ML, MLCE, Pen, WoC.*

XENOPHON 431–355 B.C. **Anabasis.** Describes the military campaigns of Cyrus of Persia and the retreat of the Greek mercenaries across Arabian deserts to the Black Sea. *McKay $3.50, Ment, Pen, SM.*

# B. Books About Greece

AGARD, WALTER R. 1894– *The Greek Mind* (1957). A stimulating philosophic interpretation of the intellectual achievements of the Greeks. *Anv.*

BOWRA, C. M. 1898– *The Greek Experience* (1958). Brilliant popular analysis of Greek life, thought, and culture. *World $6, Ment.*

BULFINCH, THOMAS 1796–1867 *Mythology.* The most convenient (but most bowdlerized and Victorian) of the many handbooks of mythology. Includes *The Age of Fable* (1855), *The Age of Chivalry* (1858), and *The Legends of Charlemagne* (1863). *Crowell $5.95, Dell (abr), Ment, MLG.*

BURY, JOHN BAGNELL 1861–1927 *History of Greece* (1900). Authoritative and entertaining account from prehistory to Alexander the Great. *St Martin's $4.75, MLG.*

DICKINSON, G. LOWES 1862–1932 *The Greek View of Life* (1896). A sound discussion of Greek thought and ideals. *Michigan $4.40, Peter Smith $3, AA, Collr.*

DURANT, WILL 1885– *The Life of Greece* (1939). Comprehensive yet most readable survey of Greek civilization from remote times to the Roman conquest. *Simon & Schuster $10.*

FARRINGTON, BENJAMIN 1891– *Greek Science* (1939). Illuminating survey of the physical and economic forces and of the speculative minds that laid foundations for modern science. *Pen.*

FINLEY, M. I. 1912– *The World of Odysseus* (1954). The best popular introduction to the world and works of Homer. *Mer.*

_____ *The Ancient Greeks* (1963). A popular but scholarly account of ancient Greek history and culture, rich in anecdote and sound in assessing Greek strengths and shortcomings. *Viking $5.*

FRAZER, JAMES GEORGE 1854-1941 *The Golden Bough* (1915). Provocative comparative analysis of primitive religions and ancient folklores. *St Martin's 13 vols $65;* abridgments: *Criterion $8.50, Macmillan $3.95, Anch, Macm.*

GOODRICH, NORMA LORRE *The Ancient Myths* (1960). A popular narration of selected myths from Greece, Rome, Persia, India, and Egypt. *Ment.*

GRAVES, ROBERT 1895– *Hercules, My Shipmate* (1945). Imaginative reconstruction of the savage, lusty, daring adventures of the Argonauts who sought the Golden Fleece. *Farrar, Straus $4.50, UL.*

_____ *The Greek Myths* (1955). The complete story of the Greek gods and heroes assembled—often with fresh insights—into one continuous narrative by a poet and novelist of great ability. *Braziller $5, Pen.*

GUTHRIE, W. K. C. 1906– *The Greeks and Their Gods* (1951). A lucid, nontechnical account of the religious background of the Greek classics. *Bea.*

HADAS, MOSES 1900– *A History of Greek Literature* (1950). A sound comprehensive survey. *Columbia $4.25, Col.*

HAMILTON, EDITH 1867–1963 *The Greek Way* (1930). Entertaining and stimulating study of Greek writers and their influence in ancient as well as modern times. *Norton $4.50, Ment.*

―――――― *Mythology* (1942). Popular, well-written short narrative of the Greek myths. *Ment, UL.*

HARRISON, JANE 1850–1928 *Prolegomena to the Study of Greek Religion* (1903). Fascinating scholarly account of deities, ceremonials, sacrifices, and other elements of primitive Greek religion. Extensively illustrated. *Mer.*

JAEGER, WERNER 1888–1961 *Paideia: Ideals of Greek Culture* (1939). Profound, difficult, but highly rewarding study of the development of Greek culture and thought. *Oxford 3 vols $7.50 ea.*

KITTO, H. D. F. 1897– *The Greeks* (1954). Focuses on social conditions in ancient Greece. *Pen.*

―――――― *Form and Meaning in Drama* (1956). A splendid analysis of the structure and themes of Greek tragedy. *Barnes & Noble $6, B&N.*

―――――― *Greek Tragedy* (3rd ed 1961). Informed, perceptive, unusually illuminating analyses of Greek tragedies and their backgrounds. *Barnes & Noble $6, Anch.*

LAWRENCE, ARNOLD WALTER 1900– *Greek Architecture* (1957). Lavishly illustrated history of Greek architecture. *Penguin $16.50.*

LIVINGSTONE, R. W. 1880–1960 (ed) *The Legacy of Greece* (1921). Stimulating essays by Gilbert Murray, W. R. Inge, other distinguished scholars on all aspects of Greek life, thought, and art. *Oxford $5.75.*

LOUŸS, PIERRE 1870–1925 *Aphrodite* (1896). Lushly detailed tragic romance of a priestess of love in rich, corrupt Alexandria. *Lance, ML.*

ROSE, H. J. 1883–1961 *A Handbook of Greek Literature* (1948). Supplies background facts simply, soundly, readably. *Dutton $7.95, Evman.*

ROUSE, W. H. D. 1863–1950 *Gods, Heroes, and Men of Ancient Greece* (1934). A racy, rapid narrative of the better-known myths. *SigK.*

STOBART, JOHN C. 1878–1933 *The Glory That Was Greece* (rev ed 1934). Greek life, art, and civilization profusely illustrated. *Ever.*

TOYNBEE, ARNOLD J. 1889– *Greek Civilization and Character* (1950). Skillfully edited collection from the Greek historians highlighting various aspects of ancient civilization. *Ment.*

WARNER, REX 1905– *The Greek Philosophers* (1958). Useful for an introductory study of the major philosophers and their predecessors. *Ment.*

WEBER, J. SHERWOOD 1918– et al. *From Homer to Joyce* (1959). Contains useful popular guides to the understanding of masterworks by Homer, Aeschylus, Sophocles, Euripides, Plato, and Aristotle. *Holt $2.50.*

## 2. Rome

**NORMAN T. PRATT, JR.,** *Indiana University*

The word "Roman" conjures up a vision of blocks of masonry—strong, massive, durable. And with reason, for many of the roads, temples, bridges, aqueducts, amphitheaters the Romans built still survive. But they made other contributions even more enduring. Their network of roads and their settlements helped give modern Europe its shape. Their language, Latin, was the main source of eight modern languages, including Italian, French, and Spanish. Their political system strongly influenced the founding fathers of America, among others. And their law is the core of one of the two major legal systems in Western civilization.

Such accomplishments of the Roman gift for organization are important, but they leave a misleading impression. Efficiency implies hard practicality, perhaps even lack of feeling. Yet the Romans, like other Mediterranean peoples, were also emotional and excitable, as their literature abundantly reveals. Though the Romans did not match the intellectual and artistic originality of the Greeks, their literature has wit, emotional insight, and esthetic power. The uniqueness of Roman literature lies in the fusion of sophistication with the moral force and earnestness produced by a strong social orientation.

A sampling will show the variety. The comedies of Plautus, written near the beginning of Latin literature, are full of lively humanity. His comic animation and chaotic plots stand in sharp contrast to Terence's quieter, more polished and sensitive comedies of manners.

In the literature of "the Ciceronian period" (the first half of the 1st century B.C.), the outstanding names are Cicero and Caesar in prose, Catullus and Lucretius in poetry. The orations and letters of Cicero reveal a skilled politician and a consummate orator. The strong and brilliant personality of Caesar appears vividly in his accounts of the Gallic and civil wars. These two writers, political enemies, help us to know well a crucial period in world history. Catullus pictures in his lyrics the sophisticated society of poets, rakes, and beauties, using his art for the spontaneous expression of erotic feeling. Lucretius, a probing and poetic thinker, undertakes in *The Nature of Things* to crush superstition and ignorance with the scientific thought of Epicureanism.

The following half-century, known as "the Augustan age," produced equally notable work. Vergil's *Aeneid*—the most significant single Latin book to know—portrays the cultural mission of Rome with intelligence and grandeur. Horace's lyrics—sometimes delicate, sometimes weighty, usually brilliant—and his pungent satires have been enjoyed by many readers. Ovid's *Metamorphoses* has left endless imprints on later literature. In a period memorable mainly for its poetry, Livy's epical history of Rome is a prose masterwork.

The reader will find much that seems contemporary in the social criticism that permeates the best writing of the early centuries A.D. The Roman precursors of the novel, Petronius and Apuleius, wrote bawdy satiric social romances. The materialism and immorality of Rome are the targets of Juvenal's blowtorch satires. Also critical of the times are Tacitus' devastating historical analysis of the emperors and Seneca's Stoic writings. Stoicism was the source of much social liberalism, as evidenced in a Senecan letter challenging slavery: "Just remember that he whom you call your slave was born from the same seed, enjoys the same sky, and equally breathes, lives, and dies."

The continuous movement from pagan to fully Christian times is reflected in the literature from the 4th century through the 6th. Jerome, whose favorite authors were Plautus and Cicero, was primarily responsible for the great Latin translation of the Bible known as the Vulgate. Augustine's *Confessions* records his conversion to Christianity from and through classical thought. Boethius clings firmly to the rationality of pagan philosophy

# ROME

as a support to the faith of Christianity. So new vitality arises from old.

## A. Literature of the Roman Era

### Collections

***Classics in Translation: Latin Literature*** (1952). Ed. by P. L. MacKendrick and H. M. Howe. Roman culture presented through a generous selection of complete works and units, both prose and poetry, mostly in new translations. *Wisconsin $5, UWis.*

***The Complete Roman Drama*** (1942). Ed. by G. E. Duckworth. 36 plays: lively comedies by Plautus and Terence bring the reader close to the life and humor of the Romans; and violent, influential melodramas by Seneca. *Random House 2 vols $15.*

***Latin Poetry in Verse Translation*** (1957). Ed. by L. R. Lind. An excellent anthology of Latin poetry from the beginnings to the Renaissance, by a number of translators. *Houghton $4.75, RivEd.*

***Roman Readings*** (1958). Ed. by Michael Grant. A tasteful, compact, well-edited anthology of Roman poetry and prose. *Pen.*

### Individual Authors

**APULEIUS, LUCIUS** c. A.D. 160 *The Golden Ass.* The only completely surviving Latin novel, about an adventurer changed to an ass and doomed to fantastic experiences until the goddess Isis allows him to resume human form. *Black, Collr, Ind, Loeb, PB.*

**AUGUSTINE, SAINT** A.D. 354–430 *The City of God.* The fall of the Roman Empire and the death of paganism interpreted by a Christian believing in Divine Providence. Possibly the most influential early Christian document. *Evman-h, Im, MLG.*

─────── *Confessions.* A searching autobiography of a brilliant wastrel converted to Christianity. *Regnery $3.75, Black, Collr, EvmanNA, Im, Loeb, Ment, ML, Nel, Pen, WSP.*

**BOETHIUS** A.D. 480–524 *The Consolation of Philosophy.* A moving dialogue concerning pagan philosophy and Christianity by "the last great pagan author." *Lib, Loeb, ML, Ungar.*

**CAESAR, GAIUS JULIUS** 100-44 B.C. *Commentaries.* The conqueror of Gaul and Britain and the victor in civil war gives clear, vivid reports of crucial campaigns and political struggles. *Evman, Evman-h, Ment, Pen.*

**CATULLUS, GAIUS VALERIUS** 84–54 B.C. *Poems.* A hypersensitive young artist expresses intense emotion in lyrics moving from personal feeling to contemporary life to the world of myth. *Dutton $3.95, Michigan $3.75, Transatlantic $2.50, AA, Lib.*

CICERO, MARCUS TULLIUS 106–43 B.C. **Selected Works.** Essays on philosophy and rhetoric, forceful orations, and revealing personal letters, written by a Roman equally active in politics and the arts. *Evman-h, ML, Pen.*

HORACE (QUINTUS HORATIUS FLACCUS) 65–8 B.C. **Poems.** Polished lyrics, sophisticated satires, and poetic essays by one who belonged to the court circle but retained independence of mind. His name symbolizes urbanity and wit. *Evman-h, Loeb, ML, Phoen, SM.*

JUVENAL (DECIMUS JUNIUS JUVENALIS) *c.* A.D. 60–140 **Satires.** Bitter, realistic attacks on vices, abuses, and follies of imperial Rome, by an idealist driven to indignation. *Cambridge $2.75, Evman-h, Ind, Loeb, Ment.*

LIVY (TITUS LIVIUS) 59 B.C.–A.D. 17 **History of Rome.** Picturesque account of the growth of the Roman state from the earliest times, emphasizing that the decline of moral values in the author's time would cause its downfall. *Loeb, Pen.*

LUCRETIUS (TITUS LUCRETIUS CARUS) *c.* 94–55 B.C. **On the Nature of Things.** Impressive philosophic poem presenting materialistic Epicureanism as the cure for superstition and human folly and hence as the salvation for man. Shows how the ancients anticipated such modern concepts as the atomic theory, conservation of matter, evolution, and survival of the fittest. *Oxford $3, Dolp, Evman, EvmanNA, Lib, Loeb, Pen.*

MARCUS AURELIUS ANTONINUS A.D. 121-180 **Meditations.** An emperor and Stoic philosopher records his thoughts as he struggles for composure and order in the face of national disaster. *Dolp, Evman-h, Gate, Lib, Loeb, WoC.*

OVID (PUBLIUS OVIDIUS NASO) 43 B.C.–A.D. 17 **The Art of Love.** Playful, risqué verses on the devices of love, full of charm and humor. The Humphries version is superior *(Ind)*. Others: *Black, Evman-h, Loeb, UL.*

———— **Metamorphoses.** Tales of miraculous transformations, by a versatile narrative poet. Its broad coverage of Greek and Roman myth has made it a most important source book. The Humphries translation is first-rate *(Ind)*. Others: *Loeb, Ment, Pen.*

PETRONIUS, GAIUS d. A.D. 66 **The Satyricon.** Picaresque novel about the adventures of three rascals, incorporating both social and literary criticism. This hilarious satire also provides useful information about Roman everyday life. The Arrowsmith translation is recommended *(AA, Ment)*. Others: *Black, Loeb.*

PLAUTUS, TITUS MACCIUS *c.* 251–184 B.C. **Comedies.** Rollicking farces about tricky servants, braggart soldiers, courtesans, etc. See **The Complete Roman Drama**, above. Also: *Lib, Loeb.*

PLUTARCH *Lives.* See "Greece," page 34.

SENECA, LUCIUS ANNAEUS *c.* 5 B.C.–A.D. 65 **Works.** Essays and letters applying Stoic thought to perennial human problems and conditions of Roman life; melodramas portraying intense emotion and violence. See **The Complete Roman Drama**, above. Also: *Lib, Loeb.*

# ROME

**TACITUS, CORNELIUS** c. A.D. 55–117 **Works.** History of the Roman Empire to A.D. 70 and of the Roman occupations in Britain and Gaul, written from a republican bias and exhibiting ironical insight as well as literary talent. *Oxford $2.40, ML, Pen.*

**TERENCE (PUBLIUS TERENTIUS AFER)** c. 195–159 B.C. **Comedies.** Polished, refined, but somewhat colorless comedies of manners stressing moderation. See **The Complete Roman Drama**, above. Also: *Anch, Lib, Loeb.*

**VERGIL (PUBLIUS VERGILIUS MARO)** 70–19 B.C. **Aeneid.** A great national epic glorifying the historical tradition and stressing the universal cultural mission of Rome. *Anch, Evman-h, Ment, HRW, ML, MLCE, Pen, Scrib, SM, WoC.*

———— **Eclogues.** Ten pastoral poems blend natural beauty and the political scene. *Evman-h, MLCE, Pen, WoC.*

———— **Georgics.** Four books on "tillage, trees, cattle, bees," written by one who knew farming and respected its rigors and rewards. *Chicago $3.75, Evman-h, MLCE, WoC.*

**VITRUVIUS POLLIO, MARCUS** c. 85–26 B.C. **On Architecture.** A unique record of Greek and Roman city planning, engineering, and construction of private and public buildings. *Loeb.*

## B. Books About Rome

**BARROW, R. H.** 1893– **The Romans** (1949). Clear sketch of their traits, history, achievements, and contributions to modern times. *Pen.*

**BULWER-LYTTON, EDWARD** 1803–1873 **The Last Days of Pompeii** (1834). A colorful historical romance about the life that perished beneath the ashes of Vesuvius. *CoNC, Dolp, Evman-h, Nel.*

**COWELL, F. R.** 1897– **Cicero and the Roman Republic** (1948). A substantial book which uses Cicero as the focus for portraying the development and nature of the Republic. *Pen.*

**DE BURGH, W. G.** 1866–1943 **The Legacy of the Ancient World** (1947). Comprehensive treatment of our cultural legacy from the Hebrews, Greeks, and Romans. *Pen.*

**DUDLEY, DONALD R.** 1918– **The Civilization of Rome** (1960). An up-to-date, popular account of Rome from 753 B.C. to A.D. 476, including history, politics, religion, art. *Ment.*

**DURANT, WILL** 1885– **Caesar and Christ** (1944). Well-informed cultural history of Rome and Christianity from their beginnings to A.D. 325. *Simon & Schuster $10.*

**GIBBON, EDWARD** 1737–1794 **The Decline and Fall of the Roman Empire** (1776–78). A monumental masterpiece of great analytical power which has become an historical classic. *Collr, Evman, MLG, Torch, Vik.*

GRANT, MICHAEL 1914– *The World of Rome* (1961). Illustrated, readable fresh interpretation of Roman history and culture and subsequent influence. *Ment.*

GRAVES, ROBERT 1895– *I, Claudius* (1934). Fictional autobiography of a strange emperor, which makes excellent use of historical sources. *ML, Vin.*

HAMILTON, EDITH 1869–1963 *The Roman Way* (1932). A readable portrayal of Rome and the Romans during four centuries. *Ment, Nort.*

_____ *Mythology.* See "Greece," page 36.

HIGHET, GILBERT 1906– *The Classical Tradition* (1949). Authoritative, engaging analysis of classical influences upon Western literature. *Oxford $7.50, GB.*

HORIA, VINTILA *God Was Born in Exile* (1961). Fascinating historical novel about Ovid in exile experiencing the coming of Christianity. *St Martin's $4.95.*

KOESTLER, ARTHUR 1905– *The Gladiators* (1939). The revolt of slaves, farmers, and gladiators under Spartacus realistically recreated in an historical novel. *Ban.*

MacKENDRICK, PAUL L. 1914– *The Roman Mind at Work* (1958). Identifies Roman attitudes and qualities, and illustrates them with translated readings from Greek and Latin sources. *Anv.*

_____ *The Mute Stones Speak* (1960). A lively, well-illustrated historical account of recent archaeological work at major Italian sites. *St Martin's $7.50.*

PATER, WALTER H. 1839–1894 *Marius the Epicurean* (1885). Many-sided picture of Roman life and thought in the 2nd century A.D. as seen by a young patrician. *Evman-h.*

RENAN, ERNEST 1823–1892 *The Life of Jesus* (1863). A moving, skeptical portrayal of the Great Teacher against the background of Roman Judaea. *Dolp, Evman-h, ML.*

ROWELL, HENRY T. *Rome in the Augustan Age* (1962). An expert analysis of the factors that made classical Rome a significant world capital. *Oklahoma $2.75.*

WILDER, THORNTON 1897– *The Ides of March* (1948). The assassination of Julius Caesar vividly re-created through imaginary letters and documents. *Harp, Sig, UL.*

YOURCENAR, MARGUERITE *Hadrian's Memoirs* (1954). Brilliant novelistic re-creation of an intelligent emperor's reflections on the world of his time. *Anch.*

# 3. India and the Far East

## NATHAN M. TALBOTT, *Iowa State College*

According to Jawaharlal Nehru, "The new awakening, the resurgence of Asia, is probably the most important event of this present generation." This "awakening" is reflected in the frequently revolutionary national aspirations of Asian peoples and in their efforts to achieve a better life. This "resurgence" is effecting dramatic changes in world affairs. Its impetus can be found in the outward thrust of European expansion which reached maturity in the middle of the last century. Asian nations were propelled into a world community dominated by Western interests and politics; in many instances they participated with reluctance and without alternative. But reluctant or not, they were soon caught up in currents of change which were to lead to the ferment of war and revolution in the 20th century. Ironically, in gaining their independence, many of the nations used ideas and methods learned from their colonial rulers.

Like other such momentous events in history, the revolution in Asia has been multiform and multilevel. Thus it is hazardous to refer to it as a single entity; yet in a sense the changes which began a little more than a century ago constitute collectively a single great revolution which has brought about a cataclysmic transformation in every area of human life—cultural, social, economic, political, religious. However, it should not be concluded that all countries thrown into the crucible of change have been molded to the same pattern. Each country responded to the impact from the West from the historical perspective of a long tradition and with the values bred of its own unique culture and institutions. The resulting alloy of native and Western elements has created a considerable challenge to those who would seek an understanding of contemporary Asian problems.

While most people in the United States have only recently become aware of the importance of Asia in their lives, the history of our relations with East Asia dates from the earliest years of our republic. An American vessel, the *Empress of China,* left Boston for Canton in 1784, and records reveal that, only five years later, fifteen ships of United States' registry did business in Whampoa harbor. Our country had a consul in China as early as 1786, and our first representative of ministerial rank, Caleb Cushing, arrived in Canton on February 24, 1844. On July 3 of the same year, Cushing signed the first treaty between this country and China. This act signaled an ever-increasing involvement by the United States in that part of the world, an involvement which was climaxed by the United States' role as a major participant in World War II and in the Korean War. The conduct of our relations with Asia is now not only one of the primary tasks of our foreign policy makers but a matter of deep concern for thoughtful private citizens as well.

The geographical area encompassed in the following book list contains more than half of the world's three billion people, whose recorded history predates the Christian era in the West by nearly a millenium. The books deal not only with economic, political, and social history and problems, but also with art, literature, philosophy, and religion. In modern thought, especially with fine arts, there is mounting awareness of the introduction of a subtle exotic flavor into many aspects of American life. Witness the extraordinary influence of Japanese esthetic values and motifs in architecture and in home construction and decor, the dilettante interest in Zen Buddhism, and the unmistakable Oriental element in some contemporary painting and ceramics. This list has been compiled then to provide not only useful information but also material which will open up new avenues of enjoyment for adventurous and perceptive readers.

Those who are encouraged to read beyond this limited list will find invaluable three annotated bibliographies published by the University of Arizona Press: *China: A*

*Critical Bibliography* by Charles O. Hucker, *India: A Critical Bibliography* by J. Michael Mahar, and *Japan and Korea: A Critical Bibliography* by Bernard S. Silberman.

## A. General

BINYON, LAURENCE 1869–1943 *Painting in the Far East* (3rd ed 1923). The standard history of the subject. *Dov.*

BOWERS, FAUBION 1917– *Theatre in the East* (1956). An introductory survey of Asian drama and dance, covering both traditional and contemporary forms in the Indian subcontinent, east Asia, and southeast Asia. *Ever.*

CONZE, EDWARD 1904– *Buddhism: Its Essence and Manifestations* (1959). Probably the best short introduction to the subject in English. *Peter Smith $3.35, Torch.*

DEAN, VERA MICHELES 1903– *The Nature of the Non-Western World* (1957). A thoughtful general introduction to how most people live, stressing the impact of the West on older traditional cultures. Chapters 4 to 7 deal specifically with India and the Far East. *Ment.*

DE BARY, WILLIAM THEODORE 1919– (ed.) *Sources of the Japanese Tradition* (1958); *Sources of Indian Tradition* (1958); *Sources of Chinese Tradition* (1960). Matchless historical surveys of religion and philosophy using new and invariably accurate translations of key primary materials supplemented by lucid explanations. Invaluable for both students and the general reader. *Columbia $7.50 ea.*

GINSBURG, NORTON 1921– (ed.) *The Pattern of Asia* (1958). A stimulating collection of essays by specialists on aspects of the physical, economic, and political geography of the area. *Prentice-Hall $11.95.*

KAHIN, GEORGE M. 1918– (ed.) *Major Governments of Asia* (1958). Government and politics of China, Japan, India, Pakistan, and Indonesia described and analyzed in a collection of first-rate introductory essays written by recognized scholars. *Cornell $7.25.*

*Pelican History of Art. The Art and Architecture of India* (1953), by BENJAMIN ROWLAND 1904– ; *The Art and Architecture of Japan* (1955), by ROBERT T. PAINE 1900– and ALEXANDER SOPER 1904– ; *The Art and Architecture of China* (1956), by LAURENCE SICKMAN 1907– and ALEXANDER SOPER 1904– . These three comprehensive surveys are uniformly handsome and readable, making visible important aspects of Oriental culture. *Penguin $12.50 ea.*

REISCHAUER, EDWIN O. 1910– and JOHN K. FAIRBANK 1907–
*East Asia: The Great Tradition* (1906). The best one-volume history of China and Japan from their beginnings to the mid-19th century. *Houghton $12.50.*

VINACKE, HAROLD M. 1893– *A History of the Far East in Modern Times* (6th ed 1959). A standard introductory account, providing some historical background but focusing on recent international affairs in East Asia. India is discussed only incidentally. *Appleton $7.*

# B. India

BASHAM, A. L. *The Wonder That Was India* (1955). The definitive history of traditional India. *Macmillan $9, Ever.*

BOWLES, CHESTER 1901– *Ambassador's Report* (1954). A perceptive and reliable appraisal of India today, indispensable for anyone interested in the subject. *Harper $5.50.*

BROWN, D. MACKENZIE 1908– *The White Umbrella* (1953). A collection of excerpts from the writings of important figures in Indian political thought from Manu to Gandhi, supplemented by acute introductory essays by the author. *Calif.*

———— *The Nationalist Movement* (1961). A sequel to the above, analyzing political thought from Ranade to Bhave. *Calif.*

BROWN, W. NORMAN 1892– *The United States and India and Pakistan* (1953). An excellent brief treatment of Indian history, culture, politics, and foreign affairs. *Harvard $5.*

FISCHER, LOUIS 1896– *Gandhi* (1954). A generally reliable biography of a great man. *Ment.*

GANDHI, MOHANDAS K. 1869–1948 *Gandhi's Autobiography* (1927–29). A revealing and always compelling document by one of modern India's most eminent and controversial figures. *Bea.*

MORGAN, KENNETH W. 1908– (ed.) *Religion of the Hindus* (1953). This collection of essays by noted scholars, though somewhat technical, contains some of the best translations and interpretations of Hindu religious scripture and philosophic literature. *Ronald $6.*

NEHRU, JAWAHARLAL 1889– *The Discovery of India* (1946). This work, primarily autobiographical, contains Nehru's views on Indian history and culture. Essential reading for anyone interested in India and its present leader. *Peter Smith $3.50, Anch (abr).*

———— *Independence and After* (1949). This significant collection of essays and speeches illumines Nehru's political views and policies. *Day $4.50.*

PALMER, NORMAN D. 1909– *The Indian Political System* (1961). An authoritative study of Indian government and politics. *Houghton $3.50, HM.*

# INDIA AND THE FAR EAST

**TAGORE, RABINDRANATH** 1861–1941 *A Tagore Reader* (1961). A superb selection from the writings of one of the world's great literary figures, edited by Amiya Chakravarty. *Macmillan $6.50.*

*Upanishads.* The sacred Hindu writings which date back to the 8th century B.C. The preferred translation is by Max Muller (*Dov*). Others: *Oxford $3.75, Ment.*

**WALLBANK, T. WALTER** 1901– *A Short History of India and Pakistan* (1958). A careful work dealing primarily with the modern period. *Ment.*

**ZIMMER, HEINRICH** 1890–1943 *Myths and Symbols in Indian Art and Civilization* (1946). A provocative interpretation by a distinguished Indologist. *Pantheon $4.50, Torch.*

──────── *The Philosophies of India* (1951). An impressive analysis of the major elements in Indian thought and religion, published posthumously. *Pantheon $6, Mer.*

## C. China

**BARNETT, A. DOAK** 1895– *Communist China and Asia* (1960). A careful analysis of the rise to power of Communist China and of its relations with its Asian neighbors. Discusses conditions on Taiwan and recommends a new approach in the U. S. policy toward both Chinas. *Harper $6.95, Vin.*

**CONFUCIUS** c. 551–479 B.C. *The Analects of Confucius.* Arthur Waley's translation and careful editing of the work which provided the basis for the Confucian system is highly preferred: *Macmillan $3.50. Vin.* Other translations under different titles: *BH, Ment, Prem, WoC.*

**CREEL, HERRLEE G.** 1905– *The Birth of China* (1937). Though technically superseded by later works, still an enthralling and reliable account of life during the Shang and early Chou periods (1400–600 B.C.), reconstructed from archaeological, linguistic, and literary evidence. *Ungar $7.50, Ungar.*

**CRESSEY, GEORGE B.** 1896–1963 *Land of the 500 Million* (1955). A comprehensive survey of the geography of China, including principal regions, terrain, climate, resources, etc. *McGraw-Hill $12.75.*

**FAIRBANK, JOHN K.** 1907– *The United States and China* (rev ed 1958). The best general introductory study of the full history of American-Chinese relationships. *Harvard $5.50, Comp.*

**FUNG YU-LAN** 1895– *A Short History of Chinese Philosophy* (1948). One of China's foremost scholars analyzes the major developments in Chinese philosophy and religion from the beginnings to the early 20th century. *Macmillan $7.50, Macm.*

**HUDSON, GEOFFREY F.** 1903–, **RICHARD LOWENTHAL**, and **RODERICK MacFARQUHAR** *The Sino-Soviet Dispute* (1961). A competent treatment of a vital subject. *Praeger $5, FAP.*

LIN YUTANG 1895– (ed. & trans.) *Famous Chinese Short Stories* (1952). An interesting collection of twenty folk tales from the T'ang (A.D. 618–907) and Sung (A.D. 960–1180) periods, adapted by a well-known interpreter of China to the West. *WSP.*

MAO TSE-TUNG 1893– *Mao Tse-tung: An Anthology of His Writings* (1962). Editor Anne Fremantle has written a long, factually reliable introduction on Mao and assembled fourteen articles from Mao's *Collected Works.* Though his revolutionary blueprint, *The New Democracy,* is not included, this book is nevertheless essential reading for anyone interested in the aims and policies of the present ruler of Communist China. *Ment.*

PAYNE, ROBERT 1911– (ed.) *The White Pony* (1947). An anthology of Chinese poetry (sometimes indifferently translated) from earliest times to the 20th century, with short biographies for each poet represented. *Ment.*

SCOTT, A. C. 1909– *An Introduction to the Chinese Theatre* (1959). The best work on the subject in English. Though Scott covers most major aspects, he devotes greatest attention to the classical theater because of its importance. *TAB.*

TSAO HSUEH-CHIN 1717–1764 *Dream of the Red Chamber.* This gigantic, complicated novel dealing with a love affair and the decline of a noble family is widely regarded as a classic of Chinese fiction. *Twayne $6, Anch (abr).*

WALEY, ARTHUR 1889– (ed. and trans.) *The Way and Its Power: A Study of the Tao Te Ching and Its Place in Chinese Thought* (1934). *The Way* is the basic document for Taoism, one of the two most important philosophic schools in China. Of the many English translations, Waley's is by far the best, and it contains an excellent introduction. *Macmillan $3.50, Ever.*

——— (trans.) *Translations from the Chinese* (1941). Beautiful, yet linguistically accurate, renderings into English of more than 200 major Chinese poems, by the most distinguished translator of the Oriental. *Knopf $7.50.*

WILLETTS, WILLIAM 1918– *Chinese Art* (1958). Authoritative, illustrated historical survey of the full wide range of Chinese art. *Braziller $5.*

# D. Japan

AKUTAGAWA RYUNOSUKE 1892–1927 *Rashomon and Other Stories* (1952). Quite uncommon tales written by a literary genius and sensitively translated by Edward Seidensticker. *Liveright $4.95, Ban.*

BOWERS, FAUBION 1917– *Japanese Theatre* (1952). The best general introduction to the subject, emphasizing the traditional forms but not neglecting the modern. Contains three translated *Kabuki* plays. *Nelson $6, Drama.*

## INDIA AND THE FAR EAST

BUNCE, WILLIAM K. *Religions in Japan: Buddhism, Shinto, Christianity* (1955). Useful, readable introduction to the history of Japanese religious beliefs and practices, including the postwar situation. *Tuttle $3, Tutle.*

BURKS, ARDATH W. 1915– *The Government of Japan* (1961). In many ways the best introduction to the subject, emphasizing recent times but also providing essential historical background. *Crowell $2.95, TYC.*

HENDERSON, HAROLD G. 1889– *An Introduction to Haiku* (1958). Skillful, sensitive translations of about 375 17-syllable *haiku*, which, though it dates from earliest times, is still one of Japan's most popular literary forms. Contains the original Japanese, translations, and helpful historical and explanatory discussion. *Doubleday $4.50, Anch.*

KEENE, DONALD 1922– (ed.) *Japanese Literature: An Introduction for Western Readers* (1953). Includes prose fiction, poetry, and drama (mainly from the classical period), plus an adept analytic discussion. *Ever.*

———— (ed.) *Anthology of Japanese Literature from the Earliest Era to the Mid-Nineteenth Century* (1955). Reliable translations of representative samples of all forms from Japan's great literary tradition. *Ever.*

———— (ed.) *Modern Japanese Literature* (1956). A companion volume to the above, covering the period from 1868 to the present day. *Grove $4.75, Ever.*

———— *Living Japan* (1959). A perceptive, sympathetic account of modern Japan, with excellent photographs. *Doubleday $7.95.*

MURASAKI, SHIKIBU 978-1015 *The Tale of Genji.* An absorbing novel about the culture of ancient Japan. The first two parts have been ably translated by Arthur Waley. *Anch, MLG.*

REISCHAUER, EDWIN O. 1910– *Japan, Past and Present* (1952). Short and accurate introduction to Japanese political and social history, with a long section on postwar Japan. *Knopf $4.*

———— *The United States and Japan* (1957). Essential for the informed reader: includes a careful description of Japanese economic, political, and social institutions and traditions; and a full account of U.S.-Japanese relations. *Harvard $5.50.*

TANIZAKI, JUN'ICHIRO 1886– *Some Prefer Nettles* (1955). Edward Seidensticker's translation of the most important novel published in post-World War II Japan. *Knopf $3.50, Berk.*

TREWARTHA, GLENN T. 1896– *Japan: A Physical, Cultural, and Regional Geography* (1945). The best introduction to the subject by a distinguished geographer. *Wisconsin $7.50.*

WARNER, LANGDON 1881– *The Enduring Art of Japan* (1952). A sound, readable introduction to Japanese art. *Harvard $6.50, Ever.*

# E. Southeast Asia

BUSS, CLAUDE A. 1903– *Southeast Asia and the World Today* (1958). Excellent introduction to the problems of the new nations and to recent developments in the area. Includes 27 well-chosen documents. *Anv.*

BUTWELL, RICHARD A. *Southeast Asia Today—And Tomorrow* (1961). Stimulating discussion of the important domestic issues in each country since its independence, with some general remarks on critical international problems. *Praeger $4.25, FAP.*

DU BOIS, CORA 1903– *Social Forces in Southeast Asia* (2nd ed. 1959). An outstanding analysis of the social forces and changes brought about by European colonial rule. *Harvard $2.50.*

GINSBURG *The Pattern of Asia.* See above, page 45.

HALL, DANIEL G. E. 1891– *East Asian History Today* (1959). The only detailed one-volume history that pays enough attention to political aspects. Contains a long bibliography. *Ox.*

KAHIN, GEORGE M. 1918– (ed.) *Government and Politics of Southeast Asia* (1959). Matches the high quality of Kahin's more general study cited above (page 45), but deals exclusively with Southeast Asia. *Cornell $6.50.*

# 4. The Middle East and Africa

## J. GREGORY OSWALD, *University of Arizona*

Greater social and political changes have occurred in Africa and the Middle East in our times than in the preceding millennium. Heirs of both an illustrious and an ignominious past, the peoples of these regions are now consciously constructing a future which will assure expression of national and individual aspirations. Stilled for centuries in the grip of colonialism or ages-old tradition, they exude a new-found enthusiasm in politics and international affairs which cries to be understood. Africa's emergent nations, politically as fertile as the soil from which they sprang, test their skills and their spiritual stamina to join the march of modern man. Iranians, Arabs, Turks, and Israelis, occupying a strategic land mass the size of continental United States, confront destiny with the zeal of dedicated men.

Both the problems and promise of these regions stagger the imagination. They are deeply rooted in a cultural continuum explained by anthropology, philosophy, political behavior, economic development, and other complex forces—some of which stretch so far back in time that they defy short summary. Carleton Coon's timeless study of people and their environment in the Middle East—*Caravan*—is a fine place to begin one's reading. H. A. R. Gibb's superb little volume—*Mohammedanism*—places Islam in focus and makes clear the Prophet's intention that Islam is not only a religion but a total way of life. Aware of this, the reader can appreciate the modern significance of Islam, the fastest-growing religion in Africa and the major barrier to secularism in the Middle East. George Antonius' *Arab Awakening* is a good introduction to Middle East nationalism, and J. Jahn's *Muntu* offers a fascinating invitation to study Africa and its exciting complexities. *Muntu* might be followed by *The Human Factor in Changing Africa* by the renowned Africanist M. J. Herskovits.

Many have profited from Sydney N. Fisher's judicious introductory survey, *The Middle East*. The book list that follows has been enriched by his assistance as well as by that of John R. Willis, Jr., African affairs advisor to the Peace Corps.

## A. The Middle East

ANTONIUS, GEORGE 1891– *The Arab Awakening* (1939). A fundamental introduction to the Arab national movement in the 20th century. *Lippincott o. p.*

*Arabian Nights* (8th to 15th century). Fascinating stories of genii and magicians, of golden palaces and beautiful gardens, of wonderful voyages and adventures, of intrigue and enchantment. The best translation is by Burton: *ML, PB*.

ATIYAH, EDWARD 1903– *The Arabs* (1955). Readable survey of the Arabs' emergence to greatness and their decline until the awakening in our times. *Pen.*

BEN-GURION, DAVID 1887– *Rebirth and Destiny of Israel* (1953). Essays on the emergence of Israel as a nation-state, 1915–1952, by its first Prime Minister. *Philosophical Library o. p.*

*The Bible.* Monumental in the history of religion and literature. See "Religion," page 212.

BURROWS, MILLAR 1889– *The Dead Sea Scrolls* (1955). Scholarly, tempered account of the discovery and contents of the scrolls, which have profoundly affected biblical studies. *Viking $6.50.*

———— *More Light on the Dead Sea Scrolls* (1958). New discoveries and interpretations, some corrections, an overall index, and extensive bibliography. *Viking $6.50.*

COON, CARLETON 1904– *Caravan* (1951). Excellent anthropological introduction to the Middle East written for layman and student by an outstanding authority. *Holt $6.55.*

CROMER, EVELYN BARING 1841–1917 *Modern Egypt* (1909). A two-volume autobiographical account of his rule of Egypt and the Sudan, 1876–1907. *Macmillan o.p.*

DIEHL, CHARLES 1859–1944 *Byzantium: Greatness and Decline* (1957). The classic study by the great French Byzantinist. Contains a fine bibliographical essay by Peter Charanis. *Rutgers $8.50.*

FISHER, SYDNEY N. 1906– *The Middle East* (1959). The best introductory historical survey of Islam, the Ottoman Empire, and

## THE MIDDLE EAST AND AFRICA

the modern Middle East; contains an excellent annotated bibliography. *Knopf $8.95.*

GIBB, H. A. R. 1895– **Arabic Literature** (1926). An introduction to the subject, with a bibliography of Arab literature in translation. *Oxford o.p.*

———— **Mohammedanism** (2nd ed. 1953). Superb succinct account of Islamic religion and culture. *GB.*

HARARI, MAURICE **Government and Politics of the Middle East** (1962). A country-by-country analysis linking the current political systems to their historical origins. The most realistic nonpartisan survey available. *Prentice-Hall $3.95, Spec.*

HITTI, PHILIP KHURI 1886– **History of the Arabs from the Earliest Times to the Present** (6th ed. 1956). The standard text for the history of the Arab peoples down to the 16th century; treats the last four centuries sparsely. *St. Martin's $9.*

HUREWITZ, JACOB COLEMAN 1914– (ed.) **Diplomacy in the Near and Middle East** (1956). An indispensable compilation of documents relating to European diplomacy from 1535 to 1956. *Van Nostrand 2 vols $7.50 & $9.50.*

KHADDURI, MAJID 1909– **Independent Iraq, 1932–1958** (1960). The most thorough, objective, and complete single volume on the emergence of Iraq as an independent Arab nation. *Oxford $7.20.*

KIRK, GEORGE EDEN 1911– **Short History of the Middle East** (5th ed. 1959). Compact factual account emphasizing the major problems of each historical era. *Praeger $6, FAP.*

———— **Contemporary Arab Politics** (1961). A concise history of the modern Arab world. *Praeger $5, FAP.*

**Koran.** The sacred scriptures of Islam by the Prophet Mohammed (570?–632). A new translation, almost literal but highly readable, by Mohammed Marmaduke Pickthall is recommended: *Ment.* Other versions: *Evman-h, Pen, WoC.*

LAWRENCE, THOMAS EDWARD 1888–1935 **Seven Pillars of Wisdom** (1935). An absorbing personal account of Lawrence of Arabia's military-political activities among the Arabs in World War I. *Doubleday $6, Dell.*

LENCZOWSKI, GEORGE 1915– **Oil and State in the Middle East** (1960). A highly informed, balanced account of the relationship between oil and international relations in the area. *Cornell $6.75.*

———— **The Middle East in World Affairs** (1962). Chronological survey of the impact of the Western world on 20th-century Middle East politics. *Cornell $8.95.*

LEWIS, BERNARD 1916– **The Arabs in History** (1950). Concise, readable interpretation of the rise of the Arabs and of the broad economic movements influencing the history of the Middle East. *Hillary $2.50, Torch.*

———— **The Emergence of Modern Turkey** (1961). A comprehensive, well-written, scholarly history of 20th-century Turkey. *Oxford $7.70.*

——— and P. M. HOLT (eds.) *Historians of the Middle East* (1962). Fascinating survey of everything of significance ever written on Middle East history, by 41 international scholars. Invaluable for an understanding of the area. *Oxford $8.*

MEHDI, MOHAMMED T. 1920– *Of Lions, Chained* (1962). An Arab professor's provocative appraisal of United States failures and successes in Middle East diplomacy since 1945. *New World Press $3.25.*

MOOREHEAD, ALAN 1910– *Gallipoli* (1956). The story of the famous campaign which might have changed the course of World War I. *Harper $5.50, Bal.*

MULLER, HERBERT J. 1905– *Loom of History* (1958). Stimulating studies of old civilizations in Asia Minor, viewed from a humanistic position with "reverence and irony." *Harper $7.50, Ment.*

NASSER, GAMAL ABDEL 1918– *Egypt's Liberation: The Philosophy of the Revolution* (1959). A fundamental statement by the ideological leader of Arab nationalism. *Public Affairs $2.50, Econ.*

OMAR KHAYYÁM d. 1123? *The Rubáiyát.* Pleasant cynicism in quatrains filled with vivid Oriental images and symbols. The splendidly poetic translation by Edward FitzGerald is available in numerous editions.

OSTROGORSKY, GEORGE *History of the Byzantine State* (1958). An uncommonly clear, scholarly one-volume history of the Byzantine Empire. *Rutgers $12.50.*

PATAI, RAPHAEL 1910– *The Kingdom of Jordan* (1958). The history of a political and economic anomaly in the Middle East. *Princeton $5.*

ST. JOHN, ROBERT 1902– *Ben-Gurion* (1959). A biography of Israel's first Prime Minister by one who understands the Middle East. *Doubleday $3.95.*

SAYEGH, FAYEZ ABDULLAH *Arab Unity* (1958). A nationalist Arab's commentary on the cultural and political aspects of Arab unity. *Devin-Adair $4.*

SUMNER, BENEDICT H. 1893–1951 *Peter the Great and the Emergence of Russia* (1949). Outstanding analysis of Russia's early 18th-century relations with the Ottoman Empire and the increasing role of Europe in Near East Affairs. *Collr.*

SYKES, PERCY MOLESWORTH 1867–1945 *A History of Persia* (1930). Distinguished history covering from 3000 B.C. to the 20th century. *St Martin's 2 vols $16.*

WATT, W. MONTGOMERY *Muhammad at Mecca* (1953), and *Muhammad at Medina* (1956). Based on wide research, these volumes discuss the religious, political, social, and military activities of the Prophet. *Oxford $4 & $7.20.*

WEIZMANN, CHAIM 1874–1952 *Trial and Error* (1949). The thoughts and political activities of the leader of Zionism during the Mandate period. *Harper $5.*

WHEELOCK, KEITH *Nasser's New Egypt* (1960). Lucid and comprehensive critical study of Egypt since the revolution of 1952. *Praeger $6.*

# THE MIDDLE EAST AND AFRICA

WILSON, EDMUND 1895– *The Scrolls from the Dead Sea* (1955). An absorbing but strongly prejudiced report of the exciting discovery of the ancient scrolls and of their implications for biblical scholarship. *Mer.*

YOUNG, DESMOND *Rommel, The Desert Fox* (1950). Biography of the renowned German general's World War II experience in Egypt and North Africa. *Harper $4.95, Berk.*

## B. Africa

BOVILL, EDWARD WILLIAM 1892– *The Golden Trade of the Moors* (1958). The centuries-old story of how Berbers, Arabs, Jews, and Christians drew on the wealth and industry of black Sudanese. *Oxford $7.*

BUELL, RAYMOND L. 1896–1946 *The Native Problem in Africa* (1928). Important for activities of colonial governments in Africa before 1926. *Macmillan o.p.*

────── *Liberia* (1947). A standard history, covering the century from 1847 to 1946. *University Museum $1.50.*

DAVIDSON, BASIL 1914– *The Lost Cities of Africa* (1959). Achievements of sub-Saharan African civilization before the colonial period. *Little $6.50, Little.*

────── *Black Mother* (1961). Informative, up-to-date account of African contact with Europe and America and of its effects. *Little $6.50.*

DUFFY, JAMES 1923– *Portuguese Africa* (1959). Portugal's historical contact with the peoples of Angola and Mozambique. *Harvard $7.50.*

FAGE, J. D. 1921– *Ghana* (1959). Scholarly reinterpretation of Gold Coast history in the light of its emergence as the independent nation of Ghana. *Wisconsin $3.*

────── *An Introduction to the History of West Africa* (1959). Short, crisp survey by a leading authority. *Cambridge $3, CUP.*

GORDIMER, NADINE 1923– *Six Feet of the Country* (1956). South Africa's most distinguished short story writer tells compellingly about life in and around Johannesburg. *Simon & Schuster $3.50.*

GROVES, C. P. 1887– *The Planting of Christianity in Africa* (1948-55). The major comprehensive history of European missionary expansion. *Butterworth 3 vols o.p.*

HAILEY, WILLIAM MALCOLM 1872– *African Survey* (rev 1956). A classic synthesis of European activities in sub-Saharan Africa during the colonial period. *Oxford $16.80.*

HERSKOVITS, MELVILLE JEAN 1895– *The Myth of the Negro Past* (1941). Explodes myths and misconceptions about the Negro and his past. *Peter Smith $4, Bea.*

_____ ***The Human Factor in Changing Africa*** (1962). A splendid anthropological study of sub-Saharan peoples past and present, with an excellent bibliography. *Knopf $6.95.*

HODGKIN, THOMAS LIONEL 1910– ***Nationalism in Colonial Africa*** (1957). Examines adjustments, compromises, and withdrawals European powers have had to make and will have to make before the claims of African nationalism. *New York Univ. $3.75, NYU.*

_____ ***African Political Parties*** (1961). A thorough analysis by one who has been and still is a leading participant in African politics. *Peter Smith $3, Pen.*

HOLT, PETER MALCOLM ***A Modern History of the Sudan*** (1961). Compact overall history of a state existing on the periphery of the Arab and African worlds. *Grove $5.95.*

JAHN, JANHEINZ ***Muntu*** (1961). Fascinating outline of neo-African culture covering art, religion, philosophy, history, the dance, and surrealism, translated from the German. *Grove $5.50, Ever.*

JONES, ARNOLD H. M. 1904– and ELIZABETH MONROE ***A History of Abyssinia*** (1935). The standard short history. *Oxford o.p.*

OLIVER, ROLAND 1923– (ed.) ***The Dawn of African History*** (1961). Men who have themselves contributed to African history discuss work presently being conducted in African history, giving a good idea of the whole subject and analyzing the many unsolved problems. *Oxford $1.70.*

_____ and GERVASE MATTHEWS (eds.) ***History of East Africa*** (1963). The first of three projected volumes in which the history of East Africa is presented from an African as well as a European point of view. *Oxford.*

PATON, ALAN 1903– ***Cry, the Beloved Country*** (1948). South Africa's most celebrated writer poignantly depicts the race question in South Africa in an intense, sometimes lyrical, novel. *Scribner $3.95, Scrib.*

_____ ***Tales from a Troubled Land*** (1961). Fiction giving insight into the human problems in South Africa. *Scribner $3.50.*

SLADE, RUTH M. ***The Belgian Congo*** (1960). An excellent short history of the period before independence. *Ox.*

_____ ***King Leopold's Congo*** (1962). The first of two interesting volumes tracing the development of race relations in the Congo Independent State to 1908. *Oxford $4.80.*

TRIMINGHAM, JOHN SPENCER ***History of Islam in West Africa*** (1962). A phenomenological study of the religious life of West Africa's Muslims, providing a much-needed account of Africa's fastest-spreading religion. *Oxford $4.80.*

# 5. Latin America

## DONALD DEMAREST, Academy Library Guild

Latin American writing has gone through three distinct stages. During its colonial period, the writers—like the artists and architects—found their models in Mother Spain. During its revolutionary period, which extended over two centuries, the literature of France—first France of the Encyclopedists, then of the Symbolists—was the vital influence. Only very recently has Latin American literature entered a renaissance; compounded of North American techniques and developing from indigenous roots, it promises to have the vitality of the plastic arts of the 1930's.

The Indian has always been a key (and problematic) figure in Latin American letters. During the colonial period he was either a quaint sort of Uncle Tom or an even more fantastic and romantic Natty Bumppo; during the various revolutionary cycles he was first a Rousseauesque Noble Savage and afterwards a faceless symbol of the oppressed. For the new generation, however—especially in Mexico (where the new artistic movements generally originate)—he is the complex protagonist of an exceptionally split but also extraordinarily rich culture. For *mestizo* writers like Juan Rulfo, Rosario Castellanos, and Carlos Fuentes, the Indian epitomizes an ancient wisdom that the Toltecs and Maya once possessed long before the conquistadors arrived on the scene.

In their creative preoccupation with who they are and what they mean, young Latin American writers have a fruitful literary tradition to explore and return to. The pre-Columbian legends—preserved by priest-ethnologists of the caliber of Sahagún and Ximénez and (today) Angel Garibay, or by Europe-educated natives such as the Inca Garcilosa—have a stylistic and symbol-packed richness resembling that of the Upanishads and the Old Testament. A work like *Chilam Balam,* compiled long after the people whose legends and history it preserves had vanished, ranges in style and theme from a Grimm (and Freudian) fairy tale, through an Ecclesiastical curse on the conquerors, to a Blakean myth of a New Jerusalem.

Even the colonial period produced some works of lasting importance. An Alarcón, a Sor Juana Inés de la Cruz —even a Lizardi, whose picaresque novel, *The Itching Parrot,* was the first written and published in this hemisphere—deserve more attention from students of international literature than they have been given.

During the revolutionary cycles (which can be divided into the 19th century wars of independence and the continuing struggles against native dictators), much of the major writing was done by intellectuals turned soldiers— from Hidalgo to Martí. Their manifestos often took the form of poetry, novels, newspaper columns, and philosophic essays. To the latter phases of the revolutions we owe such vital novels as those by Algería (Peru), Arciniegas (Colombia), Azuela (Mexico), Da Cunha (Brazil), Gallegos (Venezuela), and Quiroga (Uruguay). Most such novels suffer, however, from being written too close to the scene: either as protest novels, or as combat diaries compiled by the light of the campfire on the eve of battle. In this genre the semifictionalized accounts of the Villa campaigns by Martín Luis Guzmán are notable. Though there is still no Latin American *War and Peace,* sons of guerillas have composed battle scenes as convincing as Stephen Crane's.

The novelists and journalists fought and wrote. The poets tended to retreat to the ivory towers which Mallarmé and other Symbolists inhabited with great style. In Mexico the retreat took the form of the complex and opaque death- and God-centered poetry of Villaurrutia and Gorostiza. Enlistment in the Spanish Civil War gave Octavio Paz (as it gave Neruda) a social focus for what had been private pyrotechnics.

Meanwhile, a special genre of Latin American writing —which echoes the bitter epigrams of *Chilam Balam* and borrows from such diverse sources as La Rochefoucauld and O. Henry—deserves attention. In the field of the very short story, prose poem, or short essay such Latin Americans as José Luis Borges (Argentina), Ramón López Velarde, Julio Torri, Juan José Arreola (all of Mexico) have perfected forms as stylized as the Japanese *haiku* and as lethal as the scorpion. Combining a European elegance of style with Indian impassivity, these pieces are as far removed, in style and ferocity, from the "sick humor" of the nightclub comics as Swift's *A Modest Proposal* is from Hitchcock.

In very recent years, American publishers have responded enthusiastically to new voices coming out of Latin America. Much, of course, has been hasty political reportage, but durable literary or historical work has appeared. Two books of more than transient interest are C. Wright Mills' ebullient *Listen, Yankee* (which Latin American intellectuals found sympathetic) and Gary MacEoin's *Latin America: The Eleventh Hour* (which does not seek to absolve the United States from guilt).

We shall probably have to wait a generation, as we did after the Mexican Revolution, before writers of the stature of Rulfo and Fuentes can assess the Cuban happenings in terms of fictional art. Meanwhile, a book like Azuela's *The Underdogs* etches a timeless picture of what revolution does to the revolutionaries.

Since Latin Americans blame North Americans for long neglect of their area and problems, we should do more to find out what they have to say about themselves. A good place to begin (and to return to) is *The Labyrinth of Solitude* by Octavio Paz.

## A. Latin-American Literature

ALEGRÍA, CIRO (Peru) 1909– *The Golden Serpent* (1935). One of the great river novels, reminiscent at times of Mark Twain. A surging epic of the Marañón, which runs from the highest Andes into the Amazon, it deals profoundly and compassionately with the boatmen who live on it and the Indian villagers who live beside it. Translated by Harriet de Onís. *SigC*.

ARCINIEGAS, GERMÁN (Colombia) 1900– (ed.) *The Green Continent* (1944). Excellent anthology of writings by more than 30 Latin-American historians, biographers, essayists, and novelists, showing how our southward neighbors think and feel. *Knopf $5*.

AZUELA, MARIANO (Mexico) 1873–1951 *The Flies* (1918) and *The Bosses* (1917). Two pungent novelettes about the Mexican revolution. *Calif.*

——— *The Underdogs* (1927). A starkly incisive novel of the Mexican Revolution. Probing the symptoms of revolution and the aftereffects, Azuela shows that in the end those who are betrayed are the people themselves. *SigC.*

CASTELLANOS, ROSARIO (Mexico) 1922– *Balún-Canán (The Nine Guardians)* (1957). Rich novel about contemporary descendants of Mayan Indians. *Vanguard $3.95.*

CUNHA, EUCLIDES DA (Brazil) 1866–1909 *Rebellion in the Backlands* (1902). The wild west of the Amazon Valley erupting in dramatic action. The epic narrative of Brazil's struggle from tropic jungle toward modern civilization. *Chicago $6.50, Phoen.*

FUENTES, CARLOS (Mexico) 1929– *Where the Air Is Clear* (1960). An ambitious, controversial first novel that provides an epilogue to the revolution, especially as it has affected the second generation. Borrowing well from Dos Passos, Faulkner, Huxley, and Joyce, Fuentes has woven a rich tapestry of a metropolis, Mexico City. *Obolensky $4.95.*

GALLEGOS, RÓMULO (Venezuela) 1884– *Doña Bárbara* (1942). A symbolic novel about a femme fatale, developing the conflict between civilization and barbarism, written by a former President of Venezuela. *Peter Smith $4.*

GALVÁN, MANUEL DE JESÚS (Dominican Republic) 1834–1911 *Enriquillo (The Cross and the Sword)* (1879). Tr. by Robert Graves. About life in the Caribbean during Spain's greatest moment (c. 1503–1533). *Indiana $3.75.*

MACHADO DE ASSIS, JOAQUIM MARIA (Brazil) 1839–1908 *Epitaph of a Small Winner* (1880). Ironic psychological novel about a 19th-century Brazilian George Apley. *Farrar, Straus $3.50, Noon.*

MANACH, JORGE (Cuba) 1898– *Martí, Apostle of Freedom* (1950). Fascinating biography of the martyr of Cuban independence and forerunner of modernism. *Devin-Adair $4.50.*

MISTRAL, GABRIELA (Chile) 1889–1957 *Selected Poems* (1957). Langston Hughes' translations of representative verse by a Nobel Prize winner. *Indiana $3.*

ONÍS, HARRIET DE (U.S.A.) 1899– (ed. and trans.) *The Golden Land* (1948). A rich anthology of Latin-American writings from the Spanish conquest to 1948, chosen to show how native folklore has influenced literature. *Knopf $5.75.*

PAZ, OCTAVIO (Mexico) 1914– *An Anthology of Mexican Poetry* (1958). Published in several countries under UNESCO auspices, excellently edited with a vital introduction by the Mexican poet. In this bilingual edition the first-rate translations are by Samuel Beckett. *Indiana $3.50.*

***Popol Vuh: The Sacred Book of the Ancient Quiché Maya*** (1950).
A marvelous myth put into English by Delia Goetz and Sylvanus G. Morley. *Oklahoma $5.*

RULFO, JUAN (Mexico) 1918– ***Pedro Páramo*** (1955). Powerfully haunting novel about a ghost town in Jalisco; somewhat Faulknerian in tone, but completely indigenous and unique. *Ever.*

SUBERCASEAUX, BENJAMÍN (Chile) 1902– ***Jemmy Button*** (1954). Curious, provocative historical novel about a Fuegian Indian subjected to British culture of the 1830's. *Macmillan o.p.*

VERISSIMO, ERICO (Brazil) 1905– ***Time and the Wind*** (1949). A long novel of epic richness recounting the evolution of the state of Rio Grande do Sol. *Macmillan o.p.*

## B. Books About Latin America

ARCINIEGAS, GERMAN (Colombia) 1900– ***Caribbean: Sea of the New World*** (1946). Weaves a rich tapestry of clashing empires, merging cultures, struggle and achievement. *Knopf $6.75.*

CALDERÓN DE LA BARCA, FRANCES E. (England) 1804–1882 ***Life in Mexico*** (1931). Classic account by a 19th-century diplomat's wife, still largely accurate. *Dolp, Evman-h.*

CASO, ALFONSO (Mexico) 1896– ***The Aztecs*** (1958). A classic of style and learning. *Oklahoma $7.95.*

COVARRUBIAS, MIGUEL (Mexico) 1904–1957 ***Indian Art of Mexico and Central America*** (1957). A brilliant and handsome work, revolutionary yet definitive. *Knopf $17.50.*

CROW, JOHN (U.S.A.) 1906– ***Mexico Today*** (1957). Extraordinarily balanced account of the contemporary situation—in art, industry, politics, journalism, tourism. *Harper $5.*

DÍAZ DEL CASTILLO, BERNAL (Spain) c. 1492–1581 ***Discovery and Conquest of Mexico*** (1632). Blunt, engaging chronicle by one of Cortes' conquistadors. *Farrar, Straus $6.50, Ever, Pen.*

FLORNOY, BERTRAND (France) ***The World of the Inca*** (1956). Authoritative, literate account of a colorful vanished empire. *Vanguard $4.50, Anch.*

HERRING, HUBERT C. (U.S.A.) 1889– ***History of Latin America*** (2nd ed 1961). The standard work, tracing a kaleidoscopic interplay of varied cultures and forces upon an immense, rich continent. *Knopf $10.75.*

HITCHCOCK, HENRY RUSSELL (U.S.A.) 1903– ***Latin American Architecture Since 1945*** (1955). Daring triumphs of modern design reflecting the new civilization that is taking shape. *Doubleday $6.50.*

LEWIS, OSCAR (U.S.A.) 1914– ***The Children of Sánchez*** (1961). Tape-recorded interviews with a typical Mexico City slum family edited to produce an anthropological documentary that reads like a novel. Provides a key to the Latin-American crisis—poverty—that is more convincing than the tomes of the pundits. *Random House $7.50, Vin.*

LIEUWEN, EDWIN (U.S.A.) 1923– *Venezuela* (1961). Compact history of this cockpit country from conquistador days to the present, raising a finger to dangerous winds from right and left but pointing hopefully to the future. *Oxford $4.*

MADARIAGA, SALVADOR DE (Spain) 1886– ***The Rise of the Spanish American Empire*** and ***The Fall of the Spanish American Empire*** (1947). Brilliant, provocative attacks on "The Black Legend" of Spanish colonialism, these well-written volumes provide the essential historical background to an understanding of Latin America today. *Collr.*

MORLEY, SYLVANUS G. (U.S.A.) 1883–1948 ***The Ancient Maya*** (rev 1956). Classic account of the "Greeks" of Central America. *Stanford $10.*

MYERS, BERNARD S. (U.S.A.) 1908– ***Mexican Painting in Our Time*** (1956). Lucid, readable coverage of the Renaissance in Mexican art, beautifully illustrated. *Oxford $15.*

PAZ, OCTAVIO (Mexico) 1914– ***The Labyrinth of Solitude*** (1962). A major modern poet (currently his country's ambassador to India) analyzes the ambivalence of the Mexican—his sudden pendulum swings from sensuality to asceticism, taciturnity to rhetoric, solitariness to social explosion. The sociological and literary classic of our time provides a study in depth of the descendant of the conquistador and the Indian—and of the North American as well. *Grove $3.95, Ever.*

PRESCOTT, WILLIAM HICKLING (U.S.A.) 1796–1859 ***Conquest of Mexico*** (1843) and ***Conquest of Peru*** (1847). Colorful classics of historical writing. *Dolp, Ment, MLG.*

RODMAN, SELDEN (U.S.A.) 1909– ***Haiti, The Black Republic*** (1954). Rounded poetic view of a strange, complex country very much in the news; timely and often prophetic. *Devin-Adair $5.50.*

TORRES-RIOSECO, ARTURO (U.S.A.) 1897– ***The Epic of Latin American Literature*** (1959). A packed panorama, laden with nuggets of insight, and an excellent guide to reading in this field. *Peter Smith $3.50, Calif.*

# 6. The Middle Ages

## JULES ALAN WEIN, Pratt Institute

The thousand years of the Middle Ages are conventionally dated from the fall of Rome in the 5th century to the fall of Constantinople (Istanbul) in the 15th. The first half of this period, often called the Dark Ages, used to be regarded as a "long Gothic midnight," because the Europe-wide organization of the Roman Empire had disintegrated and because we inherit from these five centuries few noteworthy architectural monuments and relatively little of value in literature and art.

But nowadays we realize that the so-called Dark Ages were not a blackout of civilization, but a long period of incubation during which a fusion of classical and "barbarian" cultures prepared the way for the great achievements of the "high," or later, Middle Ages. Greco-Roman society was dying of its own defects long before the incursion of alien peoples administered the *coup de grâce*. It was those vigorous and independent peoples, aided by a store of classical knowledge preserved in monasteries and in daily productive work, who created the basis for social progress far beyond the capability of the ancient world. Not least among their organizational accomplishments was the replacement of the defunct international system of the Roman Empire by the international structure and ideology of the Roman Church.

Some of the notable literature of the five centuries of incubation—such as Augustine's *City of God* and Boethius' *Consolation of Philosophy*—drew inspiration from Plato and the Greco-Roman past, which became interwoven with the doctrines of Christianity. Other literary documents—such as *Beowulf*, *The Song of Roland*, the legends of King Arthur, and numerous Norse, Icelandic, and Teutonic sagas, eddas, and lieder, chanted by scops, bards, minstrels—reflect the injection into the old culture of the new values of new peoples with their characteristic cult: glorification of the conquering hero.

The medieval tales of most appeal to the reader today are the Icelandic and Norse sagas, especially the *Njal Saga* and the *Heimskringla*—and, of course, the Old English *Beowulf*. They present with vivid realism and narrative skill the seafaring adventures, family feuds, personal duels, and political history of the Scandinavian peoples from the 9th through the 12th century.

The later Middle Ages witnessed the full development of feudalism, the gallantry and sordidness of the Crusades, the struggle between popes and emperors for control of Christendom, the fragmentation of the West into segments approaching nationhood, and the economic progress and urbanization that provided material basis for the Renaissance. This is the great period of theological philosophy, of religious art and architecture, of chivalric romance, and of the troubadour poetry and religious idealism that found their consummation in Dante's *The Divine Comedy*.

The subject of *The Divine Comedy* is the Christian drama of sin and redemption, of that salvation to which man is led by his love for woman, Reason, and God's Revelation. Christian in inspiration and form, it speaks to all men in the magnificence of its poetry and the universality of its human insight. Here, and (in miniature) in *The Pearl*, a 14th-century English poem, are movingly recorded medieval man's noblest aspirations.

Medieval readers had large appetite for miscellaneous information along with their stories. Like the encyclopedic *The Divine Comedy*, many of Chaucer's poems abound in information. But this serves only to enrich the effect of Chaucer's imaginative power in works like *Troilus and Criseyde* (a superb psychological narrative poem adapted from Boccaccio's *Filostrato*) and the incomparable *Canterbury Tales*, with their brilliant portraiture, lusty realism, and healthy humor. Chaucer was a voracious reader and liked to share his harvest. In fact, he claimed to have learned about love by reading old books of romance rather than by experience. Read "The

Friar's Tale" and the whole account of the Wife of Bath, and see if you believe him.

Boccaccio, in mid-14th-century Italy, was a transitional figure—an inheritor of the Middle Ages and a shaper of the Renaissance. Poet and author, classical scholar and social philosopher, he wrote in almost every literary form available, and invented others. He is best known for his masterpiece, *The Decameron,* a work of great literary art. In form *The Decameron* is a typically medieval collection of tales, but in substance it embodies a penetrating critique of medieval values and institutions. Though *The Decameron* is most famous for its tales of illicit love, some amusing and some tragic, less than a third of its hundred stories deal with sex problems, and even these are integral to the social and philosophical themes of the work as a whole.

As Boccaccio created the realistic prose fiction of the Renaissance, so his older contemporary, friend, and mentor, Petrarch, set the pattern for Renaissance love poetry. Emulating Dante's literary passion for Beatrice, Petrarch produced, in the *Sonnets* to Laura, one of the great lyrical sequences in the long tradition that culminated in Shakespeare's sonnets. His place is also secure in intellectual history, for if any individual can be styled the "father" of the Renaissance, Petrarch is the man. A tireless scholar, writer, and searcher for ancient manuscripts, he led and inspired the generations of humanists who recovered classical literature and philosophy for the modern world.

But perhaps the medieval poet who speaks to us with the most modern accent is François Villon, vagabond-poet of 15th-century Paris. Read about his life and works in Wyndham Lewis' fascinating biography, and you will find a timeless, ageless character who is yet an epitome of the medieval temper, with its strange mixture of love-gallantry and religious ribaldry, of piety and gay wit, of gusto in sinning and lust for repentance. The side of the Middle Ages that Henry Adams omits from his *Mont-Saint-Michel and Chartres* (the greatest single American book on the Middle Ages) you will find in Villon. Like Petrarch, Boccaccio, and Chaucer, this French poet had one foot in the future. So did the earnest English cleric who wrote *Piers Plowman*. In his search for truth and justice, Langland's *Piers* is a symbol of man's eternal yearning for a social order in which to live a life fit for man. And that is still the search of the modern world.

## A. Medieval Literature

*The Age of Belief* (1954). Ed. by Anne Fremantle. Excerpts from the medieval philosophers from Augustine to Ockham, with lucid commentary by the editor. *Houghton $3, Ment.*

*Arabian Nights.* See "The Middle East and Africa," page 52.

*Aucassin and Nicolette, and Other Medieval Romances* (8th to 16th century). Delightful stories of love and adventure in the days of the troubadours. *Evman.*

AUGUSTINE *The City of God* and *Confessions.* See "Rome," page 39.

*Beowulf* (8th century). Anglo-Saxon epic of the heroic deeds of a legendary hero. *Appleton $2.25, Cambridge $6.50, Dutton $3, Houghton $3, Oxford $3.50, Pantheon $3, Calif, Collr, Ment, Pen.*

BOCCACCIO, GIOVANNI 1313–1375 *The Decameron* (c. 1348–53). A lusty age and a philosophy of life brilliantly delineated in 100 tales of love, intrigue, and adventure. *Black, Crest, Dell, Evman-h, Liv, ML, WSP.*

BOETHIUS *The Consolation of Philosophy.* See "Rome," page 39.

CHAUCER, GEOFFREY 1340?–1400 *The Canterbury Tales* (1387–1400). Medieval English life and thought entertainingly compounded in stories touched with wit, pathos, common sense, and superb literary art. *Anch, Evman-h, ML, OxA, WoC.* For good versions in modern English see the translations by Nevill Coghill *(Pen)* and R. Lumiansky *(HRW).* V. F. Hopper has done an interlinear translation *(BES).*

———— *The Portable Chaucer.* Contains selections from *The Canterbury Tales, Troilus and Criseyde* (a "psychological novel in verse"), shorter poems, and selections from other long poems in modern translations. *Vik, Vik-h.*

DANTE ALIGHIERI 1265–1321 *The Divine Comedy* (1300–1321). An epic journey through Hell, Purgatory, and Paradise, the brilliant poem is a compendium of medieval Catholic philosophy and religion, embraced in a timeless love story. The translations of "Inferno" and "Purgatorio" by John Ciardi are particularly good *(Ment).* Other translations: *Columbia $4.50, Tudor $3.98, Dolp, Evman-h, GB, HRW, ML, MLCE, OxA, Pen, SM, Vik, Vik-h, Vin, WoC.*

*English Drama before Shakespeare.* Famous medieval miracle plays and interludes, and 16th-century plays, variously anthologized

## THE MIDDLE AGES

and titled by different publishers. *Anch, Ban, BES, Evman, HRW.*

FRANCIS OF ASSISI, SAINT 1182–1226 **The Little Flowers.** A beautiful record of the kind hearts of "Il Poverello" and his friends. *Harper $4.50, Newman $3.50, EvmanNA, Im, Pen, WoC.*

FROISSART, JEAN 1333?–1400? **Chronicles of England, France, and Spain** (1373–90). The classic contemporary history of the first half of the Hundred Years' War. *Evman.*

GEOFFREY OF MONMOUTH 1100?–1154 **History of the Kings of Britain** (c. 1136). Idealized, often imaginary, history that underlies much of Arthurian romance. *Evman.*

GEOFFROY DE VILLEHARDOUIN 1160?–1212? and JEAN DE JOINVILLE 1224?–1317? **Memoirs of the Crusades** (c. 1207 and 1309). Vivid and fascinating first-hand accounts of the 4th and 7th Crusades. *Evman, Evman-h.*

LANGLAND, WILLIAM 1332?–1400? **Piers Plowman.** A powerful social protest in vigorous verse. *Oxford $2.25, Evman-h, Pen.*

MALORY, THOMAS 1430?–1471 **Le Morte d'Arthur** (1485). Sometimes lusty, sometimes idealized picture of chivalric combat and courtly love. *Appleton $1.75, Evman-h, Ment, OxA, WSP.*

MANDEVILLE, JOHN d. 1372 **Travels** (1371). An enjoyable compound of geographical facts and legendary marvels. *Evman.*

*Medieval Latin Poetry.* Delightful verse translations of medieval songs and satires are presented in two sound scholarly anthologies: HELEN WADDELL 1889– **Medieval Latin Lyrics** (5th ed 1948), *Barnes & Noble $3.50;* and GEORGE F. WHICHER 1889–1954 **The Goliard Poets** (1949), *New Directions $7.50.*

MOHAMMED **The Koran.** See "The Middle East and Africa," page 53.

*Njal Saga.* Realistic, grimly humorous story of a 12th-century Icelandic judge who could rule the republic by his justice, but could not keep his wife from feuding with beautiful neighbor Hallgerda, to Njal's undoing. *New York Univ. $6.50, Pen.*

OMAR KHAYYÁM **The Rubáiyát.** See "The Middle East and Africa," page 54.

PETRARCH (FRANCESCO PETRARCA) 1304–1374 **Sonnets and Songs.** Justly admired for centuries as the first great literary expression of romantic love. *Pantheon o.p.*

POLO, MARCO 1254?–1324? **Travels** (1300–24). Colorful autobiographical account of the adventures of a Venetian merchant who was an official in China under the great Kublai Khan. *Black, Dell, Evman-h, ML, Pen, SigC.*

*The Portable Medieval Reader* (1949). Ed. by James B. Ross and Mary M. McLaughlin. The world of the Middle Ages in 690 pages of selections from biography, history, science, theology, and poetry. *Vik, Vik-h.*

*The Romance of Tristan and Iseult* (12th century). A great medieval legend of tragic love. *Columbia $3.50, Heritage $6, Anch.*

*Selections from Medieval Philosophers* (1930). Ed. by Richard Mc-

Keon. Two volumes of selections from Augustine to Ockham, with good introductions. *ModSL, Scrib.*

THOMAS À KEMPIS 1380–1471 **The Imitation of Christ** (*c.* 1471). A famous devotional work reflecting the ideals of the medieval church. *Many editions.*

THOMAS AQUINAS, SAINT 1225?–1274 **Writings.** The greatest Catholic philosopher and theologian writes about God, man, and man's pursuit of his destiny. *Random House 2 vols $15, EvmanNA, ML.*

———— **On the Truth of the Catholic Faith.** A new, four-volume translation of *Summa Contra Gentiles,* classic manual of Christian doctrine. *Im.*

VILLON, FRANÇOIS 1431–1463? **Poems.** Compelling, illuminating lyrics by the singing rogue of old Paris. *Ban, BH, Black.*

## B. Books About the Middle Ages

ADAMS, HENRY 1838–1918 **Mont-Saint-Michel and Chartres** (1904). Penetrating, sensitive analysis of the medieval spirit in architecture and literature. *Houghton $6, Anch, Collr, Ment, SenEd.*

**The Age of Chaucer** (1954). Ed. by Boris Ford. The first volume of *The Pelican Guide to English Literature,* containing short essays on the literature of the period and an excellent collection of poems and plays. *Pen.*

ANDERSON, GEORGE K. 1901– **The Literature of the Anglo-Saxons** (1949). Excellent one-volume introduction to the whole range of Anglo-Saxon literature, with illustrative excerpts in translation and fine annotations. *Russell $8.50.*

ANOUILH, JEAN 1910– **The Lark** (1956). A thoughtful dramatic treatment of St. Joan, to be compared to Shaw's version. *Oxford $3.50, Drama.*

BLOCH, MARC 1886–1944 **Feudal Society** (1960). Very readable translation of a classic French study of the growth, nature, and broad social significance of feudalism in Western Europe. *Chicago $8.50.*

CHUTE, MARCHETTE 1909– **Geoffrey Chaucer of England** (1946). Delightful and meaty popular introduction to the poet and his time, with illuminating analyses of the major poems. *Dutton $5, Evman.*

COULTON, GEORGE G. 1858–1947 **Medieval Panorama** (1947). Richly detailed survey of the English scene from the Norman Conquest to the Reformation. *Mer.*

DRUON, MAURICE 1918– **The Accursed Kings.** A series of vivid historical novels about the French monarchy in the turbulent 14th century, including **The Iron King** (1956), **The Strangled Queen** (1957), **The Poisoned Crown** (1957), and **The Royal Succession** (1958). *Scribner $4.50 ea.*

## THE MIDDLE AGES

**DURANT, WILL** 1885– *The Age of Faith* (1950). Clear, vivid popular history of 1000 years of medieval civilization—Christian, Judaic, Islamic. *Simon & Schuster $12.*

**HUGO, VICTOR** 1802–1885 *The Hunchback of Notre Dame* (1831). The strange love of a hunchback for a dancer. A great historical novel set in 15th-century Paris. *Norton $1.65, Ban, Evman-h, ML, Nel.*

**HUIZINGA, JOHAN** 1872–1945 *The Waning of the Middle Ages* (1924). Colorful and original interpretation of the psychology of the late Middle Ages in France, based on secular and religious literature, art, and costume. *Anch.*

**KELLY, AMY** 1878– *Eleanor of Aquitaine and the Four Kings* (1950). Wife of Louis VII of France and Henry II of England, mother of Richard the Lion-Hearted and King John, Eleanor made history as a mistress of political intrigue. First-rate biography and history. *Harvard $5.50, Vin.*

**LAMB, HAROLD** 1892–1962 *The Crusades.* One-volume edition combining *Iron Men and Saints* (1930), the best popular account of the First Crusade; and *The Flame of Islam* (1931), the story of 150 years of struggle for supremacy between the Saracens and the West. *Doubleday $6, Ban.*

────── *Charlemagne* (1954). A great king and conqueror brought to life in a striking biography. *Doubleday $4.50, Ban.*

**LEFF, GORDON** 1926– *Medieval Thought from St. Augustine to Ockham* (1958). Concise survey of the philosophers and philosophies of the Middle Ages. *Quadrangle $5, Pen.*

**LEWIS, D. B. WYNDHAM** 1894– *François Villon* (1928). A fascinating biography of the great 14th-century vagabond-poet, with generous selections from his poetry both in French and in English translations. *Anch.*

**MOORE, GEORGE** 1852–1933 *Héloïse and Abélard* (1921). Fictionized version of a famous love affair. *Black.*

**MUNTZ, HOPE** 1907– *The Golden Warrior* (1949). A distinguished and beautiful novel about Harold, last of the Saxon kings, and his gallant losing fight against William the Conqueror. *Scribner $4.50.*

**OLDENBOURG, ZOË** 1916– *Destiny of Fire* (1961). A compassionate and moving novel based on the 13th-century scourge known to history as the Albigensian Crusade. *Pantheon o.p.*

**PAINTER, SIDNEY** 1902–1960 *Mediaeval Society* (1951). The complex system of medieval life lucidly summarized in a short essay. *Corn.*

**PEI, MARIO** 1901– *Swords of Anjou* (1953). Recaptures the spirit of the Middle Ages in a fast-moving romance about the Moors in Spain. *Day o.p.*

**PIRENNE, HENRI** 1862–1935 *Economic and Social History of Medieval Europe* (1937). Clear and penetrating; a rapid sketch, but a classic in its field. *Harv.*

**POWER, EILEEN** 1889–1940 *Medieval People* (1924). Fine scholarship and stylistic grace recreate six medieval lives in memorable fashion. *Peter Smith $3, Anch.*

READE, CHARLES 1814–1884 *The Cloister and the Hearth* (1861). Vigorous, realistic novel set in Flanders, France, Germany, and Italy toward the end of the Middle Ages. *CoNC, Evman, Harp, ML, Nel, SM, WSP.*

SCOTT, WALTER 1771–1832 *Ivanhoe* (1819). Romance of Old England, with Richard the Lion-Hearted, Robin Hood, tournaments, love, and robber barons. *CoNC, Collr, Dell, Dolp, Evman, Nel, SigC, WSP.*

———— *Quentin Durward* (1823). A young Scottish adventurer in France wins the king's favor and a bride. *CoNC, Dolp, Evman, ML, Nel, Scrib, SigC.*

SHAKESPEARE *Richard II, Henry IV (1 & 2), Henry V, Richard III, Henry VI (1, 2, & 3).* These historical dramas reflect the glories and violence of feudal times. See "In Tudor England," page 80, for editions.

SHAW, GEORGE BERNARD 1856–1950 *Saint Joan* (1923). A modern chronicle play with Jeanne d'Arc as its heroine. *Pen.*

TAYLOR, HENRY OSBORN 1856–1941 *The Mediaeval Mind* (4th ed 1959). The standard scholarly exposition of medieval intellectual history. *Harvard 2 vols $10.*

UNDSET, SIGRID 1882–1949 *Kristin Lavransdatter* (1920–22). A fictional trilogy of medieval Scandinavia: the passion of Kristin's bridal wreath, the tragedy of her married life at Husaby, and the cross she bore to the end. *Knopf $6.50.*

VALENCY, MAURICE 1903– *In Praise of Love* (1958). A brilliant, high-level analysis of the poetic tradition of the troubadours in its historical, social, and psychological setting. *Macmillan $3.95, Macm.*

VOSSLER, KARL 1872–1949 *Mediaeval Culture: An Introduction to Dante and His Times* (1929). Definitive study of the religious, philosophical, political, and literary background of Dante's poetry, with an analysis of *The Divine Comedy.* An education in itself. *Ungar 2 vols $9.*

WADDELL, HELEN 1889– *The Wandering Scholars* (7th ed 1949). The life and art of the lyric poets of the Latin Middle Ages, with selections from the poetry in the original and in charming translations. *Barnes & Noble $3.50, Anch.*

WHITE, HELEN 1896– *Bird of Fire* (1958). St. Francis of Assisi and his age made to live in a well-spun and soundly researched historical novel. *Macmillan $3.95, Collr.*

# 7. The Renaissance

## ON THE CONTINENT

**LOUIS C. ZUCKER,** *University of Utah*

The Renaissance nurtured the seeds of our modern culture—our art, our science, our literature. During the Middle Ages the great painters had been committed to religious symbolism: Madonna and Child, Descent from the Cross, saints and saints and saints again, rendered with pious zeal. In the Renaissance, the artists became absorbed with this world rather than the next, with humanity rather than divinity. They rediscovered what the Greeks had known and enjoyed: the eloquence of the human body and the deep delights of nature. As a result, in the painting which reached a climax with da Vinci, Michelangelo, Raphael, and Titian (even when they dealt with stock religious subjects) we find a passion for the magnificent textures of the world about them and for the beauty of mankind. Like Shakespeare's Miranda, they seem to cry:

> How beauteous mankind is! O brave new world
> That has such people in't!

Fortunately for us, several of the greatest Renaissance artists were also writers. Cellini's *Autobiography* is perhaps the best single record of the *virtù*—the bold self-assertiveness of the period. Da Vinci's *Notebooks* with their fascinating drawings show the proverbial yet incredible range of Renaissance genius. And a lesser artist of the period, Vasari, gives us in his *Lives of the Painters* an intimate, gossipy glimpse into the lives of the great men who wrought the new beauty.

As in art, so in science. Heroic navigators—Vasco da Gama, Columbus, Vespucci, Magellan—opened new horizons on earth and in the minds of men; they were rapidly followed by that astonishing swarm of explorers and colonizers who opened the continent on which we live. Similarly, Copernicus and Galileo discovered new vistas in the heavens. Da Vinci and Vesalius pioneered the new science of anatomy, helping men to learn more about their bodies and hence about themselves. All these discoveries, and others, might have been largely wasted but for one Renaissance craftsman, Gutenberg, who invented the art of printing from movable type. From 1475 to 1500 ten thousand editions of books poured from the presses in Italy alone. For most people, without printing there would have been no books to read; mass education and modern democracy would have remained the most visionary of dreams. Altogether, Renaissance science was profound in its effects and magnificent in its scope, embracing the heavens, earth, and man.

The Renaissance was speeded by the revival of ancient culture. But, like its art and science, its literature arose from that extraordinary release of creative energy which thrilled first through Italy, later through France, Spain, England, and beyond.

Consider, for instance, what lies behind such modern phrases as "a Machiavellian schemer" and "a Rabelaisian wit." The first phrase reflects the fame of a Florentine statesman whose brief volume, *The Prince,* is surely the most perceptive analysis ever written of the methods of power politics. Almost simultaneously, the counterpart of *The Prince,* More's *Utopia,* projected the soaring Renaissance dreams of social perfection.

The phrase "a Rabelaisian wit" recalls the unique comic genius of a Renaissance Frenchman. A physician and an irrepressible jester, François Rabelais had his joke even in his will, which reads: "I owe much; I have nothing; I give the rest to the poor." His *Gargantua* and *Pantagruel* are the most meaningful and tallest tall tales in literature. Rabelais was the earthiest writer of an earthy age: fanciful word inventions, ribald jests, and lusty adventures poured from him in a torrent, while he was hugely amused by the body's appetites and functions.

Meanwhile Montaigne, Rabelais's younger and more urbane contemporary, set forth in his *Essays* a timeless appraisal of men, morals, and manners. Except for Shakespeare, no man of his age plumbed human motives more fully and deeply. "Others form man," Montaigne wrote; "I only report him." And he reported himself with a poise and veracity that make him still the delight of adult minds the world over. To Montaigne, a balanced skepticism guided by the great pagan classics was the way to learn about and enjoy life. Though a conforming Catholic, he doubted that any philosopher or theologian had found ultimate truth.

To see man through the eyes of a Michelangelo or a da Vinci; to pierce the uncharted seas with Columbus; to explore the universe with Copernicus or Galileo; to meet Rabelais and Montaigne face to face—this is to sample the range, the depth, the brilliance of the Renaissance. In its creative energies set free, we mark for the first time in history the limitless potentialities of the modern mind.

## A. Continental Renaissance Literature

BOCCACCIO *The Decameron.* See "The Middle Ages," page 66.

CASTIGLIONE, BALDASSARE 1478–1529 *The Courtier* (1528). The Renaissance ideal of gentleman and lady developed in a succession of dialogues. To these, we largely owe our "old school" conceptions of the lady and the gentleman. *Ungar $2.25, Anch, Evman-h, Ungar.*

CELLINI, BENVENUTO 1500–1571 *Autobiography* (first pr. 1728). The artist-genius as hot-blooded, unscrupulous, egotistic rogue. Inside tales about his dealings, tricks, and work, involving popes, kings, nobles, other artists, and models. *Phaidon $3.50, Black, Dolp, Evman-h, Pen, WoC, WSP.*

CERVANTES SAAVEDRA, MIGUEL DE 1547–1616 *Don Quixote* (1605–15). This rambling novel is many things to many people. Underneath the richly comic surface lie deep problems of illusion and reality, of too much and too little idealism, of the weaknesses in the Spanish character. The recent translations by Samuel Putnam *(Vik, Vik-h)* and J. M. Cohen *(Pen)* are superior to others, old or new, for their accuracy, vividness, and readability. Other editions, including abridgments: *Dodd $3, Houghton $2.95, BES, Evman-h, Ment, ML, MLCE, MLG, PB.*

DA VINCI, LEONARDO 1452–1519 *The Notebooks.* Text and drawings show Leonardo's versatile powers perfecting the spiritual and esthetic heritage of his time and experimenting toward the mechanical wonders of ours. *Braziller $7.50, Ment, ML.*

ERASMUS, DESIDERIUS 1466–1536 *In Praise of Folly* (1512). Witty satire of monkish superstitions, theological squabbling, learned ignorance, war, and other human vagaries by the most influential humanist of the Renaissance. *Michigan $4.40, Princeton $3.75, AA, ML.*

*Famous Utopias of the Renaissance* (1946). Ed. by Frederic R. White. A useful collection of major Renaissance visions of a better world, including MORE, *Utopia* (1516); RABELAIS, "Abbey of Thélème" from *Gargantua* (1535); CAMPANELLA, *City of the Sun* (1623); and BACON, *The New Atlantis* (1626). *Hendricks o.p.*

MACHIAVELLI, NICCOLÒ 1469–1527 *The Prince* (1513). An influential manual for the ruler who would establish his realm and perpetuate his rule. Although Machiavelli appeals to self-interest as the core of human nature, he makes order and prosperity in the state the goal of the political leader, not the ruler's self-aggrandizement. *Appl, Evman-h, Gate, Ment, ML, MLCE, Pen, WoC, WSP.*

MONTAIGNE, MICHEL DE 1533–1592 *Essays* (1580, 1588). Personal, rambling, richly urbane discourses on the art of living humanely in a secularized society. *Knopf 3 vols $15, Stanford $5.75, Anch, Appl, ML, PB, Pen, SM.*

PETRARCH *Sonnets and Songs.* See "The Middle Ages," page 67.

*The Portable Renaissance Reader* (1953). Ed. by James B. Ross and Mary M. McLaughlin. The Continental Renaissance in 756 pages, chosen to represent all the writings of that teeming time. *Vik, Vik-h.*

RABELAIS, FRANÇOIS 1494?–1553 *Gargantua* (1535) and *Pantagruel* (1533). Although these stories of fabulously lusty giant-heroes appear to be fantastic farces, between the lines they reflect the mature Renaissance satirically disposing of the lingering old order in education and morality. The Putnam translation is recommended *(Vik, Vik-h).* Others: *Evman-h, MLG, Pen.*

VASARI, GIORGIO 1511–1574 *The Lives of the Painters* (1550). A pupil of Michelangelo and Andrea del Sarto gives reasonably accurate and acute accounts of the famous Italian painters, sculptors, and architects of his day, largely from personal knowledge. *Simon & Schuster $5, Evman-h, ML, Noon.*

## B. Books About the Continental Renaissance

BERENSON, BERNARD 1865–1959 *Italian Painters of the Renaissance* (1932). Appreciative essays about Venetian, Florentine, Central Italian, and North Italian painters by an intimate connoisseur. *Phaidon $8.50, Oxford $6.25, Mer.*

# THE RENAISSANCE

**BURCKHARDT, JAKOB** 1818–1897 *The Civilization of the Renaissance in Italy* (1860). A pioneer but still definitive work, discussing culture, politics, science; cities and institutions; realities and ideals. *Phaidon $2.95, Oxford $2.10, Peter Smith $6.75, Ment, ML, Torch.*

**CORVO, FREDERICK, BARON (FREDERICK ROLFE)** 1860–1913 *Chronicles of the House of Borgia* (1901). A powerful and wicked family is portrayed in a style brilliant and appropriately decadent. *Dov.*

**DURANT, WILL** 1885– *The Renaissance* (1953). A popular, readable survey of our Renaissance heritage and of the men who made it, stressing Italy and its art. *Simon & Schuster $10.*

**ELIOT, GEORGE** 1819–1880 *Romola* (1863). Excellent novel portraying moral deterioration in 16th-century Florence. *Evman-h, WoC.*

**LAMB, HAROLD** 1892–1962 *Suleiman the Magnificent* (1951). A romantic biography of the sultan (died 1566) who raised the Ottoman Empire to its pinnacle of success and let it begin its decline. *Doubleday $5.*

**LUCAS, HENRY S.** 1889– *The Renaissance and the Reformation* (2nd ed. 1960). Dependable summary of this most significant period of history. *Harper $8.50.*

**MATTHEWS, GEORGE T.** 1917– (ed.) *News and Rumor in Renaissance Europe (The Fugger Newsletters)* (1959). About the great German family of merchant princes, the richest family in Renaissance Europe. *Putnam $2.50, Cap.*

**MATTINGLY, GARRETT** 1900–1962 *The Armada* (1959). A masterly piece of historical writing, as readable as a novel, about the Spanish attempt to invade Elizabethan England. *Houghton $6, SenEd.*

**MEREZHKOVSKY, DMITRI** 1865–1941 *The Romance of Leonardo da Vinci* (1902). A brilliant imaginative portrait of da Vinci and a panoramic pageant of his times. *Heritage $3.95, ML, WSP.*

**MORGAN, CHARLES H.** 1902– *The Life of Michelangelo* (1960). The best one-volume account of the life and work of the greatest sculptor between Phidias and Rodin. *Reynal $6.*

**MORISON, SAMUEL ELIOT** 1887– *Admiral of the Ocean Sea* (1942). Scholarly but highly readable biography of Columbus, dealing expertly with his seamanship. *Little $8.50.*

**MOTLEY, JOHN L.** 1814–1877 *The Rise of the Dutch Republic* (1856). An excellent history of the thirty years' resistance (1555–1584) of the Protestant Netherlands against the mighty Spain of Philip II. *Evman-h.*

**PANOFSKY, ERWIN** 1892– *Meaning in the Visual Arts* (1955). A profound student of art and culture attractively describes the relations between life and art in the Middle Ages and the Renaissance. *Peter Smith $3.40, Anch.*

**PATER, WALTER** 1839–1894 *The Renaissance* (1873). Deeply felt impressions of a great era by a great critic. *Ment, Mer, ML.*

**PRESCOTT** *Conquest of Mexico* and *Conquest of Peru.* See "Latin America," page 62.

***The Renaissance Philosophy of Man*** (1956). Ed. by Ernst Cassirer *et al.* Selections from the major thinkers of the early Italian Renaissance on the central subject of the nature of man. *Chicago $5, Phoen.*

ROEDER, RALPH 1890– ***The Man of the Renaissance*** (1933). This "man" includes Aretino with his lust for living; Castiglione, the gentle knight; Machiavelli, the shrewd and subtle strategist; and Savonarola, the puritanic monk. *Mer.*

SCOTT, GEOFFREY 1885–1929 ***The Architecture of Humanism*** (1914). An eloquent vindication of Renaissance architecture as being based on the styles of Greece and Rome. *Peter Smith $3, Anch.*

SYPHER, WYLIE 1905– ***Four Stages of Renaissance Style*** (1955). Integrating the fine arts and literature, the author describes and interprets their transformations from 1400 to 1700 in a profound, difficult book. *Anch.*

WEBER, J. SHERWOOD 1918– *et al.* ***From Homer to Joyce*** (1959). Contains guides to the reading of masterworks by Boccaccio, Chaucer, Machiavelli, Rabelais, Montaigne, Shakespeare, and Cervantes. *Holt $2.50.*

YOUNG, GEORGE F. 1846–1919 ***The Medici*** (1909). A colorful verbal portrait of the Florentine merchant princes and their artists. *ML.*

ZWEIG, STEFAN 1881–1942 ***Erasmus of Rotterdam*** (1934). Readable, authoritative biography of the great Dutch humanist, the epitome of the Renaissance man of culture. *Comp.*

# IN TUDOR ENGLAND

## LESLIE M. OLIVER, Lesley College

What makes an age great? Is it merely we who think it so? Certainly, during the century and a half following the death of Elizabeth Tudor, Englishmen—always paying at least lip-service to Shakespeare, "Nature's child"—seem to have seen little to admire in the Tudor period. From the Romantics on, however, men have agreed that the 16th century in England was a period of great accomplishment.

The Tudor monarchs, from Henry VII through Elizabeth I—except for the unfortunate Mary and the sickly boy Edward, who between them ruled only eleven years—were vigorous, strongminded, active, popular rulers. They knew what they wanted for England, and how to get it. They had a way with the people. And they gave England its first century of legitimate rule, during which no king was violently removed from the throne, and each succeeding monarch had at least a strong legal claim to the succession. England was relatively prosperous during that period—and at peace throughout most of it. She was powerful enough, and wealthy enough, to be sought, courted, and sometimes attacked by the great powers of the Continent. She survived the political and doctrinal struggles of her own ecclesiastical reformation, though sowing seeds of trouble for later times to reap. France rejected and lost her Huguenots; England kept her Catholics, found an accommodation for and with them, and was the stronger for it. Is it any wonder that we see in Shakespeare a constant predilection for legitimacy and "degree"?

This time of relative peace, political stability, and economic growth helped shape the English Renaissance. Oxford and Cambridge prospered as centers of the new learning; the royal courts were abuzz with it. Even Henry VIII, in addition to being a patron of scholars, wrote poetry and composed music. And Elizabeth encouraged the arts and letters, especially the drama.

The English were in many ways half pirates: they plundered the Spanish treasure fleets and "singed the King of Spain's beard" in his own harbors; and they ransacked the literary treasures of other countries and times, translating and adapting and making their own whatever they thought they could use. Shakespeare himself levied tribute on Plutarch and Belleforest, Saxo Grammaticus and Montaigne.

The highest and most original Elizabethan achievement was in the theater. When the period opened there was already a well-developed native drama, using largely religious themes. Marlowe, Shakespeare, and a host of others expanded this drama into secular fields and enriched it with foreign and classical borrowings. Between 1590 and 1620 Englishmen enjoyed the world's richest and most varied theater; no age of the world can match it for quantity and diversity; only the classic Greek drama compares with it in quality.

Other arts were almost equally vigorous. Music was everywhere, usually vocal. Nondramatic poetry was rich and various. The English began building churches and homes for the nobility on fresher models than the old Gothic. If they had no great native painters, they attracted many continental artists, paid them well, and tried to keep them.

The language they developed—at its best, perhaps, in Shakespeare and the King James Bible—is both a cause and an effect of their greatness. Easy, flexible, varied, it was a tool expertly worked by verbal masters. Elizabethan English is proof enough, if proof were needed, that a freely used, freely changing language is in no danger of degenerating. In their unacademic linguistic freedom they produced a literature we can admire today, but cannot equal.

# A. Tudor Literature

*Anthology of English Drama Before Shakespeare* (1952). Ed. by Robert B. Heilman. A rich selection of early dramas, from the first liturgical tropes to the immediate forerunners of the Elizabethans, showing how the drama developed before it reached its climax in Shakespeare. *HRW*.

BACON, FRANCIS 1561–1626 *Essays* (1597, 1612, 1625). Project a shrewd, practical estimate of human life in aphoristic sentences. Macaulay said these essays have "moved the intellects that have moved the world." *Appl, Dolp, Evman-h, Nel, SM, WoC, WSP*.

_____ *The Advancement of Learning* (1605). An outline of the inductive system of reasoning, and an influential argument for the adoption of the scientific method. *Odyssey $2.50, Oxford $2, Evman-h, WoC*.

*Chief Elizabethan Dramatists* (1911). Ed. by William Allan Neilson. Contains 30 plays by Shakespeare's contemporaries. No one knows Shakespeare who knows Shakespeare only; these rivals of his, first-rate playwrights by any standard, will add a new dimension to one's understanding and appreciation of Shakespeare and of his time. *Houghton $8.50*.

DONNE, JOHN 1573–1631 *Poems* (1633). First of the so-called metaphysical poets, and still foremost among English poets in the brainy, sinewy quality of his verse. He writes of love as if it were a religion, of religion as if it were a passionate love affair. *Appl, Evman-h, ML, MLG, OxA, Pen*.

*Eight Famous Elizabethan Plays* (1932). Ed. by E. C. Dunn. A briefer, less expensive collection than Neilson's above. *ML, MLCE*.

HAKLUYT, RICHARD 1552–1616 *Voyages* (1598–1600). Selected reports of English voyagers and explorers, real and legendary. Most literate Elizabethans, including the playwrights, knew and liked this often fascinating book. *Evman-h, WoC*.

JONSON, BEN 1572?–1637 *Plays*. Next to Shakespeare, the best and most interesting of Elizabethan dramatists. A conscious artist, Jonson exacted high standards and created in conformity with his own clear-cut critical theories. His best play is *Volpone*. *Drama, Drama-h, Evman-h, WoC*.

KYD, THOMAS 1558–1594 *The Spanish Tragedy* (1592). This very popular stage piece set the pace for most of the tragedies that came after it, including Shakespeare's *Hamlet*. *Appl*.

*Life in Shakespeare's England* (1911). Ed. by John Dover Wilson. Selected readings in Elizabethan prose to represent the tenor of the times. *Cambridge $2, Pen*.

MARLOWE, CHRISTOPHER 1564–1593 *Plays*. If this brilliant poet-dramatist had lived longer, he might well have rivaled

Shakespeare. His principal plays are **Tamburlaine, Doctor Faustus,** and **The Jew of Malta.** *Over a dozen editions.*

MORE, THOMAS 1478–1535 **Utopia** (Latin 1516, English 1551). In this satire More pictures an ideal nation founded on liberty, toleration, and economic equality. His would be a dull world, but this is nevertheless a classic vision of what human society might be. *Cambridge $1.75, Oxford $1.30, Appl. Evman-h, SM.*

NASHE, THOMAS 1567–1601 **The Unfortunate Traveller** (1594). A picaresque forerunner of the modern novel. *Putnam $2.50, Cap.*

**The Portable Elizabethan Reader** (1946). Ed. by Hiram Haydn. The best small, yet representative, anthology of Tudor writing. *Vik, Vik-h.*

SHAKESPEARE, WILLIAM 1564–1616 **Plays.** The finest drama of the Christian world, infinitely various. Of the 35 tragedies, comedies, and history plays in his canon, perhaps the most popular are **As You Like It, Hamlet, Henry IV, King Lear, Macbeth, Midsummer Night's Dream, Othello, Romeo and Juliet, Henry V, The Tempest, Twelfth Night,** and **The Winter's Tale.** Available in countless hardcover and paperbound collections and editions. The best of the single play paperbound editions are those in *Dell, Pen,* and *SigC.*

———— **Sonnets** (1609). An uneven and puzzling sonnet sequence containing some of the world's finest sonnets and raising seemingly unanswerable questions about their author and his subjects. These and the lyrics scattered throughout his plays insure Shakespeare a secure place in the first rank of lyric poets. *Peter Pauper $1, Appl, Dell, Dolp, Pen.*

SIDNEY, PHILIP 1554–1586 **Astrophel and Stella** (1591). The first and perhaps the finest sonnet sequence in English. Not now in print, it is worth a trip to the library.

———— **Defence of Poesy** (1595). A classic of criticism. *Cambridge $1.25, B&N, SM.*

SPENSER, EDMUND 1552–1599 **Poems.** The first major English poet since Chaucer. His technical skill and rich imagery have made him the poet's poet. *Houghton $7, Evman-h, HRW, OxA.*

# B. Books About Tudor England

ADAMS, JOSEPH QUINCY 1881–1946 *A Life of William Shakespeare* (1923). Scholarly, compact, lively, and not dated. *Houghton $6.*

ANDERSON, MAXWELL 1888–1959 *Elizabeth the Queen* (1939) and *Mary of Scotland* (1934). Poetic dramas about two extraordinary women of 16th-century England. An attempt to revive on the modern stage the Elizabethan tradition of plays in verse. *HarB, Harv.*

BRADLEY, A. C. 1851–1935 *Shakespearean Tragedy* (1904). The dean of modern Shakespearean criticism gives us thorough and extremely helpful analyses of *Hamlet, Othello, Lear,* and *Macbeth*. *St Martin's $4.50, Mer.*

CHAMBERS, E. K. 1866–1954 *Shakespeare, A Survey* (1925). A stimulating collection of a great scholar's introductions to the plays. *Macmillan $4.50, Drama.*

CHUTE, MARCHETTE 1909– *Shakespeare of London* (1949). A brilliant research scholar and writer lets the facts speak for themselves in this most popular biography of the Bard and portrait of the world in which he lived. *Dutton $5.95, Evman.*

——— *Ben Jonson of Westminster* (1953). A splendid account of the life and work of the Elizabethan dramatist next in rank to Shakespeare. *Dutton $5.95, Evman.*

COLERIDGE, SAMUEL TAYLOR 1772–1834 *Lectures on Shakespeare* (1849). A great romantic poet and critic exercises his keen critical judgment on the plays, particularly on the characters. *Cap, Evman-h.*

CRAIG, HARDIN 1875– *Introduction to Shakespeare* (1952). Contains a great Shakespearean scholar's introductions and critical essays from his edition of the complete plays. *Scott, Foresman $2.95.*

ELIOT, T. S. 1888– *Essays on Elizabethan Drama* (1932). One of our most respected poets writes perceptively and engagingly on one of his chief interests. *HarB, Harv.*

GRANVILLE-BARKER, HARLEY 1877–1946 *Prefaces to Shakespeare* (1944-47). A great producer-director, who deserves more credit than any other single person for returning the plays to the open uncurtained apron stage for which they were written, writes shrewd and sensitive analyses of plot, character, and language. *Princeton 2 vols $12, PUP.*

GREG, WALTER WILSON 1875–1959 *The Shakespeare First Folio, Its Bibliographical and Textual History* (1955). A great bibliographer speaks from a long lifetime of work in this field. *Oxford $7.50.*

HACKETT, FRANCIS 1883–1962 *The Personal History of Henry VIII* (1929). Rounded portrait of a lusty monarch who ran the British nation as his private business and established the balance of power principle as the basis of English foreign policy. *Black, ML.*

HARBAGE, ALFRED B. 1901– *Shakespeare's Audience* (1941). Rich in its understanding of the world of the London theater. *Columbia $3, Col.*

HARRISON, GEORGE B. 1894– *Introducing Shakespeare* (1939). The best layman's introduction to the dramatist, his theater, and his plays. *Pen.*

HEILMAN, ROBERT B. 1906– *Magic in the Web* (1956). A stimulating study of the imagery and symbolism in *Othello*, which can teach us to read all of Shakespeare's plays—and perhaps all poetry—more perceptively. *Kentucky $5.*

HOTSON, LESLIE 1897– *The First Night of Twelfth Night* (1954). A brilliantly reconstructed moment in Shakespeare's career, by one of the liveliest of today's Elizabethan scholars. *Macmillan o.p.*

JONES, ERNEST 1879-1958 *Hamlet and Oedipus* (1949). This psychoanalysis of Hamlet—or of *Hamlet*—introduced a new method of dramatic criticism. After it no critic could ignore the dramatist's psyche, nor those of his characters. *Anch.*

LEVIN, HARRY 1912- *The Question of Hamlet* (1959). This very modern, wise, and urbane discussion of *Hamlet* presents it as a complex web of questions, doubts, and irony. *Oxford $3.75, Comp.*

MATTINGLY *The Armada.* See "The Renaissance," page 75.

PARTRIDGE, ERIC 1894- *Shakespeare's Bawdy* (rev ed 1955). This often fascinating study of Shakespeare's bawdy vocabulary will increase the reader's understanding of almost any Elizabethan text. *Evman.*

ROWSE, ALFRED L. 1903- *The England of Elizabeth* (1950) and *The Expansion of Elizabethan England* (1955). The first two volumes of a three-volume history of the period by its foremost modern historian. Vol. I: *Macmillan $10.50, Macm;* Vol. II: *St Martin's $5.75, Torch.*

SCOTT, WALTER 1771-1832 *Kenilworth* (1821). A full-dress historical novel about the period. *Collr, CoNC, Dolp, Evman-h, Nel.*

*Shakespeare's England* (1917). Ed. by Walter A. Raleigh. The standard reference, rich in colorful detail about clothes, homes, sports, trade, manners, and a host of other things. *Oxford 3 vols $12.*

SITWELL, EDITH 1887- *Fanfare for Elizabeth* (1946). A modern poet writes of the future queen's childhood on the periphery of the romantic and terrible court of Henry VIII. *Macm.*

SMITH, IRWIN 1892- *Shakespeare's Globe Playhouse, A Modern Reconstruction* (1956). Based on J. C. Adams' scholarly reconstruction, this book contains scale drawings for building a model of the Globe. *Scribner $10.*

SPENCER, THEODORE 1902-1949 *Shakespeare and the Nature of Man* (2nd ed. 1949). A brilliant analysis of the dramatist's presentation of the human condition. *Macmillan $5, Macm.*

SPURGEON, CAROLINE F. E. 1869-1942 *Shakespeare's Imagery and What It Tells Us* (1935). A basic treatment of the subject, encyclopedic in scope, vital for any serious student of the plays. All subsequent studies of Shakespeare's imagery are built on Miss Spurgeon's foundation. *Cambridge $7.50, Bea.*

STRACHEY, LYTTON 1880-1932 *Elizabeth and Essex* (1928). A subtle portrayal of Queen Elizabeth, her lover Essex, and Raleigh, Burghley, Bacon, Tyrone of Ireland, Philip of Spain, and of their effects on each other. *Harcourt $3.25.*

WEBSTER, MARGARET 1905- *Shakespeare Without Tears* (1955). America's foremost Shakespearean director narrates her experiences in staging the plays. *World $4.50, Prem.*

WINTER, CARL 1906- *Elizabethan Miniatures* (1943). Splendid color reproductions of an almost forgotten art. *Pen.*

# 8. The 17th Century

**JOSEPH A. BYRNES,** *City College of New York*

Between the Renaissance and the Age of Reason, prolonging one and preparing for the other, came the politically turbulent, intellectually active 17th century—the century of genius, as it has been called. In science, the age began with the new cosmology of Copernicus and Galileo, and ended with Newton's law of gravitation. Along the way, it saw the experimental method advocated by Bacon, the founding of the English Royal Society and the French Academy of Sciences, the invention of the telescope and microscope, the discovery of the calculus and logarithms, and Harvey's demonstration of the "Motion of the Heart and the Blood." In the arts, painting produced Rembrandt, Hals, Rubens, Van Dyck, Vermeer, and Velásquez. Music developed from polyphony to harmony, from madrigal to opera; Monteverdi, Corelli, Lulli, and England's greatest native-born composer, Purcell, established the baroque style.

These peaceful accomplishments were achieved at a time when Europe was torn by political, economic, and religious strife. During the Thirty Years' War (1618–1648), pious Catholic and zealous Protestant thoroughly devastated most of Germany. Victims of religious persecution fled: many, like the Huguenots and the Pilgrim Fathers, sought liberty of conscience in the wilderness of the New World. Spain's power was weakening; in France, the monarchy, aided by able administrators like Richelieu and Mazarin, established its supremacy over the rest of the nation, although on an uncertain financial basis. The English, during and after their Civil War (1642–1649), modified their government—in part by killing one king, expelling another, and importing a third; and in part by applying the liberal political tenets of men like

Milton and Locke. Europe's merchant classes made weapons of their wealth in their vigorous struggle for power, nowhere with more success than in England. Energetic, practical, "forward-looking," predominantly radical-Protestant, they eventually triumphed over the conservative aristocrats.

Religion, long a source of bitter controversy, found itself harassed from a new quarter by doubts induced by the "new science." The issue of faith versus reason began increasingly to trouble men's minds. Although the bulk of partisan religious writing is unreadable today, not all religion was acrimonious. Among Englishmen, Fox and Bunyan explored serene personal approaches to God; Donne and Herbert spoke for Anglican moderation.

Philosophy was concerned with its perennial problems, but especially with religion and politics. Descartes began with a complete and radical skepticism; Hobbes postulated man's inhumanity to man, advocating absolutism as the safeguard of domestic tranquillity. Locke's *Two Treatises of Government* formed part of the liberal intellectual heritage of America's founding fathers. Spinoza geometrically re-examined the fundamentals of ethics and religion; Pascal, moralist and mathematician, paradoxically exalted faith. In educational theory, the Moravian Comenius developed an idealistic project for universal free education.

This age gave us Spain's foremost contributions to European letters: Cervantes' comic knight and the dramas of Calderón and Lope de Vega. French drama likewise found its most sublime classical formulation in Corneille and Racine, and its supreme comic vision in Molière. English literature began the century with the glory of Shakespeare and the Jacobean dramatists, and with Donne and his fellow metaphysical poets, who compressed their world into intense, striking images. Unlike the metaphysicals, the greatest Puritan literary spokesman, Milton, was deeply committed to politics as well as to his attempt to "justify the ways of God to men." His rejection of royal absolutism and his fervent plea in the *Areopagitica* for the free exchange of ideas unhampered by censorship are seminal propositions in the British and American view of democratic life.

In England, after years of Puritan repression, the Restoration of 1660 ushered in a reaction well characterized by its witty rationalistic comedies about eager gentlemen in pursuit of equally eager mistresses. Life in that England of Charles II was reported with humor and frank self-revelation by the prince of diarists, Pepys. The style of verse changed, and the varied stanzas and the subtle lyrics of the metaphysicals, Herrick, and the Cavaliers were replaced by Dryden's pointed, balanced, rational, "heroic" couplets. English prose, the best of it nonpolemic, developed rapidly. What the English sentence lost throughout the century in exuberant Elizabethan length, it gained in power, precision, and suppleness. The magnificent phrasing of the King James Bible, the cadences of Sir Thomas Browne, the devotional simplicity of Bunyan, the rational power of Dryden's critical essays —all influenced the course of our language.

If, during the Renaissance, man reached the threshold of the modern world, he stepped fully into it when he entered the 17th century with its conflicts and confusions —some of which still plague us today. In coping with his problems, he forged many of the scientific and philosophic principles we live by, leaving us an enduring literary record of the agonies, delights, and accomplishments of his passage.

## A. 17th Century Literature

AUBREY, JOHN 1626–1697 *Brief Lives* (1813). Informal, revealing sketches, with often amusing details, of a host of 17th-century persons. *AA*.

*Authorized Version of the Bible* (King James translation, 1611). "The noblest monument of English prose." Available in countless editions.

BACON *Essays* and *Advancement of Learning.* See "In Tudor England," page 79.

BEAUMONT, FRANCIS 1584–1616 and JOHN FLETCHER 1579–

1625 *Selected Plays.* Excellent theater, violent and exotic; elegant, poetic, witty. *Evman-h.*

BOYLE, ROBERT 1627–1691 *The Sceptical Chymist* (1661). Empirical demolition of the myths of alchemy and other pseudochemistry, by an early exponent of the scientific method. *Evman-h.*

BROWNE, THOMAS 1605–1682 *Religio Medici* (1643). The style—stately, cadenced, lucid, and personal—distinguishes the reasoned liberalism of Browne's Platonist faith. *Cambridge $2, EvmanNA, Gate, Nel, SM.*

✗ BUNYAN, JOHN 1628–1688 *Pilgrim's Progress* (1678). A visionary tinker's allegory of the Christian's journey to self-fulfillment; the most abiding scripture of English Puritanism, with a strong influence on later English prose style. *Grosset $2.95, Lippincott $3.95, CoNC, Evman-h, HRW, Nel, OxA, WoC, WSP.*

BURTON, ROBERT 1577–1640 *The Anatomy of Melancholy* (1621). A monumental assembly of late Renaissance science and amusing pseudoscience, elaborately organized in a remarkable and frequently difficult style. *Tudor $3.95, Evman-h.*

CERVANTES *Don Quixote.* See "The Renaissance," page 73.

*Colonial American Writing* (1950). Ed. by Roy H. Pearce. Original, wide-ranging anthology marking the progress from Old England to the American Enlightenment. *HRW.*

CONGREVE, WILLIAM 1670–1729 *Comedies.* Satire on, and for, Restoration society. Brilliantly cynical situations; dialogue of amazing finish and verve. *Drama, WoC.* Congreve and his fellow Restoration dramatists are also represented in convenient collections: *Evman-h, ML, RivEd.*

CORNEILLE, PIERRE 1606–1684 and JEAN RACINE 1639–1699 *Six Plays.* These playwrights, despite individual differences, represent the quintessence of French classical drama. Polished verse and careful observance of the Aristotelian unities, often in Greco-Roman settings, mark the formal patterns of these tragedies of reason versus passion. *ML.*

DESCARTES, RENÉ 1596–1650 *Discourse on Method* (1637). Established scientific doubt and mathematical logic as the bases for modern rationalism. Not easy reading. *Evman-h, Lib, Pen.*

DONNE *Poems.* See "In Tudor England," page 79.

✗ DRYDEN, JOHN 1631–1700 *Poems.* A titan of 17th-century English literature—critic, dramatist, translator, lyric and especially satiric poet. *Houghton $8, Evman-h, HRW, Nel, OxA.*

FOX, GEORGE 1624–1691 *Journal* (1694). The Quaker leader's own account of his 34 years of "enlightening" the people. *Cambridge $4.50, Cap, Evman-h.*

GRIMMELSHAUSEN, HANS JACOB CHRISTOFFEL VON 1625?–1676 *Simplicissimus* (1669). A satiric fantasy, cast in a picaresque mold, of an innocent at large in mid-17th-century Europe, written by a veteran of the Thirty Years' War. *Bison, Lib, Ungar.*

HERRICK, ROBERT 1591–1674 *Poems* (1648). Piquant, poignant, graceful lyrics, encompassing both religious devotion and an Epicurean feeling for life and love. *Anch, Dell, OxA, Pen, WoC.*

## THE 17TH CENTURY

**HOBBES, THOMAS** 1588-1679 *Leviathan* (1651). An intriguing but difficult explanation of why government is necessary and of what it is competent to do; the classic defense of state power to end, by compact, the "war of all against all." *Macmillan $3.50, Oxford $2.40, Collr, EvmanNA, Gate, Lib.*

**LAFAYETTE, MADAME DE** 1634-1693 *The Princess of Cleves* (1678). Profound, delicate novel, notable for psychological realism, about a woman in a triangle. The preferred translation is by Nancy Mitford *(Pen)*. Others: *Anch, Macm, SigC.*

**LA FONTAINE, JEAN DE** 1621-1695 *Fables* (1668-94). Traditional beast fables from Aesop and other sources adapted to the not-too-nice world of Louis XIV. *Viking $5, Anch, Evman-h, SM.*

**LA ROCHEFOUCAULD, DUC DE** 1613-1680 *Maxims* (1665). Polished wit and courtly cynicism, reflecting the world as it was, and is, rather than as theorists would have it be. *Peter Pauper $1, Random House $3.50, Pen, Vin.*

**LEIBNIZ, GOTTFRIED WILHELM VON** 1646-1716 *Selections.* The rationalist optimism later to be Voltaire's target in *Candide. Open Court $2.50, Oxford $4, B&N, Evman-h, Scrib.*

**LOCKE, JOHN** 1632-1704 *Two Treatises of Civil Government* (1689). The source of much of the early political theory of America, especially that of Jefferson. *Appl, Evman-h, Gate, Haf, Lib, ModSL.*

———— *An Essay Concerning Human Understanding* (1690). A classic of empiricism. Seminal attack on innate ideas, appealing to experience for knowledge of nature. *Open Court $2.50, Oxford $2.40, Dov, Evman-h, Gate, Open.*

**MARVELL, ANDREW** 1621-1678 *Poems.* A Puritan politician known, surprisingly, for one of the greatest love poems in English. *Harvard $2.50, Dell, HUP.*

***Masterpieces of the Spanish Golden Age*** (1957). Ed. by Angel Flores. There was more to Spanish literature than *Don Quixote;* this convenient and representative collection introduces the range and power of Cervantes' great contemporaries and successors. *HRW.*

**MILTON, JOHN** 1608-1674 *The Portable Milton* (1949). Douglas Bush's introduction makes this one of the best, as it is one of the handiest, collections of the works of the poet ranked by many authorities next to Shakespeare. It contains the incomparable *Paradise Lost* and other poetry; and selected prose, including the *Areopagitica,* the most impassioned defense in English of free speech, *Vik, Vik-h. Over twenty other collections.*

**MOLIÈRE (JEAN BAPTISTE POQUELIN)** 1622-1673 *Comedies.* Comic genius, expert theatricalism, and classic art united in a satiric portrayal of 17th-century society. Translations of Molière are variable in quality; in general, the older ones are not very satisfactory. Richard Wilbur's *Misanthrope* is in a class by itself *(Harcourt $5).* Single plays are available in many editions; collections in *Oxford $5, MLCE, Pen, SM.*

**NEWTON, ISAAC** 1642-1727 *Principia* (1687). The foundation of modern physical science, set forth in terms of classical geometry. A seminal book, but very difficult reading. *Calif (2 vols).*

*Oxford Book of Seventeenth Century Verse* (1934). Ed. by H. J. C. Grierson and G. Bullough. The standard collection, containing over 600 poems by more than 100 poets. *Oxford $5.75.*

PASCAL, BLAISE 1623–1662 *Pensées (Thoughts)* (1670). Reflections of a sensitive mathematician on nature, man, and God. *Harper $6, Peter Smith $3, World $1.75, Anch, Dolp, Evman, Evman-h, Macm, ML, Pen.*

PEPYS, SAMUEL 1633–1703 *Diary.* Pepys reformed the Royal Navy, collected books, chased the ladies (and their maids), and recorded his observations in a shorthand deciphered years later. His is a fascinating and frank picture of work and play in the Merry Monarch's London. *British Book Centre $4.75, Peter Smith $4.50, Evman-h, Macm, ML, SM, Torch.*

RACINE See CORNEILLE, above.

SÉVIGNÉ, MARIE, MARQUISE DE 1626–1696 *Letters.* Charming, witty, natural letters which give a fine picture of the times of Louis XIV. *Dutton 2 vols $7.50, Evman-h.*

SPINOZA, BARUCH 1632–1677 *Philosophy.* Mysticism and mathematics blend to view mind and matter as demonstrable attributes of God (Nature). *Peter Smith 2 vols $7, Dov, ML, ModSL, Scrib.*

WALTON, IZAAK 1593–1683 *The Compleat Angler* (1653). Generations of fishermen have delighted in this serene recommendation of the contemplative sport, with its interpolations on literature and life. *Collr, Dolp.*

———— *Lives* (1678). Four Anglican churchmen (including Donne and Herbert) are seen as saints in "the most literary and the most readable today of the 17th-century biographies." *Oxford $2.75, WoC.*

# B. Books About the 17th Century

BREDVOLD, LOUIS I. 1888– *The Intellectual Milieu of John Dryden* (1934). Dryden seen as the figure around whom swirl the intellectual currents of the later years of the century, arising from the interaction of skepticism, religion, and the "new science." *Michigan $4.40, AA.*

CATHER, WILLA 1876–1947 *Shadows on the Rock* (1931). French pioneers on the Quebec frontier strive to maintain the decorum of their homeland. *Knopf $3.95.*

CHUTE, MARCHETTE 1909– *Two Gentle Men: The Lives of George Herbert and Robert Herrick* (1959). Caroline England gracefully evoked, with enlightening details, through the lives of two great lyric poets. *Dutton $5.*

DEFOE, DANIEL 1660–1731 *A Journal of the Plague Year* (1722). This vivid tour de force of imaginative journalism chills the reader with a nightmare of pestilence and carts piled with the dead in the London of 1665. *Evman, Evman-h, ML, SigC.*

## THE 17TH CENTURY

DUMAS, ALEXANDRE 1802–1870 *The Three Musketeers* (1844). Swashbuckling adventure in the court of Louis XIII. *CoNC, Evman-h, ML, Nel, Pyr, WSP.*

DURANT, WILL 1885– and ARIEL DURANT 1898?– *The Age of Reason Begins* (1961) and *The Age of Louis XIV* (1963). A panoramic view of Western civilization during the formative years of the modern world. Engagingly written, with a wealth of illuminating detail. *Simon & Schuster $10 ea.*

GOOCH, GEORGE P. 1873– *English Democratic Ideas in the Seventeenth Century* (rev. 1927). An important study defining the sources of some of our most cherished political ideals. *Cambridge $3.50, Torch.*

GRIERSON, HERBERT J. C. 1866–1960 *Cross Currents in 17th Century English Literature* (1929). The age-old oppositions of world, flesh, and spirit, as manifested in a complex milieu. *Peter Smith $3.75.*

HALLER, WILLIAM 1885– *The Rise of Puritanism* (1938). Even without Cromwell's New Model Army in the field, Puritanism became a force to be reckoned with. This standard study traces the movement from its humble beginnings. *Columbia $6.50, Torch.*

HAWTHORNE, NATHANIEL 1804–1864 *The Scarlet Letter* (1850). Three characters, with the Puritan society of the setting functioning as a fourth, are worked and reworked into a series of highly dramatic tableaux to dramatize the effects of sin and guilt on the human psyche. The characters are studied deeply, the style is symbolic, and there is no clear commitment to either moral liberalism or the rigorous Calvinistic code. *Many editions.*

JOHNSON, SAMUEL 1709–1784 *The Lives of the Poets* (1779–81). English poets of the 17th century appraised with sturdy independence and common sense by the 18th century's great literary dictator. *Dolp, Evman-h, SM, WoC.*

LEWIS, WARREN H. 1895– *The Splendid Century* (1953). A wide-ranging view of the great and the lowly in French society during Louis XIV's zenith. *William Sloane $5, Anch.*

MACAULAY, THOMAS B. 1800–1859 *The History of England* (1855). Scholarship and dramatic imagination brought to bear on English history. *Evman-h.*

———— *Essays.* Lively criticism of Bacon, Milton, Bunyan, and the drama. Dogmatic and even wrongheaded as Macaulay must often appear to the modern reader, his views nevertheless express much good sense. *Evman-h.*

SCOTT, WALTER 1771–1832 *Old Mortality* (1816). Presbyterian revenge, resolution, and fortitude under Royalist persecution. *CoNC, Evman-h, Nel.*

STEEGMULLER, FRANCIS 1906– *The Grand Mademoiselle* (1956). The age of Louis XIV as reflected in the activities of his somewhat unconventional cousin. *Farrar, Straus $3.75, Anch.*

TAWNEY, RICHARD H. 1880–1962 *Religion and the Rise of Capitalism* (1926). Relating the Protestant ethic to the economic development of Western Europe. *Ment.*

VAN LOON, HENDRIK W. 1882–1944 *R. V. R.: The Life and Times of Rembrandt* (1930). An imaginative reconstruction of a great man and artist in a great time. *Heritage $3.95, Avon, Black.*

WILLEY, BASIL 1897– *The Seventeenth Century Background* (1934). Primarily literary-philosophical and sometimes difficult, these essays examine English religion and poetry against contemporary climates of opinion. *Columbia $5, Anch.*

# 9. The 18th Century

**WILLIAM C. GREENE,** *Massachusetts Institute of Technology*

The ambition, the bursting out of impulse that marked the Renaissance, faded halfway through the 17th century. England, ahead of her continental neighbors politically, killed her king, consummated her revolution, and settled her political turbulence by compromise in the 17th century. France had to wait more than a hundred years for her revolution—through the extravagance of Louis XIV and Louis XV and until her whole society had gone bad economically and socially. The various Germanies and Italies had to wait nearly a hundred years further and Russia rather more than that to become modern nations. In America, however, the abundance of land and the absence of an hereditary ruling class bred an independent spirit which ultimately led to the rebellion against Britain.

The 18th was a century in which trade began to be worldwide. But trade is seldom an activity of a noble class, and its growth meant the rise to wealth of city merchants, country squires, and occasionally of clerks, yeomen, and mechanics who broke out of their social subjection and pursued their fortunes. This shifting of weight betwen classes steadily transformed England. In France the nobility held primacy somewhat longer, scorning the English as a nation of shopkeepers.

Most thoughtful men of the 18th century believed that the world was rational. A century earlier scientists had seemed to establish the laws by which physical bodies acted and the mathematics by which their motions could be predicted. Might there not be moral, social, and political laws quite as inescapably true and quite as self-operating and systematic as Newton's laws of mechanics? Could not Reason find the "right" answers to all problems?

Hence Reason replaced Faith as a guide for the intellectual leaders of the period. The philosophers from Berkeley through Hume and Kant to Condorcet, whatever their first premises, worked by Reason, and in its name the satirists such as Swift and Voltaire criticized its products. The religion of the reasonable man in the 18th century was the deism simply expressed by Franklin in his *Autobiography,* advocated with passion by Tom Paine in his *Age of Reason,* and adhered to by many of the founding fathers in America.

In political theory the way of Reason moved through the axiom that society was an agreement by all men to the practice of check-and-balance republicanism, a program deriving from John Locke in the previous century and finding outstanding exponents in Rousseau, Jefferson, and Madison. The same habit of mind was carried into economic theory by Adam Smith, whose *Wealth of Nations* gave the free-traders a rational justification for their break with the state-controlled mercantilism that had dominated Europe since the Renaissance.

A reasonable century, for which Benjamin Franklin may be considered the prototype, is not one in which extreme emotionalism or intense individualism is likely to be honored. The 18th century produced no fresh and memorable tragedy, and only toward its end any intense, moving poetry. Its plays still enjoyed today—those of Sheridan, Goldsmith, Beaumarchais, and Goldoni—evolved from the more biting satiric comedies of manners of Molière and Congreve in the 17th century. Pope, the poetic model of the century in England, believed the heroic couplet to be the one orderly form of verse. Anything may be said in the couplet, but it will render chiefly epigram, and emotion dies in its formality, as may be seen when Robert Burns tried to "rise" from his dialect to "polite" verse.

Reason and decorum are likely to be critical, but to be critical in a lucid style. The century poured out its clarity in essays such as those of *The Spectator,* in letters such as those of Lord Chesterfield, even in the conversation of Samuel Johnson, captured from loss by Boswell—and all in a prose balanced and comprehensible.

## THE 18TH CENTURY

The great creative speech of the century, however, was the novel, presenting human life in action. As early as the 1720's, Defoe was writing fabricated "eyewitness" accounts of plague and shipwreck, Le Sage had transformed the story of adventure into a to-be-continued-next-week series of pictures of backstairs life, and the Abbé Prévost published in 1731 the archetype of all French novels of fatal passion in *Manon Lescaut*.

But virtue overtook the novel, of course: in *Pamela* Samuel Richardson showed girls how to be good by a long series of letters about a servant girl who "held out for marriage." This cant so disgusted a minor playwright named Henry Fielding that he wrote a burlesque of it in *Joseph Andrews*, about Pamela's brother who fled from the ardent advances of Lady Booby. To Fielding's surprise the figures turned alive as he shaped them; and when he went on to a larger scheme, *Tom Jones*, he produced one of the greatest of all novels. Soon the novel's capacities had been extended into philosophical fable by Voltaire in *Candide*, into comic extravaganza by Sterne in *Tristram Shandy*, and into "Gothic" horror by Horace Walpole in *The Castle of Otranto*.

When man faces up to Reason, he soon decides that each individual is significant to himself; if men are equal, so are their feelings. By 1765, order and restraint were giving way to a freer expression of individual emotions. Robert Burns could then declare boldly from the depths of poverty that "a man's a man for a' that." Goethe's young Werther could value no law but his own amorous despair. Rousseau could get men to read his own egotisms and impulses. And the French Revolution could burst out into enraged murder of one's own countrymen. Burke, opposing the French Revolution, was an 18th-century gentleman trying to keep the 19th century from being born.

Yet when we speak of the 18th century today we tend to neglect the romantic. We feel the 18th century to be Franklin and Jefferson, Pope and Voltaire. It was the century in which for the first time since Periclean Athens men really began to plan their futures and to depend confidently upon their own reason to progress.

# A. 18th Century Literature

ADDISON, JOSEPH 1672–1719 and RICHARD STEELE 1672–1729 *The Spectator* (1711–12). Pleasantly witty and polished commentary on fashions and foibles and fops of Queen Anne's London. *Cambridge $1.25, Peter Pauper $2.50, St Martin's $1.50, Evman-h, HRW.*

*The Age of Enlightenment* (1956). Ed. by Isaiah Berlin. Generous selections from the major philosophers of the 18th century with helpful commentaries by the editor. *Houghton $3, Ment.*

BEAUMARCHAIS, PIERRE CARON DE 1732–1799 *The Barber of Seville* (1775) and *The Marriage of Figaro* (1778). Comedies satirizing class privilege, best known now in the opera versions by Rossini and Mozart. *BES.*

BERKELEY, GEORGE 1685–1753 *A Treatise Concerning the Principles of Human Knowledge* (1710). Platonic idealism reworked in the light of Newtonian science. *Lib, Open.*

BLAKE, WILLIAM 1757–1827 *Poems.* Simple, original, profound, many of these poems, like Blake's pictures, are unequaled. *Macmillan $2, Dell, Evman-h, ML, Nel, Ox, OxA, Pen, Vik, WoC.*

BOSWELL, JAMES 1740–1795 *London Journal* (1762–63). An intimate account of Boswell's start in London. *McGraw-Hill $6, Sig.*

_____ *The Life of Samuel Johnson* (1791). The widely ranging opinions of one of England's favorite minds, recorded by a shrewd, devoted admirer in perhaps the greatest biography ever written. Complete: *Oxford $6, Evman, MLG, OxA.* Abridged: *Collr, Dell, ML, ModSL, Scrib, SM, Vik.*

BURKE, EDMUND 1729–1797 *Reflections on the Revolution in France* (1790). A conservative defense of slow change, opposed to the violence Burke saw coming. *Dolp, Evman, GrDeb, HRW, Lib, WoC.*

BURNS, ROBERT 1759–1796 *Poems.* Songs and meditations, mostly in a Scottish dialect, that are enduringly popular. *Houghton $6, Macmillan $2, Evman, Evman-h, Nel, Nort, OxA, WoC.*

CASANOVA DE SEINGALT, GIOVANNI 1725–1798 *Memoirs* (1826–38). The main episodes are amorous; the filler pictures sketch the times. *Collr, Dov, ML.*

CHESTERFIELD, LORD 1694–1773 *Letters to His Son* (1774). Urbane 18th-century advice on manners and morals in a worldly aristocratic society. *Peter Pauper $2.50, Evman.*

*Constitution of the United States* and *Declaration of Independence.* Basic American documents every good citizen should know. Bound together: *Doubleday $1.50.* Found in almost every history of the United States and in most encyclopedias.

## THE 18TH CENTURY

CRÈVECOEUR, ST. JOHN DE 1731–1813 *Letters from an American Farmer* (1782). These letters to an imaginary friend in Europe reflect both an idealistic and a realistic view of life in the young America. *Dolp, Evman, Evman-h, SigC.*

DEFOE, DANIEL 1660–1731 *Robinson Crusoe* (1719). The original and immortal desert island story. *Many editions.*

———— *Moll Flanders* (1722). A realistic story of one woman's life through many marriages and several crimes. *Collr, Dell, Dolp, Evman-h, HRW, ML, MLCE, RivEd, WoC, WSP.*

———— *A Journal of the Plague Year.* See "17th Century," page 88.

DIDEROT, DENIS 1713–1784 *Rameau's Nephew and Other Works.* Pieces satiric and serious by the compiler of the French encyclopedia who was, after Voltaire, the most versatile French writer of the century. *Anch o.p.*

*Federalist Papers* (1787–88). Political essays by James Madison, Alexander Hamilton, and others, which influenced the acceptance of our Constitution and remain prime examples of political theory. A new edition edited by Clinton Rossiter is unusually good: *Ment.* Others: *Anch, Appl, Lib, ML.*

FIELDING, HENRY 1707–1754 *Joseph Andrews* (1742). Adventures of a chaste footman and a sturdy parson, told in mockery of 18th-century sentimentalism. *Ban, Evman-h, HRW, MLCE, Nort, RivEd, SigC, WSP.*

———— *Tom Jones* (1749). The long, zestful, carefully plotted story of a lively hero from childhood to marriage, richly filled with realistic characters and typical 18th-century adventures. *Evman-h, MLCE, Nort, SigC, Vin, WSP.*

FRANKLIN, BENJAMIN 1706–1790 *Autobiography* (1791, 1817, 1868). A great American and the prototype of the pragmatic man explains his rise to fame and fortune. *Calif, Collr, Dolp, Evman-h, HarpMC, HRW, Lib, MLCE, RivEd, SigC, WSP.*

GAY, JOHN 1685–1732 *The Beggar's Opera* (1728). Rollicking burlesque of political society; thieves, highwaymen, and harlots sing false sentiments to the tunes of street ballads. *BES.*

GIBBON *The Decline and Fall of the Roman Empire.* See "Rome," page 41.

GOETHE, JOHANN WOLFGANG VON 1749–1832 *The Sorrows of Young Werther* (1774). An early very "romantic" novel in which the hero kills himself for unrequited love. *Ungar $2.75, Ban, HRW, SigC, Ungar.*

———— *Wilhelm Meister's Apprenticeship* (1795–96). The development of a young man, partly in the theater, from yearning, through fatherhood, to maturity in work. *Collr.*

———— *Faust.* See "Poetry," page 157.

GOLDONI, CARLO 1707–1793 *Comedies.* Actable and natural comedies by one of the very best dramatists of the century. *Oxford $3.75.*

GOLDSMITH, OLIVER 1728–1774 *The Vicar of Wakefield* (1766). A novel relating the amusing tribulations of the most famous of gentle and gullible clergymen. *Ban, Collr, CoNC, Dolp, Evman, ML, Nel, PB, SigC, SM, WoC.*

———— **She Stoops to Conquer** (1773). A comic masterpiece and one of the most actable of all plays. *Appl, BES, CoNC, Drama, Evman-h, Nel, SM.*

JEFFERSON, THOMAS 1743–1826 **Autobiographical and Political Writings.** A founding father writes clearly and eloquently on many subjects still of concern to Americans. Collections under various titles: *Putnam $2.40, Cap, Lib, ML, Prem.*

JOHNSON, SAMUEL 1709–1784 **The Portable Johnson and Boswell** (1947). Representative selections from the writings of the literary dictator of his age and passages from Boswell's classic life. *Vik, Vik-h.*

KANT, IMMANUEL 1724–1804 **Critique of Pure Reason** (1781–87). A difficult book that explains intellect as the formulator of knowledge. *St Martin's $5.50, Evman-h, ML.*

———— **The Metaphysics of Morals** (1797). The basic argument for the Puritan and democratic code many people still live by. *Appl, Lib.*

LESSING, GOTTHOLD EPHRAIM 1729–1781 **Laokoön** (1766). Perhaps the most famous book of the century on the theory of the arts. *Evman-h, Lib, Noon.*

MALTHUS, THOMAS ROBERT 1766–1834 **Essay on the Principle of Population** (1798). Classic study of the relationship between population growth and means of subsistence. *AA, Evman-h, Ment, ML.*

PAINE, THOMAS 1737–1809 **Common Sense** (1776). A pamphlet that helped rouse the American colonies to independence. *Dolp, Lib.*

———— **The Rights of Man** (1791). Paine's answer to Burke's criticism of the French Revolution. *Lib.*

———— **The Age of Reason** (1794, 1796). A spirited defense of deism, the 18th-century intellectual religion. *Lib.*

POPE, ALEXANDER 1688–1744 **Poems.** The philosophy of Optimism, social satire, occasionally emotion—all in neat epigrammatic heroic couplets. *Houghton $5, Oxford $1.55, Ronald $2.75, St Martin's $3, Appl, Evman-h, HRW, ML, MLCE, Nel.*

PRÉVOST, ANTOINE 1697–1763 **Manon Lescaut** (1731). The story of a young man fascinated by a courtesan who loves him, deceives him, but never gives him up. *Dolp, Scrib, SigC.*

RICHARDSON, SAMUEL 1689–1761 **Pamela** (1740). In letters that reveal the "sentiments" of the age, a maidservant tells how she resisted her young master until he offered marriage. *Evman-h, Nort.*

ROUSSEAU, JEAN JACQUES 1712–1778 **Émile** (1762). A didactic novel, an important source of progressive education theory. *BES, Evman-h.*

———— **The Social Contract** (1762). The document that profoundly influenced the French Revolution. *EvmanNA, Gate, Haf.*

_____ *Confessions* (1781-88). Uninhibited self-revelations of a romantic egoist. *Evman-h, ML, PB, Pen.*

SHERIDAN, RICHARD BRINSLEY 1751-1816 *The Rivals* (1775) and *The School for Scandal* (1777). Two famous social comedies, noted for their wit, complicated but effective plots, and memorable caricatures (notably Mrs. Malaprop). *CoNC, Drama, Evman-h, WoC.*

SMITH, ADAM 1723-1790 *The Wealth of Nations* (1776). The classic explanation of the economic advantages of free trade and of division of labor. *Evman-h, Gate, Lib, MLG.*

SMOLLETT, TOBIAS 1721-1771 *Roderick Random* (1748). Adventures on sea and land, famous for portraying the miserable lot of 18th-century seamen. *Dolp, Evman-h, Prem, WoC.*

_____ *Humphrey Clinker* (1771). Various adventures and pictures of the times on a coaching trip through England and Scotland. *CoNC, Evman-h, HRW, Nel, SigC, WoC.*

STERNE, LAURENCE 1713-1768 *Tristram Shandy* (1759-67). Comic domestic episodes, done in all sorts of styles—whimsical, digressive, extravagant. Many editions; recommended: *HRW, MLCE, SigC.*

SWIFT, JONATHAN 1667-1745 *Gulliver's Travels* (1726). Imaginary journeys that amuse children but are really thoroughgoing and first-rate satires of man's irrational inhumanity. Many editions; recommended: *HRW, RivEd, SigC.* **The Portable Swift** contains a good cross-section of Swift's total output. *Vik, Vik-h.*

VOLTAIRE (FRANÇOIS MARIE AROUET) 1694-1778 *Candide* (1759). A short, funny, well-spiced adventure story; a masterly satire of optimism, war, religion, governments, romantic love, wealth, and a host of other things by one of the greatest minds and the most versatile literary figure of the century. *Peter Pauper $4.95, Ban, BES, ML, Pen, Scrib, SigC, SM, WSP.*

WALPOLE, HORACE 1717-1797 *Letters* (1732-97). The civilized 18th century comes to life in these letters about his friends and their activities. *Evman-h.*

_____ *The Castle of Otranto* (1764). The first famous "Gothic" novel of horror and supernatural invention. *Collr.*

# B. Books About the 18th Century

BECKER, CARL LOTUS 1873-1945 *The Heavenly City of the Eighteenth-Century Philosophers* (1932). A lively, scholarly, provocative analysis of 18th-century thought. *Yale $3.50, Yale.*

BRINTON, CRANE 1898- (ed.) *The Portable Age of Reason Reader* (1956). Many short pieces on many subjects from thought to intimate scenes, with a good introduction. *Vik, Vik-h.*

BUTTERFIELD, HERBERT 1900- *The Origins of Modern Science*

(rev ed 1957). A classic volume on the history of science, particularly good on the 18th-century developments and their effects. Macmillan $4, Collr, Macm.

CARLYLE, THOMAS 1795–1881 **The French Revolution** (1837). A long, dramatic, intensively written account, more bedazzled by Napoleon than we would be nowadays. *Evman-h, MLG.*

CASSIRER, ERNST 1874–1945 **The Philosophy of the Enlightenment** (1932). A thoughtful, balanced, illuminating corrective to Becker's **Heavenly City**. *Peter Smith $3.50, Bea.*

COBBAN, ALFRED 1901– **A History of Modern France** (1961). Regarded as the best short history of the period. *Peter Smith $3.50, Pen.*

DICKENS, CHARLES 1812–1870 **A Tale of Two Cities** (1859). A tale of self-sacrifice during the French Revolution, famous for Sidney Carton and Madame Defarge. *Many editions.*

HUGO, VICTOR 1802–1885 **Ninety-Three** (1874). A dramatic novel of France in the violent throes of revolution. *Ban.*

LEFEBVRE, GEORGES 1874–1959 **The Coming of the French Revolution** (1939). A balanced, authoritative recent history. *Vin.*

MILLER, PERRY 1905–1963 **The New England Mind** (1953). A major book by the most distinguished historian of American ideas. *Harvard $7.50, Bea.*

MORGAN, EDMUND S. 1916– **The Birth of the Republic, 1763–89** (1956). Regarded as the best recent short treatment of an often treated subject. *Chicago $3.50, CHAC.*

NOCK, ALBERT J. 1872–1945 **Jefferson** (1926). A short but penetrating life, done with sympathy. *Hill & Wang $4.50, H&W.*

ROBERTS, KENNETH 1885–1957 **Arundel** (1930), **Rabble in Arms** (1933), **Northwest Passage** (1937), **Oliver Wiswell** (1940). Scrupulously documented and vigorously narrated historical novels about military adventures and the conflicts among various classes of people during the American Revolution. *Doubleday $4–$4.95, Crest.*

SCOTT, WALTER 1771–1832 **Waverley** (1814), **Guy Mannering** (1815), **The Antiquary** (1816), **Rob Roy** (1817), **The Heart of Midlothian** (1818), and **Redgauntlet** (1824). These Scott novels deal with 18th-century events, chiefly in Scotland, the memorable characters being common folk. All available in *Evman-h* or *Nel.*

TOCQUEVILLE, ALEXIS DE 1805–1859 **The Old Regime and the French Revolution** (1855). A shrewd version of the subject by a wise Frenchman of the first half of the 19th century. *Peter Smith $3, Anch.*

VAN DOREN, CARL 1885–1950 **Benjamin Franklin** (1938). A thorough and thoroughly enjoyable biography, with generous quotations from Franklin. *Viking $7.50.*

WILLEY, BASIL 1897– **Eighteenth Century Background** (1940). A thoughtful and useful treatment of the idea of Nature in the thought of the 18th century. *Columbia $4.50, Bea.*

# LITERARY TYPES

# LITERARY TYPES

## 10. The Novel

### A. 19th Century Continental

**ARTHUR WALDHORN**, *City College of New York*

More good novels were written in Continental Europe during the 19th century than in any other place or period. It seems doubtful that this was mere happenstance. The arts flourish in peace, and there were no great wars after Napoleon's defeat in 1815. A novelist feeds on his time, and Continental Europe in the 19th century served varied and nourishing fare. Ferment in art, science, and politics leavened the age and infused the novel with new ideas and new points of view. For those with intellectual appetite, it was a zestful time to live and to write.

France and Russia showed the greatest activity. Out of the turmoil of French politics a new middle class was arising. Increasingly, careers were open to talent instead of to aristocratic privilege. The greatest French novelists —Balzac, Zola, Stendhal, Flaubert—were bourgeois, and it was the rise of their class that they portrayed with varying degrees of disapproval. Where the French Romantics saw man as a passionate individual, nobler or baser than he consistently was, Balzac placed this individual in society, and in his novels the Romantic goals of an abstract liberty or an exalted love change to money and social ambition. His *Comédie Humaine* had the most comprehensive plan any novelist ever made, nothing less than to depict in a series of novels a whole nation, the France of his time, as it actually was. For Zola, actuality was scientific: "Study men like simple elements and note their reactions," he advised. His novels about the Rougon-Macquart families shocked France to the core although they never quite achieved the scientific objectivity he aimed for: a strong moral disapproval shows through. In his three chief novels Stendhal wrote the same story three times, that of a young man making his way in the world: in *The Red and the Black*, a poor young man in a real France; in *Lucien Leuwen*, a rich young man; but in *The Charterhouse of Parma* (sometimes called the greatest French novel), a young aristocrat fails to gain happiness in an imaginary Italian principality. The actions, operatic and extravagant, are moved by a hard-boiled modern psychology.

With Flaubert's *Madame Bovary*, the novel changed. Although he was called a realist in his time, it can now be seen that he not only fused the Realistic and the Romantic ideas but he moved the novelist out of the book. The characters seem to think and act by themselves. His intense care for structure and the fall of the individual sentence gave novelists everywhere a new sense of the seriousness of their art; thus he is the bridge to Joyce and through him to the 20th century.

In Russia the situation was different. The Czars, frightened by the democratic ideas that had spread from revolutionary France, tried to shut them out by suppressing freedom of assembly and imposing a strict censorship. It is possible that most Russian novels, although politically "correct," were a defiant response to these pressures. Tolstoi was a rich nobleman, an army officer, and had none but the artist's obligation to be a novelist at all, yet in *War and Peace, Anna Karenina,* and *Resurrection,* he tries to portray the permanent, essential Russia, regardless of the accidents of politics, and his vision is so profound that he gives us not merely Russians but very human beings. After a term in Siberia as a political offender, Dostoevski was tormented by the problems of Christian belief and the existence of evil. His lifelong aim was to write a huge work called *Life of a Great Sinner*, but he never did. However, his great novels, *The Brothers Karamazov, Crime and Punishment,* and *The Possessed*, may be fragments of this work. He owed much to Dickens, but he treats his characters with a psychological penetration that often foreshadows Freud and makes Dickens seem at times naïve. Turgenev, like Tolstoi, was a rich nobleman; he was sent to jail for depicting serfs as human beings in his *Sportsman's Sketches*. In *Fathers and Sons* he examines with great clarity the impact of liberal ideas on two generations of Russians. Isolated though they were, these Russian novelists have a power and intensity that abolish national boundaries.

Other European countries had fewer great novelists, but fine novels were published nevertheless. Manzoni's *The Betrothed* and Verga's *The House by the Medlar Tree* were the best to come out of Italy. The charm of Alarcón's *The Three-Cornered Hat* and Pérez Galdós' *Doña Perfecta* makes one wish that Spain had been more prolific. Among German novels, *Wilhelm Meister*, although not Goethe's greatest work, is still a product of one of the most fertile minds of the age. Novels by Scandinavian, Polish, Hungarian, Belgian, Dutch, and Portuguese authors had merit but made little stir internationally.

In 1800 the novel had been a new thing, scarcely to be ranked with poetry or drama as serious literature. By 1900 the novel was clearly the most popular and most influential of all literary forms.

ALARCÓN, PEDRO ANTONIO DE (Spain) 1833–1891 ***The Three-Cornered Hat*** (1874). After *Don Quixote*, the most famous of Spanish tales. A clever, witty, and charming account of how a miller's wife fooled an amorous mayor. *BES*.

BALZAC, HONORÉ DE (France) 1799–1850 ***Eugénie Grandet*** (1833). One of the greatest of ***La Comédie Humaine***, Balzac's series of novels that record French life from the fall of Napoleon to 1848. Grandet, a provincial bourgeois miser, sacrifices his daughter's happiness upon the altar of greed. Powerful realism and sweeping imagination color the portrayal of emotional sterility. *Ban, Dolp, Evman-h, Nel, Pen, RivEd*.

———— ***Old Goriot*** (1834). Balzac's version of the King Lear theme, an agonizing, searing, and relentlessly objective tale of an old father's humiliation at the hands of his monstrous daughters. *Anch, Dolp, Evman-h, HRW, MLCE, Pen, Pyr, SigC, Scrib, WSP*.

———— ***Cousin Bette*** (1846). "A serious and terrible study of Parisian manners," Balzac called it. Many consider this brutal study of vice, jealousy, and vanity his finest work. Certainly the characterizations—the vindictive Bette, the debauched Hulot, and the dazzling "beast of prey" Valérie—number among his most unforgettable. *Ban, ML.*

CONSTANT, BENJAMIN (France) 1767–1830 **Adolphe** (1815). One of the earliest psychological novels, it draws upon Constant's long and dramatic relationship with Mme. de Staël. *SigC.*

DOSTOEVSKI, FEDOR (Russia) 1821–1881 **Notes from the Underground** (1864). A terrifying analysis of psychic alienation and impotence. In many ways the protagonist is the archetypal "anti-hero" of 20th-century existential fiction. *Dutton $3.75, Dell, Evman, Evman-h, SigC.*

———— **Crime and Punishment** (1866). A half-starved student with superman aspirations murders two women, then seeks a motive for his crime. On one level a superb detective story; on a deeper level a trenchant analysis of human impulses. *Macmillan $3.75, Oxford $3.75, Ban, Dell, Evman-h, HarpMC, MLCE, Pen, UL, Vin, WSP.*

———— **The Idiot** (1868–69). An eccentric epileptic emerges as a Christ figure in this complex study of unworldly saintliness in a harshly realistic world. *Macmillan $3.75, Ban, Dell, Evman-h, Pen.*

———— **The Brothers Karamazov** (1880). Dmitri Karamazov and his debauched father vie for the affections of the loose and lusty Grushenka. Smerdyakov, an illegitimate son and an epileptic, murders the father, but Dmitri is tried and convicted on circumstantial evidence. Beyond the intricate plot and compelling characterizations, the novel gains force from its profound investigation of good, evil, and faith. The climactic novel of Dostoevski's career. The Magarshack translation is recommended: *Pen.* Other unabridged versions: *Macmillan $3.75, Evman-h, HarpMC, MLCE, SigC, Vin.*

DUMAS, ALEXANDRE (France) 1802–1870 **The Count of Monte Cristo** (1844). An exciting story that dramatizes French history with melodramatic romance and adventure. *Grosset $4.95, Norton $1.85, Ban, Evman-h.*

FLAUBERT, GUSTAVE (France) 1821–1880 **Madame Bovary** (1857). Often called the first modern realistic novel, Madame Bovary reveals consummate precision in language, structure, and irony. Emma Bovary seeks vainly in a dull marriage the romance she has read and dreamed of. Disillusioned, she searches for adventure in illicit amours, but again encounters disappointment and monotony. At last she destroys herself, a victim of her own failure to distinguish appearance from reality. The Steegmüller translation is recommended: *MLCE.* Others: *Anch, Ban, Dell, Dolp, Evman-h, HRW, Pen, Scrib, SigC, UL, WSP.*

FRANCE, ANATOLE (France) 1844–1924 **The Crime of Sylvestre Bonnard** (1881). Presented against a background of gentle humor, pathos, urbanity, Bonnard is one of the most lovable characters of French literature. *Dodd $2.75.*

———— For other titles, see "20th Century Continental Novels," page 111.

# THE NOVEL: 19TH CENTURY CONTINENTAL 105

**GAUTIER, THÉOPHILE** (France) 1811–1872 *Mademoiselle de Maupin* (1835). A romantic, sensual love story by the fine poet who first preached the gospel of "art for art's sake." *o.p.*

**GOETHE** (Germany) *Wilhelm Meister's Apprenticeship.* See "The 18th Century," page 95.

**GOGOL, NIKOLAI** (Russia) 1809-1852 *Dead Souls* (1842). Chichikov, the rascally hero, journeys across Russia purchasing the names of dead serfs for their taxable value. Beneath the genial, comic surface run twin streams of satire against fraud and compassion for the underprivileged. *Evman-h, HRW, ML, Pen, SigC, WoC.*

———— *The Overcoat* (1842). "We have all come out of Gogol's overcoat," Dostoevski observed, conscious in his jest of Gogol's sure-handed style, pungent social satire, and heartfelt warmth. All appear in this curiously realistic tale that steps over into the realm of fantasy. The Magarshack translation in *Tales of Good and Evil* (which also contains *The Nose*) is recommended: *Anch.*

**GONCHAROV, IVAN** (Russia) 1812–1891 *Oblomov* (1859). Oblomov, a rich landowner, is the laziest man in the world. The account of his getting up in the morning is one of the funniest, most touching passages in fiction. *SigC.*

**HUGO, VICTOR** (France) 1802–1885 *The Hunchback of Notre Dame.* See "The Middle Ages," page 69.

———— *Les Misérables* (1862). Jean Valjean, Javert, and Fantine, three of the most memorable characterizations of the great French romanticist, act out their drama of pathos and poverty in post-Napoleonic France. *Liveright $2.20, CoNC, Evman-h, MLG, Prem.*

**HUYSMANS, JORIS KARL** (France) 1848–1907 *Against Nature* (1884). A lavish portrait of a decadent searching relief from the banality of bourgeois life. The exotic proclivities of the aristocratic Des Esseintes whetted many tastes, not least among them Oscar Wilde's; *The Picture of Dorian Gray* avowedly imitates portions of Huysmans's fascinating tale. *Pen.*

**LOUŸS** (France) *Aphrodite.* See "Greece," page 36.

**MANZONI, ALESSANDRO** (Italy) 1785–1873 *The Betrothed* (1826). A splendid historical novel of 17th-century Italy, replete with robber barons, the plague, and eternal love. *Evman, Evman-h, Prem.*

**MAUPASSANT, GUY DE** (France) 1850–1893 *Bel-Ami* (1885). A scoundrel makes his way by his good looks. *Pen, Pop.*

**MÉRIMÉE, PROSPER** (France) 1803–1870 *Carmen* (1845). Famous in story, opera, and film, this gypsy girl enslaves and destroys her lover but makes the experience seem worth while. *SigC.*

**NERVAL, GÉRARD DE** (France) 1808–1855 *Sylvie* (1853). An affecting, semiautobiographical narrative of adolescent love recollected in maturity. *Grove o.p.*

**PERÉZ GALDÓS, BENITO** (Spain) 1843–1920 *Doña Perfecta* (1876). The finest of Galdós' several portraits of Spanish life. The scene is provincial, the time before the Carlist war, the treatment at once romantic and realistic. *BES.*

STENDHAL (HENRI BEYLE) (France) 1783–1842 ***The Red and the Black*** (1830). Julian Sorel, one of the supreme opportunists and hypocrites of literature, turns profitably from "red" (the military life) to "black" (the clerical life) in this crisply drawn study of post-Napoleonic France. Brilliant characterizations, memorable episodes, and an overwhelming irony combine to make this one of the great novels of the century. *Ban, Collr, Dolp, ML, Pen, Prem, WSP.*

————— ***The Charterhouse of Parma*** (1839). An intricately wrought but colorful and forceful novel of love and politics. *Anch, Ban, Black, Pen, SigC.*

————— ***Lucien Leuwen*** (1894). One of the sharpest political novels ever written. Published in America as two novels: ***The Green Huntsman*** and ***The Telegraph: New.***

TOLSTOI, LEO (Russia) 1828–1910 ***War and Peace*** (1866). One of the supreme novels of all time. Historically, it chronicles on an epic scale Napoleon's invasion of Russia. But its grandeur and sweep derive chiefly from the pulsating force of characterization, the dynamic interplay of ideologies in conflict. Noble and base, wise and foolish, heroic and cowardly—every type finds a place in Tolstoi's all-embracing scheme. Unabridged translations: *Grosset $3.50, Evman-h, MLG, Pen, WoC.*

————— ***Anna Karenina*** (1877). An engrossing story of adultery among the Russian nobility. Thomas Mann called it the greatest novel of society in the history of the world. *Ban, Dell, Evman-h, HarpMC, MLCE, MLG, Pen, SigC, WoC.*

————— ***The Kreutzer Sonata*** (1889). An absorbing problem novel about an unconventional attitude toward marriage. *Prem, Vin, WoC.*

TURGENEV, IVAN (Russia) 1818–1883 ***Sportsman's Sketches*** (1852). A vigorous attack on Russian serfdom, defending the peasant as a man possessed of "a soul of his own." A subtle book despite its propagandistic intent. *Comp, SigC.*

————— ***Fathers and Sons*** (1862). Although Bazarov, the hero, embodies the principles of political nihilism that led to the October Revolution, he is also a spokesman for youthful rebellion against the authority of the older generation. *Ban, Collr, Evman-h, HRW, HarpMC, MLCE, SigC, WSP.*

VERGA, GIOVANNI (Italy) 1840–1922 ***The House by the Medlar Tree*** (1890). A graphic and tragic account of the lives of Sicilian fishermen. *Anch o.p.*

ZOLA, EMILE (France) 1840–1902 ***L'Assommoir*** (1877). The terrors of poverty, alcoholism, and debauchery hound Zola's tortured souls into animalized nonexistence. Some rate this novel second only to ***Germinal*** in its enormous force. The translation by Atwood H. Townsend is recommended: *SigC.*

————— ***Nana*** (1880). With stunning if sometimes excessive detail—a characteristic of his naturalistic method—Zola describes the bizarre life of a harlot during the Second Empire. *Collr, Dolp, HarpMC, ML, PB.*

————— ***Germinal*** (1885). Relatively free of the confining limitations of the "scientific method" of naturalism, the novel rages through the agonies of an unsuccessful strike by impoverished French coal miners. Scenes of brutality and bestiality, courage and compassion follow hard upon one another in this relentless but overwhelmingly moving story. The translation by L. W. Tancock is recommended: *Pen. Many other versions.*

## B. 20th Century Continental Novels

**ROBERT CLARKE WHITE, Castleton State College**

At the dawn of the 20th century Europe was relatively sound and healthy, its writers comfortably detached. By 1920 the Continent had suffered a severe stroke; its writers were disturbed, restless, and deeply engaged in the fever of events. In 1939 came a second stroke, followed since by cold wars, hot police actions, dissolving empires, bad consciences, émigré writers, spiritual drift and anguish, and, recently, new hopes. Each nation, uniquely ill, has made its separate diagnoses and prescriptions for health.

Before examining the major national literatures, we should note the dominant types in modern European fiction: the *family novel*—Mann (Germany), Couperus (The Netherlands), Martin du Gard (France); the *peasant novel*—Hamsun (Norway), Lagerlöf (Sweden), Sillanpää (Finland), Nexø (Denmark), Silone and Vittorini (Italy); the *novel of contemporary history*—Malraux (France), Koestler (Hungary, England), Ehrenburg (Russia), Seghers (Germany), Cela and Sender (Spain); and the *world survey novel* or *novel-group*—Mann's *The Magic Mountain,* Rolland's *Jean Christophe,* Romains's *Men of Good Will,* Proust's *Remembrance of Things Past.*

France, ever in the cultural van, regularly provides prototypical novels that develop and test all acts and isms. To treat her modish malady—a sick conscience—she has many doctors. François Mauriac offers the novel of Catholic faith; Gide, the honest if unorthodox search for selfhood and for right relations with man and God. The ironies of Anatole France can still bring refreshment. Sartre, Camus, and de Beauvoir, all existentialists, call for "personal responsibility" in a world that is itself godless and absurd. Malraux urges the tonic of action;

Romains the balm of brotherhood (unanimism); Chevallier and Colette the satisfactions of physical sensation; Proust and the Franco-Belgian Simenon the steadying sedatives of memory and Inspector Maigret.

Russian fiction flourished from about 1920 to 1932 when "Dr." Gorki's "social realism" pill cooled many a fine imaginative frenzy. Yet Sholokhov in Tolstoi's way and Leonov in Dostoevski's have transcended, while obeying, party-line directives. More recently, in *Not By Bread Alone* and in *Dr. Zhivago,* Dudintsev and Pasternak have transcended while "disobeying" the restrictions of Soviet censors; Nabokov (Russia, United States) has aroused attention and debate with his Moravia-like, sad sex comedy *Lolita;* and Simonov's *The Living and the Dead* exhibits the emergent effort of Russian self-criticism.

Norway and Greece have won fresh laurels by the translation into English, in 1958, of *Four Stories* by Sigrid Undset and of *The Odyssey: A Modern Sequel* by Nikos Kazantzakis. Switzerland is represented by an audacious and philosophical writer of strange suspense stories, Friedrich Duerrenmatt *(The Pledge).*

Italian fiction, until the death of Mussolini, had concerned itself primarily with an intense regionalism, a microscopic report of provincial life. The more broadly conceived novels of D'Annunzio and Fogazzaro reached English-language readers in the first decade of the century, those of the paradoxical Pirandello in the second. The more recent spate of Italian novels, together with many excellent films and some ever-glorious musical creations, give notice that the genius of Italy is again in ferment. The names of Ignazio Silone, Alberto Moravia, and Carlo Levi are perhaps the most considerable.

German storytellers produced significant fiction up to the brainwashings or flights-from-hell of Hitler's regime. Incidentally, "German" novels include some by Austrians, Swiss, and Czechs (such as Kafka). Prolifically translated but uneven in merit, German fiction that has been available in English could be cited to the extent of several pages; today, few are in print, and fewer still are read. The late Thomas Mann—erudite literary artist, at home in all countries, diagnostician of the 20th-century ills of Germany, Europe, and the world, revealer of the human and divine in the characters of Joseph and his brethren—is a Goethe *redivivus*. Erich Remarque, classic analyst of war and its aftermath; Feuchtwanger and Werfel, writers of historical novels with meanings for today; and Wassermann, depicter of the searching soul in modern man—all are novelists of stature. The sober nightmare surrealism of Kafka (Czech); the excruciating vivisections of errant Galahads by Arthur Koestler (Hungarian); the humanitarian dramas of Arnold Zweig (Austrian) belong, through language, in the roster of German novels. Czech fiction will long be remembered for the prophetic scientific fantasies, in novels as in plays, of Karel Čapek, as readable as they are wise.

The special features and saga-strength of Scandinavian life (lived so far from Rome and Paris!) may be assimilated, like blood transfusions, from the pages of Lagerlöf and Hellstrom (Sweden), Bojer and Gulbranssen (Norway), Sillanpää and Hemmer (Finland), Nexø and Jensen (Denmark), Gunnarsson and Laxness (Iceland).

Historical novels are sufficient in number and merit to form a considerable modern library. Blending keen research, fresh insights into history and human nature, and engrossing melodrama, the novels of Sholem Asch (Yiddish), Sigrid Undset (Norway), Annamarie Selinko (Austria), Zofia Kossak (Poland), and Mika Waltari (Finland) are both scholarly and popular.

Such is today's world of European fiction: sick in conscience, critical in mood, strong at heart, striving, the blood singing, indomitable.

ANDREYEV, LEONID (Russia) 1871–1919 *Seven Who Were Hanged* (1909). Revolutionary idealists pay the death penalty. *Vin.*

BEAUVOIR, SIMONE DE (France) 1908– *The Mandarins* (1956). A provocative satire of the manners and morals of postwar French intellectuals by a leading existentialist. *Mer.*

BECKETT, SAMUEL (Ireland, now France) 1906– *Molloy* (1951). The story of a crippled writer-tramp in search of his mother; the searcher is sought by Moran; both are surrogates of Beckett (and of all "I's") in defeated quest of a self. Sharp in detail; puzzling as parable; a terribly funny segment of absurdity. *Ever.*

# THE NOVEL: 20TH CENTURY CONTINENTAL

**CAMUS, ALBERT** (France) 1913–1960 *The Stranger* (1946). A compelling story of the absurdity of life when man's aspirations and values have no cosmic status. *Knopf $3, Vin.*

———— *The Plague* (1948). Bubonic plague in Oran forces men to make choices of action: bewildered faith, passivity, flight, suicide, helping fellow men. Symbolically, the story of the Occupation and of men's responses to any sort of human plague. *Knopf $3.95, ML.*

**CAPEK, KAREL** (Czechoslovakia) 1890–1938 *War with the Newts* (1937). The newts take over! Science fiction, excellent as humor, social commentary, and story. *Ban.*

**D'ANNUNZIO, GABRIELE** (Italy) 1863–1938 *The Flame of Life* (1900). Details in fictional guise the adventures in personal passion of the Ulysses-like D'Annunzio and the Circean Eleanora Duse. *Page o.p.*

**DUERRENMATT, FRIEDRICH** (Switzerland) 1921– *The Pledge* (1959). Thought-arousing *récit*, sparsely written, of a police force captain whose logic is defeated by reality. *Knopf $3.*

———— *The Quarry* (1961). Police commissioner Barlach—an old, brave, dying Christian—must find and arrest Dr. Emmenberger, surgeon-torturer and archetype of renascent Nazism. A chilling, inspiring, different detective-story myth for our times. *N. Y. Graphic $3.50, BC.*

**FRANCE, ANATOLE** (France) 1844–1924 *Penguin Island* (1908). Deceits, tricks, pathetic follies of the rich, poor, haters, lovers, predators, idealists when, as penguins changed to men, they repeatedly make and break "civilizations." *Ban, ML.*

———— *Revolt of the Angels* (1914). A guardian angel, off duty, investigates and denounces the God of the theologians and organizes a revolt of the fallen angels of Paris. *Crown.*

**GIDE, ANDRÉ** (France) 1869–1951 *The Counterfeiters* (1927). Ironic analysis of troubled youth. *Knopf $4, ML.*

**GULBRANSSEN, TRYGVE** (Norway) 1894– *Beyond Sing the Woods* (1936). Literally, getting out of the woods and ahead in the world of romance and bourgeois business. *Putnam $5.*

**HAMSUN, KNUT** (Norway) 1859–1952 *Growth of the Soil* (1920). While neighbors fret, a Norwegian farm couple grow in nature-wise serenity. *Knopf $4.75.*

**HASEK, JAROSLAV** (Czechoslovakia) 1883–1923 *The Good Soldier: Schweik* (1923). Demonstrates how sane a simple man may seem ("crazy like a fox") when operating in a wartime environment of by-the-book officialdom. *Ungar $5, SigC.*

**HESSE, HERMANN** (Germany) 1877–1962 *Steppenwolf* (1929). An introspective, psychoanalytically oriented novel that probes the dilemma of the intellectual divorced from society and terrified of isolation. Harry Haller, the autobiographical hero, confronts the "steppenwolf" (animal) of his inward self in one of the most remarkable scenes in modern fiction. *Ungar $3, HRW.*

———— *Siddhartha* (1951). A poignantly lyrical tale about a young Indian who learns to fuse the worlds of flesh and spirit. Though steeped in mysticism, the brief story speaks eloquently to Western minds struggling toward unity in a schizophrenic world. *New Directions $2, New.*

KAFKA, FRANZ (Czechoslovakia) 1883–1924 ***The Trial*** (1937). In this our life, Joseph "K." is up for trial. But for what? He is never told, is never really tried by the High Court. Yet, finally, he is taken to a quarry and stabbed to the heart. Is this a neurotic Jew's anxiety dream—or a revelation for Everyman? *Knopf $4.50, ML.*

KAPEK See CAPEK, above.

KAZANTZAKIS, NIKOS (Greece) 1885–1957 ***The Odyssey: A Modern Sequel*** (1958). Modern man's search for his soul adumbrated in a poetic epic-novel. To be compared with Joyce's *Ulysses*. *Simon & Schuster $10, S&S.*

KOESTLER, ARTHUR (Hungary, now England) 1905– ***The Gladiators.*** See "Rome," page 42.

——— ***Darkness at Noon*** (1941). Penetrating, memorable dramatization making clear the ideological and psychological factors in a Communist purge trial. *Macmillan $5, ML, SigC.*

——— ***The Age of Longing*** (1951). Ghastly forecast of what Frenchmen and Americans in France might be like awaiting conquest from the East. *Collr.*

LAGERKVIST, PAR (Sweden) 1891– ***Barabbas*** (1951). The 1951 Nobel Prize winner writes a powerful character study of the man released to the mob instead of Christ. *Ban, Vin.*

LAGERLÖF, SELMA (Sweden) 1858–1940 ***The Story of Gösta Berling*** (1891). An unfrocked priest, after a career of love-errantry, marries and dedicates himself to a life of service. Excels in humor, characterization, and dramatically significant Swedish backgrounds. *SigC.*

LAMPEDUSA, GIUSEPPE DI (Italy) 1896–1957 ***The Leopard*** (1960). Story of an aristocrat and his family in the Garibaldian era of Italy's birth as a nation. Captivating as story; winning in its patrician truthfulness; vital in characterization. *Pantheon $4.50, Sig.*

MALRAUX, ANDRÉ (France) 1895– ***Man's Fate*** (1933). Individuals —Communists and non-Communists—together yet solitary, brave yet absurd, commit themselves to danger and death in the attempt to control Shanghai during the Chinese civil war (1927). Not history but existentialist vision; no man's fate but Malraux's fate for man. *ML.*

MANN, THOMAS (Germany) 1875–1955 ***Buddenbrooks*** (1924). The ineluctable decline from wealth and honor to mean-spirited poverty and extinction of a too-complacent mercantile family. Interesting for its delineation of social changes; of temperaments, motives, marriages, and measures among the Buddenbrooks and their connections. *Knopf $5, Vin.*

——— ***The Magic Mountain*** (1924). One of the most profound and provocative novels of our time, picturing a mountaintop sanitarium as a symbol of mankind in a pathologic universe. *Knopf $6.*

——— ***The Joseph Tetralogy*** (1924–44). A vivid, highly sug-

# THE NOVEL: 20TH CENTURY CONTINENTAL 113

gestive recreation of ancient Egypt and the biblical saga of Joseph. *Knopf $7.50.*

MARTIN DU GARD, ROGER (France) 1881–1958 **The World of the Thibaults** (1922–36). A series of novels searching with Tolstoian vitality the moral forces at work in our complex world. *Viking o.p.*

MAURIAC, FRANÇOIS (France) 1885– The leading Catholic novelist of France, whose forte is the psychology of faith and sin; as brooding a moralist as Hawthorne. Representative novels include **The Desert of Love** (1949), *Farrar, Straus $3.75, Ban;* and **Flesh and Blood** (1955), *Farrar, Straus $3.50, Dell.*

MEREZHKOVSKY (Russia) **The Romance of Leonardo da Vinci.** See "The Renaissance," page 75.

MORAVIA, ALBERTO (Italy) 1907– **The Time of Indifference** (1953). That "indifference" itself is a kind of action is realized as the shocked reader watches the Marengos—mother, daughter, and son—maneuvered into sexual and moral ruin by an amoral business man. Neorealistic satire without a smile. *Sig.*

———— **The Empty Canvas** (1961). Perhaps Moravia's finest novel to date. Like Sartre's **Nausea**, a probing analysis of the sources of *ennui*, psychic emptiness. From the abyss, however, the tortured hero emerges toward awareness and hope. *Farrar, Straus $4.50, Sig.*

NABOKOV (Russia, now United States) **Lolita.** See "20th Century American Novel," page 144.

NEXØ, MARTIN ANDERSON (Denmark) 1869–1954 **Pelle, the Conqueror** (1906–11). A Communist author narrates at epic length the career of Pelle, a Danish worker-messiah and scapegoat, who, evilly beset, never ceases struggling for human betterment. *Peter Smith $6.*

PASTERNAK, BORIS (Russia) 1890–1960 **Dr. Zhivago** (1958). Yuri Zhivago, orphaned at ten, later an upper-class doctor, poet, husband, lover, philosopher, struggles successfully, despite upheavals and regimentation in his beloved Russia, to preserve his humanity and spiritual independence. *Pantheon $5, MLG, Sig.*

PIRANDELLO, LUIGI (Italy) 1867–1936 **The Late Mattia Pascal** (1905). Reveals the false counsels, character masquerades, and faithlessness to family responsibilities of the title character, who thereby suffers some loss of identity. *Dutton o.p.*

*Portable Russian Reader* (1947). Ed. by B. G. Guerney. Contains short novels by Andreyev and Chekhov, short stories, etc. *Vik, Vik-h.*

PROUST, MARCEL (France) 1871–1922 **Remembrance of Things Past** (1913–28). In recovering his past through the dedicated exercise of memory, Proust lays bare in a series of seven novels—from **Swann's Way** (the best known) to **Time Regained**—a growing self, a changing age, a many-stranded philosophy. To read Proust, slowly, is to experience, in entertaining and enlightening fashion, his special world. *Random House 2 vols $15, ML (7 vols).*

REMARQUE, ERICH MARIA (Germany) 1897– *All Quiet on the Western Front* (1929). Perhaps the best-known World War I novel; blends images of war's bestiality with scenes of the battle-born brotherhood of men. *Little $4.50, Crest.*

ROBBE-GRILLET, ALAIN (France) 1922– *In the Labyrinth* (1960). In echoing musical rhythms and macabre scenes that focus, dissolve, and return, the author adumbrates the image of a nameless, wounded, hospitalized-and-drugged soldier, who strains to deliver to an unfindable address a small brown package. *Ever.*

ROLLAND, ROMAIN (France) 1866–1944 *Jean-Christophe* (1904–12). A musical genius battles poverty, attains success, and finally wins peace in death. *MLG o.p.*

ROMAINS, JULES (France) 1885– *Men of Good Will.* A multi-volume prose epic of France from 1900 to 1933. Outstanding single novels are *Verdun* (1939), a powerful evocation of the 1917 crisis *(Knopf o.p.);* and *Seventh of October* (1946), the final volume picturing tensions and strains as of 1933. *Knopf $5.*

SARTRE, JEAN PAUL (France) 1905– *Nausea* (1938). Antoine Roquentin, the antihero protagonist, records in his diary the dizzying elements of his existential vertigo: time, things, bourgeois bad faith, others, and himself. A brilliant, disturbing, sometimes bracing portrait of Sartre's wasteland. *New.*

*Troubled Sleep* (1951). Third and most interesting of an existentialist tetralogy of Sartre novels: the revolutionizing impact of the events of June 1940, and the psychology of defeat. Earlier books: *Age of Reason* and *Reprieve. Knopf $4.50 ea., Ban.*

SCHNITZLER, ARTHUR (Austria) 1862–1931 *Ten Little Novels* (1929). A skeptical doctor's slant on ten Viennese women in love. *Simon & Schuster o.p.*

SENDER, RAMÓN (Spain) 1902– *The King and the Queen* (1948). Remarkable love story (possibly an allegory of modern Spain), suggesting a comparison with Lawrence's *Lady Chatterley's Lover. Vanguard o.p.*

SHOLOKHOV, MIKHAIL (Russia) 1905– *The Silent Don* (1934–41). Includes two novels of epic scope—*And Quiet Flows the Don* and *The Don Flows Home to the Sea*—about Russian life from late Czarist days through World War I and the revolution. *Knopf $10, SigC.*

SILLANPÄÄ, FRANS EEMIL (Finland) 1888– *Meek Heritage* (1938). Civil war between Finnish Whites and Reds; the tragedy of elemental man. *Knopf o.p.*

SILONE, IGNAZIO (Italy) 1900– *Bread and Wine* (1936). The hero, Pietro Spina, an independent Communist, is primarily a humanitarian who risks all to rally the exploited away from Mussolini. A novel that has everything: great story; memorable characterizations; humor and pathos; major implications for church, society, and the individual. *Atheneum $5.95, SigC.*

UNDSET (Norway) *Kristin Lavransdatter.* See "The Middle Ages," page 70.

# THE NOVEL: 20TH CENTURY CONTINENTAL

VITTORINI, ELIO (Italy) 1908– *Conversation in Sicily* (1937). An affirmative Italian story of mother and son; a modern parable of fine earthy quality. *Pen.*

WALTARI, MIKA (Finland) 1908– *The Egyptian* (1945). Novelized history, dramatic and authentic, of the times of youthful Pharaoh Akhenaton. *Putnam $5, PB.*

WERFEL, FRANZ (Austria) 1890–1945 *The Forty Days of Musa Dagh* (1934). Saga of seven Armenian villages resisting the Turks in 1915. *PB.*

## C. 19th Century British Novels

### EDWARD S. LE COMTE, *Columbia University*

In *The Progress of Romance* (1785), Clara Reeve stated that "the Novel is a picture of real life and manners and of the times in which it is written." By her implied distinction, of the two figures who loom largest in the second decade of the 19th century in England, Jane Austen wrote novels, Sir Walter Scott, romances. Writing admiringly to Miss Austen, Scott called himself the author of "Big Bow-wow stories." Scott meant his historical romances, which legions of readers have found unsurpassed for adventure and descriptions of natural scenes—all full of the joy of living and the glory of the past. Emerson said that Scott gave him a feeling of longevity, a sense of the oneness of the pageant of humanity. If you would live 700 years of English history—from the 12th century through the 18th—you can do so by reading a selection of Scott's romances, beginning with the stories of Richard the Lion-Hearted and Robin Hood in *Ivanhoe* and ending with the humble Scottish cottagers of Scott's own youth in *The Heart of Midlothian*.

While Scott wove large and colorful tapestries, Jane Austen stitched in *petit point* the minute details of the small world she knew. She herself said she created on "a little piece of ivory of two inches wide," on which she worked "with a brush too fine to get any large effect." But what she may have lacked in breadth she gained in depth of perception—in her delicate, witty delineation of people and manners. We find her deft reporting of homely details as absorbing as our own plotless lives.

The age of the machine had arrived in England, and the first steps in reform legislation had been taken by the time Charles Dickens began to write in the 1830's. The experiences of his own boyhood (imaginatively projected into *David Copperfield*) and his sympathy for the poverty-ridden class produced melodramatic novels animated by social awareness. Humanitarian Dickens dramatized the abuses of factory, school, church, and the courts. Possibly the best-remembered portrayal of a "have-not" in a cruelly heedless society is Oliver Twist in the workhouse. The Dickens gallery of original portraits is tremendous in its scope. Perennial favorites are those touched with his characteristic humor—Pickwick, Micawber, Barkis, Sarah Gamp. In comic character and situation, Dickens is a master. His later novels are better structured but more serious.

More than a century ago, in 1847 and 1848, Thackeray wrote a novel never absent from "best book" lists: *Vanity Fair,* in which we get to know the world's most designing female, Becky Sharp; her hapless husband; sweet, patient Amelia; and dashing but faithless George Osborne—and we never forget them.

Although Thackeray may not have been deeply moved by the social changes of 19th-century England, they presented him with models for snob, climber, rogue, hypocrite—a parade in which he also poses for us the sweet but vapid, the dull, the spoiled. But Thackeray, satirist and moralist, does not preach; consequently, he entertains superbly. For a fictionalized version of his own life story read *Pendennis,* with its reflection of the life of a favored young man of the 19th century.

A new psychological study of man, a highly intellectualized probing of motives, conduct, and emotions, is blended in the novels of George Eliot (Mary Ann Evans), with understanding, sympathy, and humor. Her genre novels of English country folk, *Adam Bede* and *The Mill on the Floss,* have never lost their appeal. *Middlemarch* exhibits her powers on a grand scale.

Another challenging writer, one who calls upon his readers for concentration and patience, is George Meredith. In penetrating studies of late Victorian society he employs devastating ridicule to punish those who offend. His two most frequently read novels, written twenty-six years apart, are *The Ordeal of Richard Feverel* and *Diana of the Crossways.*

Toward the close of the century that began with Scott,

who nearly always provided happy endings, came Thomas Hardy, in whom deterministic melancholy reached the depths of the Greek tragedies. The futility of human struggle against unpredictable nature and chance pervades his somber novels, of which *Tess of the d'Urbervilles* and *The Return of the Native* have been most esteemed for their structural precision and bitter ironic force.

To name these seven novelists as representing the main streams of imaginative writing in Victoria's century is not to deny the importance of such a novelist as Trollope, with his lively and intimate pictures of a cathedral town, or such individual masterpieces as *Jane Eyre, Wuthering Heights, The Cloister and the Hearth, Dr. Jekyll and Mr. Hyde,* and *Esther Waters*.

AUSTEN, JANE 1775–1817 *Sense and Sensibility* (1811). A striking contrast of two sisters—one the prototype of common sense, the other of romantic "sensibility"—with simple domestic scenes of rural England forthrightly portrayed and flavored with pleasing humor. *Over fifteen editions.*

──────── *Pride and Prejudice* (1813). Concerned mainly with the conflict between the prejudice of a young lady and the well-founded though misinterpreted pride of the aristocratic hero. The heroine's father and mother cope in very different ways with the problem of marrying off five daughters. A masterpiece of gentle humor. *Over twenty editions.*

──────── *Emma* (1816). Story of a girl who tries to regulate the love affairs of others without success, yet who, despite her meddling, endears herself to the reader. *Over a dozen editions.*

BLACKMORE, R. D. 1825–1900 *Lorna Doone* (1869). A historical romance blending revenge, love, and adventure. *Over a dozen editions.*

BRONTË, CHARLOTTE 1816–1855 *Jane Eyre* (1847). Modern realism and wildest melodrama in a story that four generations of readers have found fascinating. What secret of his past and in his house makes Mr. Rochester hesitate to marry the governess whom he desperately loves? *Over twenty editions.*

BRONTË, EMILY 1818–1848 *Wuthering Heights* (1847). A tale of psychological horror deriving from the morbid passions of an ill-treated and vindictive waif. The attraction between Heathcliff and Catherine lies deeper than sex. The tale weirdly continues into the second generation and beyond the grave. *Over twenty editions.*

BULWER-LYTTON *The Last Days of Pompeii.* See "Rome," page 41.

# THE NOVEL: 19TH CENTURY BRITISH

**BUTLER, SAMUEL** 1835–1902 *Erewhon* (1872). A satire upon shams in education, religion, social customs, and ethics. As sharply pointed as Aristophanes, as modern as today's headlines. *Collr, Dolp, Evman-h, ML, SigC.*

———— *The Way of All Flesh* (1903). A semiautobiographical account of a son struggling to find himself and break free of the restrictions of Victorian convention and parental authority. Ernest Pontifex has the doubts and struggles that we now recognize as modern. One of the best books ever written about education—in both the narrow and the broad sense. *Over a dozen editions.*

**CARROLL, LEWIS (CHARLES L. DODGSON)** 1832–1898 *Alice in Wonderland* (1865). A masterpiece of inimitable fantasy and deft satire. Its inseparable sequel is *Through the Looking-Glass* (1872). Each in over fifteen editions.

**COLLINS, WILKIE** 1824–1889 *The Moonstone* (1868). Mystery thriller about a priceless diamond stolen from a Hindu shrine. *Dolp, Evman-h, MLG, Nel, Pyr, WoC.*

**CONRAD, JOSEPH** 1857–1924 *Almayer's Folly* (1895). Story of a lone white man in Malaya destroyed by a dream of gold. *CoNC, Dell, Nort.*

———— *The Nigger of the Narcissus* (1897). Extraordinary delineation of a common man of the sea. *Over ten editions.*

———— Later Novels. See "20th Century British Novels," page 126.

**DICKENS, CHARLES** 1812–1870 *Pickwick Papers* (1837). Not exactly a novel, but rather a series of loosely connected incidents. Extravagantly funny, rich in memorable characters. *Over a dozen editions.*

———— *Oliver Twist* (1838). The underworld and "culture of poverty" of early 19th-century London portrayed by a reformer. *Over a dozen editions.*

———— *David Copperfield* (1850). Dickens' own favorite, perhaps because it reflects the author's own youth. *Over fifteen editions.*

———— *Bleak House* (1853). A long-drawn-out lawsuit blights the innocent young and brings in its train murder, madness, shame, poverty, in one of the biggest—in every sense—of Dickens' novels. *Oxford $4 CoNC, Evman-h, Nel, RivEd, SM.*

———— *A Tale of Two Cities.* See "The 18th Century," page 98.

———— *Great Expectations* (1861). A mocking narrative of absurd waiting for legacies. Dickens' best-plotted—and in many ways best—novel. *Over fifteen editions.*

**ELIOT, GEORGE (MARY ANN EVANS)** 1819–1880 *Adam Bede* (1859). The simple charm of the English countryside pervades this story of two brothers, a girl who murders her illegitimate baby, and Dinah Morris, a Methodist preacher whose healing influence works on all. *Over a dozen editions.*

———— *The Mill on the Floss* (1860). Revelation of youthful perplexities in the person of Maggie Tulliver—sensitive, impulsive, strong-willed, misunderstood, destined to sorrow. *Over a dozen editions.*

*Silas Marner* (1861). Sentimental story of a victim of deceit restored to happiness through the love of a child. *Over twenty editions.*

*Middlemarch* (1872). A novel of great cumulative power dealing with two unhappy marriages in a provincial community that becomes as familiar to us as our own home. *Harcourt $3.50, Collr, Evman-h, RivEd, SigC, WoC, WSP.*

GASKELL, ELIZABETH 1810–1865 *Cranford* (1853). Delightful picture of quaint characters and customs in a quiet village. *Dolp, Evman-h, Nel, Nort, WoC.*

GISSING, GEORGE 1857–1903 *New Grub Street* (1891). Deals movingly with the problem of being honest—and not becoming a hack—in the literary world, where the slow and unpopular writer starves, along with any family he may have. *RivEd, WoC.*

HARDY, THOMAS 1840–1928 *Far From the Madding Crowd* (1874). The drab existence of country people is made vivid and vital. *Evman-h, HarpMC, HRW, Prem, RivEd, SigC, SM.*

*The Return of the Native* (1878). A story of joy, sorrow, and tragedy told against the somber background of Egdon Heath. *Over a dozen editions.*

*The Mayor of Casterbridge* (1886). The worldly rise and fall of a man who, while drunk, sold his wife to a stranger. *Over a dozen editions.*

*Tess of the d'Urbervilles* (1891). The poignant tragedy of a woman who tells the truth to a husband not ready to receive it. Whenever happiness seems within grasp, the mocking Fates snatch it away. *Dell, Dolp, HarpMC, MLCE, Nort, RivEd, SM, WSP.*

*Jude the Obscure* (1896). A tragic, powerful study of ambition thwarted by weak will and poor environment. *Collr, Dell, Dolp, HarpMC, ML, SigC, SM.*

JAMES See "19th Century American Novels," page 136.

KINGSLEY, CHARLES 1819–1875 *Westward Ho!* (1855). Bitterly anti-Jesuit, but a thrilling adventure story of the time when Elizabeth knighted sea captains for piracy against the Spaniards. *Evman-h, Nel.*

MEREDITH, GEORGE 1828–1909 *The Ordeal of Richard Feverel* (1859). The hero bitterly resents the smug inhumanity and human destructiveness of his father's educational system. *Evman-h, ML, MLCE, SigC, WSP.*

*The Egoist* (1879). A novel satirizing man's inherent selfishness. *Dolp, ML, RivEd, SigC, WoC.*

*Diana of the Crossways* (1885). A brilliant woman's struggle for independence in a man's world. *o.p.*

MOORE, GEORGE 1852–1933 *Esther Waters* (1894). The misfortunes and brief happiness of a servant girl portrayed sympathetically by a follower of Zola's "naturalism." *Black, Evman-h, Nort, Prem, RivEd.*

*Héloïse and Abélard.* See "The Middle Ages," page 69.

# THE NOVEL: 19TH CENTURY BRITISH

**READ** *The Cloister and the Hearth.* See "The Middle Ages," page 70.

**SCOTT, WALTER** 1771–1832 For his ever-popular historical novels dealing with the Middle Ages, the Renaissance, the 17th Century, and the 18th Century, see pages 70, 82, 89, 98.

**SHELLEY, MARY WOLLSTONECRAFT** 1797–1851 *Frankenstein* (1818). A man-made monster destroys all whom his master loves. *Collr, Dolp, Evman, Evman-h, Pyr.*

**STEVENSON, ROBERT LOUIS** 1850–1894 *Treasure Island* (1883). A delightful yarn of buried gold, pirates, mutiny, and a brave cabin boy. *Over twenty editions.*

_____ *Kidnapped* (1886). A young Scot's romantic adventures on sea and land. *Over twenty editions.*

_____ *The Strange Case of Dr. Jekyll and Mr. Hyde* (1886). Psychological study of the struggle between good and evil within a human soul. *Coward-McCann $3.50, Evman, Evman-h, Nel, Nort.*

_____ *The Master of Ballantrae* (1889). A feud between brothers begins in Scotland, comes to an eerie end in the wilderness of America. Unique combination of domestic character study and adventure story. *Evman-h, HRW, Nel, Nort, WoC.*

**THACKERAY, WILLIAM MAKEPEACE** 1811–1863 *Vanity Fair* (1847–48). Essentially an unsparing portrayal of a designing female, who succeeds until retribution sets in. Fascinating, selfish Becky Sharp contrasts with sweet, simple Amelia Sedley, whose brother and husband are but two of the men Becky attracts. *Over fifteen editions.*

_____ *Pendennis* (1848–50). A typical young man displays typical faults and mistakes, the chief of which is selfishness. *Evman-h.*

_____ *The Newcomes* (1853–55). Memorable for a portrait of Colonel Newcome, formerly of the army in India, who keeps his honor, but not his fortune, in a world of snobs and schemers. *Evman-h.*

**TROLLOPE, ANTHONY** 1815–1882 *The Warden* (1855). A brash young reformer stirs up trouble and raises delicate questions of conscience in a hitherto outwardly quiet ecclesiastical town. *Over a dozen editions.*

_____ *Barchester Towers* (1857). Animates with zest and humor the small-town middle-class life of Victorian England, making interesting the intrigues and gossip of petty church officialdom. *Over a dozen editions.*

**WILDE, OSCAR** 1854–1900 *The Picture of Dorian Gray* (1891). Dorian is doomed to keep the unsullied exterior splendor of youth while the gradual deterioration of his portrait reveals his accumulating internal depravity. *Dell, Dolp, ML, Pen, Pyr, SigC.*

## D. 20th Century British Novels

ARTHUR ZEIGER, *City College of New York*

In the decade preceding World War I some very impressive British novels were written: John Galsworthy's *The Man of Property* (1906), first volume of *The Forsyte Saga;* Arnold Bennett's *The Old Wives' Tale* (1908); H. G. Wells' *Tono-Bungay* (1909). Produced by perceptive novelists who respected truth and their craft, these are serious and substantial works.

Yet the younger novelists found them unsatisfying. Galsworthy had conceived his Philistine saga ironically, but in execution the iron melted. The author became the novelist member of the Forsyte family, esteeming them—and their solid possessions—almost as much as they did. Sentiment blurred his vision, and the Forsytes seem never wholly in focus.

Bennett built compacter, perhaps more durable, structures. In his best, most deeply felt novel, he placed two sisters against a drab industrial background—Bursley, one of the "five towns" of Staffordshire. He pictured their unlovely, joyless lives in immense and accurate detail, so that one knows all *about* them—but never quite *knows* them, never feels their life as they felt it. Like other naturalistic novels, *The Old Wives' Tale* impresses by its massed data, not by the immediacy with which it enables us to know the characters it describes.

H. G. Wells had formidable novelistic equipment: curiosity, intelligence, social conscience, fertility of invention, and an incapacity for dullness. Yet, proudly regarding himself as a journalist and deprecating the artist's role, he willfully sacrificed form to social reform. His people seem frequently to illustrate a thesis rather than to live even a fictitious life.

Admitting the virtues of Wells, Bennett, Galsworthy,

and their industrious school, Virginia Woolf, the most articulate spokesman for the opposition, denounced their resolute externality, their documentary materialistic bias, their refusal to immerse in the stream of consciousness. *To the Lighthouse* (1927) illuminates her strictures. The author enters the consciousness of her characters, reproduces sensitively the quality and content of their feeling, and herself intrudes only obliquely. From the subtle, lambent prose, one deduces not only the characters and their relationships but also the environment itself. An admirable stylistic achievement, *To the Lighthouse* becomes at times impalpable and rarefied as the shadow of a flame. One admires, but longs for plot and incident, for more solidity, more substance.

Virginia Woolf did not of course inaugurate the subjective novel: she acknowledges two great ancestors, Henry James and James Joyce. James's involute sentences, which at first block the reader's progress and obscure the dramatic structure of his fiction by their dislocated clauses, fragmented phrases, displaced adverbs, piled-up punctuation, and wrenched rhythms, seem ultimately right; for they capture the delicate, fleeting, apparently ineluctable nuance of feeling. Joyce's mythic ordering of the flux of contemporary experience, his dedication to the word, his comic vision, and above all his power of rendering the inward life of his characters, make *Ulysses* a triumph of the introvertive method.

Because of the compelling examples of Joyce, James, and (to a lesser extent) Virginia Woolf, many novelists since have progressively shunned external reality, preferring instead to record—intensively, almost raptly—the feelings and thoughts it induces. The unhappy fact, however, is that the reality itself often attenuates or disintegrates. As practiced by most contemporary English writers—for example, Philip Toynbee (whose *Tea with Mrs. Goodman* [1947] explores the "events" occurring at a tea)—the novel has lost force and breadth (and readability) and gained technique. Writers in our decade generally have turned their backs on the elements that vitalize technique.

But charting the development of the 20th century thus

broadly, one inevitably distorts. A number of writers refuse to submit to facile classification. Two with whom Virginia Woolf associated herself in the revolt against the realistic and naturalistic novel, E. M. Forster and D. H. Lawrence, escape the perils incident to both the extrovertive and introvertive novel. Each novelist has a central, governing theme. Forster, beautifully, lucidly, penetrates the moral situation of our time, the difficulties we have "connecting" with one another, establishing truly human attitudes. Lawrence, in passionate, thrusting prose, probes the vital relationship between men and women, their failures to achieve fulfillment, the deepest longings of their subterranean beings.

And there are writers so sharply individual that only an arbitrary critic will name them within a paragraph. Perhaps most eccentric, Ivy Compton-Burnett has written her characteristic novel since the 1920's (though not until recently has her reputation approached her performance): through the witty, stylized conversation of her country-house characters, the reader comes to learn of monstrous doings afoot—the urbanity enhancing the melodrama. Henry Green writes in a lower, more modulated key. Though his novels, too, unfold through conversation, it is accurately reproduced conversation that brilliantly reveals his characters, the world surrounding them, the atmosphere they inhabit.

Other names arise to undermine generalizations concerning the progressive inwardness of the novel during this century. Aldous Huxley, Evelyn Waugh, and George Orwell have attained notable success in satire, a genre which, requiring a definite credo, finds the climate of our divided age inhospitable. Nevertheless, Huxley, Waugh, and Orwell, men firmly grounded in belief (the first in Vedanta, the second in Roman Catholicism, the last in socialism), have withstood the forces impelling to unbelief.

Finally, traditional novelists—novelists who have never abjured plot, chronology, climax, never renounced the world outside us from which presumably our impressions derive—have flourished. Somerset Maugham, an astute craftsman, until recently has produced clever and extremely readable novels, though hardly anyone would claim that they were searching or powerful creations, enlarging our apprehension or increasing our sensibility. Christopher Isherwood has not realized the promise of his Berlin novels—penetrating, moving, prophetic evocations of pre-Hitler Germany; but *The Last of Mr. Norris* and *Goodbye to Berlin* stand, perhaps, as the best "social" fiction in this century. Graham Greene freights his well-made novels of suspense with theological insight—unlikely matter, but far from capsizing, it imparts gravity and dimension to them. Joyce Cary, nearly alone among his contemporaries, has dedicated his splendid novelistic abilities—a marvelous creative vigor, a warm and sympathetic insight into human imperfections, a flexible and resilient style—to celebrating the enduring, vaulting spirit of man.

Though C. P. Snow and Lawrence Durrell received most attention, the 1950's were dominated by the Angry Young Men—writers like Kingsley Amis, John Wain, J. P. Donleavy, Alan Sillitoe, and John Braine. "Angry" certainly seems an inappropriate designation for most of them: far more they are disaffected, disassociated, or "disaffiliated." No member of the group (whether he voluntarily enlisted or was dragooned by the critics) has yet published a great novel. And, in spite of their various excellences, the novels they have so far produced bear too marked a resemblance to one another.

Nevertheless, the members are young (most of them about 40), talented, energetic; and, happily, discontent with their achievements. The best, in fact, have seceded. Iris Murdoch, for example, whose early fiction looked more than a little like Amis's, has recently attempted novels in the "crystalline mode"—novels informed by myth, structured by symbol. While perhaps they say something essential about the substrata of reality, they scant or distort reality itself.

But already British writers are formulating a new ideal, painfully working toward it. In novels to come, the shape, direction, and meaning of our age will be shown forth by characters inhabiting the real world and bound to it. It promises to be an exciting development.

AMIS, KINGSLEY 1922– **Lucky Jim** (1954). A funny, at times cruel, story of a young, inept instructor on probation at an English college, his difficulties and fortunes in love. *Comp.*

BECKETT **Molloy.** See "20th Century Continental Novels," page 110.

BEERBOHM, MAX 1872–1956 **Zuleika Dobson** (1911). Undergraduate Oxford is disrupted by the maddening beauty of Zuleika in this deft comic fantasy. *Dodd $6, Heritage $6, ML.*

BENNETT, ARNOLD 1867–1931 **The Old Wives' Tale** (1908). Slowly, almost imperceptibly, the grimy Midlands town presses life from Sophia and Constance Baines. *HarpMC, ML, SigC.*

BOWEN, ELIZABETH 1899– **The Death of the Heart** (1938). A deeply moving tragedy of adolescence, brought about by adult cruelty and insensitivity. *Knopf $4.95, Vin.*

BRAINE, JOHN 1922– **Room at the Top** (1957). A brilliant chronicle of the fortunes—and ultimate misfortune—of a young man who knows all prices but no values. *Houghton $3.75, Sig.*

CARY, JOYCE 1888–1957 **The Horse's Mouth** (1944). Last of a trilogy including **Herself Surprised** (1941) and **To Be a Pilgrim** (1942). Exuberant history of Gulley Jimson, visionary painter and outrageous person, told by himself. (In the other volumes, Sarah, his lady love, and Wilcher, his lawyer rival, tell their complementary stories.) *HarpMC, UL.*

COMPTON-BURNETT, IVY 1892– **Bullivant and the Lambs** (1948). A comedy of manners, couched in antinaturalistic epigrammatic dialogue, involving a stingy father, his sinister children, and Bullivant, the butler, who never loses control. *Knopf o.p.*

CONRAD, JOSEPH 1857–1924 **Early Novels.** See "19th Century British Novels," page 119.

———— **Lord Jim** (1900). The hero suffers dishonor through cowardice; he atones, endures heroic defeat, and gains redemption. *Over a dozen editions.*

———— **Heart of Darkness** (1902). A short novel revealing the heart's darkness, deeper than Africa's. *Dell, Nort, SigC.*

———— **Nostromo** (1904). An intricately structured political novel, recounting in full detail the genesis and course of a South American revolution and pointing up the corrupting power of silver. *Heritage $6, Dell, HRW, ML, Pen, SigC.*

DONLEAVY **The Ginger Man.** See "20th Century American Novels," page 141.

DOUGLAS, NORMAN 1868–1952 **South Wind** (1917). Amusing, cynical symposium on conventional morality. The setting is a Mediterranean island whose shifting winds effect shifts in moral values among the visitors. *Ban, ML, Pen, UL.*

DURRELL, LAWRENCE 1912– **Justine** (1957), **Balthazar** (1958), **Mountolive** (1959), **Clea** (1960). A stunning baroque "Quartet" of novels about Alexandria—the shimmering, monstrous, beautiful, unreal city—and the "truth" about some exotic people who live there told from shifting perspectives. *Evman, PB.*

FORSTER, E. M. 1879– **The Longest Journey** (1907). A sensitive young man regularly accepts illusion for reality, an error that leads to an unhappy marriage and ultimate destruction. *Knopf $4, Vin.*

———— *A Passage to India* (1924). Focusing on a dramatic situation, this philosophical novel explores the tensions between Englishmen and Indians—and, symbolically, other, more basic tensions as well. *HarB.*

GALSWORTHY, JOHN 1867–1933 *The Forsyte Saga* (1906–21). A series of 12 novels affectionately centering on a large, wealthy, middle-class family from 1886 to 1920, and tracing the effect on them of property and the possessive instinct. The three best-known titles are available in *Scribner $7.50.*

GARNETT, DAVID 1892– *Lady into Fox* (1922). A modern fantasy, with ironic overtones, about a beautiful woman transformed into a vixen and the consequences to her doting husband. *o.p.*

GOLDING, WILLIAM 1911– *Lord of the Flies* (1954). "Boys will be boys"—which, Golding implies in this brilliant, merciless allegory, means they will be, quite literally, savage. *Coward $5, Cap.*

GREEN, HENRY (HENRY VINCENT YORKE) 1905– *Loving* (1945). A comic-pathetic realistic novel, set against a romantic Irish background: the story concerns the love of Edith, a housemaid, for Raunce, a butler, *Anch.*

GREENE, GRAHAM 1904– *Brighton Rock* (1938). One of Greene's "entertainments," involving pursuit, gang warfare, and murder; encompassed by terror—and informed with theological doctrine. *Viking $3.50, Comp.*

———— *The Heart of the Matter* (1948). A "theological thriller," but equally a tale of frustrated goodness and thwarted love. *Viking $3.50, Comp.*

HUDSON, W. H. 1841–1922 *Green Mansions* (1904). Romantic tale, set in the tropical forests of South America, recounting the ill-starred love of Rima, the "bird-girl," and the narrator, Mr. Abel. *Knopf $6.95, Ban, HarpMC, ML, Nort, UL.*

HUGHES, RICHARD 1900– *A High Wind in Jamaica* (also titled *The Innocent Voyage*) (1929). A revealing study of the separate world of childhood: a group of children, captured by pirates, undergo a violent voyage into experience. *HarpMC, SigC.*

HUXLEY, ALDOUS 1894–1963 *Point Counter Point* (1928). Through "parallel contrapuntal plots," Huxley atomizes the upper-class world in pursuit of "pleasure"—its sensuality, debauchery, parasitism, and purposelessness. *Avon, HarpMC, ML, Torch.*

———— *Brave New World* (1932). Satire on the mechanized, dehumanized world of the future; the time is 632 A.F. (After Ford). *Harper $3.50, Ban, HarpMC, ML, Torch.*

ISHERWOOD, CHRISTOPHER 1904– *The Berlin Stories* (1946). Two short novels that hauntingly evoke Berlin in the five years before Hitler—its degeneration, futility, ominous brutality. *New Directions $3.50, New.*

JOYCE, JAMES 1882–1941 *Portrait of the Artist as a Young Man* (1916). A semiautobiographical "novel of initiation": the young artist strives to gain his freedom—from religion, country, family —to practice his art untrammeled. *Viking $3.50, Comp.*

*Ulysses* (1922). Ostensibly the record of a single day filtered through the consciousness of Leopold Bloom and Stephan Dedalus; but more than that, a great comic-epic poem, a paradigm of modern man's search for values. *Random House $6, MLG.*

KIPLING, RUDYARD 1865–1936 *Kim* (1901). A vivid picture of India and her people is given in this exciting tale of secret-service activity. *Doubleday $2.95, Collr, Dell, ML.*

LAWRENCE, D. H. 1885–1930 *Sons and Lovers* (1913). A semiautobiographical novel, powerfully dramatizing the sexually inhibiting force of excessive mother-love. *Comp, ML.*

*The Rainbow* (1915). An analysis (sometimes concrete, sometimes mystical) of the nature of sexuality, divisive and unifying—and ultimately insufficient. *Comp, ML.*

*Lady Chatterley's Lover* (1928). Long censored because of the author's unreticent description of the processes of passionate love, the novel seems a bit old-fashioned today in spite of the plain language, but is still valid as a study in contrasts —industrialism versus "nature," the decadent upper class versus the vigorous lower. *BC, ML, PB, Sig.*

MAUGHAM, W. SOMERSET 1874– *Of Human Bondage* (1915). An engrossing "educational novel," based on the author's life: the hero comes to the realization of his individual identity through suffering, defeat, and tragic love. *Doubleday $4.95, ML, Vin.*

*The Moon and Sixpence* (1919). This *roman à clef* (the prototype of the hero is Paul Gauguin, the French impressionist painter) tells of an artist whose only morality is in his art. *Ban, ML.*

MURDOCH, IRIS 1919– *The Flight from the Enchanter* (1956). Fascinating simply as story, this symbolic "fantasia" centers on a group of Londoners drawn into the orbit of the powerful, shadowy enchanter, Mische Fox, and how each suffers change or extinction. *o.p.*

*A Severed Head* (1961). A "metaphysical examination of love," in its several varieties, through shock narrative. *Viking $3.95, Comp.*

O'FLAHERTY, LIAM 1897– *The Informer* (1926). Dublin during "the Trouble" is the scene: what passed through the mind of a man who betrayed his best friend to the English enemy. *SigC.*

ORWELL, GEORGE 1903–1950 *Animal Farm* (1945). Brilliant satirical allegory on dictatorship, especially on its penchant for devouring its own. *Harcourt $2.95, SigC.*

*1984* (1949). A nightmare projection of a future police state ruled by "Big Brother," where "War is Peace" and all values are transvalued. *Harcourt $4.75, SigC.*

PATON *Cry, the Beloved Country.* See "The Middle East and Africa," page 56.

# THE NOVEL: 20TH CENTURY BRITISH

**POWELL, ANTHONY** 1905– *A Question of Upbringing* (1951), *A Buyer's Market* (1952), *The Acceptance World* (1955), *At Lady Molly's* (1957), *Casanova's Chinese Restaurant* (1960), *The Kindly Ones* (1962). **A Dance to the Music of Time**—the general title for the series (six novels yet to come)—chronicles urbanely and wittily the small adventures of Nicholas Powell and his odd acquaintances between two wars, their multiple amours, their excursions into the world of art, their frustrated attempts at fulfillment—all the changes wrought by time's kaleidoscope. *Little $4.50–$5.95.*

**PRIESTLEY, J. B.** 1894– *The Good Companions* (1929). Long, diverting picaresque tale involving a troupe of wandering English players. *Harper $6.50.*

**SILLITOE, ALAN** 1928– *Saturday Night and Sunday Morning* (1958). The career of a young worker, trapped by the system and angry with it, described authentically from a proletarian (even a lumpenproletariat) point of view. *Knopf $3.75, Sig.*

———— *The Loneliness of the Long-Distance Runner* (1959). A short novel, the quintessence of "disaffiliation," about a Borstal boy who deliberately refuses to win a race—rejecting any triumph, no matter how gratifying, which gratifies the authorities as well. *Knopf $3.50, Sig.*

**SNOW, C. P.** 1905– *The Masters* (1951). Absorbing neorealistic account of the election of a new master to a Cambridge college. *Scribner $4.50, Anch.*

———— *The Conscience of the Rich* (1958). Warmly and perceptively, Snow draws the portraits of the Marches, a family of great Jewish financiers. *Scribner $4.50, Scrib.*

These two volumes are part of a continuing sequence—**Strangers and Brothers** (1940– )—a rich and complex panorama of modern society, mostly set in the corridors (rather than chambers) of power. So far published, in addition to the above: *Strangers and Brothers* (1940), *Scribner $4.50, Scrib; The Light and the Dark* (1947), *Scribner $4.95; Time of Hope* (1949), *Scribner $4.50, Scrib; The New Men* (1954), *Scribner $4.50, Scrib; Homecoming* (1956), *Scribner $4.50;* and *The Affair* (1960), *Scribner $4.50, Scrib.* Three projected volumes will complete the series.

**SPARK, MURIEL** 1918– *Memento Mori* (1959). A group of oldsters, their prepossessions and prejudices merely ossified by time, take brief positions in this funny and sad dance of death. *Lippincott $3.95, Mer.*

**WAUGH, EVELYN** 1903– *A Handful of Dust* (1934). A satire of the contemporary wasteland: the career of Last, the man of good will, ends in tragic-absurd fashion, as captive reader to a Dickens-loving lunatic. *Dell.*

———— *Brideshead Revisited* (1945). A muted satirist in this novel written from a Catholic stance, Waugh presents dissipation, boredom, and insurmountable hopelessness as the only alternative to faith and works. *Dell.*

**WEBB, MARY** 1881–1927 *Precious Bane* (1924). Somber, poetic novel of the Shropshire country, in the tradition of Hardy. *Dutton* $4.95, ML.

WELLS, H. G. 1866–1946 ***Tono-Bungay*** (1908). Vigorous history of the rise and fall of the promoters of a patent-medicine fraud, with perceptive sidelights on the evils commercialism breeds. ML, SigC.

WOOLF, VIRGINIA 1882–1941 ***To the Lighthouse*** (1927). From shifting centers of consciousness, this beautifully textured symbolic novel shows rather than describes Mrs. Ramsey and her widening effect (even after she has died) on the lives that touch hers. HarB.

———— ***Orlando*** (1928). The hero turns heroine in this pseudo-biography, which is also a survey of England's history and literature since Elizabethan times. SigC.

# E. 19th Century American Novels

## DANIEL GERZOG, Pratt Institute

The story of the American novel from its beginnings through the first half of the 19th century is mainly the story of a second struggle for independence from England. In the manner of Richardson, scores of young American heroines relived Pamela's moral anguish. Charles Brockden Brown transported Godwin's and Walpole's eerie "Gothic" castles to the outskirts of Philadelphia. H. H. Brackenridge fashioned a Pennsylvania Don Quixote and an Irish Sancho Panza, set them on the western frontier, and acknowledged his satiric debt to Fielding and Swift. Some of these early attempts have their moments, but none is an enduring work of art.

The first important American novelist, James Fenimore Cooper, consciously imitated Sir Walter Scott. Because America lacked knights in full panoply and the romance of the Highlands, he exploited the closest parallels—the frontier, with its noble savages and dauntless pioneers; and the Revolution, with its larger-than-life heroes on both land and sea. Like Scott, Cooper created some unforgettable scenes and characters, but his adventure stories are best read in adolescence. Sophisticated readers have found, however, that the Cooper novels concerned with American social problems—*The Pioneers* and *The Prairie* (the best of the Leatherstocking Series); the "Rent-War" trilogy, especially *Satanstoe;* and *Homeward Bound* and *Home as Found*—yield rewarding if highly opinionated insights into the growing pains of our turbulent formative years.

While the American novel can be said to have started slowly and imitatively, it came of age in that creative efflorescence of the early 1850's that has come to be known as the first American renaissance. In successive years, two of the greatest novels in any nation's literature were published—Hawthorne's *The Scarlet Letter* and Melville's *Moby Dick*.

Not only had America discovered a subject matter in its own past and present, but it had found a form in which to present it. Although both novels are, in the broadest sense, romances (neither Hawthorne's Salem nor Melville's *Pequod* is a world that ever was), both men create out of the materials of romance rich fabrics of highly complex symbolism, woven through with the dark threads of enigmatic moral and metaphysical inquiry. In Melville's words, they "dove deep" and surfaced with treasures that lie unseen by those who swim in the shallows of human awareness. Because Hawthorne and Melville raised troublesome questions in an essentially optimistic age, neither was fully appreciated in his day. But in our darker times, they are rightly considered two of the giants of American—and world—letters. The depth of psychological insight and the profundity of theme in these novels will sustain the reader through several re-readings and many hours of reflection.

Hawthorne went on to write other provocative romances, but he never again achieved the economy of expression and tightness of form that elevate *The Scarlet Letter* and the best of his short stories to the highest level of art.

*Moby Dick* marks the high point of Melville's output. Of the five novels he produced in the five years before its publication, four are fictionalized accounts of his adventures at sea. One, *Mardi*, does attempt the philosophic scope of his masterpiece, but fails to achieve its dramatic and poetic power. After *Moby Dick*, Melville's somber vision produced two more novels, but neither strikes the happy balance between exciting realism and significant speculation that we experience following Ahab in search of the white whale. Late in life, in the short novel *Billy Budd*, Melville again used shipboard life as a microcosm to illuminate man's metaphysical dilemma. Read with a proper awareness of its author's sharp satiric bent and powerful irony, it reaffirms the dark genius of the mind that spawned America's greatest novel.

# THE NOVEL: 19TH CENTURY AMERICAN

The strength that the romance had achieved with Hawthorne and Melville was quickly dissipated in the hands of what Hawthorne called a "damned mob of scribbling women." The serious literary figures from 1830 to 1870—perhaps still imprisoned by the Puritan skepticism of "story telling"—wrote poetry or essays. The novelists ground out precursors of today's sentimental soap operas. *Little Women* illustrates the type, although it far surpasses in quality the trivia produced. From this genre, too, came *Uncle Tom's Cabin,* important for its pervasive effect on the antislavery movement. We might pause to consider *Elsie Venner* by Dr. Oliver Wendell Holmes, whose medical interest in the nature of the mind and in the moral and social problems raised by psychological determinism has new significance in our post-Freudian times. But not until the novel received vital transfusions from two regenerative springs did it regain its lost power.

The United States emerged as a nation from the Civil War, and with the awareness of wider vistas came the desire to create real pictures of the sprawling country. The best of the "local color" writing appeared in short stories, but at least one of the novels arising from the movement, G. W. Cable's *The Grandissimes,* etches sharp portraits not only of individuals but of the impact of slavery and miscegenation on the culture of antebellum New Orleans. The movement helped encourage Mark Twain to write the novels whose wit, humor, and sharp social and political satire dominate the last quarter of the century. In his greatest novel, *Huckleberry Finn,* we travel down the mainstream of the nation on a raft—seeing not only the Mississippi but the world through the eyes and mind of a wise-innocent boy through whose vision Mark Twain has created a memorable work of art. Twain chose satire as his weapon to attack the far-from-idyllic America of the 70's and 80's. Although he can hardly be called gentle or subtle, until late in his life he always made men laugh at what angered him.

The second powerful influence brought with it the seeds of a much harsher form of social criticism. William Dean Howells, who had spent the war years in Italy, brought home the gospel of realism. Howells was primarily concerned that the novel reflect a true image of the situations it portrayed. He wrote as he preached, observing carefully, but rarely penetrating the surface of what he saw. Perhaps more important than his novels was his pervasive influence as editor and literary critic. He praised, justly, De Forest's *Miss Ravenal's Conversion* for its realistic scenes; encouraged writers as different as Henry James and Mark Twain; and fought to gain public acceptance for younger writers like Garland, Crane, and Norris.

This new realism took vastly divergent paths. Henry James used it as a magnifying glass to explore human consciousness in depth in novels that are subtle, carefully wrought studies of the motivations and interactions of real people. But for the younger group, the new realism was a harsh white spotlight to be cast, in the manner of Zola, into the dark corners of the contemporary scene. Stephen Crane wrote *Maggie* in 1893 and *The Red Badge of Courage* in 1895. Norris was soon to follow with *McTeague* and Dreiser with *Sister Carrie* in 1900.

The troublesome social and economic conditions that had prompted Twain's satire and Bellamy's utopian prescription in *Looking Backward* gave rise to a full-fledged literature of protest, which carried the American novel into its position of dominance as a literary form in the 20th century.

ALCOTT, LOUISA MAY 1832–1888 **Little Women** (1868). A sentimental, rather dated story of domestic life in New England. The characters, nevertheless, exude a certain charm while living as we'd like life to be rather than as it is. *Crowell $3.50, Dutton $2.75, Little $3, Collr, Dolp, Evman-h, Nel, Nort, Pen.*

BELLAMY, EDWARD 1850–1898 **Looking Backward** (1888). One of the most popular utopian romances in English: a vision of our nation in the year 2000, showing how economic planning and nationalization of industry can create prosperity of both body and spirit. *Dolp, HarpMC, MLCE, RivEd, SigC.*

CABLE, GEORGE WASHINGTON 1844–1925 **The Grandissimes** (1880). Episodic but rich, sensitive treatment of the New Orleans of the year of the Louisiana Purchase, by a man who loved the South while repudiating its values. *AmCen.*

COOPER, JAMES FENIMORE 1789–1851 **The Pioneers** (1823). The earliest and least idealized of the Leatherstocking Tales. Cooper's pioneer hero, Natty Bumppo, past middle age, struggles against the encroachments of civilization on the New York State frontier in 1793. *Dolp, HRW, WSP.*

_____ ***The Prairie*** (1827). The most lasting of the Leatherstocking Series—tied together by the force of the Great Plains themselves. Natty Bumppo lives out his last days reflecting on and waiting for death among a cast of characters that ranges the social gamut from naked savage to born-to-the-blood aristocrat. *Dolp, Evman-h, HRW.*

_____ ***Satanstoe*** (1845). The first novel in a trilogy which presents the author's brief for the necessity of a landed aristocracy. In this story of the youthful adventures of Cornelius Littlepage, colonial life on three social levels is vividly portrayed. *Bison, Dolp.*

CRANE, STEPHEN 1871–1900 ***Maggie: A Girl of the Streets*** (1893). A short, brutally naturalistic novel that had to fight its way into print, about a young New York streetwalker. Social protest etched in the acid of bitter irony. *Prem, WSP.*

_____ ***The Red Badge of Courage*** (1895). This Civil War story divests that overromanticized war—or any war—of much of its false glory. So vivid that its readers cannot believe that Crane had never known war firsthand, yet subtly symbolic and farreaching in its implications. *Over twenty editions.*

DE FOREST, JOHN WILLIAM 1826–1906 ***Miss Ravenal's Conversion from Secession to Loyalty*** (1867). A surprisingly realistic novel of manners, delineating characters neither good nor bad, and projecting a well-balanced view of the Civil War. *HRW.*

FREDERIC, HAROLD 1856–1898 ***The Damnation of Theron Ware*** (1896). The story of a Methodist minister whose superficial faith, based on self-satisfaction, crumbles as he begins to see more deeply. By implication, the story symbolizes America's loss of innocence. *Harvard $4.50, Dolp, HRW, Prem.*

HAWTHORNE, NATHANIEL 1804–1864 ***The Scarlet Letter.*** See "The 17th Century," page 89.

_____ ***The House of Seven Gables*** (1851). A novel about sinister hereditary influences within an old New England family, sunnier than Hawthorne's other works despite its grim subject. *Houghton $4, Collr, Dell, Evman-h, HRW, SigC, WSP.*

_____ ***The Marble Faun*** (1860). The Fall of Adam reset amidst the ruins and art treasures of Rome. *Dell, Dolp, SigC.*

HOLMES, OLIVER WENDELL 1809–1894 ***Elsie Venner*** (1861). A young woman's struggle with a hereditary moral flaw raises important questions of moral and social responsibility in a novel that would be greater if it had a less creaky structure. *SigC.*

HOWELLS, WILLIAM DEAN 1837–1920 ***A Modern Instance*** (1882). A realistic study of average people, a young newspaperman and his wife, and of their marital difficulties. *RivEd.*

_____ ***The Rise of Silas Lapham*** (1885). A self-made man chooses not to recoup his losses at the expense of others and thus "rises" morally if not socially and financially. Made less trite than the plot line would suggest by Howell's careful attention to realistic detail and characterization. *Collr, Dolp, HarpMC, HRW, MLCE, RivEd, SigC.*

*A Hazard of New Fortunes* (1890). Howells' best novel, written when his moral outrage at the injustices of industrial conflict had driven him toward a Tolstoian socialism. A personal experience with socio-economic injustice awakens the novel's protagonist to his total involvement with his fellow men. *Ban, Dolp, Evman-h.*

JAMES, HENRY 1843–1916 *The American* (1877). Wealthy, capable, candid Christopher Newman came to Paris to "live" and to get a wife who would be "the best article on the market." An early novel, direct in style, and a good introduction to James. *Dell, HRW, RivEd, SigC.*

*The Portrait of a Lady* (1881). Isabel Archer, the counterpart of Christopher Newman, hopes to find in Europe the best of life and men. Another incisive contrast of American and European types and codes. *Collr, Dell, MLCE, Pen, RivEd, SigC, WoC, WSP.*

*The Turn of the Screw* (1898). A fascinating psychological ghost story. *Dell, Evman-h, ML, SigC.*

*The Wings of the Dove* (1902). Kate Croy and Merton Densher weave a subtle scheme to enmesh the American heiress, Milly Theale, who surprisingly reveals them to themselves in a complicatedly psychological novel whose background is stately London residences, shabby lodging houses, and twisting Venetian canals. *Dell, ML.*

*The Ambassadors* (1903). James's richest novel, contrasting the European and American traditions. Slowly, slowly, in a novel of great psychological suspense, the American Lambert Strether falls under the spell of the liberal European way of life and sheds his new-world provincialism. *Evman, Evman-h, HRW, Nort, Prem, RivEd, SigC, WSP.*

*The Golden Bowl* (1905). In this story set in Victorian London, a beautiful but flawed golden bowl symbolizes the marriage of the Italian prince, Amerigo, and the wealthy American girl, Maggie Verver, who eventually surmounts all difficulties in another working-out of James's "international theme." *BC, Dell, Ever.*

MELVILLE, HERMAN 1819–1891 *Typee* (1846). A fictionalized account of Melville's stay in the Marquesan Islands. Chiefly descriptive of the natives' simple and lovely way of life and critical of civilized ways. *Dodd $4.50, Farrar, Straus $3.50, Ban, Dolp, Evman, HarpMC, WoC, WSP.*

*Omoo* (1847). Well-developed episodes and twenty characters sharply realized as Melville recounts in fictional form his Tahiti adventures. *Dodd $4.50, Farrar, Straus $3.50, Dolp.*

*Moby Dick* (1851). A rich, complex, highly symbolic narrative which explores the deepest reaches of man's moral and metaphysical dilemma at the same time that it tells a gripping realistic sea story. A paean to the human spirit which nevertheless faces up to its darker, less comforting side. Perhaps Melville

# THE NOVEL: 19TH CENTURY AMERICAN

raises more questions than he answers, but this is as it should be in the highest order of literary art. Soaring poetic prose, dramatic conflict, unforgettable characterizations—in a book to be read and reread. *Over twenty unabridged editions.*

———— *Billy Budd* (c. 1891, pub. 1924). Goaded beyond endurance, Adam-like Billy strikes down his satanic persecutor and is executed in a scene suggesting the Crucifixion in this ironic quasi-allegory of human and divine justice. *Dolp, Evman, Phoen, SigC, WSP.*

NORRIS, FRANK 1870–1902 *McTeague* (1899). A realistic study of the disintegration of character, ending in murder. *HRW, Prem.*

———— *The Octopus* (1901). The story of battles between California wheatgrowers and the intruding railroad "octopus" is the beginning volume of a naturalistic trilogy Norris never completed. *AmCen, Ban, RivEd.*

STOWE, HARRIET BEECHER 1811–1896 *Uncle Tom's Cabin* (1852). Powerful antislavery propaganda in sentimental fiction filled with stereotyped characters. *Collr, Dolp, Evman-h, ML, Nel, RivLib, WSP.*

TWAIN, MARK (SAMUEL LANGHORNE CLEMENS) 1835–1910 *The Adventures of Tom Sawyer* (1876). This book for young and old pictures boys' life in little, lazy Hannibal, Missouri, contrasting their superficial cussedness with their inner decency. *Over a dozen editions.*

———— *The Adventures of Huckleberry Finn* (1885). Mark Twain's imagination elevates this tale of a boy seeking freedom on a raft he shares with a runaway slave into a true comic epic of American life. Huck—who sees the world with a marvelous combination of wisdom and innocence—tells his own story in a direct, colloquial idiom that is a perfect vehicle for Mark Twain's social satire. *Over twenty editions.*

———— *A Connecticut Yankee in King Arthur's Court* (1889). A modern American finds himself among the Knights of the Round Table and discovers that Yankee ingenuity is more than a match for medieval magic and superstition. *Harcourt $3.50, Harper $3.95, AmCen, ML, SigC, WSP.*

———— *Pudd'nhead Wilson* (1894). A nonconformist too wise for his backwoods community, Wilson solves several mysteries. Partly a triumph of bitter humor, partly a daring treatment of miscegenation. *Harcourt $3.50, Harper $3.95, Ban, Ever, SigC.*

# F. 20th Century American Novels

## HARRY T. MOORE, Southern Illinois University

The American novel in the 20th century is a medley of opposing tendencies. Only one trend, the realist-naturalist, has been in any way dominant. Among the novelists of various schools, or of none, no 20th-century writer has attained the stature of Herman Melville, achieved the gigantic and ferocious poetry of a *Moby Dick*. Whether any recent American novelist measures up to Henry James or even Nathaniel Hawthorne remains to be seen.

Historically, Dreiser begins the century with *Sister Carrie* in 1900. This book was part of the realist-naturalist trend of the time, but its challenge to convention caused it to be muffled for several years. Dreiser was eventually heard, however, and stands out today as an important figure—craggy, crude, forceful. His most faithful follower has been James T. Farrell.

The 1920's—that was the great time, and some of its luster glowed on through the generally drab 1930's. These two decades were brightened by the occasionally first-rate work of F. Scott Fitzgerald and by the earlier, better writings of Ernest Hemingway and William Faulkner. In 1925 Dreiser produced his last impressive novel, *An American Tragedy*. Willa Cather, who knew the western Middle West better than anyone else, began the most important phase of her own career in 1918 with *My Ántonia*, and in several other fine novels wrote of the region she remembered; she was less effective in her pallid evocations of a further past. Sherwood Anderson was another important writer of the 1920's beginning with his 1919 collection of stories that has the force of a novel: *Winesburg, Ohio*, which established him as the miniaturist of the corn-belt towns. The satiric laughter of Sinclair Lewis at the expense of small-town and small-city ritualists of tribal manners sounded through these years, and the expressionist prose of John Dos Passos jerkily projected the lives of city dwellers.

These writers and their fellows rarely approach the traditionally heroic or tragic: the nerve-splintering effect of two massive wars, leading to the possibility of total extermination, has been reductive; and the first-rate writers, visionary explorers of humanity, have felt this. The direction now is toward the type of protagonist whom Dostoevski called the Underground Man; he is the "hero"—or antihero—of recent European novels and plays by Albert Camus, Samuel Beckett, and many of their contemporaries, and he is now invading American literature in the fiction of various writers, including James Purdy and James Baldwin, and in such plays as those by Edward Albee.

What readers of the far future will think of the authors and books listed below, who can tell? At that time Dr. Johnson's common reader is supposed to take over; but tomorrow's common reader may not be so far removed from today's critics and professors as Johnson's mythical figure was supposed to be.

Some of the newer American novelists are included in the list below on a shakily tentative basis. They are—well, they are what we have, even if some will prove not to belong so much to contemporary literature as to temporary literature. But just now they look most promising.

ALGREN, NELSON 1909– *The Man with the Golden Arm* (1949). Chicago's West Side provides the brutal and vivid setting of this pungently idiomatic story of the Polish Frankie Machine, whose "golden arm," used for dealing in a gambling house, is too often punctured by a dope-dealing needle. *Doubleday o.p.*

ANDERSON, SHERWOOD 1876–1941 *Winesburg, Ohio* (1919). In the vein of Edwin Arlington Robinson's Tilbury Town of New England and of Edgar Lee Masters' Midwestern Spoon River, this unified medley of tales—Anderson's finest work—is the prose equivalent of those poems, a portrait gallery of the frustrated men and women of a small town at the end of the last century. *Viking $3.50, Comp, ML.*

———  *Poor White* (1920). A novel emblematic of the arrival of the industrial revolution in the Middle West, this is the story of Hugh McVey, the Lincolnian and Huck Finn-like folk-hero inventor, and of his attempt to launch a successful marriage. In *Portable Sherwood Anderson: Vik, Vik-h.*

BALDWIN, JAMES 1924– ***Go Tell It on the Mountain*** (1953). At once ironic and intense, this novel (largely autobiographical) traces the several lines of force which meet in the conversion of the Negro boy who is the central character. The vividly realized culminating scene is perhaps the most sustained description of a religious seizure in modern American literature. *Sig, UL.*

_____ ***Another Country*** (1962). An abrasive, often brutal novel about interracial and homosexual relations in Harlem and Greenwich Village. Sometimes the plot creaks and the style grows shrill, but Baldwin's impassioned intensity and superb intelligence compel attention. *Dial $5.95, Dell.*

BARTH, JOHN 1930– ***The Sot-Weed Factor*** (1960). Perhaps a freewheeling picaresque novel, a Rabelaisian satire of human pretensions, a bawdy prose extension of Ebenezer Cook's 18th-century lampoon *The Sot-Weed Factor*, or a "moral allegory cloaked in the material of colonial history" (as the author affirms), Barth's narrative is certainly an astonishing fusion of witty tour de force and comic epic. *Doubleday $7.50.*

BELLOW, SAUL 1915– ***The Victim*** (1947). Bellow's finest short novel so far is this intense study of anti-Semitism in which the persecutor is his own victim. *Comp.*

_____ ***The Adventures of Augie March*** (1953). This plump novel about the wanderings of a young man from Chicago, with episodes taking place in a Mexican village and on the ocean during a shipwreck, makes a valiant attempt to revive picaresque fiction. *Viking $5. Comp.*

BOURJAILY, VANCE 1922– ***The End of My Life*** (1947). The adventures of a cynical American college boy, as an ambulance driver for the British Field Service in the Levant and in Italy, parallel his search for values—emblemized by his projected football game between the "Yes" team (Lincoln, Lenin, D. H. Lawrence, Christ, and others) against the "No" team (including Swift, Hemingway, Eliot, Voltaire, and Freud). *Dial $4.50, Ban.*

BOYLE, KAY 1903– ***The Crazy Hunter*** (1940). Reprinted in the paperback ***Three Short Novels***, this novella about a blind horse and a girl's fight to save him from being put to death is one of the most skillful and intense fictional projections of our time. Known mostly for her incomparable short stories, Kay Boyle is one of the best but most neglected novelists of modern America. *Bea.*

CALDWELL, ERSKINE 1903– ***God's Little Acre*** (1933). The Georgia mountaineer, Ty Ty Walden, and his daughters Rosamund and Darling Jill are the hilariously grotesque central characters of this notable American folk comedy. *ML, Sig.*

CAPOTE, TRUMAN 1924– ***Other Voices, Other Rooms*** (1948). A sensitive boy undergoes some weird experiences in a Southern-Gothic atmosphere. *Sig. Vin.*

CATHER, WILLA 1873–1947 ***My Ántonia*** (1918). The red grass and white snows of the Nebraska prairies provide the scenery for this compelling story of a 19th-century immigrant girl and her American friends. *Houghton $5, SenEd.*

_____ ✓ ___ *The Professor's House* (1925). There are two houses in Professor St. Peter's life, and two worlds representing different values, in this impressive scrutiny of American civilization in terms of a family's experiences. *Knopf $3.95.*

DONLEAVY, J. P. 1926– *The Ginger Man* (1955). Although for some years a resident of England, Donleavy may still be counted as an American writer, notably for this vigorously funny picaresque story of a young American's adventures and misadventures in Dublin and London. *Obolensky $3.95, Random House $3.95, Berk.*

DOS PASSOS, JOHN 1896– *U. S. A.* (1937). This trilogy—made up of *42nd Parallel* (1930), *1919* (1932), and *The Big Money* (1936) —is an expressionistic panorama of the experiences of various Americans, ordinary and famous, during the first three decades of this century. *Houghton 3 vols. $10, MLG, SenEd, WSP.*

_____ *Midcentury* (1961). Using some of the expressionistic techniques of *U. S. A.*, Dos Passos creates a valuable sociological exploration of mid-century, partly attacking labor unions and partly (however unconsciously) big business. *Houghton $5.95, PB..*

DREISER, THEODORE 1871–1945 *Sister Carrie* (1900). Helped along by various lovers, Carrie Meeber rises from poverty in Chicago to fame on the New York stage of the 1890's. *AmCen, Ban, Dell, Dolp, HRW, ML, RivEd, SigC.*

_____ *The Titan* (1914). The centerpiece of Dreiser's trilogy about Frank Cowperwood (which also includes *The Financier*, 1912, and *The Stoic*, 1947), *The Titan* is the clumsily powerful story of a robber-baron type of magnate who, in the late 19th century, takes over Chicago's traction system and is eventually ruined by his enemies. *World $3.75, Dell.*

_____ *An American Tragedy* (1925). The story of Clyde Griffiths, an overambitious poor young man electrocuted for murder, is a gripping and naturalistic indictment of the social system that made Clyde what he was. *World $4.95, Dell, Mer, ML.*

ELLISON, RALPH 1914– *The Invisible Man* (1952). In this compelling story which is symbolic of modern man's alienation, an anonymous Negro undergoes a series of baffling adventures, first in the South and later in New York, during a fervent quest for his identity. *Random House $4.95, Sig.*

FARRELL, JAMES T. 1904– *Studs Lonigan* (1935). The Lonigan trilogy (made up of *Young Lonigan*, 1932; *The Young Manhood of Studs Lonigan*, 1934; and *Judgment Day*, 1935) tells the story of the middle-class Irish on Chicago's South Side, seen in terms of the degenerating effects of the environment upon the weak, bragging Studs in the years between World War I and the Depression, *Vanguard $6, MLG, Sig.*

FAULKNER, WILLIAM 1897–1962 *The Sound and the Fury* (1929). Using the stream-of-consciousness technique, Faulkner projects, through their own visions, the members of the decaying Compson family, concentrating on three brothers (one an idiot) and their magnetic, intense sister. *ML, Vin.*

_____ *As I Lay Dying* (1930). The Bundren family take the ripening corpse of Addie, wife and mother, on a gruesomely comic journey that is interrupted by such elemental matters as fire and flood. *ML* (with *The Sound and the Fury*).

_____ *Light in August* (1932). A day of violence, including murder and a pursuit, shows the part-Negro Joe Christmas going through a series of complicated and fatal adventures. *ML*.

_____ *Absalom, Absalom!* (1936). The Civil War, miscegenation, and murder run through this macabre and complex story of a Southern family. *ML*.

FITZGERALD, F. SCOTT 1896–1940 *The Great Gatsby* (1925). A scrutiny of American values, this brilliant tour de force is the story of a magnificent impersonation amid the yellow cocktail music and blue lawns of the jazz age, a masquerade leading to a somewhat melodramatic disaster. *Scribner $3.50, Scrib.*

_____ *Tender Is the Night* (1934). Almost a tragedy in the classic style, this is the story of a doctor with high ambitions as both healer and theorist, a man slowly destroying himself after marrying an heiress-patient who eventually discovers that she no longer needs him. Little appreciated when it appeared, the novel is now widely regarded as one of the finest American novels of our time. *Scribner $4.50, Ban, Scrib.*

GLASGOW, ELLEN 1874-1945 *Barren Ground* (1925). A poor Virginia girl with aristocratic connections, Dorinda Oakley is betrayed by a weak-natured young doctor in this tale of madness and murder, written elegantly but powerfully. *Peter Smith $3.50, AmCen.*

_____ *Vein of Iron* (1935). Ada Fincastle, daughter of a scholarly former Presbyterian minister in Virginia, loses the man she loves but finally regains him and, despite losses from the Depression, turns to encounter life with her "vein of iron." *HarB.*

GOLD, HERBERT 1924– *The Man Who Was Not With It* (1956). This novel about carnival people, narrated in their own pungent idiom, is an often comic but predominantly dramatic story of a man's regeneration and his failure to help the man who had saved him. *Little $3.75.*

_____ *Therefore Be Bold* (1960). This gracefully written novel describes young love in the Cleveland suburbs in the 1930's and presents a lively and amusing portrait gallery of a gang of adolescents. *Dial $3.95, Lance.*

GOVER, ROBERT 1929– *One Hundred Dollar Misunderstanding* (1962). A hilarious story of a "square" college boy and a Negro prostitute, each of whom speaks a different argot, this little fable is a comedy of communications, or lack of them, leading to semantic and financial confusions neatly presented by a promising new novelist. *Grove $3.95, Bal.*

HAWKES, JOHN 1925– *The Lime Twig* (1961). The author of the fine first novel *The Cannibal* (1949) writes a novel of "Gothic" atmosphere and force about the English underworld, the theft of a racehorse, and the violent death of a man under the hoofs of horses during a race. *New.*

## THE NOVEL: 20TH CENTURY AMERICAN

**HELLER, JOSEPH** 1923– *Catch-22* (1961). An American bomber squadron in World War II is full of zany characters whose antics the author narrates with a fine comic gusto. *Simon & Schuster $5.95, Dell.*

**HEMINGWAY, ERNEST** 1899–1961 *The Sun Also Rises* (1926). In one of the 20th century's most influential novels, Hemingway's hero, Jake, blasted in the war, lives in Paris among Left Bank expatriates who make side trips to Spain for the bullfighting and search for values through the alcoholic fog of the "lost generation." *Scribner $3.95, Scrib.*

———— *A Farewell to Arms* (1929). Told in terse and rhythmic understatement, with nicely calculated repetitions, this star-crossed romance of an American ambulance driver and an English nurse in the Italy of 1917 is one of the finest war novels of our time. *Scribner $4.50, Scrib.*

**JAMES** See "19th Century American Novels," page 136.

**JONES, JAMES** 1921– *From Here to Eternity* (1951). This stark picture of barracks life in Hawaii just before Pearl Harbor is notable particularly for its portrait of Sergeant Warden, the professional soldier who controls the entire army post—enlisted men, officers, and officers' wives. *Scribner $5.95, Sig.*

**KEROUAC, JACK** 1922– *On the Road* (1957). In this, as in Kerouac's other fiction, the headlong prose, sometimes shoddy and sometimes streaked with a fierce poetry, chronicles the experiences of the "beat generation" in its frenetic wanderings and its inhaling of "tea" in the clan's "pads." *Comp, Sig.*

**LEWIS, SINCLAIR** 1885–1951 *Main Street* (1920). A doctor's wife and minor-league Madame Bovary, Carol Kennicott, in her ill-considered attempts to bring culture to the Midwestern town of Gopher Prairie, is severely defeated. *HarB, SigC.*

———— *Babbitt* (1922). A monstrously clownish businessman in the mythical city of Zenith, George F. Babbitt, whose last name has come to stand for the type that is at once hustler and conformist, tries in this satirical novel to break away from the grip of tribal customs—and fails grotesquely. *HarB, SigC.*

———— *Arrowsmith* (1925). A young doctor who becomes a bacteriologist has to battle both germs and the materialistic institutionalism of his colleagues. *HarB, SigC.*

**LONDON, JACK** 1876–1916 *The Call of the Wild* (1903). The finest book of London—the socialist who became a millionaire noted for his stories about brutal supermen on ships—is this story about a dog of the Alaskan wilderness. *Dial $6, Ban, RivLit, SigC, WSP.*

**McCULLERS, CARSON** 1917– *The Heart Is a Lonely Hunter* (1940). A bizarre group in a Southern town—a man who owns a lunch counter, a girl with musical ambitions, an alcoholic radical, and a Negro doctor—confide their troubles to a mute in this story which Mrs. McCullers has never since equaled. *Houghton $4, Ban.*

**MAILER, NORMAN** 1923– *The Naked and the Dead* (1948). A collective picture of a reconnaissance squad in action against the Japanese on an island in the Pacific, this is one of the finest and grimmest of American war novels of World War II, and by far Mailer's best book to date. *Grosset $2.49, Holt $5, ML, Sig.*

MALAMUD, BERNARD 1914– *The Assistant* (1957). In this effective and affective story, a criminal who falls in love with a storekeeper's daughter tries to find redemption through her and through religion. *Farrar, Straus, $3.50, Sig.*

MARQUAND, J. P. 1893–1960 *The Late George Apley* (1937). Ostensibly a biographical tribute by a friend, this neat satire of a proper Bostonian shows the dignified and not unlovable Apley and his tribal rituals in a dry comic light. *Little $5, ML, UL, WSP.*

MILLER, HENRY 1891– *Tropic of Cancer* (1931). Miller's exuberant, influential, and controversial masterpiece records, in simple but ecstatic prose, the adventures of an American vagabond merrily sponging on his Left Bank friends. *Grove $7.50, BC.*

MOORE, BRIAN 1921– *The Lonely Passion of Judith Hearne* (1955). Moore's finest novel so far is his first, the tenderly comic story of a frustrated, dream-tormented woman existing amid the pubs and lodging houses of foggy Belfast. *Dell.*

NABOKOV, VLADIMIR 1899– *Lolita* (1955). This hilarious novel by the Russian-born Nabokov is as full of satiric surprises as *Candide* as it reverses the Henry James theme by showing an underage American girl (a "nymphet") making a lovesick fool out of a sophisticated European. *Crest.*

NORRIS See "19th Century American Novels," page 137.

O'CONNOR, FLANNERY 1925– *The Violent Bear It Away* (1960). The story of an ancient man and his young great-nephew, set in a backwoods corner of Tennessee, is full of fiercely primitive religion and fiercely macabre humor. *Farrar, Straus $3.75, Sig.*

O'HARA, JOHN 1905– *Appointment in Samarra* (1934). In his first novel, a compact one unlike his loose-jointed later attempts, the prolific O'Hara tells a striking story strikingly well, unreeling a little saga of the country-club set in a Pennsylvania town during the bootleg era, when the flashy Julian English drove himself down the highway of self-destruction. *Random House $3, ML, SigC.*

PORTER, KATHERINE ANNE 1894– *Pale Horse, Pale Rider* (1939). These three short novels include the title story, which concerns a young newspaperwoman in love with a soldier who dies in the 1918 influenza epidemic; *Noon Wine,* the narrative of a shooting in the glare of a Texas midday; and *Old Mortality,* a three-stage account of a Southern family that tries to believe its own myths about itself. *Sig, SigC.*

———— *Ship of Fools* (1962). Miss Porter's first full-length novel, a contrived allegorical story of a shipload of varied people, mostly abstract types, going from Mexico to Germany in 1931, became an immediate best seller. *Little $6.50, Sig.*

PURDY, JAMES 1923– *Malcolm* (1959). In a novel that captures the avant-garde and "Gothic" qualities of his short stories, Purdy narrates the adventures of a complicatedly simple young man who, before he dies unexpectedly, meets a bizarre group of people, including a midget, a Negro undertaker, a wealthy woman who calls her home "The Château," and the torch singer whom he marries. *Farrar, Straus $3.95, Avon, Noon.*

ROBERTS, ELIZABETH MADOX 1886–1941 **The Time of Man** (1926). A fine prose craftsman tells the story of Ellen Chesser and her rootless existence as the daughter of Kentucky tenant farmers in a novel combining the harshly realistic with the colorfully romantic. *Comp.*

_____ **The Great Meadow** (1930). This sound historical novel tells the tale of Diony Hall and her life at Fort Harrod, Kentucky, in the second half of the 18th century. *SigC.*

RUMAKER, MICHAEL 1932– **The Butterfly** (1962). A young man first seen in a mental hospital finds his way toward personal integration with the help of a wise doctor and an understanding girl, in a finely poised novel whose dramatic tensions are balanced by lyric ease, and whose characters enlist the reader's sympathy. *Scribner $3.95, Scrib.*

SALINGER, J. D. 1919– **The Catcher in the Rye** (1951). In his own brand of flavorful but sometimes monotonous slang, a prep-school adolescent named Holden Caulfield relates his attempts to evade adulthood in this mischievous and slyly comic novel of perennial appeal to the young. *Grosset $1.95, Little $4.50, ML, Sig.*

_____ **Franny and Zooey** (1961). These two stories deal with the members of the Glass family mentioned in the title, a college girl and her older brother who gives his twitching sister a sleeping pill in the form of a statement to the effect that the mythical Fat Lady their brother Seymour (who killed himself) used to talk about is none other than Christ—thus providing a new image for modern readers groping toward religious values. *Little $4.*

SINCLAIR, UPTON 1878– **The Jungle** (1906). An impressive piece of dramatized journalism which in the Theodore Roosevelt era brought about sanitary reforms in the meat-packing industry, this novel paints a grim picture of the Chicago stockyards of the period. *HarpMC, SigC.*

STEIN, GERTRUDE 1874–1946 **Three Lives** (1909). The three novellas in this book present Gertrude Stein at her experimental best, particularly in the story of a Negro girl, *Melanctha*, which is written, as Katherine Mansfield noted, "in syncopated time." *New, Vin.*

STEINBECK, JOHN 1902– **In Dubious Battle** (1936). Across the years, this forcefully dramatized story of a fruit pickers' strike in California has remained Steinbeck's most impressive novel. *Ban, Comp, ML.*

_____ **The Grapes of Wrath** (1939). Although the 1962 Nobel Prize winner has disappointingly failed to develop as a writer, his most famous novel, which describes the misadventures of dispossessed Oklahoma tenant farmers during the Depression, must be praised for its vivid picture of the conditions of the time and for its compassion, but criticized for its mawkishness and melodrama. *Viking $6, Ban, Comp.*

**STYRON, WILLIAM** 1925– *Lie Down in Darkness* (1951). One of the brilliant younger members of the Southern school here tells a powerful story of the decay of a Virginia family; drunkenness, incest, and suicide are all evoked with force in a novel that has a haunting, nightmare quality. *Comp, Sig.*

**THOMAS, NORMAN** 1926– *Ask at the Unicorn* (1963). A lively poetic style and a gallery of picturesque characters distinguish this story of the quest of a young Californian who revisits his native Wales to discover his identity by exploring the reality of his remembered past. *New.*

**UPDIKE, JOHN** 1932– *Rabbit, Run* (1960). Written rather breathlessly in the present tense, the typically American story of Rabbit Angstrom is that of the former star athlete who cannot reach maturity and whose later life, without the excitement and applause of the games, seems an anticlimax: here, Rabbit leaves his wife, dashes through various escapades, and keeps on running. *Knopf $4, Crest.*

**WARREN, ROBERT PENN** 1905– *All the King's Men* (1946). The best novel of a fine American poet, critic, and scholar tells the story of a corn-pone dictator, undoubtedly based on Huey Long. Remarkable not only for dramatic present-day scenes but also for its flashbacks written in ripe Victorian-type prose and telling about a mid-American journey before the Civil War. *Harcourt $5.75, Ban, ML.*

**WESCOTT, GLENWAY** 1901– *The Grandmothers* (1927). From the stories told by his grandmother and other relatives, and from the evidence in family albums, a Wisconsin boy pieces together the vivid story of his pioneer heritage. *Athen, HarpMC.*

**WEST, NATHANAEL** 1906–1940 *The Complete Works of Nathanael West* (1957). This omnibus volume reprints West's four novels, of which the best is *Miss Lonelyhearts* (1933), the story of an unhappy newspaperman who, assigned to write the lovelorn column, is scornful of the stricken people who write in but gradually feels himself involved in their destinies as his own life becomes increasingly unhappy. *Farrar, Straus $5.*

**WHARTON, EDITH** 1862–1937 *The House of Mirth* (1905). A compelling novel of manners in which the glamorous, well-connected, but poverty-ridden Lily Bart desperately goes toward her doom. *Peter Smith $3.50, Ban, HRW, RivEd, Scrib, SigC.*

———— *Ethan Frome* (1911). Grim and icy New England dominates this story of a farmer who falls in love with the cousin of his wife, who, after a catastrophe to the lovers, triumphs bitterly over them. *Scribner $3, Scrib.*

**WILDER, THORNTON** 1897– *Heaven's My Destination* (1934). A great modern comic novel, this is the story of a traveling textbook salesman, a priggish amateur evangelist whose quixotic attempts to meddle in the lives of others usually end in hilarious but at the same time pathetic disasters. *Harper $4.50, Anch.*

———— *The Ides of March.* See "Rome," page 42.

**WILLINGHAM, CALDER** 1922– *End as a Man* (1947). The sardonic and sadistic adventures of Jocko De Paris as a cadet in an all too painfully recognizable Southern military school where young men go wild in a rigid environment—all naturalistically depicted. *Vanguard $3.75, Dell.*

**WOLFE, THOMAS** 1900–1938 *Look Homeward, Angel* (1929). Wolfe's best novel tells, in occasionally forceful but too often rhetorical prose, the story of the turbulent Eugene Gant's first nineteen years in his native Southern town and at his state university. *Scribner $5.95, Scrib.*

———— *The Short Novels of Thomas Wolfe* (1961). Five novellas, some of which lost their force when diffused through Wolfe's sprawling novels, represent the author at his strongest. *Scribner $4.50.*

**WRIGHT, RICHARD** 1908–1960 *Native Son* (1940). Crude but magnetic, this story of Bigger Thomas, the Negro who would not submit, remains, through its violence and bitterness, an unusually effective novel of social protest. *HarpMC, SigC.*

## II. The Short Story

### WILLIAM PEDEN, *University of Missouri*

Story-telling is among mankind's oldest arts; brief tales, narrative sketches, and stories of character and situation are common to all early literatures. As a distinct and independent literary type, however, the short story was born in the early 19th century in America; and Washington Irving, Edgar Allan Poe, and Nathaniel Hawthorne are usually considered its "fathers."

The short story has always been characterized by flexibility, vigor, and variety; no other literary form is so close to the pulse of the times in which it is written. The first great generation of American short story writers were essentially Romantics—Irving with his richly tinted excursions into the American past, Poe with his engrossing tales of suspense and terror, Hawthorne with his probings into the New England moral and historical condition. By the first decades of the 20th century, however, the short story had become increasingly realistic. More and more modern short story writers—American, English, Russian, French, Irish, Dutch, South African—shared with the Sicilian Giovanni Verga or the Russian master Anton Chekhov or James Joyce or Henry James or Sherwood Anderson the conviction that the lives of "ordinary" or "nonexceptional" people provide the artist with an endless source of fictional materials and themes. Particularly since World War II, in a period increasingly fragmented and uncertain, most short story writers have rejected the melodrama, sensationalism, and romanticism of the past. In the contemporary short story, large-scale heroics, romantic improbabilities, contrivance, and melodrama are for the most part resolutely shunned.

Whatever its mutations, the short story continues to delight, to inform, or to disturb, regardless of changes of

# THE SHORT STORY

literary fashion and international relations, in spite of politics, nuclear fission, and the exploration of space. The form is spacious enough to accommodate the glowing escapism of Kipling's *Jungle Books* or the spare simplicities of Hemingway; it can serve as a vehicle for the most ardent social or moral convictions, or it can be a fully plotted adventure story. Like the stories of Henry James, it can be a quiet character study rich in psychological undertones, or it can be alive with the robust good humor of Faulkner's "Spotted Horses."

Rather than pondering the eternal verities which engrossed the traditional novelists and dramatists, the short story writer has tended to focus his attention on one aspect of life; he reveals briefly the essence of a character or a situation, and then passes on. Increasingly, the short story seems to be the literary form most compatible with the spirit and temper of an age in which the new may be obsolete by tomorrow and in which only change seems permanent. More and more the short story occupies a contemporary position similar to that of drama in the Elizabethan Age or the novel during the 19th century. It seems increasingly possible that the short story is the major literary achievement of the post-World War II years.

Volumes listed in earlier chapters that contain short narratives include AESOP's *Fables* ("Greece"), OVID's *Metamorphoses* ("Rome"), *Arabian Nights* and the Bible ("The Middle East and Africa"), BOCCACCIO's *The Decameron* and CHAUCER's *The Canterbury Tales* ("The Middle Ages"), CERVANTES' *Don Quixote* ("The Renaissance"), and ADDISON and STEELE's *The Spectator* ("The 18th Century").

There are countless useful paperbound and hardcover anthologies of short stories old and new.

ANDERSON *Winesburg, Ohio.* See "20th Century American Novels," page 139.

BABEL, ISAAC 1894–1938 *Collected Stories* (1955). Stories of civil war and of Russian life before and after the Revolution by a Russian master believed to have died in a concentration camp. *Criterion $5, Mer.*

BENÉT, STEPHEN VINCENT 1898–1943 *Selected Works of Stephen Vincent Benét* (1942). Colorful, romantic stories dealing mostly with America's past. *Holt $6.*

BIERCE, AMBROSE 1842–1914 *In the Midst of Life* (1898). Sardonic sketches of soldiers and civilians in the terrifying world of our Civil War and after. *SigC.*

BRADBURY, RAY 1920– *The Golden Apples of the Sun* (1953). A first-rate collection of tales of fantasy and science fiction by a master of the genre. *Ban.*

CALDWELL, ERSKINE 1903– *Complete Stories* (1953). Tales of ribald humor, social protest, and poignant tragedy by the author of *God's Little Acre. Little $5.95, Sig.*

CAPOTE, TRUMAN 1924– *The Grass Harp and A Tree of Night and Other Stories* (1950). Nebulous, haunting stories by an imaginative, sensitive writer. *Sig.*

CHEKHOV, ANTON 1860–1904 *Short Stories.* Carefully wrought, skeptical commentaries on Russian life and character. Chekhov's indirect, implicational narrative technique has profoundly influenced 20th-century fiction. *Over a dozen editions.*

COLETTE 1873–1954 *My Mother's House* (1953). Reminiscences of childhood by one of the most celebrated French writers of this century. *Anch.*

COPPARD, A. E. 1878–1957 *Collected Tales* (1948). Delightful stories by a British master, ranging from naturalism to fantasy and symbolism. *Knopf $5.75.*

CRANE, STEPHEN 1871–1900 *Stories.* Long narratives by a pioneer of realism in America. *Avon, HRW, Vin, WSP.*

DE LA MARE, WALTER 1873–1956 *The Collected Tales* (1950). Fascinated by the "twilight side of life," de la Mare created stories and tales of an unforgettable world of fantasy, dreams, and the supernatural. *Knopf o.p.*

DINESEN, ISAK (BARONESS KAREN BLIXEN) 1885–1962 *Seven Gothic Tales* (1934). Jewel-like, richly embroidered tales of a romantic past peopled by cavaliers, maidens, and ghosts. *ML.*

*Famous Chinese Short Stories* (1952). Retold by Lin Yutang, these provide a good introduction to the rich field of Chinese short fiction. *WSP.*

FARRELL, JAMES T. 1904– *Stories.* Representative collections of stories of 20th-century urban America by the author of *Studs Lonigan. Vanguard $6.50 and $3.50, UL.*

FAULKNER, WILLIAM 1897–1962 *Collected Stories* (1950). Richly varied short fiction ranging in time from the early settling of Mississippi to post-World War II days, by a master of form, subtlety, symbolism, and psychological insight. *Random House $6.50.*

FITZGERALD, F. SCOTT 1896–1940 *Stories* (1951). 28 gay and tragic stories by the sad young spokesman for the Jazz Age. *Scribner $5.50*

*44 Irish Short Stories* (1955). An excellent anthology edited by Devin Garrity: from Yeats and Joyce to O'Connor, O'Faolain, and McLaverty. *Devin-Adair $5.*

*French Stories and Tales* (1954). Representative collection from

## THE SHORT STORY

Balzac and Flaubert to Gide, edited by Stanley Geist. *Knopf $4.50, WSP.*

GORDIMER *Six Feet of the Country.* See "The Middle East and Africa," page 55.

*Great American Short Stories* (1959). From Poe to the present, edited by Mary and Wallace Stegner. *Dell.*

*Great English Short Stories* (1959). Representative collection edited by Christopher Isherwood. *Dell.*

*Great German Short Novels and Stories* (1952). Ed. by Victor Lange. 15 stories and short novels, including GOETHE's *Sorrows of Young Werther* and MANN's *Death in Venice. ML.*

*Great Russian Short Stories* (1959). A stimulating collection edited by Norris Houghton. *Dell.*

HAWTHORNE, NATHANIEL 1804-1864 *Tales and Stories.* Deeply symbolic and carefully wrought studies of sin and retribution, and romantic tales of colonial New England, by a master who helped establish the form as a serious literary type. *Doubleday $4.95, Knopf $4.50, Evman-h, HRW, MLG, Vik, Vik-h, Vin.*

HEMINGWAY, ERNEST 1899-1961 *Short Stories* (1954). Contains the best short fiction of one of the most significant, influential, and controversial writers of our time. *Scribner $6.*

HENRY, O. (WILLIAM SYDNEY PORTER) 1862-1910 *Short Stories.* Ingenious, swiftly paced, skillfully plotted trick- or surprise-ending stories by a most widely read and imitated practitioner. *Doubleday $2.50, ML, WSP.*

IRVING, WASHINGTON 1783-1859 *Sketch Book* (1820). Warmly colored, romanticized sketches, tales, and essays, such as "Rip Van Winkle" and "Legend of Sleepy Hollow." *Dolp, SigC.*

JACKSON, SHIRLEY 1919- *The Lottery* (1949). Terrifying vignettes of tensions underlying contemporary life. *Farrar, Straus $3.50.*

JAMES, HENRY 1843-1916 *Short Stories.* Intricate analyses of conflicting personalities and their psychological and emotional reactions, by a consummate craftsman. *Ban, HRW, MLG, Pen, SigC, Vik, Vik-h.*

JOYCE, JAMES 1882-1941 *Dubliners* (1914). Joyce sought his material in the lives of insignificant people in "dear, dirty Dublin"; rich in insight, subtly symbolic, essentially simple in structure, *Dubliners* is a towering landmark in the evolution of the short story. *Comp, ML, Vik-h.*

KAFKA, FRANZ 1883-1924 *Short Stories.* Searching, strikingly original commentaries on modern life presented in terms of grotesque imagery and fantastic symbols. *ML.*

KIPLING, RUDYARD 1865-1936 *Stories.* Representative collections of a celebrated British teller of tales. *Doubleday $6.95, Anch, Bal, Prem.*

LARDNER, RING 1885-1933 *Short Stories.* Satirical tales—sometimes humorous, often bitter—debunking hypocrisy in American life. *Scribner $4.50, Scrib.*

LAWRENCE, D. H. 1885-1930 *Stories.* Often compelling tales by a much imitated craftsman and controversial thinker. *Comp, Vik, Vik-h.*

LONDON, JACK 1876–1919 **Best Short Stories.** Stories of action, violence, and atmosphere, set from the Far North to the South Seas. *Doubleday $2, Prem.*

MALAMUD, BERNARD 1914– **The Magic Barrel** (1958). Ironic, highly individualistic stories of American Jews at home and abroad, tempered by nostalgia for the Jewish past. *Farrar, Straus $3.75, Vin.*

MANN, THOMAS 1875–1955 **Long Stories.** Masterful lengthy short stories on subjects ranging from the adolescent to the artist. "Tonio Kröger" and "Death in Venice" are among the finest stories ever written. *Knopf $5.75, MLG, Vin.*

MANSFIELD, KATHERINE 1888–1923 **Short Stories.** Penetrating character studies of ordinary Englishmen in the Chekhov manner, and impressionistic portraits of situations. *Knopf $6.75, Vin.*

MAUGHAM, W. SOMERSET 1874– **Stories.** Dramatic accounts by a popular raconteur, mostly dealing with strange people in faraway places. *Avon, Bal, ML.*

MAUPASSANT, GUY DE 1850–1893 **Short Stories.** Realistic impressions of French life, deftly constructed and brilliantly ironic. *BH, Dell, Evman, Evman-h, ML, Pen, Pyr, Vik, Vik-h.*

MELVILLE, HERMAN 1819–1891 **Stories.** Impressive, usually provocative tales by the author of **Moby Dick.** *HRW, MLG, Vik, Vik-h.*

O'CONNOR, FLANNERY 1925– **A Good Man Is Hard To Find** (1955). Remarkable artistry, high social awareness, and a preoccupation with the grotesque characterize these stories of the contemporary South. *Harcourt $3.75, Sig.*

O'CONNOR, FRANK 1903– **Stories** (1952). Humor, insight, and satire mark these representative stories by a leading Irish writer-critic. *Knopf $4.50, Vin.*

O'FAOLAIN, SEAN 1900– **The Man Who Invented Sin** (1948). 15 narratives of contemporary Ireland selected by the author as his most characteristic. *Devin-Adair $2.75.*

O'HARA, JOHN 1905– **Selected Short Stories** (1956). Short works of a prolific social satirist with a sharp eye for individual and societal absurdity, and an uncanny ear for American speech. *ML.*

PARKER, DOROTHY 1893– **Stories.** Sophisticated sketches of American life in the Jazz Age. *ML, Vik, Vik-h.*

POE, EDGAR ALLAN 1809–1849 **Tales.** Memorable stories of atmosphere, horror, and ratiocination by a founder and master of short fiction. *More than fifteen editions.*

PORTER, KATHERINE ANNE 1894– **Short Stories.** Beautifully wrought and subtle stories of varied moods, themes, and settings. *Harcourt $4.75, Dell, Delta, HarB, Harv, ML, Sig, SigC.*

PRITCHETT, V. S. 1900– **The Sailor, Sense of Humour, and Other Stories** (1956). Mostly about the "double lives" of middle-class Britishers tormented by changing social forces. *Knopf $5.*

PURDY, JAMES 1923– **Color of Darkness** (1957). A haunting novella

("63: Dream Palace") and moving, poignant stories of emotional misfits confined to the purgatories of the unloved, the unwanted, and the lonely. *New Directions $3.50, Key.*

ROTH, PHILIP 1933– **Goodbye, Columbus, and Five Short Stories** (1959). In this National Book Award-winning novella and stories Roth writes with irony and understanding of the American Jew in a variety of settings ranging from army training camp to big city. *Houghton $3.75, Ban, Mer.*

SAKI (H. H. MUNRO) 1870-1916 **Short Stories.** Facetious treatment of affectations of English society; stories of fantasy and surprise. *Comp, ML.*

SALINGER, J. D. 1919– **Nine Stories** (1953). Subtle, often moving defense of childhood and the childlike mind through revealing histories of people slightly off center. *Little $3.75, Sig.*

SHAW, IRWIN 1913– **Mixed Company** (1950). Talented, versatile exponent of the socially conscious story. *Random House $3.95.*

**Spanish Stories and Tales** (1956). A representative collection edited by Harriet de Onís. *PB.*

STAFFORD, JEAN 1915– **Children Are Bored on Sunday** (1953). Disturbing pictures of neuroses in contemporary society by a discriminating craftsman. *Random House $3.*

STEELE, WILBUR DANIEL 1886– **The Best Stories of Wilbur Daniel Steele** (1946). Ingeniously plotted stories of suspense, melodrama, and mystery, with psychological undertones. *Doubleday o.p.*

STEINBECK, JOHN, 1902– **Short Stories.** Powerful short fiction by a leading contemporary writer and a winner of the Nobel Prize. *Ban, Vik, Vik-h.*

THOMAS, DYLAN 1914–1953 **Adventures in the Skin Trade** (1955). Includes individualistic short stories and sketches, employing melodrama, fantasy, humor, and surrealism. *New Directions $3.50, SigC.*

TWAIN, MARK (SAMUEL L. CLEMENS) 1835–1910 **Short Stories.** Generous selections from the shorter works of America's greatest humorist. *Doubleday $3.95, Ban, Dell, SigC.*

UPDIKE, JOHN 1932– **The Same Door** (1959) and **Pigeon Feathers** (1962). Frustrations and small pleasures of nonexceptional people in suburbia, small town, and metropolis by one of the most gifted young American writers. *Knopf $3.75 & $4, Crest.*

VERGA, GIOVANNI 1840–1922 **Little Novels of Sicily** (1883). Stories reconstructing Sicilian life in the 1860's by a highly skilled but never very popular artist. *Ever.*

WELTY, EUDORA 1909– **Short Stories.** Sensitive, masterfully worked stories about contemporary Mississippi. *Harcourt $3, ML.*

WOLFE, THOMAS 1900-1938 **The Hills Beyond** (1941). Semiautobiographical stories reminiscent of his novels and generally more carefully and economically written. *Harper $5, Pyr.*

# 12. Poetry

**ROBERT C. POOLEY,** *University of Wisconsin*

Poetry so often probes the imponderable elements of human experience that, like them, it is almost incapable of exact definition. Everyone, hearing such words as "soul" or "spirit," knows what area of man's life is meant, though scarcely ever will two people agree on exact definitions. Poetry, too, is experience in words that can be shared by all without precise definition. Nevertheless, what poets have said about poetry furnishes clues to gaining the greatest rewards from reading it. The man who closes his ears to poetry shuts out a realm of riches in human understanding, in personal insight, in awakened sensitivity. The effort required to understand and enjoy poetry pays as rich returns as any form of human endeavor.

Even though poetry eludes exact definitions, an examination of what it is and what it does opens the way to understanding and appreciation. To start with one aspect, many poets agree that poetry is the expression of the best, the finest, and the most significant of all human knowledge. Shelley puts it, "Poetry is the record of the best and happiest moments of the happiest and best minds"; and Matthew Arnold parallels him closely with, "Poetry is simply the most beautiful, impressive, and widely effective mode of saying things." All who have "traveled in the realms of gold" agree that poetry is the essence of man's unceasing effort to discover, retain, and express in imperishable form that which surpasses the ordinary, the best that life reveals, the most profound and meaningful—sometimes the painful and ugly, along with the happy and beautiful.

The technical aspects of poetry are occasionally mistaken by the uninitiated for poetry itself, as one at times judges a person by his clothes only rather than by his whole character. Rhythm, rhyme, repetition, meter, imagery—devices of form which enhance poetry—are not in themselves the substance of poetry, though in the analysis of a true poem it is not possible to isolate form and substance from each other. Poetry is life itself—tied inseparably to the words which shape it. Robert P. Tristram Coffin says, "Poetry is no marginal decoration, no luxury, no froth or fringe or frame on life. It is the solid center.... The poet is not a dreamer.... The poet is the man who is trying to see things as they are for the first time." As the rough diamond becomes a gem of beauty by cutting and polishing, so is the substance of poetry set glowing by its form. But there must be a diamond to start with.

If the reading of poetry offers difficulties, there are valid reasons. The appreciation of excellence, like excellence itself, requires sustained effort. One characteristic of poetry is compression. Emerson says, "Poetry teaches the enormous force of a few words." A poem must often be lived with patiently for the wholeness of its treasure to be released. Furthermore, poets suggest rather than state the truths they would manifest. When an ancient poet wrote, "The Lord is my shepherd," he suggested in an extended metaphor a relationship which has enriched the lives of countless thousands of persons. Had he attempted to define his idea explicitly, his words would have been forgotten before the end of his life. Most important to realize is that while some poetry seems universal in its appeal, much poetry is more particular. Coleridge cautions, "A poem is not necessarily obscure because it does not aim to be popular. It is enough if a work be perspicuous to those for whom it is written." If, therefore, a particular poem seems to say nothing on first reading, there is no cause for despair; the effort to understand often rewards with enlightenment. In other cases, the poem must be laid aside for a time of richer experience, greater knowledge, for "How can we reason but from what we know?"

# A. Guides and Anthologies

## Standard

BROOKS, CLEANTH 1906- and ROBERT PENN WARREN 1905- (eds.) *Understanding Poetry* (3rd ed 1960). An anthology of English and American poetry with extensive and subtle critical interpretations. *Holt $8.30.*

CIARDI, JOHN 1916- (ed.) *Mid-Century American Poets* (1950). Principles of poetry by the poetry editor of the *Saturday Review*, with generous selections from each of the fifteen contributors. *Twayne $5.*

CREEKMORE, HUBERT 1907- (ed.) *A Little Treasury of World Poetry* (1955). Poetry in translation from the great poets of the world, ancient and modern. *Scribner $5.*

ENGLE, PAUL 1908- and WARREN CARRIER 1918- (eds.) *Reading Modern Poetry* (1955). A rich modern anthology with valuable critical analyses of many persons. *Scott $2.95.*

FRIAR, KIMON and JOHN MALCOLM BRINNIN 1916- (eds.) *Modern Poetry* (1951). Selection of recent American and British verse with brilliant introductions and useful explications. *Appleton $4.*

MATTHIESSEN, F. O. 1902-1950 (ed.) *The Oxford Book of American Verse* (1950). A standard anthology of high literary merit and with a fine introduction. *Oxford $7.*

PALGRAVE, FRANCIS 1824-1897 (ed.) *The Golden Treasury* (1861). A standard collection for over a century. *Many editions.*

ROSENTHAL, M. L. 1917- and A. J. M. SMITH 1902- *Exploring Poetry* (1955). A stimulating introduction to poetry through the analysis of many particular poems. *Macmillan $5.50.*

UNTERMEYER, LOUIS 1885- (ed.) *Modern American Poetry; Modern British Poetry* (rev ed 1962). Two earlier anthologies revised and combined in one volume; a widely used and highly regarded collection. *Harcourt $11.*

## Paperbound

ELLIOTT, GEORGE P. 1918- (ed.) *Fifteen Modern American Poets* (1956). *HRW.*

HALL, DONALD *et al.* (eds.) *New Poets of England and America.* *Mer.*

HARRISON, G. B. 1894- (ed.) *A Book of English Poetry* (1950). *Pen.*

HUMPHRIES, ROLFE 1894- (ed.) *New Poems by American Poets* (1953). *Bal.*

IVES, BURL 1909- (ed.) *The Burl Ives Song Book* (1953). *Bal.*

## POETRY

SPEARE, M. E. (ed.) *Pocket Book of Verse. WSP.*

SWALLOW, ALAN 1915– (ed.) *Rinehart Book of Verse. HRW.*

UNTERMEYER, LOUIS 1885– (ed.) *Story Poems. WSP.*

WHICHER, GEORGE F. 1889–1954 (ed.) *Poetry of the New England Renaissance, 1790–1890* (1950). *HRW.*

WILLIAMS, OSCAR 1900– (ed.) *Silver Treasury of Light Verse* (1957). *Ment.*

# B. Poets to 1900

For the poetry of Greece, Rome, the Orient, the Near East, Latin America, The Middle Ages, the Renaissance, the 17th century, and the 18th century, see Chapters 1 through 9.

ARNOLD, MATTHEW 1822–1888 *Poems.* Thoughtful, mature, carefully wrought poetry by a master of English. *Over ten editions.*

BLAKE *Poems.* See "The 18th Century," page 94.

BROWNING, ELIZABETH BARRETT 1806–1861 *Sonnets from the Portuguese.* Intellectual poetry of a deeply personal character. *Crowell $2, Harper $2.50, Peter Pauper $1, Avon, Dolp.*

BROWNING, ROBERT 1812–1889 *Poems.* Rugged expression from a poet intellectually brilliant and morally courageous, the master of the dramatic monologue. *Over fifteen editions.*

BURNS *Poems.* See "The 18th Century," page 94.

BYRON, GEORGE GORDON 1788–1824 *Poems.* The outpouring of a rebellious, sensitive, and freedom-loving soul. *Over fifteen editions.*

CHAUCER *The Canterbury Tales.* See "The Middle Ages," page 66.

COLERIDGE, SAMUEL TAYLOR 1772–1834 *Poems.* Haunting poetry of beauty and terror by one of the most fertile imaginations in English literature. *Over fifteen editions.*

DANTE *The Divine Comedy.* See "The Middle Ages," page 66.

DICKINSON, EMILY 1830–1886 *Poems.* Brilliant and beautiful short lyric verse by a recluse who probed deeply into the human spirit. *Harper $5.50, Little $4.75, Macmillan $2, Anch, Dell, ML.*

DONNE *Poems.* See "In Tudor England," page 79.

DRYDEN *Poems.* See "The 17th Century," page 86.

EMERSON, RALPH WALDO 1803–1882 *Poems.* Vision and wisdom coupled with a stern but kindly morality. *Van Nostrand $1.75, Dell, HRW, Ment, ML, RivEd, Vik.*

GOETHE, JOHANN WOLFGANG VON 1749–1832 *Faust* (1808–32). The dramatic expression of a modern man seeking restlessly for the solution to the problem: What is the purpose of life? Recommended translation: C. F. MacIntyre (*New*). *Many other translations and editions.*

HEINE, HEINRICH 1797–1856 ***Poems.*** Powerful lyrics which successfully survive translation. *Heritage $5, Pittsburgh $4, Evmanh.*

HERRICK ***Poems.*** See "The 17th Century," page 86.

HOLMES, OLIVER WENDELL 1809–1894 ***Poetical Works.*** The beloved physician whose clever, polished verse graced many public occasions. *Houghton $5.50.*

HOMER ***Iliad*** and ***Odyssey.*** See "Greece," pages 33–34.

HOPKINS, GERARD MANLEY 1844–1889 ***Poems.*** Powerful verse of social criticism in unusual metrical form. *Oxford $5, Pen.*

HOUSMAN, ALFRED EDWARD 1859–1936 ***A Shropshire Lad*** (1896). Cool but lovely lyrics catching the passions and disillusionments of youth. *Peter Pauper $1, Avon, BH.*

KEATS, JOHN 1795–1821 ***Poems.*** An inspired genius who wrote a lifetime of great poetry in a few years. *Over twenty editions.*

LANIER, SIDNEY 1842–1881 ***Selected Poems.*** The lyric voice of the South in clear and graceful verse. *Johns Hopkins $6.*

LONGFELLOW, HENRY WADSWORTH 1807–1882 ***Poems.*** Until the current generation, America's most beloved poet. *Houghton $6.75, Dell, Evman-h, ML.*

LOWELL, JAMES RUSSELL 1819–1891 ***Poems.*** A scholar-poet, most original in his unscholarly ***Biglow Papers,*** satirizing American life. *Houghton $5.50, Odyssey $2.50.*

MARVELL ***Poems.*** See "The 17th Century," page 87.

MILTON ***Poems.*** See "The 17th Century," page 87.

OMAR KHAYYÁM ***The Rubáiyát.*** See "The Middle East and Africa," page 54.

POE, EDGAR ALLAN 1809–1849 ***Poems.*** Verse of high musical quality on themes of imagination and fantasy. *Over ten editions.*

POPE ***Poems.*** See "The 18th Century," page 96.

RIMBAUD, JEAN ARTHUR 1854–1891 ***The Illuminations*** (1886). A tortured spirit whose powerful verse has influenced many 20th-century poets. *New.*

SHAKESPEARE ***Sonnets.*** See "In Tudor England," page 80.

SHELLEY, PERCY BYSSHE 1792–1822 ***Poems.*** Poetry of sheer beauty with urgent messages to all mankind. *Over fifteen editions.*

SPENSER ***Poems.*** See "In Tudor England," page 80.

SWINBURNE, ALGERNON CHARLES 1837–1909 ***Poems.*** The spirit of romance in rich, sensuous verse. *Harcourt $5.75, St Martin's $1.75, Pen, WoC.*

TENNYSON, ALFRED 1809–1892 ***Poems.*** A late romantic and typical Victorian of rare singing quality whose greatness is sometimes lost in familiarity. *Over twenty editions.*

VERGIL ***Aeneid.*** See "Rome," page 41.

VILLON ***Poems.*** See "The Middle Ages," page 68.

POETRY 159

WHITMAN, WALT 1819–1892 *Leaves of Grass* (1855). The most original American poet sings his songs of democracy and the individual. *Over a dozen editions.*

WHITTIER, JOHN GREENLEAF 1807–1892 *Poems.* This Quaker poet sang of the nature he loved and the freedom of man, for which he fought. *Houghton $6, Dell.*

WILDE, OSCAR 1854–1900 *Poems.* Best known for "The Ballad of Reading Gaol" but a lyric poet of rare gifts. *Collins $1.85, BH, Evman-h, ML, Vik.*

WORDSWORTH, WILLIAM 1770–1850 *Poems.* One of England's greatest poets, who revealed the extraordinary beauty and significance of simple people and things. *Over twenty editions.*

## C. Modern Poets

AIKEN, CONRAD 1889– *Selected Poems* (1961). A musical poet with a special interest in psychoanalysis. *Oxford $4.75.*

AUDEN, W. H. 1907– *Selected Poetry* (1959). A poet's reactions to the crosscurrents of thought and the changing aspects of a restless period. *ML.*

BENÉT, STEPHEN VINCENT 1898–1943 *John Brown's Body* (1928). A vigorous epic of the Civil War and one of the best long narrative poems written in America. *Holt $3.50.*

CULLEN, COUNTEE 1903–1946 *On These I Stand* (1947). Integrity of purpose, honesty of expression, by a gifted Negro poet. *Harper $3.*

CUMMINGS, E. E. 1894–1962 *100 Selected Poems.* Deep poetic insight expressed powerfully in unorthodox forms and manners. *Ever.*

DE LA MARE, WALTER 1873–1956 *Rhymes and Verses* (1947). The magic and mystery of life in haunting melody. *Holt $5.*

ELIOT, T. S. 1888– *Complete Poems and Plays, 1909–1950* (1952). One of the most original and influential of modern poets and verse dramatists, independent in thought and form. *Harcourt $6.*

——— *The Waste Land and Other Poems. Harv.*

FROST, ROBERT 1874–1963 *Poems.* From his New England countryside Frost viewed quietly, thoughtfully, lyrically the meaning of human experience. *Holt $6, HRW, WSP.*

LINDSAY, VACHEL 1879–1931 *Collected Poems* (1925). A minstrel who beat out the rhythms of America as he felt them. *Macmillan $7.95.*

LOMAX, JOHN AVERY 1872–1948 and ALAN LOMAX 1915– (eds.) *Cowboy Songs and Other Frontier Ballads* (rev ed 1938). The outstanding collection of Western folk poetry. *Macmillan $8.75.*

**MacLEISH, ARCHIBALD** 1892– *Collected Poems* (1952). A deeply patriotic critic and prophet of American democracy. *Houghton $5, SenEd.*

**MacNEICE, LOUIS** 1907–1963 *Eighty-Five Poems* (1950). A classical scholar deals with contemporary British ideas with liberal views and traditional forms. *Oxford $3.50.*

**MASEFIELD, JOHN** 1878– *Selected Poems* (1950). A teller of tales in rhythmic verse, he delights many who love the life of action. *Macmillan $2.50.*

**MILLAY, EDNA ST. VINCENT** 1892–1950 *Sonnets.* An important American poet who sings of the richness of life in traditional verse forms. *Harper $6, WSP.*

**MOORE, MARIANNE** 1887– *Collected Poems* (1951). Fresh and musical verse in the modern manner by a Pulitzer Prize winner and a strong force in modern poetry. *Macmillan $3.95.*

**NASH, OGDEN** 1902– *Poems.* A humorist of brilliant wit and preposterous rhymes. *ML, PB, UL.*

**PARKER, DOROTHY** 1893– *Poems.* A sophisticated and often cynical wit. *ML, Vik.*

**POUND, EZRA** 1885– *Selected Poems* (1957). An expatriated and obscure American poet whose influence has been widely felt by Eliot, MacLeish, and many young poets. *New.*

**RANSOM, JOHN CROWE** 1888– *Selected Poems* (1945). An intellectual poet criticizes the defects of American industrial society. *Knopf $3.50.*

**ROBINSON, EDWIN ARLINGTON** 1869–1935 *Collected Poems* (1937). Serious lyrics, powerful narratives, unforgettable characters in blank verse and other metrical forms. *Macmillan $12.*

**SANDBURG, CARL** 1878– *Complete Poems* (1950). A modern minstrel who sings the songs of America and American people. *Harcourt $8.*

**SPENDER, STEPHEN** 1909– *Collected Poems* (1955). Lyrics of social significance in the language and imagery of today. *Random House $4.*

**STEVENS, WALLACE** 1879–1955 *Collected Poems* (1954). Intricate counterpoint of reality and imagination, with a diapason of exquisite melody by a major 20th-century poet. *Knopf $7.50, Vin.*

**THOMAS, DYLAN** 1914–1953 *Collected Poems* (1953). An extraordinary artist of Welsh background whose poetry is the most impressive of the 20th century. *New Directions $3.75.*

**WYLIE, ELINOR** 1887–1928 *Collected Poems* (1932). Delicate, witty, and thought-provoking verse. *Knopf $5.75.*

**YEATS, WILLIAM BUTLER** 1865–1939 *Collected Poems* (1951). The leading poet of the Irish Renaissance, a singer of rare lyric power and considerable contemporary influence. *Macmillan $6.50.*

# D. Poetry on Records

(Note. All recordings are 33 rpm LP's unless otherwise noted.)

## Poets Reading from Their Own Work

AIKEN, CONRAD 1889– Wistful reading of the colloquial but contemplative "Blues of Ruby Matrix" and "A Letter from Li Po." *(Caedmon).*

AUDEN, W. H. 1907– An intelligent interpretation that captures both the wit and seriousness of his poetry. The record contains also readings by Richard Eberhart and Mark Van Doren. *(Library of Congress).*

BENÉT, STEPHEN VINCENT 1898–1943 Contains "Portrait of a Southern Lady" and "Ballad of William Sycamore." *(National Council of Teachers of English, 78 rpm).*

COFFIN, ROBERT P. TRISTRAM 1892–1955 Includes "The Secret Heart," with an explanation of its origin; "The Fog"; "The Lantern in the Snow." *(National Council of Teachers of English, 78 rpm).*

ELIOT, T. S. 1888– A cultivated voice, sometimes ironic, sometimes sepulchral—always effective. "The Waste Land," "Ash Wednesday," "Sweeney Among the Nightingales," etc. *(Library of Congress);* "Prufrock," "Portrait of a Lady," "Preludes," etc. *(Caedmon).*

FROST, ROBERT 1874–1963 His own unmistakable voice in many of his best-known poems. *(Caedmon, Library of Congress).*

LINDSAY, VACHEL 1879–1931 Reads with chanting voice and powerful rhythm "The Congo" and other poems. *(Caedmon).*

NASH, OGDEN 1902– A selection of old favorites and some lesser-known poems read in a sprightly style. *(Caedmon).*

*Pleasure Dome.* An anthology of poets reading from their own works: Cummings, Eliot, Moore, Nash, Williams, etc. *(Columbia).*

SANDBURG, CARL 1878– Our most famous midwestern "minnesinger" enthralls listeners with his earnest humanity in *The People, Yes* and *Sandburg Reads Sandburg. (Decca).*

THOMAS, DYLAN 1914–1953 The notable quality of his poetry and prose and his remarkable vocal range and projection make his readings inimitable. *(Caedmon).*

## Readings from the Classics

*Beowulf* and CHAUCER. One record combining portions of *Beowulf* (including the fight with Grendel and the banquet scene) read by Helge Kokintz, and selections from Chaucer read by John C. Pope. *(Lexington).*

CHAUCER, GEOFFREY 1340?-1400 *The Canterbury Tales.* The BBC dramatization of the "Prologue" and five tales in Nevil Coghill's skillful modernization. *(Spoken Word).*

DICKINSON, EMILY 1830-1886 68 Dickinson poems are read by Lucyle Hook with narration by Henry W. Wells. *(National Council of Teachers of English).*

*Early English Ballads.* A fine selection, read by Kathleen Read. *(Folkways).*

*Elizabethan Verse and Its Music.* The reading by W. H. Auden is accompanied by the musical settings of these madrigals and lute songs. *(Columbia).*

SHAKESPEARE, WILLIAM 1564-1616 *Sixteen Sonnets.* David Allen's voice and interpretation are almost perfect; the harp backgrounds are intrusive. *(Poetry).*

WHITMAN, WALT 1819-1892 *Leaves of Grass.* David Allen brings a supple voice and poetic intelligence to the best-known Whitman poems. *(Poetry).*

WORDSWORTH, WILLIAM 1770-1850 *The Poetry of Wordsworth.* Sir Cedric Hardwicke reads the "Ode on Intimations . . . ," "Tintern Abbey," sonnets, and other famous poems. *(Caedmon).*

## Recorded Poetry Anthologies

*Anthology of Negro Poets in the U.S.A.* Arna Bontemps reads gracefully from a 200-year span of American Negro poetry ranging in mood from innocence to anger, in manner from bold simplicity to subtle, complex imagery and rhythm. *(Folkways).*

*Caedmon Treasury of Modern Poets.* Over 20 major poets of today read one or more of their own creations. *(Caedmon).*

*Elizabethan Lyrics and Shakespearean Sonnets.* Short poems by Donne, Marlowe, Sidney, Shakespeare read by Anthony Oneiyl. *(Spoken Arts).*

*Great Poets of the English Language.* David Allen reads effectively 29 popular poems. *(Poetry).*

*Great American Poetry.* Various able interpreters read from Anne Bradstreet to Stephen Crane. *(Caedmon).*

*No Single Thing Abides.* Standard classics, such as Gray's "Elegy" and Shelley's "Ozymandias" read by David Allen. *(Poetry).*

*Palgrave's Golden Treasury.* Well-known poems by major English poets (from Shakespeare on) read by several interpreters. *(Caedmon).*

# 13. Drama

**J. SHERWOOD WEBER,** *Pratt Institute*

Reading a play is at best only an expedient substitute for seeing it on the stage or hearing it on records. Because a play is properly a story acted on a stage before an audience, its printed version is only a partial art form. Story, dialogue, some few stage directions are supplied, but missing are scenery, costumes, stage movement, inflection, timing, gesture, sometimes music—all of which are part of the dramatist's original conception, none of which clearly translates to the printed page. Yet plays can be read—and with considerable understanding and satisfaction, for a good play retains much of its dramatic power even when merely read.

When only read, however, a play is a highly condensed, closely packed, carefully structured literary form; it lacks the novel's expanse, full detail, and orientation to the reader. The reader of plays must therefore supply through a developed dramatic imagination what theatrical production normally adds to enhance the playwright's dialogue. Only during a second reading (or a third) will analogies, symbols, overtones become clear—elements that would cause only few puzzled brows if the same play were well produced in the theater.

Because a play must immediately excite an audience or fail in production, the drama is a thoroughly social art. It must speak movingly and persuasively to large groups of people, or quickly perish. Thus great playwrights were publicly acclaimed during their lifetimes. To win this recognition the dramatist had to employ action, conflict, character, theme emanating from the bedrock of all lasting art, our common humanity.

On this bedrock of what is common to all of us, men have built many different theatrical structures, ranging from the huge, formal open-air amphitheater of the Greeks through the intimate, flexible apron stage of the Elizabethans to the detached picture-frame or versatile epic stages of today. It has nurtured many forms, running from slapstick farce to austere poetic tragedy—all of which involve an orderly distortion of reality through dramatic art and artifice. It has employed the sister arts—of music, dance, architecture, painting, sculpture—to express itself vividly, and it has combined these elements with endless variation. Through continual adaptation to contemporary needs, the theater has remained vital. The play reader can learn about theater history and development through Macgowan and Melnitz's handsomely illustrated *The Living Stage*.

One unchanging factor in the theater is the audience's desire to be entertained—though ideas as to what constitutes entertainment have shifted greatly through the ages. Playwrights, always mindful of popular acclaim, have developed a sneaking fondness for the spectacular, the melodramatic, the sentimental. In almost every age the plea of the minority—from Aristotle to Walter Kerr and Kenneth Tynan—has been for less show and more art.

Perhaps the best way to learn to read plays perceptively is in a critical, skillfully edited anthology such as Goodman's *Drama on Stage,* Bentley's *The Play,* or Brooks and Heilman's *Understanding Drama.* All of these contain a variety of theater classics from Sophocles to Miller as well as apparatus for developing a capacity to visualize imaginatively. Paperbound anthologies generally provide the most good plays for the least money, and the following book list favors them. By browsing in them the reader can discover periods of the drama and specific playwrights that he wishes to explore further—in books, on records, or on the stage.

Earlier chapters of this book contain selective material on the classic dramatic localities: Greece with its unrivaled quartet of Aeschylus, Sophocles, Euripides, and Aristophanes; Tudor England with Marlowe, Shakespeare, Jonson; 17th-century France with Corneille, Molière, Racine; Restoration England with Congreve and Sheridan. All of these, and many others, helped build the solid foundations of modern drama.

Since the late 19th century the world has taken such a lively interest in the social art of drama that it has vied with the novel for popularity. Thirteen Nobel prizes for literature have been awarded to playwrights, and the familiarity of such names as Ibsen, Chekhov, Pirandello, Shaw, O'Neill, Eliot, Camus, Brecht, Williams makes one realize how large the dramatist bulks in the total literary scene.

Today in America and elsewhere the drama has flourished—quantitatively if not always qualitatively—in the motion picture and in television as well as in the legitimate theater. Though some form of realism has been the prevailing mode, experimentation abounds. In recent decades the theater has become at its best a forum for provocative social thought: O'Casey, Sartre, Rice, Odets, Hellman, Miller, Beckett, Albee have written plays that are both eminently theatrical and socially alert. To read representative contemporary American, British, and European plays is to become aware of the most challenging and disturbing developments in our confused and absurd day.

## A. Anthologies

***Anchor Anthology of Jacobean Drama*** (2 vols) (1963). Ed. by Richard C. Harrier. A representative collection of early 17th-century plays. *Anch.*

***Anthology of English Drama Before Shakespeare.*** See "In Tudor England," page 79.

***Anthology of Russian Plays*** (2 vols) (1961, 1963). Ed. by F. D. Reeve. One of several good paperbound collections of a great body of dramatic literature. *Vin.*

BENTLEY, ERIC 1916– (ed.) ***The Play: A Critical Anthology*** (1951). One play each by Sophocles, Molière, Ibsen, Strindberg, Rostand, Wilde, and Miller, and two by Shakespeare, plus illuminating critical analyses, constitute an excellent introduction to the study of drama. *Prentice-Hall $6.60.*

———— (ed.) ***The Modern Theatre*** (6 vols) (1955–60). Stimulating collections containing 30 otherwise hard-to-find modern European and American plays, including dramas by Anouilh, Brecht, Giraudoux, Gogol, Schnitzler. *Anch.*

———— (ed.) *The Classic Theatre* (4 vols) (1958–63). Good collections from major dramatic periods: Vol. 1—six Italian plays by Machiavelli, Goldoni, *et al;* Vol. 2—five German plays by Goethe, Kleist, Schiller; Vol. 3—Spanish classics by Calderón, Cervantes, Lope de Vega; Vol. 4—French dramas by Beaumarchais, Corneille, Molière, Racine. *Anch.*

BENTLEY, GERALD E. 1901– (ed.) *The Development of English Drama* (1950). Well-edited collection of 23 plays from the miracle plays to Pinero. *Appleton $7.*

CERF, BENNETT A. 1898– and VAN H. CARTMELL 1896– (eds.) *24 Favorite One-Act Plays* (1958). A good collection showing the variety of form and subject used by modern masters of the short play. *Doubleday $4.95, Dolp.*

DOWNER, ALAN S. 1912– (ed.) *The Art of the Play* (1955). A basic guide to intelligent playreading through analysis of 9 great dramas from the Greeks to O'Neill. *Holt $8.65.*

———— (ed.) *American Drama* (1960). Traces the history of playwriting in America through specimen plays. *Crowell $5.95, TYC.*

*Eight Great Comedies from Aristophanes to Shaw* (1957). *Ment.*

*Eight Great Tragedies from Aeschylus to O'Neill* (1957). *Ment.*

GASSNER, JOHN 1903– (ed.) *A Treasury of the Theater* (2 vols) (1950, 1960). A monumental collection of 65 plays (not all in the best translations) covering dramatic history from classical Greece to recent Broadway—each with a helpful introduction. *Holt $5.50 & $10.50.*

GOODMAN, RANDOLPH (ed.) *Drama on Stage* (1961). A first-rate introduction to the serious study of plays, containing illustrative dramas from major periods as well as many essays about theaters, dramatic production, acting, etc. *Holt $6.50, HRW.*

LIND *Ten Greek Plays in Contemporary Translations.* See "Greece," page 32.

*Six Restoration Plays* (1959). Masterworks of Wycherley, Congreve, and others, with good background essays by J. H. Wilson. *RivEd.*

WALLEY, HAROLD R. 1900– (ed.) *The Book of the Play* (1950). An introduction to drama study through 12 plays of all types and from many periods, accompanied by extensive study aids. *Scribner $5.*

# B. Classics of the Drama

For plays by, and books about, the classical Greek dramatists (AESCHYLUS, SOPHOCLES, EURIPIDES, ARISTOPHANES) see "Greece," pages 32 to 36. For Roman drama, see "Rome," pages 39 to 42. Elizabethan drama, including SHAKESPEARE, is treated in the

Tudor England section of "The Renaissance," pages 79 to 82. For 17-century French drama (CORNEILLE, MOLIÈRE, RACINE), see "The 17th Century," pages 86 to 90. Distinctive plays from all the great dramatic periods are contained in many of the critical and standard anthologies cited above.

## C. Modern Drama

Many plays by modern and contemporary dramatists are inexpensively available in anthologies such as those cited above. Only collections of a single playwright's work are given below. The latest *Paperbound Books in Print* contains an up-to-date listing of single plays in paperbound trade editions.

ALBEE, EDWARD 1928– *The American Dream and The Zoo Story* (1962) and *Who's Afraid of Virginia Woolf?* (1963). Short and long plays by the brightest new dramatist, whose verbal pyrotechnics delight, anger, and sometimes irritate. *Sig* and *Atheneum $5*, *Athen.*

ANDERSON, MAXWELL 1888–1959 *Four Verse Plays* (1959). Contains the best tragedies—*Elizabeth the Queen, High Tor, Winterset, Mary of Scotland*—of a modern playwright who tried with varying success to blend poetry and social commentary with his own tragic vision. *Harv.*

ANOUILH, JEAN 1910– *Five Plays* (2 vols) (1958–59). Ten distinctive and diverse plays by a contemporary French master of theatricalism. *Drama, Drama-h.*

BECKETT, SAMUEL 1906– *Waiting for Godot* (1954), *Endgame* (1958), *Krapp's Last Tape and Other Dramatic Pieces* (1960). Ambiguous, sensitive, controversial plays by a creator of the theater of the absurd. *Ever.*

BRECHT, BERTOLT 1898–1956 *Parables for the Theater* (1957). The best-known "epic theater" dramas—*The Good Woman of Setzuan* and *The Caucasian Chalk Circle*—by a skillful Communist playwright who used the stage for social protest. *Grove $3.50, Ever.*

CHEKHOV, ANTON 1860–1904 *Plays.* There are many good inexpensive collections of this realist's subtle analyses of timeless human nature. *Ban, Evman, HRW, ML, Pen, UL, Vik, Vik-h.*

ELIOT *Complete Poems and Plays.* See "Poetry," page 159.

GIRAUDOUX, JEAN 1882–1944 *Four Plays* (1958). Four theatricalist dramas, including *The Madwoman of Chaillot*, in Maurice Valency's first-rate translations and adaptations. *Drama.*

HELLMAN, LILLIAN 1905– *Six Plays* (1960). A realist, moralist, and superb dramatic craftsman analyzes contemporary society; includes *The Children's Hour* and *The Little Foxes. ML.*

IBSEN, HENRIK 1828–1906 *Plays.* Naturalistic, symbolic, poetic plays that have significantly shaped both the form and content of drama since his time. The new translations by Rolf Fjelde are superior: *Ment.* Many other translations and editions.

IONESCO, EUGÈNE 1912– *Plays* (1958–60). Antirealistic, symbolic plays, long and short, by a leading exponent of the experimental European theater. *Ever (4 vols).*

LORCA, FEDERICO GARCÍA 1899–1936 *Three Tragedies* (1956). Powerful poetic tragedies by the leading author of 20th-century Spain. *New.*

MILLER, ARTHUR 1915– *Collected Plays* (1957). All the plays up to 1957 by the author of tragedies and social parables that cause some critics to rate him with O'Neill. *Viking $6.*

O'CASEY, SEAN 1884– *Three Plays* (1957). The three best plays—*Juno and the Paycock, The Shadow of a Gunman,* and *The Plough and the Stars*—by the most powerful and influential Irish playwright. *SM.*

ODETS, CLIFFORD 1906–1963 *Six Plays* (1939). The early, and only important, plays of a once-potent social critic. *ML.*

O'NEILL, EUGENE 1888–1953 *Three Plays* (1961). The best-known tragedies—sometimes overlong but always deeply probing—that make O'Neill the major American playwright; includes *Desire Under the Elms, Strange Interlude, Mourning Becomes Electra. Vin.*

PIRANDELLO, LUIGI 1867–1936 *Naked Masks* (1952). In five enigmatic, provocative dramas, an Italian playwright of first importance probes into the confusing nature of reality. *Evman, EvmanNA.*

SARTRE, JEAN PAUL 1905– *No Exit and Three Other Plays* (1955). Incisive dramatizations of French existentialist thought by its leading literary spokesman. *Vin.*

SHAW, GEORGE BERNARD 1856–1950 *Plays.* Witty, talky dramas dedicated to the rule of goddess Reason among 20th-century man. Individual plays: *Pen.* Collections: *Dodd, Mead $7.50, Dell, Dodd, HRW, ML, SigC.*

STRINDBERG, AUGUST 1849–1912 *Plays.* Misogynic, moving dramas by a mordant Scandinavian playwright, important for his psychological plays and perhaps more for his symbolist "chamber plays." *Humphries 3 vols $3.75 ea., Anch, Ban, Evman.*

WILDER, THORNTON 1897– *Three Plays* (1957). Includes *The Skin of Our Teeth* and *Our Town,* experimental but always lucid plays by a modern who retains his faith in both man and God. *Harper $5.50, Ban, HarpMC.*

WILLIAMS, TENNESSEE 1914– *Plays.* Strange poetic tragedies about warped, frustrated lives by the dramatic successor of Sherwood Anderson. *The Glass Menagerie* included in *6 Great Modern Plays, Dell;* others in individual volumes: *New Directions $3–$3.75 ea., Sig.*

## D. History and Criticism

ABEL, LIONEL 1910– *Metatheatre: A New View of Dramatic Form* (1963). An interesting, sophisticated, but difficult study of modern drama, arguing that "metatheatre" (dramatization of self-consciousness) is our characteristic form of drama. *Hill & Wang $3.95, Drama.*

BENTLEY, ERIC 1916– *The Playwright As Thinker* (1955). Perceptive, informed analyses of the thought in drama of Cocteau, Ibsen, Pirandello, Sartre, Shaw, Strindberg—most useful after the reader knows the plays discussed. *Mer.*

CHENEY, SHELDON 1886– *The Theatre* (rev ed 1959). A popular, well-illustrated introductory history of three thousand years of drama, acting, and stagecraft; particularly informative on early periods. *McKay $9.50.*

ESSLIN, MARTIN *The Theatre of the Absurd* (1962). A critical analysis of recent playwrights whose experimental forms mirror their convictions about life's absurdity—Albee, Beckett, Genet, etc. *Peter Smith $3.50, Anch.*

FERGUSSON, FRANCIS 1904– *The Idea of a Theatre* (1949). An often profound, and sometimes difficult, study of ten great plays from *Oedipus Rex* to *Murder in the Cathedral* with focus on the changing art of the theater. *Anch.*

GASSNER, JOHN 1903– *Masters of the Drama* (1954). A sound, readable, basic study of the world's major playwrights. *Dover $6.95.*

MACGOWAN, KENNETH 1888– and WILLIAM MELNITZ *The Living Stage* (1955). Fascinating, lively, handsomely illustrated history of the world theater. *Prentice-Hall $11.*

NICOLL, ALLARDYCE 1894– *World Drama* (1949). Thorough, scholarly, lucid history of drama from Aeschylus to Anouilh. *Harcourt $9.*

TYNAN, KENNETH 1927– *Curtains* (1961). A stimulating collection of essays and theatrical reviews by a critic with taste, convictions, and style. *Atheneum $7.95.*

WRIGHT, EDWARD A. *A Primer for Playgoers* (1958). A generally helpful though sometimes pedestrian guide to richer understanding and appreciation of stage, cinema, and TV dramatic productions. *Prentice-Hall $7.*

## E. Drama on Records

Listening to recordings of plays is of course a compromise measure—usually more satisfying than reading them and less rewarding than seeing them. Only a few recorded plays are listed below; your record dealer can supply you with a complete catalog, such as Schwann's. Today, many libraries have record collections of drama as well as of music and poetry. Read the play first; then listen.

ALBEE, EDWARD 1928– *Who's Afraid of Virginia Woolf?* A superb reading by the Broadway cast of a play rich both in meaning and in lush verbal texture. *(Columbia, 4LP).*

BECKETT, SAMUEL 1906– *Waiting for Godot.* A fine recording of a provocative and highly controversial symbolist drama. *(Columbia, 2LP).*

ELIOT, T. S. 1888– *Murder in the Cathedral:* Robert Donat and the "Old Vic" company *(Angel, 2LP). The Cocktail Party:* Alec Guinness with the Broadway cast *(Decca, 2LP).* Expert performances of Eliot's two best-known verse plays.

*The First Stage: A Chronicle of the Development of English Drama from Its Beginnings to the 1580's.* 13 one-hour dramatizations from the BBC's Third Programme, tracing in illuminating fashion the development of English drama before Shakespeare. *(Spoken Word, 6 albums).*

MILLER, ARTHUR 1915– *Death of a Salesman.* A major modern tragedy performed by the Broadway cast. *(Decca, 2LP).*

*Monuments of Early English Drama.* Seven great pre-Shakespearean plays—including *Abraham and Isaac, Second Shepherd's Play, Everyman, Doctor Faustus*—effectively performed. *(Caedmon, 4LP).*

O'CASEY, SEAN 1884– *Juno and the Paycock.* Fine reading of a great, richly Irish play. *(Angel, 2LP).*

SHAKESPEARE, WILLIAM 1564–1616 The Cambridge University Marlowe Society has done from good to superb performances of more than 20 plays, including all the best-known ones. *(London, 3–5LP ea.).* John Gielgud in *Hamlet (Victor, 4LP),* Alec Guinness in *Macbeth (Victor, 2LP),* and the Dublin Gate Company in five plays *(Spoken Word, 3–4LP ea.)* give other noteworthy productions.

SHAW, GEORGE BERNARD 1856–1950 *Don Juan in Hell.* Charles Laughton, Charles Boyer, Agnes Moorhead, and Sir Cedric Hardwicke give a spirited reading of the third act of *Man and Superman (Columbia, 2LP). Saint Joan:* Siobhan McKenna in the Cambridge Drama Festival production *(Victor, 3LP).*

SOPHOCLES 496–406 B.C. *Oedipus Rex.* The soundtrack from the impressive film performed by the Canadian Stratford Players. *(Caedmon, 2LP).*

SYNGE, JOHN MILLINGTON 1871–1909 *The Playboy of the Western World.* Cyril Cusack and Siobhan McKenna head a fine cast in a lively reading of this roistering comedy. *(Angel, 2LP).*

THOMAS, DYLAN 1914–1953 *Under Milk Wood.* The author, one of the great reciters of our time, is a featured player in his lyrical Welsh comedy. *(Caedmon, 2LP).*

WILDE, OSCAR 1854–1900 *The Importance of Being Earnest.* An elegant cast supports John Gielgud in this dry, witty, sophisticated farce. *(Angel, 2LP).*

# 14. Biography

## WAINO S. NYLAND, University of Colorado

The lives of famous men and women, or even of infamous rascals, can make profitable as well as entertaining reading. If the purpose of creative composition is, as the ancients said, to please and to instruct, then a good biography has everything: it delights while it gives information. From the lives of others we can learn to understand ourselves and to respect the mysteries of relationship between a self and the world.

Where shall you start reading in biography? One method is to begin with something easy but substantial, like Franklin's *Autobiography*. The next step would be to take on something a little more remote, like Cellini's *Autobiography* or Armitage's *The World of Copernicus*. Thus one would be prepared to digest and enjoy the richness of detail in such volumes as Sandburg's *Abraham Lincoln*, Jones's *The Life and Work of Sigmund Freud*, or Edel's *Henry James*. Then even the masterpieces would be assimilable: such works as Boswell's monumental *Johnson* or the philosophic *Education of Henry Adams*.

Another and less cautious plan is to begin with a few of the greatest biographies and work out, or down, from them. By this method you might read Boswell first of all, then Krutch's modern interpretation of Johnson. Similarly, the solid *Autobiography* of John Stuart Mill might come before the saltier *Queen Victoria* by Strachey.

A third system for biographical reading may be called chronological. As Carlyle said, "History is the essence of innumerable biographies." Certainly history reduced to its elements is a combination of the lives of many folk. To understand your own place in the present confusion, it is helpful to look into the confused past. This is not the first time that mankind has considered himself at the crossroads of fateful decisions. A mature reader may untangle some of the apparent contradictions in the record of mankind by wisely adopting a chronological program of biographical reading.

The Bible is a good place to begin: with the lives of Jacob and Joseph in Genesis, and of Moses in Exodus. Next should come several of Plutarch's parallel *Lives*. The Four Gospels can be reread as parallel lives, with Renan's *Life of Jesus* included for comparison, or Sholem Asch's imaginative interpretations of Jesus, Paul, and Mary. Then, to see something of the two sides of Rome, the reader can proceed to the *Meditations* of the pagan emperor Marcus Aurelius and the *Confessions* of the Christian Saint Augustine. From the Middle Ages down to the age of atomic power and space flight there has been such a profusion of life-writing, by and about both saints and sinners, that the systematic reader must select on some basis of specialized interest.

For every reader of biography there is a sharp and difficult question. Is it not self-evident that the first merit of a life should be its truth, its factual reliability? Yet, almost all biographies and autobiographies are tinted by the prejudices of their authors, and are more or less shaded to protect or condemn their subjects. Even Boswell, Strachey, Sandburg, and Edel are necessarily limited by the bias of their social backgrounds. The reader naturally makes allowances for human fallibility.

Historical and other sections of *Good Reading* include numerous biographies not listed below—of artists, musicians, scientists, religious leaders, political leaders, philosophers, and others.

ADAMS, HENRY 1838–1918 *The Education of Henry Adams* (1906). Traces the earnest efforts of one sensitive man to find a meaning for his life. *Houghton $6, ML, SenEd.*

ALLEN, GAY WILSON 1903– *The Solitary Singer* (1955). The definitive biography of Walt Whitman: the scholarly evidence thoroughly sifted, the poems acutely criticized. *Macmillan $10.50, Ever.*

ARMITAGE, ANGUS 1902– *The World of Copernicus* (1947). A life story of the great Renaissance astronomer who overthrew the theory of the earth as the center of the universe. *Ment.*

# BIOGRAPHY

ARVIN, NEWTON 1900–1963 *Herman Melville* (1950). A lucid, scholarly account of the author of America's greatest novel. Sloane $4.75, Comp.

AUGUSTINE *Confessions.* See "Rome," page 39.

BOSWELL *London Journal* and *The Life of Samuel Johnson.* See "The 18th Century," page 94.

BOWEN, CATHERINE DRINKER 1897– *Yankee from Olympus* (1944). Fascinating record of a remarkable personality, Oliver Wendell Holmes, Justice of the Supreme Court. Little $5, Ban, RivLit.

———— *John Adams and the American Revolution* (1950). Highly readable re-creation of a man and an era. Little $7.50, UL.

BROOKS, VAN WYCK 1886–1963 *The Ordeal of Mark Twain* (rev 1933). An important—and much disputed—study of America's most famous humorist and social critic in the Gilded Age. Mer.

CELLINI *Autobiography.* See "The Renaissance," page 73.

CHUTE *Geoffrey Chaucer of England.* See "The Middle Ages," page 68.

———— *Shakespeare of London.* See "In Tudor England," page 81.

CUNLIFFE, MARCUS *George Washington, Man and Monument* (1958). A successful effort to re-create Washington's life as it really was rather than as legend and myth have recorded it. Little $4, Ment.

CURIE, EVE 1904– *Madame Curie* (1937). Sympathetic portrayal of the spirit of pure science incarnate. Doubleday $5, PB, RivLit.

DANA, RICHARD HENRY 1815–1882 *Two Years Before the Mast* (1840). Young Harvard graduate's adventures and hardships aboard a windjammer over a century ago. Ban, Dolp, ML, Nel.

DARWIN, CHARLES 1809–1882 *The Voyage of the Beagle* (1840). A trip around the world, both travel-adventure and significant scientific document. Anch, Ban, Evman, Evman-h.

DE QUINCEY, THOMAS 1785–1859 *Confessions of an English Opium-Eater* (1822). Ever-popular story of a drug addiction told in brilliant and beautiful prose. Dolp, Evman, Evman-h, WoC.

EDEL, LEON 1907– *Henry James* (1953–62). Scholarly, detailed, yet eminently readable account of a very important man in the history of the contemporary novel. Lippincott 3 vols $24.

ELLMANN, RICHARD 1918– *James Joyce* (1959). The nearly definitive biography of the great novelist, meticulously researched and gracefully written. Oxford $12.50.

FISCHER *Gandhi.* See "India and the Far East," page 46.

FRANK, ANNE 1929–1945 *Diary of a Young Girl* (1952). The unforgettable story of a Jewish girl who hid with her family in an Amsterdam attic before capture and death in a German concentration camp. Doubleday $3.95, ML, PB.

FRANKLIN *Autobiography.* See "The 18th Century," page 95.

FREEMAN, DOUGLAS SOUTHALL 1886–1953 *Robert E. Lee* (1934–35). The great Confederacy general enthusiastically delineated in a monumental work of historical scholarship. *Scribner 4 vols $10 ea.*

HART, MOSS 1904–1961 *Act One* (1959). A gay, witty, frank story of the rise to theatrical success of the late playwright and director. *Random House $5, ML, Sig.*

HECHT, BEN 1894– *A Child of the Century* (1954). Tangy memoirs of a bold, buoyant man with an insatiable zest for life. *Simon & Schuster $5, Sig.*

JOHNSON, EDGAR 1901– *Charles Dickens* (2 vols) (1952). A brilliantly realized picture of Dickens and his times plus discerning analyses of his novels. *Simon & Schuster o.p.*

JONES, ERNEST 1879–1958 *The Life and Work of Sigmund Freud* (1953–57). Superb three-volume biography of one of the shapers of the modern mind. Scholarly and readable. *Basic Books 3 vols $21, Anch (abr).*

KENNEDY, JOHN F. 1917–1963 *Profiles in Courage* (1956). Short readable studies of American statesmen who defied the majority and endured calumny and vilification, by a President who could write. *Harper $3.95, PB.*

LORANT, STEFAN 1901– *The Life of Abraham Lincoln* (1941). A text-and-picture biography that presents Lincoln as a student, husband, father, and statesman. *Ment.*

LUDWIG, EMIL 1881–1948 *Cleopatra* (1937). The unquiet history of Cleopatra as a lover, mother, warrior, and queen. *Ban.*

MATTHIESSEN, F. O. 1902–1950 *The James Family* (1947). A century of American life reflected in the personalities, writings, and relationships of four remarkable Americans. *Knopf $7.50.*

MAUGHAM, W. SOMERSET 1874– *The Summing Up* (1938). A popular writer's disarmingly candid observations on himself as a man and a writer, and on philosophical aspects of life. *Doubleday $3.95, Ment.*

MENCKEN, HENRY L. 1880–1956 *Days of H. L. Mencken* (1940–43). Self-portrait by the great iconoclast of the 1920's, always bold, sometimes devastating and bludgeoning. *Knopf 3 vols $12.*

MERTON, THOMAS 1915– *The Seven Storey Mountain* (1948). Account of an American poet who, converted to Roman Catholicism, entered a Trappist monastery in Kentucky. Direct, realistic, challenging. *Harcourt $3.95, Sig.*

MILL, JOHN STUART 1806–1873 *Autobiography* (1873). How an infant prodigy became one of the most important of modern economists. *Columbia $2.50, Illinois $5.50, Col, Dolp, Lib, WoC.*

MIZENER, ARTHUR 1907– *The Far Side of Paradise* (1951). Thorough, fascinating biography of a man who epitomized the Jazz Age, F. Scott Fitzgerald. *Vin.*

MONTAIGNE *Essays.* See "The Renaissance," page 74.

MORGAN *The Life of Michelangelo.* See "The Renaissance," page 75.

MORISON *Admiral of the Ocean Sea.* See "The Renaissance," page 75.

MORTON, FREDERIC 1925– *The Rothschilds* (1962). Account

## BIOGRAPHY

of a family dynasty that dominated the financial centers of Europe for two centuries. *Atheneum $5.95, Crest.*

NEHRU, JAWAHARLAL 1889– *Toward Freedom* (1941). The great leader of modern India recounts his struggle toward the dream of justice and freedom. *Day $7.50, Bea.*

NEWMAN, JOHN HENRY 1801–1890 *Apologia pro Vita Sua* (1864). Intimate account of the religious experience of one of the great minds of the 19th century. *Evman-h, Im, ML, RivEd.*

NUTTING, ANTHONY 1920– *Lawrence of Arabia* (1961). A competent portrayal of one of the most controversial figures of the last generation. *Potter $5, Sig.*

PARKMAN, FRANCIS 1823–1893 *The Oregon Trail* (1849). The classic, eyewitness story of the westward trek. *Doubleday $2.95, Holt $3.75, ML, SigC, WSP.*

PEPYS *Diary.* See "The 17th Century," page 88.

PLUTARCH *Lives.* See "Greece," page 34.

POLO *Travels.* See "The Middle Ages," page 67.

RENAN *The Life of Jesus.* See "Rome," page 42.

RIIS, JACOB 1849–1914 *The Making of an American* (1901). A classic in the literature of U. S. immigrants. Riis came from Denmark and became a successful journalist and an effective reformer. *Macmillan $5.50.*

ROOSEVELT, ELEANOR 1884–1962 *This I Remember* (1949). Absorbing reading, chiefly for the intimate, candid glimpse of the democratic way of life at the White House. *Harper $6.50, Dolp.*

ROUSSEAU *Confessions.* See "The 18th Century," page 97.

SANDBURG, CARL 1878– *Abraham Lincoln* (1926). Lincoln pictured against his natural background—the prairie. Rich in detail, poetic in phrasing. *Harcourt $5.95, Dell.*

SCHWEITZER, ALBERT 1875– *Out of My Life and Thought* (1933). The life story of the remarkable teacher and theologian who became a doctor-missionary in Africa. *Holt $4, Ment.*

SELL, HENRY B. 1889– and VICTOR WEYBRIGHT 1903– *Buffalo Bill and the Wild West* (1955). Well-illustrated life story of the man and the legend. *SigK.*

SHERWOOD, ROBERT E. 1896–1955 *Roosevelt and Hopkins* (rev ed 1950). Superlative portrayal of crucial years by an intimate friend of both men. *Harper $10, UL.*

SOUTHEY, ROBERT 1774–1843 *Life of Nelson* (1813). This masterpiece among lives of heroes has been widely read for more than a century. *Evman-h.*

STEEGMÜLLER, FRANCIS 1906– *Flaubert and Madame Bovary* (1950). A brilliant account of how a great novel came into being. *Vin.*

STEFFENS, LINCOLN 1866–1936 *Autobiography* (1931). One of the most interesting reports about graft and corruption in American city politics during the early decades of this century. *Harcourt $7.50, HarB.*

STONE, IRVING 1903- *The Agony and the Ecstasy* (1961). A biographical novel portraying the supreme craftsman of the Renaissance, Michelangelo. *Doubleday $5.95, Sig.*

STRACHEY, LYTTON 1880–1932 *Queen Victoria* (1921). A vivid picture of the Queen-Empress in the enthusiasm of youth, the loneliness of middle age, and the eccentricities of old age. *HarB.*

SWANBERG, W. A. 1907- *Citizen Hearst* (1961). A thorough and very readable document of the newspaper magnate whose fantastic exploits in publishing, art collecting, real estate plunging, and political dabbling were compelling topics of this country for a half century. *Scribner $7.50, Ban.*

THOMAS, BENJAMIN P. 1902- *Abraham Lincoln* (1952). The first modern one-volume biography to make extensive use of the new material from the papers of Robert Todd Lincoln. *Knopf $6.50.*

THOREAU, HENRY DAVID 1817–1862 *Walden* (1854). A great individualist records his experience in living alone with nature; direct and powerful, an antidote for "togetherness." *Over fifteen editions.*

TRUMAN, HARRY S. 1884- *Memoirs* (1955–56). Often fascinating memoirs of a recent President. *Doubleday 2 vols $4.50.*

WASHINGTON, BOOKER T. c. 1856–1915 *Up From Slavery* (1901). How the Negro educator and scientist, who is criticized today for compromising with whites, struggled to rise above his environment. *Doubleday $3.50, Ban.*

WEIZMANN *Trial and Error.* See "The Middle East and Africa," page 54.

WRIGHT, RICHARD 1908–1960 *Black Boy* (1945). Grim autobiography of a Southern Negro who yearned for the intellectual and physical freedoms forbidden where he was born. *Sig.*

# 15. Essays, Letters and Criticism

## CHARLES B. GOODRICH, Indiana University

It is unfortunate that the term *essay* may bring back to the present or former college student unpleasant memories of a book called *Freshman Essays* or the like which stifled in him any desire to read any more of them. It may be a shock for such a reader to learn that in his other reading he has encountered and enjoyed the essay unaware of the form. It is found, for example, on the editorial page and in the book and drama reviews of the daily newspaper. Much of our reading, whether Walter Lippmann, Norman Vincent Peale, "Red" Smith, advice to the lovelorn, the pages of *Time* or *The Nation*—almost all the nonfiction we read, in fact—is in essay form.

The essay, like most art forms, is difficult to define precisely; it is generally defined as a short prose piece focusing on one subject and reflecting the personal thoughts and feelings of the writer. This vague definition suggests the wide range to be found: Bacon may pinpoint the nature of friendship, Lamb may joke about the origin of roast pig, Richard Rovere may discuss a meeting of foreign ministers, and T. S. Eliot may tell us that Shakespeare failed in writing *Hamlet*. Thus, there is no restriction on the subject matter or its treatment; the writer is free to choose his subject, whether trivial or earthshaking, and to treat it in any way he sees fit.

The important matter for the reader of an essay is the personality of the writer. We demand that he have something new, something interesting, to say on a subject. But, even more, we want him to attract us as a person, for we react to the essayist as to the people we meet daily: with some we come to an immediate understanding, others we have to know for some time before admitting them to our friendship, and still others we never want to meet again. Some of our feeling against the essay may be swept away when we realize that we must make the same effort to relate to the essayist as to a close friend. We have to explore with him those subjects which interest him and try to see in them what he sees. As in all good relationships, we will often find ourselves putting in a word or two of opposition. All in all, the appreciation of the essay is a personal matter, and we must approach it as such, choosing those writers we would like to know. Fortunately, the range is wide, and all of us can find many friends among the writers of essays from Montaigne to E. B. White.

The letter is the most personal of essays, since the writer reveals himself to his intimates. Often, through the letters of famous and not-so-famous people we come to know them and their times better than we might even through an autobiography. Those interested in history will find that the letters of those who lived in any era can bring back the times better than a history book; those who want to know more about a work of art will see in the artist's letters the agonizing steps which led to the finished work. One may follow the daily progress of *Madame Bovary* or see the changing ideas of D. H. Lawrence, and come away with greater appreciation of the man's work. Any confirmed reader of the "Letters to the Editor" section of his paper will recognize how the letter reveals the mind and soul of the writer; with the letters of great men the revelations are simply more rewarding.

Criticism is a specialized form of the essay, an interpretation of a work of art which aims at better understanding of it. Like the essay, it is a late form in the history of civilization—although one may be sure that as soon as the first cave artist drew his first bison on the wall, a friend soon came by to criticize the technique. In any case, when the Greeks developed drama and other forms of literature, Plato and Aristotle began to analyze the results; and the practice has continued.

As with the essay, criticism is found on many levels, from the hurried newspaper review of last night's opening play or TV show to the carefully formulated reflections of one who has spent a lifetime looking at plays, reading poetry or novels, viewing paintings, or listening to music. Again, the approach is personal, and the reader will finally choose those critics in whom he has most trust. It must be noted, however, that one can find in any fine critic new insights, even though one may not always agree with the critic's final conclusions; and one may learn much through being irritated. Since there are so many critical systems, almost as many as there are critics, the reader will have no difficulty in finding what he wants. One may enjoy the Romantic approach of Coleridge or Hazlitt, the psychological probing of F. L. Lucas, the close examination of the text by I. A. Richards or Cleanth Brooks, the theological views of T. S. Eliot, or any other of the multitudinous critical tactics. The acute reader will probably not accept completely any of the possible interpretations of a work, but he will find in each new insights which will send him back to the work of art itself and help him make up his own mind.

**ESSAY ANTHOLOGIES.** Good essay collections abound. The following paperbound anthologies represent the scope and variety of the essay and include examples from many essayists of diverse interests and techniques: *American Essays*, ed. by Charles B. Shaw, *Ment*; *A Book of English Essays*, ed. by W. E. Williams, *Pen*; *Great English and American Essays*, ed. by Douglass S. Mead, *HRW*; and *Great Essays*, ed. by Houston Peterson, *WSP*.

**ADDISON and STEELE** *The Spectator.* See "The 18th Century," page 94.

**AGEE, JAMES** 1909–1955 *Letters of James Agee to Father Flye* (1962). One of our potentially great authors and a fine film critic writes about his frustrations and conflicts over his writing to his substitute father. *Braziller $5.*

**AUDEN, W. H.** 1907– *The Dyer's Hand* (1962). An important poet-critic has collected, and edited, his favorites among his own critical works, dealing with matters as diverse as the detective story and Shakespeare. Written in the form of a critic's notebook, Auden's book is both significant and irritating. *Random House $8.50.*

———— and **LOUIS KRONENBERGER** 1904– *The Viking Book of Aphorisms* (1962). Over 3000 pithy and witty general truths on all phases of life. A book to browse through for insights into the human condition. *Viking $5.95.*

**AUERBACH, ERICH** 1892–1957 *Mimesis* (1946). A classic study of the ways Western writers from Homer to Virginia Woolf have used language and rhetoric to project their unique versions of reality. *Anch.*

BACON *Essays.* See "In Tudor England," page 79.

BATE, WALTER 1918– *Prefaces to Criticism* (1959). The introductions to the major critics, from Aristotle to T. S. Eliot, make a comprehensive history of literary criticism. *Anch.*

BENCHLEY, ROBERT C. 1889–1945 *The Benchley Roundup* (1954). Nathaniel Benchley has chosen some 90 pieces, representing the best of his father's reactions to the petty irritations of daily life, for a collection of humor which should endure. *Harper $4.95, Delta.*

BOTKIN, BENJAMIN ALBERT 1901– (ed.) *Treasury of American Folklore* (1944). Although not strictly essays, these tall tales, songs, and legends show the heroes and the bad men and make clear the vitality of our nation. *Crown $5.95.*

BROOKS, VAN WYCK 1886–1963 *The Flowering of New England* (1936), *New England: Indian Summer* (1940), *The World of Washington Irving* (1944), *The Times of Melville and Whitman* (1947), *The Confident Years* (1952). A comprehensive view of American literature and society by one of the first critics to believe both to have serious merit. *EvmanNA.*

CAMUS, ALBERT 1913–1960 *The Myth of Sisyphus and Other Essays* (1955). The French novelist's searching personal essays on the absurdity of human life and on the necessity for carrying it on. *Knopf $4, Vin.*

CHESTERFIELD *Letters to His Son.* See "The 18th Century," page 94.

COLERIDGE *Lectures on Shakespeare.* See "In Tudor England," page 81.

CONRAD, JOSEPH 1857–1924 *Letters from Joseph Conrad* (1928). These letters to his friend and editor, Edward Garnett, give special insight into Conrad's life and writings. *Chart.*

COWDEN, ROY W. (ed.) *The Writer and his Craft* (1954). Twenty contemporary writers and critics advise the hopeful writer. *Michigan $4.40, AA.*

COWLEY, MALCOLM 1898– *Exile's Return* (rev ed 1951). Recollections of the "lost generation" of the 1920's and its writers by one who shared their lives and ideals. *Peter Smith $3.25, Comp.*

────── *The Literary Situation* (1954). Surveys books, authors' working conditions, and other literary matters. *Peter Smith $3.25, Comp.*

CRÈVECOEUR *Letters from an American Farmer.* See "The 18th Century," page 95.

*Crosscurrents: Modern Techniques.* A continuing series, ed. by Harry T. Moore, on contemporary writers and literary movements, each by an authority. Subjects thus far include Cather, Beckett, Orwell, the college novel. *Southern Illinois $4.50 ea.*

DREW, ELIZABETH 1887– *Discovering Poetry* (1933). A splendid introduction to the understanding and appreciation of poetry. *Norton $3.95, Nort.*

ELIOT, T. S. 1888– *Selected Essays* (1950). The poet and critic surveys literature and religion in one of the classics of modern criticism. *Harcourt $5.75.*

EMERSON, RALPH WALDO 1803–1882 *Essays.* The views of an important transcendentalist on a number of matters. *Many editions.*

EMPSON, WILLIAM 1906– *Seven Types of Ambiguity* (1930, 1955). A profound and provocative analysis of poetry through the subtleties of language; not for the beginner. *New Directions $4.50, Mer.*

FLAUBERT, GUSTAVE 1821–1880 *The Selected Letters of Gustave Flaubert* (1954). An excellent selection edited by Francis Steegmüller, showing the life and work that went into the writing of *Madame Bovary* and hence a useful guide to the novel. *Farrar, Straus $4.75.*

FORSTER, E. M. 1879– *Aspects of the Novel* (1927). A conversational and penetrating treatment of the novel as an art form by one of England's most civilized novelists and essayists. *Harcourt $3.95, Harv.*

———— *Two Cheers for Democracy* (1951). Urbane familiar essays, some on political matters, others on literary, all written with wit and tolerance. *Harv.*

GOLDEN, HARRY 1902– *Only in America* (1958), *For 2¢ Plain* (1959), *Enjoy, Enjoy!* (1960). The warm, witty editor of *The Carolina Israelite* writes about New York's Lower East Side, segregation, and America in general. *World $4 ea., PB, Perm.*

GOODMAN, PAUL 1911– *The Structure of Literature* (1954). A highly personal and most enjoyable discussion, with examples, of the value of formal literary analysis. The point of departure is Aristotle's *Poetics*. *Chicago $5, Phoen.*

GRAVES, ROBERT 1895– *Oxford Addresses on Poetry* (1962). Witty, audacious criticism of poets and poetry, advocating attention to "the White Goddess . . . the Mother of All Living." *Doubleday $4.95.*

HAZLITT, WILLIAM 1778–1830 *Table Talk* (1821). A most likable man writes of his personal reactions to people and the passing show. *Evman-h.*

———— *Hazlitt on Theatre* (1895). Ed. by William Archer and Robert Lowe. One of the best of the Romantic critics writes on the theater and the acting of his day and gives his views on Shakespeare and others. *Hill & Wang $3, Drama.*

HIGHET, GILBERT 1906– *The Anatomy of Satire* (1962). A classicist, known to many for his radio talks, defines satire with ably told examples and much wit. *Princeton $5.*

HOWE, IRVING 1920– (ed.) *Modern Literary Criticism* (1958). A good introduction to modern British and American literary criticism: Richards, Woolf, Yeats, and others. *Beacon $6.50, Ever.*

ISAACS, JACOB 1896– *The Background of Modern Poetry* (1952). A lucid and informative introduction to modern poetry addressed to the puzzled general reader. *Evman.*

JARRELL, RANDALL 1914- *Poetry and the Age* (1953). A good poet writes about modern poetry and the conditions under which it is written. *Vin.*

KEATS, JOHN 1795–1821 *Letters 1814–1821* (1958). Ed. by Hyder Rollins. The definitive edition of Keats' letters, which read almost as well as his poetry. *Harvard 2 vols $20.* Shorter collections: *Anch, Ban, HRW, Nel, RivEd, WoC.*

KRUTCH, JOSEPH WOOD 1893- *The Measure of Man* (1954). Provocative thinking and effective writing on freedom, human values, survival, and the modern temper. *Chart, UL.*

LAMB, CHARLES 1775–1834 *Essays of Elia* (1823, 1833). Sometimes gentle, always incisive, these essays fit the definition of the form; the picture of a warm, kind man comes through. *Dolp, Evman-h, Nel, SM, WoC.*

LAWRENCE, D. H. 1885–1930 *The Collected Letters of D. H. Lawrence* (2 vols) (1962). Ed. by Harry T. Moore. The always natural, sometimes shocking, outpouring of one of England's most controversial writers. *Viking $17.50.*

LINCOLN, ABRAHAM 1809–1865 *Speeches and Letters.* Lincoln's depth of character is easily seen in the dignity and directness of his personal communications. *Evman-h, HRW, MLG.*

LUCAS, F. L. 1894- *Literature and Psychology* (1957). An English critic shows the insight psychology can bring to great works of English and American literature. *AA.*

LYNN, KENNETH S. 1923- (ed.) *The Comic Tradition in America* (1958). An anthology which displays the character and wealth of American humor from Benjamin Franklin to Henry James. *Anch.*

MACHIAVELLI, NICCOLÒ 1469–1527 *The Letters of Machiavelli* (1961). Tr. and ed. by Allan H. Gilbert. These personal letters of the man whose name has wrongly become a word for political evil help us to understand the Renaissance mind and to explain *The Prince. Cap.*

MANDEL, OSCAR *A Definition of Tragedy* (1961). The author defines tragedy after evaluating critics from Aristotle to I. A. Richards. A good attempt to define a subject which constantly needs redefining. *New York Univ. $4.50, NYU.*

MANN, THOMAS 1875–1955 *Essays of Three Decades* (1947). The noted novelist and critic discusses some of the great artists: Goethe, Tolstoi, Wagner, Freud, Cervantes. *Knopf $5, Vin.*

MAUGHAM, W. SOMERSET 1874- *Points of View* (1959). Essays, mostly on writers and writing, by one of our age's most civilized authors. *Doubleday $4.50, Ban.*

MENCKEN, H. L. 1880–1956 *Prejudices: A Selection* (1958). A collection of the most lasting essays from the great shocker and debunker of the 1920's. *Vin.*

MONTAIGNE *Essays.* See "The Renaissance," page 74.

MOZART, WOLFGANG AMADEUS 1756–1791 *Mozart's Letters* (1956). Ed. by Eric Blom. Perhaps the most delightful and the most unhappy of composers reveals his problems and his great moments. This edition comes close to being a biography. *Pen.*

## ESSAYS, LETTERS AND CRITICISM

OLDSEY, BERNARD S. 1923– and ARTHUR O. LEWIS, JR. (eds.) *Visions and Revisions in Modern American Literary Criticism* (1962). Nineteen critics, from Spingarn to Philip Young, are represented in this collection which documents the range of American criticism from 1911 to 1960. *Evman.*

ORWELL, GEORGE 1903–1950 *A Collection of Essays* (1954). The author of *1984* discusses books, humor, language, politics, and provides, unintentionally, a good introduction to his novels. *Anch.*

*Pamphlets on American Writers.* A continuing series of 50-page essays on American authors, mostly of the 20th century, done with conciseness and insight—each by a different authority. *Minnesota 65¢ ea.*

RAHV, PHILIP 1908– *Image and Idea* (1957). In some 20 essays, the co-founder of *Partisan Review* examines modern literature. *New.*

READ, HERBERT 1893– *The Tenth Muse* (1958). Genius in the arts is the subject of attention here, with essays on artists, writers, and philosophers. *Horizon $4.50.*

RICHARDS, I. A. 1893– *Practical Criticism* (1929). A pioneer and classic work in modern criticism, placing emphasis on close examination of the poem itself. *Harv.*

ROSENFELD, ISAAC 1918–1956 *An Age of Enormity: Life and Writing in the Forties and Fifties* (1962). Incisive, and sometimes bitter, comments on the major and minor figures and movements of this dramatic period. Subjects range from the *New Yorker* to Gandhi. *World $5.*

RUSKIN, JOHN 1819–1900 *Sesame and Lilies* (1865). His most popular work, giving his views on the importance of education and the arts. *Evman-h, WoC.*

SARTRE, JEAN-PAUL 1905– *Literary Essays* (1957). An existentialist view of some French and American writers. *WL.*

——— *What Is Literature?* (1962). One of France's leading existentialist writers defines the art of writing, its purpose, and its audience. A fascinating historical treatment of the role of the writer in society. *Ctdl.*

SCOTT, WILBUR 1914– *Five Approaches of Literary Criticism* (1962). Moral, Psychological, Sociological, Formalistic, and Archetypal approaches are analyzed and each illustrated by three essays by well-known critics. Most helpful in giving an overall view of modern criticism. *Collr.*

SEWALL, RICHARD B. 1908– *The Vision of Tragedy* (1959). Brilliant inquiry into the nature of tragedy through examination of eight works from Job to Faulkner. *Yale $4, Yale.*

SHAW, GEORGE BERNARD 1856–1950 *Advice to a Young Critic* (1955). Ed. by E. J. West. Letters to Reginald G. Bright, illustrating both Shaw's insight into the problems of the theater and his business ability. *Cap.*

STEVENSON, ROBERT LOUIS 1850–1894 *Virginibus Puerisque* (1881). Gracefully written informal essays in the Lamb tradition. *Evman-h, Nel, SM.*

STRACHEY, LYTTON 1880–1932 *Portraits in Miniature and Other Essays* (1931). Witty essays on minor, but quite interesting, English eccentrics, by the man who did much to make history and biography readable. *Nort.*

THOREAU *Walden.* See "Biography," page 176.

THURBER, JAMES 1894–1961 *The Owl in the Attic* (1931). One of our greatest humorists discusses the English language and other difficulties of modern life. *UL.*

———— *Thurber Country* (1953). Thurber's mad and threatening world is brilliantly captured here. *Simon & Schuster $3.75, S&S.*

*Treasury of the World's Great Letters* (1940). Ed. by M. L. Schuster. Interesting and significant letters from ancient times to the present. *Simon & Schuster $5.95, S&S.*

*Twentieth Century Views Series.* Ed. by Maynard Mack. Collections of 20th-century critical essays, each volume devoted to one writer—from Homer to Sartre. *Prentice-Hall varying prices.*

*United States Authors Series.* Ed. by Sylvia E. Bowman. Some 30 volumes have been published of a projected 70, which are to cover both minor and major American authors to show the range of our literature. *Twayne varying prices.*

WALPOLE *Letters.* See "The 18th Century," page 97.

WATSON, GEORGE 1927– *The Literary Critics* (1962). This perceptive survey of English descriptive criticism has as its thesis that the great critics are not representative of contemporary thinking, but rather are revolutionaries. *Pen.*

WELLEK, RENÉ 1903– and AUSTIN WARREN 1899– *Theory of Literature* (1956). An excellent introduction of the "New Criticism" (concentration on the structure and detail of a work rather than on its historical and social background). *Harv.*

WESCOTT, GLENWAY 1901– *Images of Truth* (1962). Subjective criticism of the writer's friends—Porter, Maugham, Colette, Dinesen, Mann, Wilder—characterized by Wescott's enjoyment of the important writers. *Harper $6.*

WHITE, E. B. 1899– *The Points of My Compass* (1962). The *New Yorker*'s superb writer of personal essays looks back at the past with nostalgia and at much of the present with horror. *Harper $4.*

———— and KATHERINE S. WHITE 1892– (eds.) *Subtreasury of American Humor* (1941). The classic collection. *Cap.*

WILDE, OSCAR 1854–1900 *The Letters of Oscar Wilde* (1962). Ed. by Rupert Hart-Davis. These letters bring alive the wit and tragedy of the leader of the esthetic movement. *Harcourt $15.*

WILLIAMS, WILLIAM CARLOS 1883–1963 *In the American Grain* (1925). An important American poet discusses the makers of American history. *New.*

WILSON, EDMUND 1895– (ed.) *The Shock of Recognition* (1943, 1955). A collection of literary documents from Lowell to Sherwood Anderson, writers dealing mostly with their contemporaries. *Farrar, Straus $6.50, MLG, UL.*

———— *A Piece of My Mind* (1956). The great critic, at 60,

brings his vast reading and observation to bear on such topics as religion, science, and sex. *Farrar, Straus $3.75, Anch.*

WOOLF, VIRGINIA 1882–1941 *The Common Reader* (1925). Comments on literary themes and people by one of England's most perceptive novelists and critics. *Harv.*

ZABEL, MORTON D. 1901– (ed.) *Literary Opinion in America* (rev ed 1962). A most valuable survey of American criticism from Howells to the moderns, illustrated with essays by the critics. *Torch.*

# Magazines

The little magazines of the 1920's—*Dial, Broom, transition, Hound and Horn*—invigorated the creative impulse of their times, nourishing Eliot, Pound, and Cummings among the poets, Stein, Hemingway, and Faulkner among the prose writers. Today's quarterly magazines of literature—larger, more sedate, longer lived—abet the critical rather than the creative. In the vanguard of the "schools" are critics like Edmund Wilson and Malcolm Cowley, poet-critics like John Ciardi and John Crowe Ransom, novelist-critics like Robert Penn Warren. All contribute regularly to the modern quarterlies. Although poems, short stories, and even segments of novels in progress do appear, the chief function of these magazines is to illuminate—to explicate—the work of art (or some integral part of it). Despite an occasional descent to pedantry or a flight into the bizarre, the quarterly magazines provide their readers with insights into modern literature unavailable in either newspaper book reviews or in popular literary journals.

But literature does not hold the field alone. Nonliterary quarterlies offer informed and provocative discussions in many other areas. These journals range widely and probe deeply into politics and contemporary affairs (regional and global), economics, history, philosophy, religion, art, and psychology. In most of these magazines the writing is lucid, the arguments cogent, and the tone intellectual—though rarely academic or pompous.

Good reading abounds in weekly and monthly magazines too. Factual and interpretive surveys of current events are presented in *Time, Newsweek, The Reporter*, and *U. S. News and World Report*. Each month *Harper's Magazine* and *The Atlantic* appraise social and political developments and trends with the high seriousness and acute perceptivity that have characterized these maga-

# ESSAYS, LETTERS AND CRITICISM

zines for a century. *Commentary,* though only a quarter century old, has won respect for its outstanding essays on social and cultural problems. *Saturday Review* provides valuable weekly reports on new books, plays, films, and records (both classical and popular), plus stimulating, challenging articles and editorials. Finally, no lover of good reading should neglect *The New Yorker.* Weekly, it relies on brilliant, urbane wit to point its gently satiric thrusts at the doings and inhabitants of an absorbing but absurd world.

*The Atlantic* (Boston, Mass.). Fiction, poetry, and informed essays on a consistently high level for the general reader. (Monthly—$7.50 per year).

*Bulletin of the Atomic Scientists* (Chicago, Ill.). Essays by prominent nuclear scientists on the implications for good or ill of atomic science, aimed at the worried layman. (Monthly, Sept.–June—$6 per year).

*Challenge* (New York). A readable, informed periodical specializing in economics and related areas. (10 issues per year—$3 per year).

*Criticism* (Wayne State Univ., Detroit). A review of serious essays on the arts designed for the advanced reader. (Quarterly—$6 per year).

*Foreign Affairs* (Council on Foreign Relations, New York). Contains authoritative articles on world affairs contributed by outstanding statesmen. (Quarterly—$6 per year).

*Harper's Magazine* (New York). One of the oldest publications in the country, it publishes fiction and essays for the general intelligent reader. (Monthly—$7 per year).

*Hudson Review* (New York). One of the most important literary magazines, publishing fiction, poetry, drama, and criticism by some of the most sensitive and astute writers of our day. (Quarterly—$4 per year).

*Kenyon Review* (Kenyon College, Ohio). Like the *Hudson,* an influential periodical, known for its critical articles. (Quarterly—$5 per year).

*Modern Fiction Studies* (Purdue Univ.). Committed to criticism of American, English, and European fiction since 1880, it devotes two issues each year to single authors. (Quarterly—$2 per year).

*The Nation* (New York). One of the oldest liberal weeklies, it has articles on domestic and world politics, as well as literary and dramatic criticism. (Weekly—$10 per year).

*New Republic* (Washington). Like *The Nation,* a weekly with a long tradition of liberal reporting and criticism. (Weekly—$8 per year).

*Newsweek* (New York). A sound summary of all the important weekly news. (Weekly—$6 per year).

*New Yorker* (New York). Urbane, witty fiction, criticism, and biography, plus cartoons, pointing up the madness of our modern world. (Weekly—$7 per year).

*Saturday Review* (New York). A magazine reviewing books, drama, and music, and featuring articles on education, science, and politics. (Weekly—$7 per year).

*Scientific American* (New York). A handsomely illustrated magazine containing articles of wide-ranging scientific interest for the educated mind. (Monthly—$6 per year).

*Sewanee Review* (Univ. of the South, Tennessee). The oldest literary quarterly in the U. S. (1892) and the most important critical publication in the South, its point of view is in no way limited by regional interests. (Quarterly—$5 per year).

*Time* (Chicago). A general news review magazine, written in a contrived but often lively style. (Weekly—$7 per year).

*Virginia Quarterly Review* (Univ. of Virginia). Perceptive, well-written essays on literary subjects, on national and international affairs, and on specific problems of the South. (Quarterly—$4 per year).

*Yale Review* (Yale Univ.). A major periodical whose articles range from philosophy to international politics, from poetry to economics. (Quarterly—$4 per year).

# HUMANITIES, SOCIAL SCIENCES, AND SCIENCES

# HUMANITIES, SOCIAL SCIENCES, AND SCIENCES

## 16. Fine Arts

**ATWOOD H. TOWNSEND,** New York University

Art begins in primitive, practical handicraft; it climaxes as ultimate, exalted expression of truth and beauty.

The Stone Age men who shaped sticks, stones, shells, and bones into useful implements contrived—generation after generation—to make their hammers, scrapers, stabbers ever better and neater, more efficient and more shapely. Thus, many millennia ago, they illustrated one basic principle of artistic design: that form and function are interrelated, that beauty is a reflection of truth. This principle seems to be valid generally both in the plant and animal worlds, and in man-made artifacts: that whatever is proper, true, and good for its function is also beautiful and pleasing in its form.

Our paleolithic progenitors not only designed hand tools, clay pots, and clothing, but also built huts and daubed them with colored mud, or carved patterns on their timbers (architecture). Very early they began to make pictures of animals, people, things—scratched on bone or wood or shell, hewed from logs or shaped from clay, drawn in color on cliffs and cavern walls (painting and sculpture). On joyous occasions and at solemn rituals they jigged and chanted, clapped hands and banged on hollow logs (music and dance). Out of such primitive folkways evolved those sophisticated refinements of artistic creation which we call ballet, symphony, opera—just as the supreme glory of the Parthenon is an idealized refinement of cabins made of logs set on their butts, the crude shelters in which the early Greeks housed themselves and their gods.

A false notion, unfortunately widespread, holds that art is fancy, special, remote from the facts of life. People who call themselves "practical" sometimes sneer at art as trivial and trifling, mere foolish ornament, silly extravagance beneath the dignity of solid citizens. In truth, any genuine, vital art is the essence of life itself in finest, truest expression. Art is not rare, remote, precious, restricted to old pictures in museums or symphonies in concert halls. Art is intimately, essentially interwoven with every thread of daily life—in the neckties, scarves, clothes we wear; in the design of our chairs, rugs, kitchens; in the style of the homes we build and the autos we buy; in the shows we enjoy on stage, screen, TV; in the melodies we whistle or sing or dance to. A life deprived of the treasures and pleasures that art affords us would be no life at all—at least not on the human level. Man *is* man, significantly more than a dumb beast, because man as man has always been a creative artist, and still is. Man's creativity is what makes progress possible, the ever-repeated reaching toward a finer refinement, toward a truer truth. This is what makes the human adventure continuously exciting.

From another point of view, art can be defined as lying between the ignorance of fumbling beasts, morons, or savages who know not what they do, and the science which (in so far as it comes close to perfect knowledge) permits exact mastery over materials and forces toward predetermined ends. Art is wiser than ignorance, but never as precise as science. Art is always more free, more casual, and more personal, in a certain sense even more experimental, than science itself. Two scientists performing the same experiment will normally arrive at exactly the same result. Two artists painting the same scene must, if they are genuinely creative, produce pictures characteristically different. That is one reason why art is so infinitely entertaining; it is ever-changing, various as the waves of the sea, never to be fixed, standardized, or routinized (even though certain cults or styles have prevailed for centuries); always zestfully seeking the unknown and the untried.

It is conventional to restrict the label "Fine Arts" to a few traditionally honored fields of artistic endeavor, and to call other arts "crafts" and their practitioners "artisans." In the broad sense, however, silversmiths, gardeners, industrial designers, modistes, hairdressers, rug weavers can be and often are as truly artists in their respective lines as sculptors, composers, or choreographers.

As a rule, before you can care for a person deeply, you have to get to know him pretty well. Similarly, before you can really grasp what it is you like in various forms of art, you will have to take time to acquire a certain amount of informed understanding so as to appreciate fully. You can take delight in Beethoven and Tchaikovsky, or Renoir and Matisse, without knowing a thing about the men or their works; but if you do know something about the personalities involved and their backgrounds, something about Classicism and Romanticism in music, about Impressionism and Abstract Expressionism in painting, then you are prepared to hear in the symphonies or to see in the paintings significances and subtleties which the uninformed never know are there. By cultivating sympathetic understanding of what artists are striving toward, you develop your capacity to live more fully, to probe more deeply, to enjoy more keenly and richly.

The books listed below are means whereby your eyes and ears can be opened wider, and your intelligence keyed up, so that you may be among those equipped to relish fully the finest achievements of the greatest creative artists of all times. With the help of such books you can qualify yourself for a full, rich, truly civilized life. By cultivating the raw material of your native intellect, and by preparing it to react sympathetically to the most admirable products of the mind of man, you will ripen yourself to appreciate the sometimes sharp, sometimes exquisite delights of "the adventure of a soul among masterpieces."

# A. Basic Principles

EDMAN, IRWIN 1896–1954 *Arts and the Man* (1939). A primer of esthetics, explaining why objects have beauty. *Nort.*

FRY, ROGER E. 1866–1934 *Vision and Design* (1920). A famous art critic and former curator of the Metropolitan Museum discusses the relation between perception and esthetic form. *Peter Smith $3.50, Mer.*

GHISELIN, BREWSTER 1903– (ed.) *The Creative Process* (1952). Symposium by painters, sculptors, musicians, writers about the processes of creation. *Ment.*

GOMBRICH, E. H. J. 1909– *The Story of Art* (9th ed 1958). The artistic aims of architecture, painting, sculpture, in their historical development. *Oxford $5.50.*

JOHNSON, MARTIN C. 1896– *Art and Scientific Thought* (1949). Attempts to show that art and science are not basically antagonistic. *Dov.*

LE CORBUSIER (CHARLES EDOUARD JEANNERET) 1887– *The Modulor* (2 vols) (1954, 1958). Provocative, intensely personal argument for an ideal system of proportions based on the human body and the golden mean. *Harvard $6 & $8.*

PANOFSKY *Meaning in the Visual Arts.* See "The Renaissance," page 75.

# B. Painting, Sculpture, Photography

To enjoy fully great works of art, reading about them is less valuable than looking at them, studying them, getting to know them—as originals in museums, as prints on your own walls, and especially as reproductions in the rich variety of excellent art books, hardcover and paperbound, now available. Five series are outstanding:

*Complete Library of World Art.* 150 volumes, each presenting in black-and-white and in color the works of a great artist, together with a biographical sketch, critical comment, etc. *Hawthorn $3.95 ea.*

*Library of Great Painters.* Series of beautiful portfolio books on individual artists, including Cézanne, El Greco, Renoir, Van Gogh. *Abrams $12.50 up.*

*Pelican History of Art.* A superbly written and handsomely illustrated series of books on the art and architecture of various countries and periods. *Penguin $12.50 up.*

# FINE ARTS

***Phaidon Press Books.*** A series of excellently printed volumes of reproductions (partly in color), from Etruscan sculpture to Cézanne. Each includes informative discussions of painters, places, and periods. *Doubleday $2.95 up.*

***Skira Art Books.*** Magnificent volumes with illuminating text and accurate, full-color reproductions of paintings by particular artists and of significant countries, periods, or places. *Skira $3.50 up.*

Also extremely useful are these smaller, less ambitious, less expensive and amazingly well printed series:

***Aldine Library of Artists.*** *Tudor $1 ea.*
***Art of the East Library.*** *Crown 95¢ up.*
***Barnes & Noble Art Series.*** *Barnes & Noble 75¢ ea.*
***Compass History of Art Series.*** *Viking $2.25 ea.*
***Mentor-UNESCO Art Series.*** *New American Library 95¢ ea.*
***Pocket Library of Great Art.*** *Abrams 95¢ ea.*

ADAM, LEONARD 1891– ***Primitive Art*** (3rd ed 1954). Social meaning of art and anthropology from prehistory to today. *Pen.*

BARR, ALFRED H., JR. 1902– ***What Is Modern Painting?*** (rev ed 1958). A clear introductory explanation. *Doubleday $1.25.*

———— (ed.) ***Masters of Modern Art*** (rev ed 1959). 350 fine reproductions, some in color, of chief treasures of the Museum of Modern Art in New York, summarizing major trends of modern experimentation. *Doubleday $16.50.*

BERENSON, BERNARD 1865–1959 ***Aesthetics and History in the Visual Arts*** (1948). A master critic analyzes the reasons for changing styles in art. *Anch.*

———— ***Italian Painters of the Renaissance.*** See "The Renaissance," page 74.

BETHERS, RAY 1902– ***Composition in Pictures*** (3rd ed 1962). Graphic description of pictorial composition. *Pitman $6.75.*

BINYON ***Painting in the Far East.*** See "India and the Far East," page 45.

BOAS, FRANZ 1858–1942 ***Primitive Art*** (1927). The classic study of the subject by a distinguished anthropologist. *Peter Smith $4, Dov.*

BOECK, WILHELM 1908– and JAIME SABARTES 1881– ***Picasso*** (1955). Detailed analysis of the artist's various periods, with incisive, authoritative interpretation. *Abrams $20.*

BOWIE, HENRY ***On the Laws of Japanese Painting*** (1952). Clear, fascinating explanation. *Dov.*

CELLINI ***Autobiography.*** See "The Renaissance," page 73.

CHENEY, SHELDON 1886– ***Primer of Modern Art*** (rev ed 1958). Readable account of modern techniques. *Liveright $5.95.*

CLARK, KENNETH M. 1903– ***The Nude*** (1956, 1959). Witty, learned, graceful analysis of the nude through the ages as an expression of imaginative, idealized experience. *Pantheon $7.50, Anch.*

_____ *Leonardo da Vinci* (1958). The most readable of the many biographies of the Renaissance genius; illustrated with 67 plates. *Cambridge $7.50, Pen.*

COVARRUBIAS *Indian Art of Mexico and Central America.* See "Latin America," page 61.

CRAVEN, THOMAS 1889– (ed.) *Treasury of Art Masterpieces* (rev ed 1958). Full color reproductions from the Renaissance on. *Simon & Schuster $7.95.*

DA VINCI *Notebooks.* See "The Renaissance," page 73.

*Family of Man* (1955). Reproducing the famous photographic exhibition—503 pictures from 68 countries—created by Edward Steichen for the Museum of Modern Art. *Simon & Schuster $2.95, PB.*

FLANAGAN, GEORGE A. *Understand and Enjoy Modern Art* (1962). Readable explanation of the backgrounds, meaning, motivations of modern art. *Crowell $7.95.*

FLEXNER, JAMES THOMAS 1908– *Pocket History of American Painting* (1950). Useful, compact introduction. *WSP.*

GARDNER, HELEN d. 1946 *Art Through the Ages* (4th ed 1959). A standard one-volume history, profusely illustrated; somewhat dated, but still useful. *Harcourt $9.50.*

GROSSER, MAURICE R. 1903– *The Painter's Eye* (1951). Explains what to look for when viewing paintings. *Ment.*

HAUSER, ARNOLD 1892– *The Social History of Art* (1951). A thousand pages with scores of illustrations summarizing the interrelation of social forces and the graphic arts. *Knopf $7.50, Vin.*

HUNTER, SAMUEL 1923– *Modern American Painting and Sculpture* (1959). Explains the development of such abstract and expressionist artists as Marin, Demuth, Pollock, etc. *Dell.*

LARKIN, OLIVER W. 1896– *Art and Life in America* (rev ed 1960). Scholarly, readable study of the relationship of the visual-plastic arts to the growth of American civilization. *Holt $11.55.*

LULLIES, REINHARD 1907– and MAX HIRMER *Greek Sculpture* (rev ed 1957). Superior photographs, mostly of Greek originals, illuminated by authoritative criticism of the successive trends correlated with the history of the period. *Abrams $15.*

MEREZHKOVSKY *The Romance of Leonardo da Vinci.* See "The Renaissance," page 75.

MORGAN *The Life of Michelangelo.* See "The Renaissance," page 75.

MYERS, BERNARD S. 1908– *Fifty Famous Artists* (1953). *Ban.*

_____ *Modern Art in the Making* (2nd ed 1959). Unexcelled guide for professional and layman. *McGraw-Hill $10.95.*

_____ *Mexican Painting in Our Time.* See "Latin America," page 62.

# FINE ARTS

NEWTON, ERIC 1893– *European Painting and Sculpture* (1949). Excellent introduction and summary. *Pen.*

OZENFANT, AMÉDÉE 1886– *The Foundations of Modern Art* (1952). A scholarly investigation of backgrounds. *Dov.*

POLLACK, PETER *The Picture History of Photography* (1958). From the earliest experiments to the latest triumphs of the best photographers. *Abrams $17.50.*

PRAZ, MARIO 1896– *The Flaming Heart* (1958). Learned and fascinating essays on metaphysical and baroque art in the 17th century. *Anch.*

READ, HERBERT 1893– *Art Now* (2nd ed 1961). Good introduction to the theory of modern painting and sculpture. *Pitman $8.50.*

RICE, D. TALBOT 1903– *Byzantine Painting* (1948). A standard study. *Transatlantic $3.*

RITCHIE, ANDREW C. *Sculpture of the 20th Century* (1952). Rodin, Maillol, Moore and others interpreted and exemplified in 181 illustrations. *Museum of Modern Art $1.*

ROBB, DAVID M. 1903– *The Harper History of Painting* (1951). A first-rate survey of Western painting since the Old Stone Age, with over 500 illustrations. *Harper $13.50.*

SELTMAN, CHARLES T. 1886–1957 *Approach to Greek Art* (1960). How Greek civilization expressed its ideas and ideals in jewelry, coins, vases, sculpture, poetry, drama. *Evman.*

STONE, IRVING 1903– *Lust for Life* (1944). A romanticized and fictionalized biography of van Gogh. *ML, PB.*

STRUPPECK, JULES 1915– *The Creation of Sculpture* (1952). Analysis of the nature and techniques of sculpture for those who wish to appreciate or produce it. *Holt $12.40.*

SYPHER *Four Stages of Renaissance Style.* See "The Renaissance," page 76.

TAYLOR, FRANCIS HENRY 1903–1957 *Fifty Centuries of Art* (rev ed 1960). A thorough survey of art history from Egyptian to modern times. *Harper $6.95.*

VAN LOON *R.V.R.: The Life and Times of Rembrandt.* See "The 17th Century," page 90.

VASARI *Lives of the Painters.* See "The Renaissance," page 74.

WARNER *The Enduring Art of Japan.* See "India and the Far East," page 49.

WILENSKI, REGINALD HOWARD 1887– *Modern French Painters* (1940). Correlates the principal artists and movements with social and cultural trends from 1863 to 1938. *Vin.*

WILLETTS *Chinese Art.* See "India and the Far East," page 48.

WINTER *Elizabethan Miniatures.* See "In Tudor England," page 82.

# C. Architecture and Design

ADAMS *Mont-Saint-Michel and Chartres*. See "The Middle Ages," page 68.

FAULKNER, RAY N. 1906– et al. **Art Today** (3rd ed 1956). Traces the influence of form, color, and design in our daily lives. *Holt $10.10*.

GIEDION, SIGFRIED 1888– **Space, Time, and Architecture** (4th ed 1962). A fundamental text illuminating our times and the interrelation of materials, techniques, and human needs in terms of architectural design and city planning. Fascinatingly illustrated. *Harvard $12.50*.

GLOAG, JOHN 1896– **Guide to Western Architecture** (1959). Comprehensive and illuminating. *Macmillan $10, Ever*.

GREENOUGH, HORATIO 1805–1852 **Form and Function** (1957). Selected writings by a prophet of modern architecture. *Calif*.

HAMLIN, TALBOT FAULKNER 1889–1956 **Architecture Through the Ages** (rev ed 1953). Excellent illustrated survey. *Putnam $8.50*.

HITCHCOCK, HENRY RUSSELL 1903– **Architecture of the 19th and 20th Centuries** (1958). Encyclopedic summary of major movements and significant architects. *Pen*.

———— *Latin American Architecture Since 1945*. See "Latin America," page 61.

KAUFMANN, EDGAR, JR. 1910– **What Is Modern Interior Design?** (1953). Principles of design in home planning and furnishing. *Museum of Modern Art $1.25*.

LAVEDAN, PIERRE 1885– **French Architecture** (1956). A readable informed introduction. *Pen*.

LAWRENCE *Greek Architecture*. See "Greece," page 36.

*Makers of Contemporary Architecture*. A series of well-illustrated studies of influential modern architects, including Fuller, Johnson, Kahn, Saarinen, Tange. *Braziller $4.95 ea*.

*Masters of World Architecture*. A series of compact analyses of the works of outstanding modern architects and designers, with illustrations and bibliographies. Volumes to date include studies of Aalto, Gaudi, Gropius, Le Corbusier, Mendelsohn, van der Rohe, Nervi, Neutra, Niemeyer, Sullivan, and Wright. *Braziller $4.95 ea*.

MUMFORD, LEWIS 1895– **The Culture of Cities** (1938). The past, present, and hoped-for future of urban civilization—a panoramic survey rich with factual data and provocative positions. *Harcourt $7.50*.

———— *Sticks and Stones* (rev ed 1955). Critical analysis of

FINE ARTS 199

American architecture from the 18th into the 20th century, focusing on integration of structure with site. *Dov.*

PEVSNER, NIKOLAUS 1902– *An Outline of European Architecture* (rev ed 1960). A first-rate introduction with pointed incisive comment. *Pen.*

RICHARDS, JAMES M. 1907– *Introduction to Modern Architecture* (1956). New ways of building to fit today's needs. *Pen.*

SCOTT *The Architecture of Humanism.* See "The Renaissance," page 76.

SCOTT, ROBERT GILLAM 1907– *Design Fundamentals* (1951). Analysis of problems of visual relationships illustrated through step-by-step designing of this book. *McGraw-Hill $8.95.*

TUNNARD, CHRISTOPHER 1910– *The City of Man* (1953). Stimulating and richly illustrated commentary on the development of American city design. *Scribner $6.50.*

VITRUVIUS *On Architecture.* See "Rome," page 41.

WRIGHT, FRANK LLOYD 1869–1959 *Writings and Buildings* (1960). Chronological summary of the master architect's major periods, with photographs, drawings, floor plans, and illustrative writings. *Horizon $3.95, Mer.*

# D. Music

AUDEN, W. H. 1907– et al. (eds.) *An Elizabethan Songbook* (1955). Lute songs, madrigals, and rounds. *Anch.*

BARZUN, JACQUES 1907– (ed.) *The Pleasures of Music* (1951). Fascinating anthology of "words on music" culled from varied sources. *Comp.*

_____ *Berlioz and His Century* (1956). Splendid evocation of a man and his time. *Mer.*

_____ *Music in American Life* (1956). Provocative study of the esthetic and economic problems facing composer and performer in this age of stereo, TV, and jukebox. *Peter Smith $2.75, Ind.*

BAUER, MARION 1889–1955 and ETHEL PEYSER 1887–1961 *Music Through the Ages* (rev ed 1951). Useful basic text summarizing chief composers and main trends. *Putnam $5.50.*

BERNSTEIN, MARTIN 1904– *An Introduction to Music* (2nd ed 1951). Good guide to intelligent listening. *Prentice-Hall $10.*

BIANCOLLI, LOUIS 1907– (ed.) *The Opera Reader* (1953). Essential data, synopses, and commentary for 90 operas by 39 composers, plus criticism from many sources. *Grosset $3.95.*

BLOM, ERIC 1888–1959 (ed.) *Mozart's Letters* (1956). The intimate record of genius. *Pen.*

BROCKWAY, WALLACE 1905– and HERBERT WEINSTOCK 1905– *Men of Music* (rev ed 1950). Good critical biographies. *Simon & Schuster $6.95, S&S.*

BURK, JOHN N. 1891– *The Life and Works of Beethoven* (1946). Comprehensive biography and analysis. *ML.*

COPLAND, AARON 1900– *Our New Music* (1941). Illuminating commentary on recent European and American composers. *McGraw-Hill $5.*

———— *What to Listen For In Music* (rev ed 1957). Lucid explanation of the interrelation of rhythm, melody, harmony, and tone color in musical patterns. *McGraw-Hill $4.95, Ment.*

EINSTEIN, ALFRED 1880–1952 *A Short History of Music* (1936). Inclusive and informative. *Knopf $5, Vin.*

EWEN, DAVID 1907– *A Journey to Greatness* (1956). Revealing biography of George Gershwin from boyhood through show business to worldwide fame. *Holt $5.*

GROUT, DONALD JAY *Short History of Opera* (1947). The best introduction. *Columbia $6.*

HILL, RALPH 1900–1950 (ed.) *The Symphony* (1949). Useful basic guide to an understanding of symphonic masterpieces. *Pen.*

———— *The Concerto* (1952). Excellent guide to the understanding of musical structure. *Pen.*

HODEIR, ANDRÉ 1921– *Jazz* (1956). A French critic traces the evolution of jazz and describes its essence. *Grove $2.45, Ever.*

HOWARD, JOHN TASKER 1890– *Our American Music* (3rd ed 1955). Scholarly historical survey to mid-century. *Crowell $12.95.*

———— and JAMES LYONS 1925– *Modern Music* (rev 1957). A popular guide explaining the experiments of modern composers (Debussy, Stravinsky, Gershwin, Bartók, etc.) with dissonance, impressionism, atonality, polytonality, jazz rhythms, etc. *Crowell $3.95, Ment.*

LANG, PAUL HENRY 1901– *Music in Western Civilization* (1941). The definitive one-volume history—scholarly, detailed, yet readable. *Norton $15.*

LOESSER, ARTHUR 1894– *Men, Women, and Pianos* (1954). A fascinating history of keyboard instruments and their makers, and of outstanding piano virtuosi. *Simon & Schuster $7.50.*

LOMAX, ALAN 1915– *Mister Jelly Roll* (1950). Documentation of how underworld phenomena inspired "Jelly Roll" Morton's jazz compositions. *UL.*

MACHLIS, JOSEPH 1906– *The Enjoyment of Music* (shorter ed 1957). Persuasive instruction in music appreciation for the average listener. *Norton $7.35.*

McKINNEY, HOWARD D. 1889– and W. R. ANDERSON 1891– *Music in History* (1940). Relationship of music to the other fine arts. *American $7.25.*

NEWMAN, WILLIAM S. 1912– *Understanding Music* (1953). Basic approaches to melody, rhythm, texture, form in a survey of music in Western civilization. *Harper $6.*

SACHS, CURT 1881–1959 *The History of Musical Instruments* (1940). The evolution of rhythmic sound instruments from prehistory to the modern symphony, jazz band, and electronic devices. *Norton $10.*

SANDBURG, CARL 1878– *The American Songbag* (1927). Unexcelled for background of 280 songs, ballads, ditties with music. *Harcourt $5.95.*

SCHONBERG, HAROLD C. 1916– *The Great Pianists* (1963). The music critic of *The Times* writes engagingly and knowledgeably about pianism and pianists for the music-lover as well as for the specialist. *Simon & Schuster $6.95.*

SHAPIRO, NAT and NAT HENTOFF (eds.) *The Jazz Makers* (1957). Colorful factual sketches by various jazz critics on 21 key figures, such as Morton, Beiderbecke, Waller, Goodman, Ellington, Gillespie. *Holt $4.95.*

SPAETH, SIGMUND 1885– *A History of Popular Music in America* (1948). Pleasantly readable story of the part popular songs have played in American life. *Random House $5.*

STEVENS, DENIS W. (ed.) *History of Song* (1961). Includes all noteworthy song composers in 15 Western countries from the Middle Ages to today. *Norton $7.50.*

SULLIVAN, J. W. N 1886–1937 *Beethoven* (1927). Masterly interpretation of perhaps the greatest composer of them all. *Knopf $3.50, Vin.*

ULRICH, HOMER 1906– *Chamber Music* (1948). Summarizes evolution of music for string groups from early *canzones* and *sonatas* through Haydn, Mozart, Beethoven to the present. *Columbia $6.75.*

# E. The Dance

BALANCHINE, GEORGE 1904– *Complete Stories of the Great Ballets* (1954). Stories of more than 100 ballets which are currently performed, a guide to watching ballet, a history of ballet, and a discussion of the study of ballet—all directed to the ballet-goer. *Doubleday $5.95.*

BOWERS *Theatre in the East.* See "India and the Far East," page 45.

DE MILLE, AGNES 1908– *Dance to the Piper* (1952). Entertaining autobiography of a significant contributor to the development of ballet today. *Little $5.50.*

HASKELL, ARNOLD 1903– *Ballet* (1938). Illustrated guide to appreciation of the ballet as an art form. *Pen.*

———— *The Wonderful World of Dance* (1960). The best introduction to the dance, surveying, through text and illustrations, the history of the dance in all major cultures, and showing that how people dance reveals their way of living and thinking. *Doubleday $2.95.*

HUMPHREY, DORIS 1895–1958 *The Art of Making Dances* (1959). Illustrated guide to an appreciation of American modern dance as an art form by a great dancer and choreographer. *Holt $6.50, Ever.*

KROKOVER, ROSALYN *The New Borzoi Book of Ballets* (1956). Explains what modern dance is and discusses those who have contributed to it creatively. *Knopf $6.75.*

MUIR, JANE *Famous Dancers* (1956). Biographies of famous dancers, among them Pavlova, Duncan, Nijinsky, Graham. Though written for teen-agers, the book is equally appealing to adults for its picture of the dancer's world. *Dodd $3.*

SACHS, CURT 1881–1959 *World History of the Dance* (1937). A scholarly history of the dance (defined as rhythmical motion not related to the work motif) in different cultures. *Norton $7.50, Nort.*

SORELL, WALTER 1905– (ed.) *The Dance Has Many Faces* (1951). A collection of essays by dancers and dance experts on different aspects of the art. *World $5.*

# 17. Philosophy

### LOYD D. EASTON, Ohio Wesleyan University

Like mountain climbing, philosophy undertakes hazardous but challenging tasks—exhilarating because of their difficulties and rewarding because of the significant vistas they yield. To scan the very horizons of human experience through the lens of sustained reflection can yield a panoramic view of man and his place in the universe. Philosophy is often blamed for its high abstractions and detachment from ordinary life, but these are, in part, the price of its final satisfactions. The perspectives of philosophy require objectivity and distance to correct the distortions of familiar but fragmentary views of life.

Through many ages philosophical thinking has had essentially one basic goal—a reflective view of experience in its ramifications and relationships. The philosopher is primarily preoccupied with overall connections—not, as the scientist, with the details of a limited area. Thus, in all its varieties philosophy has maintained a unity of aim, no matter how much men have argued over specific answers.

To the general reader, a philosophy is best understood as a personally synthesized view of life or as a rationale for the way of life of a culture or a historical period. To the scholar, however, the history of philosophy is a succession of possible answers to particular technical problems involving theories of mind, knowledge, morality, or existence—and perhaps also general theories concerning the nature of beauty, society, or man's historical destiny.

To read philosophers in historical sequence provides a panorama of the development of man's basic values and ideas. As one surveys the changing cultural setting, he sees the continuing function of philosophy as a guide through the problems of life and as a record of the paths of solution men's minds have followed. The great thinkers loom as signposts, junction points, on the highways of man's intellectual journeyings. Sometimes pleasant and smooth, at other points rugged and steep, the road of great thinkers beckons the amateur as well as the professional philosopher. Often, too, great thinkers have the gift of a pleasing, vivid style—for example, Plato, Descartes, William James. But those who write more difficult prose—Aristotle, Kant, or Dewey—cannot be bypassed on the highroads of philosophy.

The beginner can well start with the paths first laid out by the great Greeks—Plato, Aristotle, Epictetus—and by Romans such as Lucretius and Marcus Aurelius. Then, with classical humanism behind him, he can follow the harder foothill pathways of Plotinus and of early Christian thought to reach St. Augustine's confessional Platonism. Next, even if he sidesteps the technicalities of Anselm and Abelard, he must survey the world view of St. Thomas Aquinas—the great medieval synthesis of Aristotelian and Christian thought which even today is fundamental for Roman Catholicism. And so on—through the Renaissance humanism of Bruno and Bacon; the 17th-century geometrical reasoning of Descartes, Spinoza, and Leibniz; the emphasis on physics and scientific method of Hobbes and Locke; the 18th-century appeal to reason, culminating in Voltaire and Kant; 19th-century philosophies of history and evolution by Hegel, Marx, and Spencer; down to 20th-century emphasis on practice, process, and logical analysis in Dewey, Whitehead, and Russell, and the more recent development of existentialism.

You need not, however, retrace 25 centuries to understand the present. You can quite as well begin with problems of contemporary thought and trace them back to their roots in the past. But if you seek philosophic insight, you cannot rest content with the flat-projection map of historical lines and connections. Some integrating and organizing focus is needed to place before the mind's eye a living landscape, a viable understanding of the actualities of your life. Such understanding, as rewarding as it is rare, comes only from that unusually persistent questioning and reflection which philosophy demands of its devotees.

## A. General Anthologies and Histories

ANDERSON, PAUL 1907- and MAX FISCH 1900- (eds.) *Philosophy in America from the Puritans to James* (1939). Substantial selections from major philosophical writings with clear and helpful introductions to their historical settings. *Appleton o.p.*

COMMINS, SAXE 1892?-1958 and ROBERT N. LINSCOTT 1886- (eds.) *The World's Great Thinkers* (1947). A monumental collection of widely read essays and selections from major speculative, social, political, and scientific philosophers. *Random House 4 vols $14.95.*

DURANT, WILL 1885- *The Story of Philosophy* (rev ed 1933). A popular, interesting, selective account of Western thinkers from Socrates through Kant and Schopenhauer to Dewey. *Simon & Schuster $5, S&S, WSP.*

EDMAN, IRWIN 1896-1954 and HERBERT W. SCHNEIDER 1892- (eds.) *Landmarks for Beginners in Philosophy* (1941). Whole writings and some selections ranging from Plato through Descartes and Kant to Bergson, with brief but illuminating introductions. *Holt $8.*

HOFFDING, HARALD 1843-1931 *A History of Modern Philosophy* (1900). A Danish philosopher's detailed but readable account of men and movements from the Renaissance to late 19th century. *Peter Smith 2 vols $8, Dov.*

LAMPRECHT, STERLING P. 1890- *Our Philosophical Traditions* (1955). Chronological presentation of the major thought of Western civilization arranged to highlight influential trends and movements. *Appleton $5.75.*

LIN YUTANG 1895- (ed.) *The Wisdom of China and India* (1942). Major sacred and philosophical writings from Hindu, Buddhist, Confucian, and Taoist traditions. *MLG.*

WINDELBAND, WILHELM 1848-1915 *A History of Philosophy* (1901). A thorough account of major Western ideas and movements from the 7th century B.C. to the mid-19th century, widely regarded as a classic study. *Torch.*

# B. Ancient and Medieval Thought

*The Age of Belief.* See "The Middle Ages," page 66.

ARISTOTLE *Ethics, Poetics,* and *Politics.* See "Greece," page 33.

AUGUSTINE *Confessions.* See "Rome," page 39.

BURNET, JOHN 1863-1928 *Early Greek Philosophy* (1930). Detailed and generally clear interpretation of writings of early cosmologists, Thales to Leucippus, with many of the main primary sources in translation. *Mer.*

LUCRETIUS *On the Nature of Things.* See "Rome," page 40.

MARCUS AURELIUS *Meditations.* See "Rome," page 40.

PLATO *Republic* and *Other Dialogues.* See "Greece," page 34.

PLOTINUS 205-270 *The Enneads.* Plato lives again in this involved philosophical search for the ineffable One. *Loeb.*

*Stoic and Epicurean Philosophers* (1940). Ed. by W. J. Oates. Complete extant writings, in standard translations, of Epicurus, Lucretius, Epictetus, and Marcus Aurelius. *Random House $3.75.*

THOMAS AQUINAS *Writings.* See "The Middle Ages," page 68.


# C. Modern Thought

*The Age of Ideology* (1956). Ed. by Henry Aiken. Selections of important, well-known writings of 19th-century philosophers—Kant, Hegel, Spencer, Comte—with connecting interpretations and suggestive commentaries. *Houghton $3, Ment.*

BERKELEY, GEORGE 1685-1753 *Three Dialogues Between Hylas and Philonous* (1713). Provocative conversations on whether material substances are anything more than collections of ideas. *Lib, Mer, Open.*

DESCARTES *Discourse on Method.* See "The 17th Century," page 86.

*English Philosophers from Bacon to Mill* (1939). Ed. by E. A. Burtt. Selections plus several whole writings mentioned in this section and Bacon's *Novum Organum* (1620), a Lord Chancellor's popularization of "true induction," exposing "idols" which mislead inquiry. *MLG.*

HEGEL, GEORG 1770-1831 *The Philosophy of History* (1837). A difficult but important panorama of civilizations as the struggle toward rational freedom or wholeness, a view attacked by Kierkegaard and revised by Marx. *Peter Smith $3.85.*

## PHILOSOPHY

HOBBES *Leviathan.* See "The 17th Century," page 87.

HUME, DAVID 1711–1776 ***Enquiry Concerning Human Understanding*** (1748). Knowledge of the self and causality as based on experience rather than logical necessity. The strongly argued view which awakened Kant. **Oxford $2.90,** *Gate, Lib, Open, WSP.*

_____ ***Dialogues Concerning Natural Religion*** (1779). Thought-provoking conversations in an easy style dealing with skepticism, arguments for theism, and the problem of evil. *Haf, Lib.*

KANT, IMMANUEL 1724–1804 ***Prolegomena to Any Future Metaphysics*** (1783). How knowledge is tied to perception, though "God, freedom, and immortality" may be rationally established through ethics. Less difficult than most of Kant's writings. **Barnes & Noble $2.20,** *Lib, Open.*

_____ ***Fundamental Principles of the Metaphysics of Morals*** (1785). Difficult but important analysis of duty proceeding from common moral knowledge to strict impartiality treating all men as ends-in-themselves. *Lib.*

KIERKEGAARD, SOREN 1813-1855 ***Fear and Trembling*** (1843) and ***The Sickness Unto Death*** (1849). A father of existentialism vividly examines faith and despair in attacking Hegel's system. *Anch.*

LOCKE *An Essay Concerning Human Understanding.* See "The 17th Century," page 87.

MARX, KARL 1818–1883 and FRIEDRICH ENGELS 1820–1895 ***The German Ideology*** (1846). Basic, concrete statement of Marx's turning point, relating man's self-estrangement to Feuerbach's humanism, Hegel's theory of history, and utopian socialism. *NWP.*

MILL, JOHN STUART 1806–1873 ***On Liberty*** (1859) and ***Utilitarianism*** (1863). Concrete and highly lucid defenses of the "greatest happiness" principle as the basis of justice and individual freedom. **On Liberty:** *Appl, EvmanNA, Gate, Lib, WoC;* **Utilitarianism:** *EvmanNA, Lib, Mer.*

NIETZSCHE, FRIEDRICH 1844–1900 ***The Portable Nietzsche*** (1954). Tr. and ed. by Walter Kaufmann. Colorful defense of noble individuality and self-assertion against mediocrity. Includes ***Thus Spake Zarathustra*** (1883 ff.). *Vik, Vik-h.*

PASCAL *Pensées.* See "The 17th Century," page 88.

SCHOPENHAUER, ARTHUR 1788–1860 ***Philosophy.*** Clearly written, pessimistic view of the world as ever-struggling Will crystallized in ideas. *B&N, ML, Scrib.*

SPINOZA *Philosophy.* See "The 17th Century," page 88.

VOLTAIRE (FRANÇOIS MARIE AROUET) 1694–1778 ***The Portable Voltaire.*** Satirical novels, selections from ***Philosophical Dictionary,*** and letters—all defending reason against superstition. *Vik, Vik-h.*

# D. Contemporary Thought

*The Age of Analysis* (1955). Ed. by Morton White. Important selections for the general reader from 20th-century philosophers—Moore, Croce, Husserl, Carnap, Wittgenstein—with connecting interpretations and thoughtful commentaries. *Ment.*

AYER, ALFRED J. 1910– *Language, Truth and Logic* (1936). Lucid exposition of logical empiricism viewing metaphysics as meaningless, ethics as emotive, philosophy as analysis. *Dov.*

BERDYAEV, NICOLAS 1874–1948 *The Beginning and the End* (1957). The final book of a perceptive religious philosopher, presenting "existential metaphysics" for the serious reader in relation to German philosophy, creativity, personality, and society. *Peter Smith $3.50, Torch.*

BERGSON, HENRY 1859–1941 *Introduction to Metaphysics* (1912). Best preface to Bergson's other writings, memorably explaining how intuition rather than intellect reaches reality. *WL.*

BUBER, MARTIN 1878– *Between Man and Man* (1947). An eminent social philosopher and Zionist clearly relates the "I-Thou" principle to communication, society, education, and modern philosophies. *Bea.*

CASSIRER, ERNST 1874–1945 *An Essay on Man* (1944). For nonspecialists, the human significance of symbolic forms in religion, art, history, and science. *Yale $5, Yale.*

COHEN, MORRIS R. 1880–1947 *Reason and Nature* (rev ed 1953). Lucid, direct account of how science and philosophy reveal the rational structure of existence and conduct. *Free Press $7.50.*

*Contemporary Philosophy* (1954). Ed. by James Jarrett and Sterling McMurrin. Widely read essays and chapters from such influential thinkers as Croce, Santayana, Wisdom, Wittgenstein, and Heidegger on knowledge, value, religion, and history. *Holt $9.45.*

DEWEY, JOHN 1859–1952 *Reconstruction in Philosophy* (1920). A vigorous, concrete presentation of experimentalism as a coherent whole in relation to science, history of philosophy, logic, ethics, and social goals. *Bea.*

———— *Experience and Nature* (1925). Lectures for professionals and laymen on the continuity of nature and experience in relation to existence, ideas, and values. *Open Court $5, Dov, Open.*

EDMAN *Arts and the Man.* See "Fine Arts," page 194.

*Existentialism from Dostoevsky to Sartre* (1956). Ed. by Walter Kaufmann. For nonspecialists, selections and whole writings, some newly translated, from Kierkegaard, Jaspers, Heidegger, and others who view truth as "subjectivity." *Peter Smith $3.50, Mer.*

## PHILOSOPHY

FRANK, PHILIPP 1884– *Modern Science and Its Philosophy* (1949). A founder of logical positivism relates for the general reader recent developments in physics to the logic of science, metaphysics, humanistic education, and social conditions. *Braziller $3, Collr.*

HYDE, WILLIAM DE WITT 1858–1917 *The Five Great Philosophies of Life* (rev ed 1928). A nontechnical interpretation of Epicureanism, Stoicism, Platonism, Aristotelianism as guides to daily life culminating in Christianity, with illustrations from literature. *Macmillan $4.50, Collr.*

*Importance of Language* (1962). Ed. by Max Black. Semipopular essays by eminent literary, sociological, and philosophical writers on the varied uses and intellectual perils of language. *Spec.*

JAMES, WILLIAM 1842–1910 *Pragmatism* (1907). Highly influential and delightful interpretation of truth in terms of practical consequences. *Mer, WSP.*

JASPERS, KARL 1883– *Reason and Existenz* (1935). Lectures for philosophically-interested laymen on relations of Kierkegaard and Nietzsche, reason and "the Encompassing" to self-existence. *Farrar, Straus $3.50, Noon.*

LOVEJOY, ARTHUR O. 1873– *The Great Chain of Being* (1936). Traces the unit-idea of Being closely and in detail through Western thought. *Harvard $6, Torch.*

MOORE, G. E. 1873– *Some Main Problems of Philosophy* (1953). Highly careful, incisive, influential lectures showing philosophy as analysis of ideas on truth and falsity, time and infinity, propositions and things in relation to concrete cases from common sense. *Macmillan $5.25, Collr.*

PEIRCE, CHARLES S. 1839–1914 *Philosophical Writings* (1955). Ed. by Justus Buchler. Popular and technical essays on logic, evolution, and the cosmos, presenting key ideas which unlocked new doors in American thought. *Dov.*

ROYCE, JOSIAH 1855–1916 *The Religious Aspect of Philosophy* (1885). For both students of philosophy and laymen, a close examination of ethics, error, doubt, and religious belief as implying an eternal Infinite Thought. *Peter Smith $3.75.*

RUSSELL, BERTRAND 1872– *The Problems of Philosophy* (1912). Straightforward and interesting introduction to such issues as the existence of matter, grounds of induction, and limits of knowledge, *GB.*

———— *Mysticism and Logic* (1917). Sharp, witty, popular essays, containing "A Free Man's Worship" and essays closely analyzing knowledge and causality. *Barnes & Noble $2.75, Anch.*

SANTAYANA, GEORGE 1863–1952 *Philosophy.* In moving prose various books and essays trace the adventure of Mind in a world of Matter. *AA, Collr, Dov, Torch.*

STEBBING, L. SUSAN 1885–1943 *Thinking to Some Purpose* (1939). A practical, easy presentation of elements of logic as guides against mistaken generalization and irrelevant conclusions. *Pen.*

SUZUKI, D. T. 1870– *Zen Buddhism* (1956). The search for what is entirely and vividly concrete, explained by a master in relation to the "doctrine of no-mind," practical methods, and the history of ideas. *Anch.*

TILLICH, PAUL 1886– *The Courage To Be* (1952). A philosophical theologian suggestively relates "courage" to historic philosophies, existentialism, despair, and "the God above God." *Yale $3.75, Yale.*

UNAMUNO, MIGUEL DE 1864–1936 *The Tragic Sense of Life* (1912). Masterpiece of an influential Spanish thinker in quest of the "saving incertitude" for life's despair. *Peter Smith $3.75, Dov.*

WHITEHEAD, ALFRED NORTH 1861–1947 *Science and the Modern World* (1925). Sweeping, path-breaking, difficult interpretation of the universe in terms of events, organisms-in-process. *Macmillan $6, Ment.*

———— *Modes of Thought* (1938). Pointed but subtle lectures on the relations of value to language, and physics to life. *Macmillan $3.75, Cap.*

# 18. Religion

### ANNA ROTHE, *Good Counsel College Library*

In one sense all learning is a record of man's quest for meaning. Religion is the specific form of learning that states the question in spiritual terms: What is man's spirit? His individual worth? His goal? Unto what far reaches does his imagination carry him? How can he express the perceptive flashes by which in certain moments the universe around him seems ordered? Religion emphasizes personal values, the nonphysical and immeasurable qualities of man, life, and God.

Nearly every religion is expressed in three forms: its basic scriptures, which reveal, often in poetic or narrative forms, the fundamental perceptions on which it rests; its theology, the conceptualized statements of its beliefs and dogma; and its church, the institution which has been created by this belief.

Sacred scriptures, like all great literature, defy effective paraphrase. Fortunately, the major documents of the world's religions are available in good—occasionally in superb—English translations; reading them quickens the spirit and imagination and intelligence. For many, the greatest of the scriptures is the King James version of The Holy Bible, a literary masterwork of our language. The low-priced Mentor Religious Classics series includes good translations of sacred Oriental writings—of Buddhism, Hinduism, Taoism, and Islam. Frazer's *The Golden Bough* is the important guide to primitive beliefs.

Theology is a highly specialized study, but a meaningful view of the original writings of Christian theologians can be gained from *The Wisdom of Catholicism* and *Great Voices of the Reformation*.

## A. The Basic Scriptures

*The Holy Bible* (800 B.C.–A.D. 300). The Holy Scriptures of Israel and Christendom is the present-day best seller. Possibly the best-loved of the English translations is the King James (Authorized) Version (1611), one of the 50 representative translations since Wycliffe's in 1382. Today the King James Version is issued by more than 30 publishers. Among modern translations, the work of councils of churchmen and lay scholars, are the English Revised Version (1881), the American Revised Standard Version *(Nelson,* 1946–52), and the *New English Bible* (New Testament, *Oxford-Cambridge,* 1961). Among the translations by individual Protestant scholars are those by James Moffatt, Edgar J. Goodspeed, J. B. Phillips, and E. V. Rieu.

The Rheims-Douay translation (1582, 1609–10), the Challoner revision (1749), the Confraternity version (1941), and the translation by Ronald Knox *(Sheed and Ward,* 1944) are the work of Roman Catholic scholars. While most of the 14 books of the *Apocrypha* (200 B.C.–A.D. 100) are included in the Bibles authorized by the Catholic hierarchy, several of the books appear as appendices in some of the Protestant versions.

In 1917 the Jewish Publication Society issued *The Holy Scriptures* in English, according to the Masoretic text; and a revision was begun in 1955.

For nearly all versions of the Bible there are guides, commentaries, and dictionaries too numerous to list. Two of the more useful of many concordances are worth noting: *Cruden's Complete Concordance to the Holy Scriptures,* ed. by A. D. Adams and others, *Holt $4;* and *Harper's Topical Concordance,* ed. by Charles R. Joy, *Harper $8.95.*

*The Bible Designed to Be Read as Living Literature* (1936), edited by Ernest Sutherland Bates, is a handsomely printed modern arrangement of the King James text, with some omissions. *Simon & Schuster $7.50.*

*The Dartmouth Bible* (1950), edited by Roy B. Chamberlin and Herman Feldman, is an abridgment of the King James Version and is well-equipped with aids to understanding: prefaces, notes, maps. Favored for college courses. *Houghton $10.*

*The Modern Reader's Bible* (1907), edited by Richard G. Moulton, is the English Revised Version. Because of the wealth of its notes and comments, it remains the most useful book for the examination of the Bible as literature. *Macmillan $7.95.*

*Bhagavad-Gita* (5th to 3rd century B.C.) The most popular book in Hindu religious literature. *Ment.*

# RELIGION

BUDDHA 563–483 B.C. *The Teachings of the Compassionate Buddha.* An anthology of the basic texts of Buddhism, with introduction and notes by E. A. Burtt. *Ment.*

CONFUCIUS *Analects.* See "India and the Far East," page 47.

LAO-TZU *The Way of Life.* See "India and the Far East," page 48. (under WALEY, *The Way and Its Power*).

LIN YUTANG *The Wisdom of China and India.* See "Philosophy," page 205.

MOHAMMED *Koran.* See "The Middle East and Africa," page 53. (under *Koran*).

## B. Writings of the Great Theologians

AUGUSTINE *The City of God* and *Confessions.* See "Rome," page 39.

FOSDICK, HARRY EMERSON 1878– (ed.) *Great Voices of the Reformation* (1952). Major writings of Protestant reformers, from Wycliffe to Wesley. *MLG.*

FRANCIS OF ASSISI *The Little Flowers.* See "The Middle Ages," page 67.

GOLDIN, JUDAH 1914– (tr. & ed.) *The Living Talmud; the Wisdom of the Fathers* (1957). The oral law of the Jews, with rabbinical discussion dating from the 6th century A.D. *Chicago $4, Ment.*

HUNT, GEORGE L. (ed.) *Ten Makers of Modern Protestant Thought* (1958). Barth, Buber, Niebuhr, Schweitzer, and Tillich are among those whose influence has been most important since 1900. *Refl.*

PEGIS, ANTON C. 1905– (ed.) *The Wisdom of Catholicism* (1949). Significant writings of Catholics through the centuries: Church Fathers, scholastic philosophers, ecclesiastics, and mystics, to the works of modern laymen and religious. *MLG.*

THOMAS À KEMPIS *The Imitation of Christ.* See "The Middle Ages," page 68.

THOMAS AQUINAS *Writings.* See "The Middle Ages," page 68.

## C. Books on Religion and the Churches

BARISH, LOUIS 1912– and REBECCA BARISH *Basic Jewish Beliefs* (1961). Answers questions about the four groups comprising Judaism, discusses its problems. Some of its 14 chapters are on God, prayer, the soul, and after-life. *Jonathan David o.p.*

BEEGLE, DEWEY M. *God's Word into English* (1960). A history, with studies and comparisons, of the translations and revisions of the Bible since 1382, in the light of old and modern scholarship. Harper $3.50.

BUNCE *Religions in Japan.* See "India and the Far East," page 49.

BURROWS *The Dead Sea Scrolls* and *More Light on the Dead Sea Scrolls.* See "The Middle East and Africa," page 52.

CAVERT, SAMUEL McCREA 1888- *On the Road to Christian Unity* (1961). Surveys gains and discusses prospects of the ecumenical movement among Protestant and Eastern Orthodox churches; covers the 25-year history of the World Council of Churches. Harper $3.75.

CHASE, MARY ELLEN 1887- *The Bible and the Common Reader* (rev 1952). Vividly written study of the Scriptures as literature and history, with emphasis on the Old Testament, King James Version. Macmillan $4.95, Macm.

ELLIS, JOHN T. 1905- *American Catholicism* (1956). Chronological, well-documented review of the growth of the Catholic Church in the United States since colonial times, coordinating ecclesiastic and secular history. Chicago $3.50, CHAC.

FOSDICK, HARRY EMERSON 1878- *The Man from Nazareth* (1949). A study of the acts and teachings of Jesus as the author believes they influenced the twelve disciples, the masses, and other groups of the Palestinian population. Harper $4.

FRAZER *The Golden Bough.* See "Greece," page 35.

GLAZER, NATHAN 1923- *American Judaism* (1957). Historical study of Judaism in America since 1654, with sociological considerations and religious insight. Chicago $3.50, CHAC.

GRAVES *The Greek Myths.* See "Greece," page 35.

GUILLAUME, ALFRED 1888- *Islam* (1954). Mohammed, the Koran, the evolution of Mohammedanism with its various schools of thought, and the place of Islam in the world today. Pen.

HILL, CAROLINE MILES 1866-? (ed.) *The World's Great Religious Poetry* (1938). Extensive anthology of the poetic expression of man's religious thought and experience. Macmillan $5.50.

HUDSON, WINTHROP 1911- *American Protestantism* (1961). Evaluation of the development of Protestant churches in the United States from Puritan times; a history of both religion and culture. Chicago $3.95, CHAC.

HUMPHREYS, CHRISTMAS 1901- *Buddhism* (rev 1958). Exposition of the different schools of Buddhism, including Zen Buddhism, by the leader of the Buddhist Society in England. Pen.

JAMES, WILLIAM 1842-1910 *Varieties of Religious Experience* (1902). The classical study of religious experiences as psychological phenomena—revelation, conversion, fears, hopes, mysticism, etc. Collr, Dolp, Ment, ML.

JURJI, E. J. 1907- (ed.) *The Great Religions of the Modern World* (1946). Ten authorities explain simply and objectively the ten

## RELIGION

great living religions. Judaism and the three divisions of Christianity are treated at greatest length. *Princeton $6.*

LATOURETTE, KENNETH S. 1884– *A History of Christianity* (1953). A definitive, well-rounded work. *Harper $11.*

MARTINDALE, CYRIL C. 1879– *The Faith of the Roman Church* (1950). A lucid setting forth of Catholic doctrines. *Sheed & Ward o.p.*

NICHOLS, JAMES H. 1915– *Primer for Protestants* (1947). Historical and doctrinal exposition of Protestantism, written with clarity and freshness. *Association Press $2.50, Refl.*

NOSS, JOHN B. *Man's Religions* (rev 1956). Excellent discussion of leading faiths, making use of original sources. *Macmillan $6.25.*

SHAPLEY, HARLOW 1885– (ed.) *Science Ponders Religion* (1960). Leading scientists reflect on the problem of the "co-existence" of religion and natural science. *(Appleton) Meredith $5.*

SPENCE, HARTZELL 1908– *The Story of America's Religions* (1960). Full description of 14 religious bodies—origins, traditions, rituals, sociological attitudes. *Holt $4, Apex.*

SUZUKI *Zen Buddhism.* See "Philosophy," page 209.

SWEET, WILLIAM WARREN 1881– *The Story of Religion in America* (1939). The churches in our national life in relation to social, economic, and political trends. *Harper $3.75.*

THIELEN, THORALF T. 1921– *What Is an Ecumenical Council?* (1960). The nature, scope, and accomplishments of the Roman Catholic councils; and a forward look to the projects of the Second Vatican Council, which began in 1962. *Newman $2.95.*

UNDERHILL, EVELYN 1875–1941 *Mysticism* (1911). A classic study of the history and manifestation of mysticism, with material drawn from St. Teresa of Avila, Meister Eckhart, St. John of the Cross, and William Blake. *Evman, Mer.*

WATTS, HAROLD H. 1906– *The Modern Reader's Guide to the Bible* (rev 1958). Perhaps the best guide to the Bible as Judaeo-Christian history, poetry, drama, and fiction. Considers some books of the *Apocrypha.* Text quoted is from the King James translation. *Harper $5.50.*

WILSON *The Scrolls from the Dead Sea.* See "The Middle East and Africa," page 55.

ZERNOV, NICOLAS *Eastern Christendom* (1961). A study of the origin and development of the national divisions of the Eastern Orthodox Church—its doctrinal issues, form of worship, sacraments. *Putnam $7.50.*

# 19. History

**AUSTIN VENABLE and BERNERD WEBER,**
*University of Alabama*

Carl Becker once defined history as "a knowledge of things said and done." But history at its best does more than present a miscellaneous collection of the varied experiences of man. It may show, although sometimes imperfectly, the whole spectrum of human behavior and belief, and illustrate the range and depth of man's experience on earth. A knowledge of history can serve as a valuable corrective to the common habits of vague generalization or of too narrow particularism. Historical knowledge explains how things have come to be what they are and hence helps to make the world more intelligible. The more one delves into the past, the deeper and broader will be his comprehension of the present and his insight into the future. The value of a knowledge of the past to the understanding of society today has been recognized by all the major historians from Thucydides on. Sir Charles Firth clearly expressed this idea: "History is not easy to define; but to me it seems the record of the life of societies of man, of the changes which those societies have gone through, of the ideas which have determined the actions of those societies, and of the material conditions which have helped or hindered their development."

By its very nature history is vibrant with life and inevitably concerns each one of us. The 19th-century British historian Edward A. Freeman defined history as "past politics," but this definition is no longer considered adequate. Modern historians in writing about the past have increasingly turned attention to what James Harvey Robinson termed "the new history"—in other words, to economic, social, and cultural behavior as well as to political, military, and constitutional events. Geographically, too, the whole base of history has broadened. No longer are historians concerned just with Europe or the Americas: Africa, Asia, and the island world of the Pacific are all part of the total drama of human experience and endeavor. Thus, all that all men have thought and done on this earth falls within the province of history.

One of the pleasures of history grows out of its relationship with literature. Since the time of Herodotus of Halicarnassus, written history has been a major form of literary expression, and many major historians of the past have been distinguished men of letters. Not only have historians created literature by writing history, but in varying degrees a knowledge of the history they write is necessary for an understanding and appreciation of the poetry, drama, essays, novels of any country or period.

History thus represents the sum of the total past experience of the world. If it is read and studied to any purpose, it is not "a confused heap of facts" (Lord Chesterfield) or "always tedious" (Anatole France), but makes an intelligent and often fascinating relationship between cause and effect that contains wisdom for all ages.

Many important historical books, too numerous for cross reference here, are listed in other chapters of this book. See especially the nine chapters in "Regional and Historical Cultures" ("Greece" through "The 18th Century"). For specialized histories, see "Fine Arts," "Philosophy," and "Religion." For more recent history, see all the chapters that follow this one—but especially "Politics," "Economics," and "Geography." For dates and other valuable reference data, extremely useful volumes include *Annals of European Civilization, 1501–1900* (1949), by Alfred Mayer; *Encyclopedia of American History* (1953), edited by Richard B. Morris; *An Encyclopedia of World History* (rev ed 1948), edited by William L. Langer; and *Historical Atlas* (8th ed 1956), by William R. Shepherd.

# A. General

ATIYAH *The Arabs.* See "The Middle East and Africa," page 52.

BASHAM *The Wonder That Was India.* See "India and the Far East," page 46.

BRINTON, CLARENCE CRANE 1898– *Ideas and Men: The Story of Western Thought* (1950). A carefully written analysis of major ideas and concepts which have helped to shape the course of Western civilization. *Prentice-Hall $9.*

———— et al. *A History of Civilization* (2nd ed 1960). Perhaps the best, and certainly the most readable, of the many general and encompassing histories of civilization. *Prentice-Hall 2 vols $8.50 ea.*

CERAM, C. W. (KURT W. MAREK) 1915– *Gods, Graves, and Scholars* (1951). A vivid and lively introduction to the field of archaeology, covering the entire area of the ancient Orient. *Knopf $5.75.*

CHURCHILL, WINSTON S. 1874– *History of the English-Speaking Peoples* (1956–58). The great English statesman presents in his inimitable style the history of England, the United States, and the British Commonwealth as a unified story. *Dodd 4 vols $6 ea., Ban.*

CLYDE, PAUL H. 1896– *The Far East* (3rd ed 1958). A general account clearly organized and particularly useful for its description of the impact of the West upon eastern Asia. *Prentice-Hall $11.95.*

CREEL *The Birth of China.* See "India and the Far East," page 47.

DEAN *The Nature of the Non-Western World.* See "India and the Far East," page 45.

FAIRBANK *The United States and China.* See "India and the Far East," page 47.

FISHER *The Middle East.* See "The Middle East and Africa," page 52.

HALECKI, JOHN OSKAR VON 1891– *A History of Poland* (1956). A readable survey by a Polish-born scholar. *Roy $4.25.*

HERRING *History of Latin America.* See "Latin America," page 61.

HITTI *The Arabs.* See "The Middle East and Africa," page 53.

KIRK *Short History of the Middle East.* See "The Middle East and Africa," page 53.

KNOLES, GEORGE H. 1907– and RIXFORD K. SNYDER 1908– (eds.) *Readings in Western Civilization* (3rd ed 1960). An excellent collection of primary source readings, accompanied by helpful explanatory introductions. *Lippincott $7.50.*

LATOURETTE *A History of Christianity.* See "Religion," page 215.

# HISTORY

LEWIS and HOLT *Historians of the Middle East.* See "The Middle East and Africa," page 54.

MAHAN, ALFRED T. 1840–1914 *The Influence of Sea Power upon History, 1660–1783* (1890). A classic work by an American admiral emphasizing the theme that sea power has frequently played a pivotal role in international relations. *Little $7.50, AmCen.*

MULLER *The Loom of History.* See "The Middle East and Africa," page 54.

PINSON, KOPPEL S. 1904–1961 *Modern Germany* (1954). A modern, clear, readable survey. *Macmillan $7.50.*

RANDALL, JOHN H. 1899– *The Making of the Modern Mind* (rev ed 1940). An incisive, stimulating, but difficult explanation of the forces from the Middle Ages on that have contributed to the way we think and act today. *Houghton $6.*

ROMIER, LUCIEN 1885–1944 *A History of France* (1959). Tr. and completed by A. L. Rowse. A readable account, giving much attention to personalities. *St. Martin's $6.50, SM.*

ROWSE *The England of Elizabeth* and *The Expansion of Elizabethan England.* See "In Tudor England," page 82.

SANSOM, GEORGE B. 1883– *The Western World and Japan* (1950). An excellently written account by one who served as an envoy to Japan. *Knopf $8.50.*

TOYNBEE, ARNOLD J. 1889– *A Study of History* (1934–61). A masterly monumental inquiry into the causes of the rise and decline of civilizations. *Oxford 12 vols $74.20.* A two-volume abridgment of the first ten volumes, by D. C. Somervell: *Oxford $6 and $5, GB.*

TREVELYAN, GEORGE M. 1876–1962 *History of England* (3rd ed 1945). A classic synthesis written by an outstanding English historian. Presupposes some knowledge of English history. *Anch.*

WALLBANK *A Short History of India and Pakistan.* See "India and the Far East," page 47.

## B. Ancient and Medieval

ADAMS *Mont-Saint Michel and Chartres.* See "The Middle Ages," page 68.

BARROW *The Romans.* See "Rome," page 41.

*The Bible.* See "Religion," page 212.

BLOCH *Feudal Society.* See "The Middle Ages," page 68.

BURY *History of Greece.* See "Greece," page 35.

CHILDE, V. GORDON 1892–1957 *What Happened in History* (1946). A rapid and clear survey of prehistory and ancient history by a distinguished archeologist. *Pen.*

DAWSON, CHRISTOPHER 1889– *The Making of Europe* (1933). A clear scholarly account from a Catholic point of view. *Sheed & Ward $4.50, Mer.*

DIEHL *Byzantium*. See "The Middle East and Africa," page 52.

DUDLEY *The Civilization of Rome*. See "Rome," page 41.

GIBBON *The Decline and Fall of the Roman Empire*. See "Rome," page 41.

GRANT *The World of Rome*. See "Rome," page 42.

HUIZINGA *The Waning of the Middle Ages*. See "The Middle Ages," page 69.

KITTO *The Greeks*. See "Greece," page 36.

MacKENDRICK *The Mute Stones Speak*. See "Rome," page 42.

PARKES, HENRY B. 1904– *Gods and Men* (1959). A good narrative account of the origins of Western culture, with a critical analysis of the important shaping ideas and ideals. *Knopf $7.50.*

PAINTER *Medieval Society*. See "The Middle Ages," page 69.

PIRENNE, HENRI 1862–1935 *Medieval Cities* (1925). A brief informed account of town origins and of the classes of society, government, and life found in medieval urban communities. *Peter Smith $3, Anch.*

_____ *Economic and Social History of Medieval Europe*. See "The Middle Ages," page 69.

PLUTARCH *Lives*. See "Greece," page 34.

POWER *Medieval People*. See "The Middle Ages," page 69.

SCHEVILL, FERDINAND 1868–1954 *The Medici* (1949). Traces with vivid detail the origin and growth of the commune of Florence down to the 16th Century. *Peter Smith $3.50, Torch.*

STEPHENSON, CARL 1886–1954 *Medieval Feudalism* (1956). One of the best introductory manuals on the subject. *Corn.*

TAYLOR *The Mediaeval Mind*. See "The Middle Ages," page 70.

THUCYDIDES *The Peloponnesian Wars*. See "Greece," page 34.

TOYNBEE *Greek Civilization and Character*. See "Greece," page 36.

## C. Modern, 1500–1900, Other Than American

ALBRECHT-CARRIÉ, RENÉ 1904– *A Diplomatic History of Europe Since the Congress of Vienna* (1958). A recent one-volume treatment of a complex subject, complete with excellent maps and an extensive topical bibliography. *Harper $8.*

ALLEN, HARRY C. *Great Britain and the United States* (1955). An interesting account of Anglo-American relations from 1783 to 1952, written from the British point of view. *St Martin's $10.*

BAINTON, RONALD H. 1894– *The Age of the Reformation* (1956). A brief summary illustrated with excerpts from primary sources of the period. *Anv.*

# HISTORY

*The Berkshire Studies in European History.* A series of popularizations by distinguished historians. The more than twenty 100–150 page monographs include such items as WALLACE K. FERGUSON *The Renaissance* and GEORGE L. MOSSE *The Reformation*. *Holt various prices.*

BRYANT, ARTHUR 1899– *Age of Elegance* (1951). A vivid description of English life during the Napoleonic era and immediately afterward. *Harper $5.*

BURCKHARDT *The Civilization of the Renaissance in Italy.* See "The Renaissance," page 75.

BUTTERFIELD *The Origins of Modern Science.* See "The 18th Century," page 97.

CARLYLE *The French Revolution.* See "The 18th Century," page 98.

COBBAN *A History of Modern France.* See "The 18th Century," page 98.

CLOUGH, SHEPARD B. 1901– and CHARLES W. COLE 1906– *Economic History of Europe* (3rd ed 1952). A basic account focusing on the period since 1500. *Heath $8.50.*

GRIMM, HAROLD J. 1901– *The Reformation Era, 1500–1650* (1954). A solid, clear, judicious appraisal of a complex era. *Macmillan $6.75.*

HALLER *The Rise of Puritanism.* See "The 17th Century," page 89.

IRVINE, WILLIAM 1906– *Apes, Angels, and Victorians* (1955). A fascinating discussion of the conflict between religion and science in Victorian England occasioned by Darwin, Huxley, and the theory of evolution. *Mer.*

LEFEBVRE *The Coming of the French Revolution.* See "The 18th Century," page 98.

LEWIS *The Splendid Century.* See "The 17th Century," page 89.

LUCAS *The Renaissance and the Reformation.* See "The Renaissance," page 75.

MACAULAY *The History of England.* See "The 17th Century," page 89.

MADARIAGA *The Rise of the Spanish American Empire* and *The Fall of the Spanish American Empire.* See "Latin America," page 62.

MATTINGLY *The Armada.* See "The Renaissance," page 75.

MORISON *Admiral of the Ocean Sea.* See "The Renaissance," page 75.

MOTLEY *The Rise of the Dutch Republic.* See "The Renaissance," page 75.

PALMER, ROBERT R. 1909– *The Age of the Democratic Revolution* (1959). A provocative and illuminating account of the interrelationships of the various revolutionary movements of the 18th century. *Princeton $7.50.*

PRESCOTT *Conquest of Mexico* and *Conquest of Peru.* See "Latin America," page 62.

RIASANOVSKY, NICHOLAS V. 1923– *A History of Russia* (1963). A lucid, scholarly, up-to-date account, emphasizing the period after 1500 and carefully balancing the political, social, economic, and cultural aspects of Russian history. *Oxford $10.50.*

*The Rise of Modern Europe.* A series of more than a dozen reliable interpretations by specialists in various areas, such as GEOFFREY BRUUN *Europe and the French Imperium, 1799–1814,* MYRON P. GILMORE *The World of Humanism, 1453–1517,* and FREDERICK L. NUSSBAUM *The Triumph of Science and Reason, 1660–1685. Harper $5 ea.*

ROWSE *The England of Elizabeth* and *The Expansion of Elizabethan England.* See "In Tudor England," page 82.

SELLERY, GEORGE C. *The Renaissance: Its Nature and Origins* (rev ed 1962). An interesting broad survey of the entire movement. *UWis.*

SIMPSON, LESLEY B. 1891– *Many Mexicos* (3rd ed 1952). Probably the best one-volume history. *Calif.*

SUMNER *Peter the Great and the Emergence of Russia.* See "The Middle East and Africa," page 54.

TAWNEY *Religion and the Rise of Capitalism.* See "The 17th Century," page 89.

THOMAS, ALFRED B. 1896– *Latin America* (1956). This survey of the history of Latin America aims to clarify the forces operating in its culture and the continuity of its development. *Macmillan $6.75.*

THOMPSON, JAMES M. 1878–1956 *The French Revolution* (5th ed 1955). A vivid, detailed narrative of the events from 1789 to 1794. *Oxford $6.*

YOUNG *The Medici.* See "The Renaissance," page 76.

YOUNG, GEORGE M. 1882–1959 *Victorian England* (2nd ed 1953). One of the best historical portraits of an age. *Ox.*

# D. Contemporary (Since 1900), Other Than American

BARNETT *Communist China and Asia.* See "India and the Far East," page 47.

BRINTON, CLARENCE CRANE 1898– *The Temper of Western Europe* (1953). Are Europeans decadent? Is Europe in decline? The author does not think so as he analyzes the history of Europe since World War II. *Harvard $2.50.*

BUSS *Southeast Asia and the World Today.* See "India and the Far East," page 50.

CHURCHILL, WINSTON S. 1874– *The Gathering Storm* (1948), *Their Finest Hour* (1949), *The Grand Alliance* (1950), *The*

## HISTORY

*Hinge of Fate* (1950), *Closing the Ring* (1951), *Triumph and Tragedy* (1953). The very titles suggest the forceful, colorful style which Sir Winston uses in *The Second World War,* his multi-volume personal narrative of vital and dramatic years. *Houghton $6.50 ea., Ban.*

EISENHOWER, DWIGHT D. 1890– *Crusade in Europe* (1948). The commander's report to the public on his assignment: clear, concise, judicious, and interesting. *Doubleday $4.50, Dolp.*

FAY, SIDNEY B. 1876– *Origins of the World War* (rev ed 1948). The causes of World War I traced from 1871 to 1914. *Macmillan $7.50.*

HERSEY, JOHN 1914– *Hiroshima* (1946). A stark but subdued report of what happened when the first atomic bomb fell on a city. *Knopf $3, Ban, ML.*

HOFER, WALTHER 1920– *War Premeditated–1939* (1955). Immediate backgrounds of World War II told briefly and cogently. *Longmans o.p.*

HOLT *A Modern History of the Sudan.* See "The Middle East and Africa," page 56.

KOGON, EUGEN 1903– *Theory and Practice of Hell* (1950). A calm, objective description of the Nazi concentration camp system and of a Christian's six years at Buchenwald. *Berk.*

LIE, TRYGVE 1896– *In the Cause of Peace* (1954). The United Nations' first Secretary-General gives an account of the first seven years of that organization. *Macmillan o.p.*

RAUCH, BASIL 1908– *Roosevelt from Munich to Pearl Harbor* (1950). An analysis of the development of the Roosevelt foreign policy from Munich to Pearl Harbor, challenging the views of extremists of both the right and the left. *Creative Age o.p.*

REISCHAUER *Japan, Past and Present.* See "India and the Far East," page 49.

SETON-WATSON, HUGH 1916– *From Lenin to Malenkov* (1953). Surveys and analyzes the successes and failures of the Communist movement in the world up to the death of Stalin. *Praeger $6.*

SHIRER, WILLIAM L. 1904– *Berlin Diary* (1941). A graphic account of Germany from the year after Hitler came into power (1933) until the Nazi war machine had overrun much of northern and western Europe. *Pop.*

———— *The Challenge of Scandinavia* (1955). A history of the Scandinavian countries—Norway, Sweden, Denmark, and Finland—since the 1930's, with the emphasis on the high level of social and economic well-being they have achieved. *Little $6.50.*

———— *The Rise and Fall of the Third Reich* (1960). A monumental and absorbing account of the rise and fall of Hitler based on personal observation and on the examination of voluminous documents. *Simon & Schuster $10, Crest.*

SNYDER, LOUIS L. 1907– (ed.) *Fifty Major Documents of the Twentieth Century* (1955). An invaluable compilation, including the Austro-Hungarian ultimatum to Serbia in 1914, the

224 GOOD READING

Munich agreement of 1939, the enfranchisement of women in Britain and the United States in 1918-19, the Nuremberg Laws on race, Churchill's "Blood, Toil, Tears, and Sweat" address, the secret Yalta agreement, and the Truman Doctrine. *Anv.*

VINACKE *A History of the Far East in Modern Times.* See "India and the Far East," page 46.

WOLFE, BERTRAM D. 1896– *Three Who Made a Revolution* (1948). A biographical history of the men and the forces that brought on the Russian Revolution, focusing on Lenin, Trotsky, and Stalin. *Dial $7.50, Bea.*

## E. The United States

ADAMS, JAMES TRUSLOW 1878–1949 *The Epic of America* (rev ed 1933). Stirring pageant of our national spirit and character, stressing "the American dream" of a better life for the common man. *Little $6.50.*

ALLEN, FREDERICK L. 1890–1954 *Only Yesterday* (1931). The years following World War I, treating the Teapot Dome scandals and the "flaming youth" period with equal charm and deftness. *Harper $5, Ban.*

BAILEY, THOMAS A. 1902– *A Diplomatic History of the American People* (6th ed 1958). A popular, authoritative survey. *Appleton $7.*

BEARD, CHARLES A. 1874–1948 and MARY BEARD 1876–1958 *Rise of American Civilization* (1949). An outstanding historical analysis of the factors (mainly economic) behind the emergence of modern America. *Macmillan $8.50.*

BOWERS, CLAUDE G. 1879–1958 *The Tragic Era* (1929). Dramatic, vigorous account of the revolutionary decade following the Civil War, sternly critical of those who made the era more tragic than necessary. *Houghton $6, SenEd.*

BROWN *The United States and India and Pakistan.* See "India and the Far East," page 46.

*Chronicles of America.* Over fifty small volumes written by distinguished scholars. Extraordinarily readable, accurate accounts of all phases of our history. *Yale about $3 ea.*

COMMAGER, HENRY STEELE 1902– (ed.) *America in Perspective* (1947). Accounts of the U. S. made by foreigners after traveling through our country—often illuminating, often disturbing. *Ment.*

CRAVEN, AVERY O. 1886– *The Growth of Southern Nationalism, 1848–1861* (1953). How sectionalism developed in the South, resulting in the Civil War. *Louisiana State $7.50.*

────── *The Coming of the Civil War* (2nd ed 1957). Readable, timely, scholarly, objective account, developing the thesis that

## HISTORY

the democratic process in the United States "failed in the critical period that culminated in the Civil War." *Chicago $6.50.*

CURTI, MERLE E. 1897- *The Growth of American Thought* (2nd ed 1951). An excellent study of American social, intellectual, and scientific thought. *Harper $9.*

*Federalist Papers.* See "The 18th Century," page 95.

FAIRBANK *The United States and China.* See "India and the Far East," page 47.

FREEMAN, DOUGLAS S. 1886-1953 *Lee's Generals* (1942-44). A splendid account of the campaigns of the Confederate Army of Northern Virginia. *Scribner 3 vols $10 ea.*

GRANT, ULYSSES S. 1822-1885 *Personal Memoirs of U. S. Grant* (1885-86). A straightforward account of the important events of his time. *Peter Smith $2.50, Prem, UL.*

HACKER, LOUIS M. 1899- *The Triumph of American Capitalism* (1940). American history to 1900, in terms of the economic and political forces that have molded our culture. *Columbia $6.*

HEFFNER, RICHARD D. (ed.) *A Documentary History of the United States* (rev ed 1956). 25 basic American "documents," each with an introduction and some interpretation. Includes not only such standard selections as Washington's Farewell Address and F. D. Roosevelt's Four Freedoms speech, but also F. J. Turner's classic explanation of the influence of the frontier, Hoover's views on rugged individualism, and the Marshall Plan. *Indiana $4.95, Ment.*

HENRY, RALPH SELPH 1889- *The Story of the Confederacy* (rev ed 1957). A distinguished account characterized as "the book with which to begin one's study of the period . . ." *Bobbs $6.*

*History of American Life Series* (1927-48). Ed. by Arthur M. Schlesinger. Twelve studies of economic, social, and cultural life in the United States. Examples are E. B. GREENE *Revolutionary Generation, 1763-1790;* A. C. COLE *Irrepressible Conflict, 1850-1865;* A. NEVINS *Emergence of Modern America, 1865-1878;* and D. WECTER *Age of the Great Depression, 1929-1941. Macmillan $6 ea.*

HOOVER, HERBERT C. 1874- *Memoirs* (1951-52). One of the most controversial figures in recent American history recounts his terms as Cabinet member and President. *Macmillan 3 vols $6 ea.*

MORGAN *The Birth of the Republic.* See "The 18th Century," page 98.

MUMFORD, LEWIS 1895- *The Brown Decades* (1931). A study and critique of three decades (1865-1895) of American architecture, city planning, landscaping, and painting. *Dov.*

PERKINS, DEXTER 1889- *History of the Monroe Doctrine* (rev ed 1955). The definitive account of this famous policy. *Little $6, Little.*

PHILLIPS, ULRICH BONNELL 1877-1934 *Life and Labor in the Old South* (1929). An interesting analysis of the forces which molded the antebellum South, and of the relations between the races. *Little $6, Little.*

PYLE, ERNIE 1900–1945 *Brave Men* (1944). A very compassionate war correspondent describes what he saw and heard, from the landing in Sicily to the liberation of Paris, in World War II. *Grosset $1.98, Pop.*

REISCHAUER *The United States and Japan.* See "India and the Far East," page 49.

*The Rivers of America.* Each volume of the popular series, edited by Carl Carmer, gives the history and folklore of the area through which a river flows. The collection now covers more than 50 rivers—from the Allegheny to the Yazoo. *Holt $3.50 up.*

SHERWOOD *Roosevelt and Hopkins.* See "Biography," page 175.

TURNER, FREDERICK JACKSON 1861–1932 *The Frontier in American History* (1920). An historically important essay analyzing the characteristics of the shifting frontier and advancing the theory that the frontier gave Americans certain distinctive national traits. *Holt $5.45, HRW.*

VAN DOREN, CARL 1885–1950 *The Secret History of the American Revolution* (1941). A fascinating account, giving much attention to conspiracies, particularly that of Benedict Arnold. *Viking o.p.*

WEBB, WALTER PRESCOTT 1888–1963 *The Great Plains* (1931). An original scholarly interpretation of the Great Plains by a distinguished authority, showing the importance of the horse, the six-shooter, the wire fence, and the windmill in the successful settlement of the huge area. *Ginn $8, UL.*

WILEY, BELL I. 1906– *The Life of Billy Yank* (1952). A fascinating study of the common soldier in the Union armies. His counterpart in the Confederate service is equally well drawn in the same author's *The Life of Johnny Reb* (1943). *Chart.*

# 20. Politics

JAMES TRACY CROWN, *New York University*

Politics may be simply defined as the study of the theory and practice of government. Political scientists—as opposed to those who just "talk politics"—attempt to systematize and refine political observations and perceptions.

But contributions to the study of politics are made by many writers other than scholars. Politics provided the stuff of tragedy and comedy for Sophocles and Aristophanes as well as for Shakespeare and Shaw because it displays both man's highest aspirations and his deepest depravity, presents a being who seems at times not distantly related to the angels and at times nearly kin to the devil. For George Orwell in *1984*, Aldous Huxley in *Brave New World Revisited*, or C. Wright Mills in *The Causes of World War III*, new developments in politics have inspired thrillers whose final chapters are yet to be written—presumably by readers, who must determine whether in the world of tomorrow mankind can survive, or will even want to. Very many thoughtful people read these books, though they seem absurd exaggerations. Why? Why do people gather together in more and more homes, cafés, libraries, and classrooms, not to plot the overthrow of governments, but to discover more about them? The reason is that in this supposed age of complacency more and more people are seriously questioning most of the age-old assumptions about government.

Many American citizens today seek new answers to old questions which once intrigued only philosophers, such as Plato, Aristotle, Machiavelli, Marx, and John Stuart Mill. They want to probe the strategic political problems: Why do we have states? Who should rule, and to what ends? How can power be obtained and maintained? What is the proper line separating state control and individual freedom? How far should the state carry out the wishes of its people? The study of political theory and constitutions ponders these questions, among others.

How government really works and how we can get it to work the way we want it to—this is the important province of "practical politics." Yet even at its most practical, politics cannot wholly divorce itself from philosophy—cannot evade the question put to Alice by Humpty Dumpty (though in a different context): "Which is to be master?" Is it to be the philosopher-king of Plato? The proletariat of Marx? The "elites" of Mosca or Ortega? "The people"? Or, in terms of the next American election, the Democrats or Republicans? The endeavor to answer the last question can reduce political writing to the level of the racing form, but it can also serve as an introduction to sound political research—as in V. O. Key's *Politics, Parties, and Pressure Groups*.

International affairs examines the relations of sovereign nations with one another, considers the ways in which they can live together. We can understand international affairs only after we know something about comparative government, the area of politics that attempts to explain why various societies have evolved different kinds of governments, and with what consequences.

For the purpose of organizing good reading in politics, then, books have been divided into categories of Theory, Constitutions, Practical Politics and Government in General, and International Affairs and Comparative Government. In this highly selective list the discriminating reader can find, in readable prose, most of the possible answers to the basic questions in politics.

# A. Theory

ARISTOTLE *Ethics* and *Politics*. See "Greece," page 33.

CROSSMAN, RICHARD H. S. 1907– (ed.) *The God That Failed* (1949). Essays by famous ex-Communists or fellow-travelers on why they sympathized with and then left communism. *Ban, CN.*

EBENSTEIN, WILLIAM 1910– (ed.) *Great Political Thinkers* (3rd ed 1960). Selected readings from famous theorists, from Plato to the present, with excellent commentaries. *Holt $8.50.*

GABRIEL, RALPH H. 1890– *The Course of American Democratic Thought* (2nd ed 1956). Lucidly traces democratic thought in this country from 1815 to the present. *Ronald $6.50.*

HOBBES *Leviathan*. See "The 17th Century," page 87.

LINDSAY, ALEXANDER D. 1879–1952 *The Modern Democratic State* (1947). Makes the reader aware of how difficult it is to define democracy in the Western sense. This gem of political thought does not simplify the task, but gives one of the most satisfactory explanations. *Oxford $3.25, GB.*

LOCKE *Two Treatises of Civil Government*. See "The 17th Century," page 87.

MACHIAVELLI *The Prince*. See "The Renaissance," page 74.

MARX, KARL 1818–1883, FRIEDRICH ENGELS 1820–1895, and V. I. LENIN 1870–1924 *The Essential Left*. Contains by no means all, but certainly the most fundamental of Communist writings: the brief, clear, and powerful *Manifesto;* critiques of liberal socialism and political economy; and Lenin's *State and Revolution*, the prescription for the transformation of capitalistic economies. Each document itself is worth a hundred pages of commentary. *B&N.*

MOSCA, GAETANO 1858–1941 *The Ruling Class* (1939). An explanation of the "circulation of elites" in terms of invariable social laws. Though difficult to read, its attempts to reconcile elites with democracy has stimulated much serious thought. *McGraw-Hill $10, McGH.*

ORTEGA Y GASSET, JOSÉ 1883–1955 *The Revolt of the Masses* (1932). A frank plea for the assumption of rule by an intellectual aristocracy and for the suppression of "mass-man." *Norton $3.95.*

ORWELL *1984*. See "20th Century British Novels," page 128.

PLATO *Republic* and *Other Dialogues*. See "Greece," page 34.

ROUSSEAU *The Social Contract*. See "The 18th Century," page 96.

SABINE, GEORGE H. 1880–1961 *A History of Political Theory* (3rd ed 1961). A trenchant, invaluable analysis of political thought from the Greeks to the present, requiring careful reading. *Holt $7.50.*

WILSON, EDMUND 1895– *To the Finland Station* (1940). The development of European radicalism from the French Revolution through the life and work of Marx to the outbreak of the Russian Revolution. *Peter Smith $3.25, Anch.*

## B. Constitutions

BARNES, WILLIAM R. 1866–1945 (ed.) *Constitution of the United States* (8th ed 1956). A surprisingly fascinating starting point for reading about American government. *B&N.*

CORWIN, EDWARD S. 1878– *The Constitution and What It Means Today* (12th ed 1958). A phrase-by-phrase exposition of fundamental American law. *Princeton $6, Athen.*

*The Federalist Papers.* See "The 18th Century," page 95.

MARKE, JULIUS J. 1913– (ed.) *Holmes Reader* (1955). The core thought of a foremost American jurist. *Oce.*

NEWMAN, EDWIN S. 1922– (ed.) *The Freedom Reader* (1955). Essays on the theory and practice of individual liberties. *Oce.*

ZURCHER, ARNOLD J. 1902– (ed.) *Constitutions and Constitutional Trends Since World War II* (rev ed 1955). The best analysis. *New York Univ. o.p.*

## C. Practical Politics and Government in General

BARTH, ALAN 1906– *The Loyalty of Free Men* (1951). A critical and readable examination of our loyalty program and of our search for "security." *Viking o.p.*

BEARD, CHARLES A. 1874–1948 *An Economic Interpretation of the Constitution of the United States* (1913). An early attempt to give a realistic interpretation of the forces which shaped the Constitution. Endless subsequent efforts to refute this work have only further established its importance. *Macmillan $4.75, Macm.*

BRYCE, JAMES 1838–1922 *The American Commonwealth* (1888). A lucid, brilliant analysis by an Englishman of the American people and their government. *Macmillan $6.75, Putnam $5, Cap.*

CORWIN, EDWARD S. 1878– *The President: Office and Powers* (4th ed 1957). A standard, but somewhat legalistic and difficult, examination of an amazingly flexible American institution. *New York Univ. $6.50.*

## POLITICS

**DIMOCK, MARSHALL E.** 1903– *A Philosophy of Administration* (1958). Emphasizes the creative and cooperative nature of successful administration; challenges some traditional power concepts. *Harper $4.*

**GOLDMAN, ERIC F.** 1915– *Rendezvous With Destiny* (1952). Perceptive, absorbing description of modern reform movements for beginning or advanced readers. Suggests that idealism, though sometimes impractical, keeps American life from sinking to mere money-grabbing. *Knopf $6.95, Vin.*

**GROSS, BERTRAM M.** 1912– *The Legislative Struggle* (1953). Highly intellectual and realistic approach to the legislative process. *McGraw-Hill $7.25.*

**HUXLEY, ALDOUS** 1894–1963 *Brave New World Revisited* (1958). Forcefully indicates that drastic action is required to halt the drift toward thought control and chaotic overpopulation. Huxley, whose vision has several times proved correct, writes with sufficient clarity for any reader to understand the impact of technology on government. *Harper $3.50, Ban, HarpMC, Torch.*

**KEY, VALDIMER O.** 1908–1963 *Politics, Parties, and Pressure Groups* (5th ed 1962). A clear, scholarly exposition of how politics works in the U.S.A. Its carefully reasoned pages should convince readers that much newspaper and TV reporting of politics is superficial if not unsound. *Crowell $7.*

**KOHN, HANS** 1891– *Nationalism, Its Meaning and History* (1955). An interesting, not-too-difficult, authoritative examination of the strongest emotional force in modern politics. *Anv.*

**LASSWELL, HAROLD D.** 1902– *Politics: Who Gets What, When, How* (1958). A lucid introduction to how practical politics works. *Mer.*

**PARKINSON, C. NORTHCOTE** 1909– *Parkinson's Law and Other Studies in Administration* (1957). Explains how all forms of social organization tend to strangle themselves by organizational hypertrophy. Written with tongue in cheek, the book reminds us that politics without humor can become monstrous. *Houghton $3, SenEd.*

**PELTASON, JACK W.** 1923– and **JAMES M. BURNS** 1918– *Functions and Policies of American Government* (2nd ed 1962). A sound yet imaginative introduction to the subject. *Prentice-Hall $5.95.*

**TOCQUEVILLE, ALEXIS DE** 1805–1859 *Democracy in America* (1835, 1840). The pertinent views of a shrewd, observant Frenchman on American government and American political behavior in the Age of Jackson. *Knopf 2 vols $7.50, Ment, Vin, WoC.*

# D. International Affairs and Comparative Government

BURKS, *The Government of Japan.* See "India and the Far East," page 49.

CORBETT, PERCY E. 1892– *The Study of International Law* (1955). Defines international law as "law, perhaps, in the making," and shows why this is so. For those with some background, this small book does more than any other to clarify this rather murky subject upon which the future of all government may depend. *Random House 95¢.*

DEAN *The Nature of the Non-Western World.* See "India and the Far East," page 50.

*Everyman's United Nations* (7th ed 1963). A useful brief reference book on the organization, work, and history of the United Nations. Easily read, the book makes most readers realize how little they have known about the varied work of this unique organization. *United Nations $1.95.*

HARARI *The Government and Politics of the Middle East.* See "The Middle East and Africa," page 53.

KAHIN *Major Governments of Asia.* See "India and the Far East," page 45.

KENNAN, GEORGE F. 1904– *Realities of American Foreign Policy* (1954). A series of lectures by a profound expert on Soviet affairs. Kennan calls for less illusion and emotionalism, and for more realism, in dealing with international politics. *Princeton $2.75.*

MacDONALD, AUSTIN F. 1898–1962 *Latin American Politics and Government* (2nd ed 1954). A short but comprehensive text on the governments of Central and South America. *Crowell o.p.*

MILLS, C. WRIGHT 1916–1963 *The Causes of World War III* (1958). Deliberately provocative arguments about political responsibility at the top level. *Simon & Schuster $3.50, Bal, S&S.*

MORGENTHAU, HANS J. 1904– *Politics Among Nations* (3rd ed 1960). The classic defense of the power-centered view of international relations. Not hammock reading, the book argues powerfully for pursuing the national self-interest and suffering any consequences. *Knopf $10.*

NEUMANN, ROBERT G. 1916– *European and Comparative Government* (3rd ed 1960). Clear but high-level explanation of several governmental systems with some thoughtful comparisons of their relative values. *McGraw-Hill $8.75.*

PALMER *The Indian Political System.* See "India and the Far East," page 46.

## POLITICS

**RIENOW, ROBERT** 1907– *Introduction to Government* (2nd ed 1956). Simplified but neverthless sound introduction to the serious study of comparative political systems. *Knopf $5.75.*

**SCHUMAN, FREDERICK L.** 1904– *International Politics* (6th ed 1958). A clear, though somewhat advanced treatment of diplomatic machinery, international law, and historical forces in the struggle for power balances, this book explains why war is a built-in part of the national state system, not an exceptional occurrence. Explains more cogently than any other book why the world is continually "on the brink of war." *McGraw-Hill $7.75.*

**STOUT, HIRAM M.** 1905– *British Government* (1953). Sound general introduction to one of the most fascinating government systems. *Oxford $5.50.*

**TINKER, HUGH** *India and Pakistan* (1962). A brief, easily read political analysis by an observer who has spent much time in the area. *FAP.*

**WHITING, KENNETH R.** 1926– *The Soviet Union Today* (1962). A brief, balanced introductory survey of a subject about which we still have very limited information. *FAP.*

# 21. Economics

**RICHARD A. LESTER,** *Princeton University*

Economists analyze the processes by which man makes his living and the problems encountered in operating an industrial economy. It is enlightening to learn how production and employment are guided and what affects the wealth and material strength of nations. And one need not accept the Marxian theory of economic determination to recognize that the economy of a country directly influences not only the inhabitants' living standards but also individual freedom, the distribution of political power, and the country's culture.

The ramifications of economic inquiry are wide indeed, ranging from modern technology to human motives, from the individual's wage to the clash between capitalism and communism.

Within its broad scope, economics provides intellectual stimulus and interesting reading for persons with widely different tastes and talents. Some look upon economics as a science which is primarily theoretical and deals with uniformities and causal relationships. To others it is essentially an art which combines practical experience with policy recommendations for both industry and government. Almost every economist is, of course, a mixture of the pure and applied, part theoretician and part institutionalist.

For the general reader, the historical approach to economics provides a good introduction and orientation, combining theory and practice in a meaningful manner. One can begin with an engaging popular account of the ideas and lives of the great economists, such as Robert Heilbroner's *The Worldly Philosophers* or George Soule's *Ideas of the Great Economists*. Then he can move in two directions: read about the development of national economies in economic histories like those of Huberman and Ware, and get to know some of the classics in economics by men such as Adam Smith, Alfred Marshall, and John Maynard Keynes, perhaps along with their biographies.

Another approach would be to select a lively, provocative textbook like Samuelson's *Economics: An Introductory Analysis* as a jumping-off point. If Samuelson seems a bit difficult as a starter, simpler works like Soule's and Crane's might be sampled first. Thereafter, one could examine in more detail the operation and the economic institutions of American capitalism in books by Berle and Means, Galbraith, Hansen, and Ross.

Whether one starts with the historical or the modern approach, he will wish to read some recent works on the overriding issue of capitalism versus communism. Hoover and Wilcox *et al.* attempt to assess the strengths and weaknesses of different economic systems.

BERLE, ADOLPH A. 1895– and GARDINER C. MEANS 1896– *The Modern Corporation and Private Property* (1932). A thorough study of the ownership and control of huge corporations; almost a classic. *Macmillan $6.50.*

BEVERIDGE, WILLIAM H. 1879– *Full Employment in a Free Society* (1945). The foundations for a full-employment economy presented in simple language by a world-renowned political economist. *Norton o.p.*

BROWN, HARRISON 1917– *et al. The Next Hundred Years* (1957). A sometimes informed, sometimes superficial, often provocative projection of the human and raw materials requirements of the American economy in the next century. *Viking $4.75, Comp.*

BURNS, ARTHUR F. 1904– (ed.) *Wesley Clair Mitchell* (1952). Essays on the life and contributions of a great American student of business cycles who applied quantitative methods to social science. *Princeton o.p.*

CLARK, JOHN MAURICE 1884– *Economic Institutions and Human Welfare* (1957). A vigorous analysis of the relation of economic thought to the broad issues of modern life. *Knopf $4.*

CRANE, BURTON ?–1963 *Getting and Spending* (1956). A thoroughly understandable and wise, though sometimes oversimplified, analysis of basic economic problems. *Harcourt o.p.*

*Economic Report of the President* (January of each year). An invaluable annual compendium of current information on the functioning of our economy as well as a statement of the economic philosophy of the administration in power. Hard reading but required for those who would be informed. *U. S. Government Printing Office $1.25.*

GALBRAITH, JOHN KENNETH 1908– *American Capitalism* (1956). A challenging critique of current economic thought and an analysis of the economy based on the thesis that power begets countervailing offsets. *Houghton $3.50, SenEd.*

_____ *The Affluent Society* (1958). A stimulating antidote to conventional thinking about the operation and goals of our economy. *Houghton $5.*

HANSEN, ALVIN H. 1887– *A Guide to Keynes* (1953). A clear, helpful guide to Keynes' *General Theory* (see below). *McGraw-Hill $5.50, McGH.*

_____ *Economic Issues of the 1960's* (1960). A forceful statement of the main economic problems we face and an incisive blueprint for solving them. *McGraw-Hill $7.50, McGH.*

HAYEK, FRIEDRICH AUGUST VON 1899– *The Road to Serfdom* (1944). A tract opposing government controls and intervention, and favoring free markets. *Chicago $5.75, Phoen.*

HAZLITT, HENRY 1894– *The Failure of the "New Economics"* (1959). A systematic, vigorous, sometimes convincing attack on Keynes' *General Theory* (see below). *Van Nostrand $7.50.*

HEILBRONER, ROBERT L. 1919– *The Worldly Philosophers* (rev ed 1961). Lively, exciting accounts of the great economic thinkers and their doctrines. *Simon & Schuster $5, S&S.*

_____ *The Making of Economic Society* (1962). A lucid account of the stages in the development of European and American capitalism, placing today's problems in a historical framework. *Prentice-Hall $4.95.*

_____ *The Great Ascent* (1963). Readable, perceptive, informed, highly recommended account of the difficulties inherent in the economic development process and of their consequent political accompaniments. *Harper $4.*

HIRSCHMAN, ALBERT O. 1915– *The Strategy of Economic Development* (1958). A sophisticated and underdocumented analysis of the major problems of economic development; more understandable to the lay reader than Nurkse (see below). *Yale $5, Yale.*

HOOVER, CALVIN B. 1897– *The Economy, Liberty and the State* (1959). General analysis of the transformation of American capitalism and of the development of the Soviet economy and of the mixed economies of Western Europe by an expert on economic systems. *Twentieth Century Fund $5, Anch.*

HUBERMAN, LEO 1903– *Man's Worldly Goods* (1936). Skilled exposition of the development of economic institutions and doctrines by a socialist writer. *Harper $3.*

JARRETT, HENRY (ed.) *Perspectives on Conservation* (1958). A collection of essays of varying quality on America's natural resources and on planning their future use. *Johns Hopkins $5.*

KEYNES, JOHN MAYNARD 1883–1946 *Essays in Biography* (1933). Engaging biographical studies of the Cambridge economists—

Malthus, Marshall, Edgeworth—as well as of political figures of the 1920's. *Nort.*

———— *The General Theory of Employment, Interest and Money* (1936). The most influential economic tract published in this century. Although sparkling in spots, it is written primarily for economists, and the general reader may prefer to approach its logic through popular interpretations such as those by Beveridge or Hansen (see above). *Harcourt $6.*

MALTHUS *Essay on the Principle of Population.* See "The 18th Century," page 96.

MARSHALL, ALFRED 1842–1924 *Principles of Economics* (1890). A restatement of the whole structure of economic thought in the grand tradition and with a view toward economic progress. *Macmillan 2 vols $15.*

MYRDAL, GUNNAR 1898– *Rich Lands and Poor* (1957). Brief, lucid account of the differing economic requirements of the developed international economies as well as of those of nations seeking development. *Harper $3.*

NURKSE, RAGNAR 1907–1959 *Problems of Capital Formation in Underdeveloped Countries* (1953). The standard scholarly study on problems of economic development, more comprehensive but less comprehensible to the lay reader than Hirschman (see above). *Oxford $2.90.*

PHELPS, EDMUND S. 1933– (ed.) *The Goal of Economic Growth* (1962). A balanced selection of papers on the national goal of economic growth and on policies for achieving that aim. *Nort.*

———— (ed.) *Public Wants and Private Needs* (1962). A collection of views by prominent economists on the proper size and scope of government spending. *Nort.*

Rockefeller Brothers Fund. *The Challenge to America* (1958). An assessment of the economic and social problems that are confronting America during this decade, by a panel of 17 experts. *Dday.*

ROSS, ARTHUR M. 1916– *Trade Union Wage Policy* (1956). A realistic analysis of American unionism in political as well as economic terms. *California $3.*

SAMUELSON, PAUL A. 1915– *Economics: An Introductory Analysis* (5th ed 1961). The leading elementary text ever since first publication in 1948, skillfully written by an outstanding American economist. *McGraw-Hill $7.95.*

SCHUMPETER, JOSEPH A. 1883–1950 *Capitalism, Socialism, and Democracy* (3rd ed 1950). An economist-philosopher examines two competing economies, forecasting the supplanting of capitalism by socialism though favoring the former. *Harper $6, Torch.*

SCHWARTZ, HARRY 1919– *Russia's Soviet Economy* (2nd ed 1954). Comprehensive picture of the operation of the Soviet economy, based on discriminating use of factual material. *Prentice-Hall $10.35.*

SMITH *The Wealth of Nations.* See "The 18th Century," page 97.

SOULE, GEORGE 1887– *Introduction to Economic Science* (1948). A first reader written interestingly and clearly. *Ment.*

─────── *Ideas of the Great Economists* (1952). Concise, deft treatment of the panorama of economic thought from the Greeks to Keynes. *Ment.*

TAYLOR, OVERTON H. 1897– *Economics and Liberalism* (1955). Philosophical, thought-provoking essays on the foundations and limitations of classical liberalism. *Harvard $5.*

VEBLEN, THORSTEIN 1859–1929 *The Theory of the Leisure Class* (1899). Barbed, pungent study of the "conspicuous consumption" of the rich and near-rich. *ML, Ment.*

─────── *The Portable Veblen* (1948). Contains the first half of *Theory* and generous selections from other works, including essays on economists. *Vik, Vik-h.*

VERNON, RAYMOND 1913– *Metropolis: 1985* (1960). A thorough, fascinating, but deeply disturbing pioneer summary of the economic planning problems facing the Greater New York metropolitan area. *Harvard $5, Anch.*

WARE, NORMAN JOSEPH 1886– *Wealth and Welfare* (1949). Popular history detailing the background of American economic structures and issues. *Holt o.p.*

WILCOX, CLAIR 1898–, W. D. WEATHERFORD, JR. 1916–, and H. D. HUNTER 1921– *Economies of the World Today* (1962). A skillful assessment of the organization, development, and performance of the economies of Soviet Russia, Great Britain, Communist China, India, and the United States. *HB&W.*

## 22. Geography

**TRUMAN M. TALLEY,** *New American Library*

The science of geography arises from man's exploration of our planet. The desire for conquest, the search for trade routes, scientific curiosity, missionary efforts, or simply the love of travel and adventure—all have played their part in discovering the world we live in.

This process of discovery—still very much with us today—had its origins in prehistoric times. There is evidence, for example, that—about 5000 B.C.—trade routes had already been established to bring obsidian blades from Lake Van in Turkey and shells from the Red Sea to the tiny communities on the foothills around the Tigris and Euphrates Valley. Coastal and river transport was well developed by 3000 B.C. By 1400 B.C. the Phoenicians had opened trading stations throughout the Mediterranean; a thousand years later their maritime network included the west coast of Africa, the Atlantic coast of Europe, and even the Azores.

The maritime trade of the Greek city-states, the conquests of Alexander, and the rise of the Roman Empire each gave impetus to new explorations extending as far eastward as China. Then, for almost 1200 years after the collapse of the Roman Empire, the curtain came down, and in Christian Europe "the conception of the globe degenerated to that of a flat disc with Jerusalem at the center."

Only in northern Europe and the Moslem world was the spark of exploration kept alive. In the middle of the 9th century the Vikings discovered the North Cape, and about a century later Leif Ericson sailed to America. In the Middle East, Arabic geographers continued to develop the science of cartography. The geographic renaissance in Europe began in the 13th century with the Asian travels of Carpini and Marco Polo. Two centuries later the magnetic compass and the astrolabe led to exploration of the oceans and exploitation of the New World.

As the unknown became more and more known, geography began to take on a new dimension: systematic comparison of geographic regions. Many different kinds of geographies evolved—economic, political, social, biological, botanical, and physical. Recently the minds of men have turned to the ocean depths and outer space as new areas of exploration. Concepts of geography have been modified and extended—forerunners of a new comprehension of our planet as well as of the still unknown universe.

ANDERSON, WILLIAM R. 1921– *Nautilus 90 North* (1959). Full account of the first voyage under the top of the world. *World $3.95.*

ARCINIEGAS, GERMÁN 1900– *The Life and Times of A. Vespucci* (1955). A brilliant, scholarly reappraisal of the first explorer to proclaim that a new world had been found. *Knopf $5.75.*

AYRES, EUGENE 1891– and CHARLES A. SCARLOTT *Energy Sources: The Wealth of the World* (1952). Where sources of energy are found today, and where they may come from in the future. *McGraw-Hill o.p.*

BASCOM, WILLARD 1916– *A Hole in the Bottom of the Sea* (1961). The director of the Mohole project describes the first effort to penetrate the crust of the earth. *Doubleday $4.95.*

BATES, MARSTON 1906– *Where Winter Never Comes* (1952). The tropics interpreted in a "new and truer light." *Scrib.*

BETTEX, ALBERT 1906– *The Discovery of the World* (1960). A lucid, illuminating history of great explorers and what they found, from Marco Polo to recent Antarctic explorers. *Simon & Schuster $22.50.*

BROWN, LLOYD A. 1907– *The Story of Maps* (1949). An account of mapping and map makers throughout history. *Little $12.50.*

CALDER, RITCHIE 1906– *After the Seventh Day* (1961). Fascinating history of human geography. *Simon & Schuster $6.95, Ment.*

CARMER, CARL 1893– *The Hudson* (1939). Delightful collection of facts and legends. One of the generally excellent *Rivers of America* series, which now numbers about 50 titles. *Holt $6, HRW.*

CARSON, RACHEL 1907– *The Sea Around Us* (1951). The origin, history, and dynamic nature of the sea as the original home of life. *Oxford $5, Ment.*

# GEOGRAPHY

**COOK, JAMES** 1728–1779 *Captain Cook's Voyages of Discovery* (1954). Ed. by John Barrow. The three voyages of one of the world's greatest navigators. Cook sailed around the South Pole and for the first time scientifically charted the islands of the Pacific. *Evman-h.*

**COUSTEAU, JACQUES-YVES** 1910– and **FREDERIC DUMAS** *The Silent World* (1953). Pioneers of skin diving report their first undersea explorations. *Harper $5.50, PB.*

**CRESSEY, G. B.** 1896–1963 *Asia's Lands and Peoples* (2nd ed 1951). A geography of one-third of the earth and two-thirds of its people. *McGraw-Hill $9.50.*

———— *Land of the 500 Million.* See "India and the Far East," page 47.

**DARWIN** *The Voyage of the Beagle.* See "Biography," page 173.

**DEBENHAM, FRANK** 1883– *Discovery and Exploration* (1960). A Cambridge geographer and Antarctic explorer traces the expansion of the human race over the earth, as reconstructed by archaeologists and ethnologists, from primitive man to today. *Doubleday $9.95.*

**FARB, PETER** *Face of North America* (1963). A readable, thorough natural history of the North American continent. *Harper $6.50.*

**FINCH, VERNOR C.** 1883– et al. *Elements of Geography* (4th ed 1957). A valuable introductory text to the whole subject. *McGraw-Hill $8.50.*

**FISHER, WILLIAM B.** 1916– *The Middle East: A Physical, Social, and Regional Geography* (rev ed 1961). Peoples, human society, and historical geography of a complex and increasingly important region. *Dutton $9.75.*

**FREEMAN, O. W.** 1889– (ed.) *Geography of the Pacific* (1951). The Pacific Ocean, its climates, currents, and features; the Pacific islands; the peoples, resources, and industries. *Wiley $8.95.*

**GOTTMANN, JEAN** 1915– *A Geography of Europe* (3rd ed 1954). A leading presentation of newer ideas on human geography. *Holt $15.95.*

**GOUROU, PIERRE** 1900– and **E. D. LABORDE** *The Tropical World* (3rd ed 1961). A geographic analysis of a large, little understood area. *Wiley $4.*

**HAKLUYT** *Voyages.* See "In Tudor England," page 79.

**HARE, FREDERICK K.** 1919– *The Restless Atmosphere* (1953). An authoritative study of climatology designed for the general reader. *Hillary $2.50, Torch.*

**HERRMANN, PAUL** 1905– *Conquest by Man* (1954). How man, from the Stone Age to historical times, driven by curiosity, greed, accident, and ingenuity, discovered the lands and seas around him. *Harper $7.50.*

**HUNTINGTON, ELLSWORTH** 1876–1947 *Mainsprings of Civilization* (1945). Explains how human vitality was affected by climate, geography, migration, and the concept of kiths. *Ment.*

## GOOD READING

HURST, HAROLD E. 1880– *The Nile* (rev ed 1957). A general account of the river and the utilization of its waters, essential to the understanding of a huge section of Africa. *Dover $5.50.*

JAMES, PRESTON E. 1899– *Latin America* (3rd ed 1959). Covers South America, Mexico, Central America, and the islands of the Caribbean. *Odyssey $8.*

JONES, CLARENCE F. 1893– and GORDON G. DARKENWALD 1906–1961 *Economic Geography* (rev ed 1954). A clear discussion of the distribution of economic resources. *Macmillan $7.75.*

KIMBLE, G. H. T. 1908– and DOROTHY GOOD 1906– (eds.) *Geography of the Northlands* (1955). Systematic and regional geography including physiography, weather, climate, marine life, and people. *Wiley $9.25.*

LEBON, H. G. *An Introduction to Human Geography* (1952). Clear, readable survey of man's physical relationship to his environment. *Hillary $2.50.*

LEITHAUSER, JOACHIM G. 1910– *Worlds Beyond the Horizon* (1955). Engrossing narrative of exploration and discovery, from ancient times to the space age, emphasizing exploits in the Western Hemisphere. *Knopf $6.75.*

MORISON *Admiral of the Ocean Sea.* See "The Renaissance," page 75.

POLO *Travels.* See "The Middle Ages," page 67.

PRESCOTT *Conquest of Mexico* and *Conquest of Peru.* See "Latin America," page 62.

RUSSELL, RICHARD J. 1895– and FRED B. KNIFFEN 1900– *Culture Worlds* (1951). Regional human geography integrated with that of physical resources. *Macmillan $7.75.*

SPATE, OSKAR H. K. and W. GORDON EAST 1902– (eds.) *The Changing Map of Asia* (rev ed 1959). A good political geography. *Dutton $6.95.*

TREWARTHA, GLENN THOMAS 1896– *An Introduction to Climate* (3rd ed 1954). The best presentation of climatic factors. *McGraw-Hill $8.25.*

———— *Japan: A Physical, Cultural, and Regional Geography.* See "India and the Far East," page 49.

VAN VALKENBURG, SAMUEL 1891– and CARL L. STOTZ 1908– *Elements of Political Geography* (1954). Geographical factors having to do with national power. *Prentice-Hall $10.65.*

WHITE, C. L. 1897– and E. J. FOSCUE 1899– *Regional Geography of Anglo-America* (2nd ed 1954). A geography of the United States, Canada, and Alaska. *Prentice-Hall $8.95.*

WOOLRIDGE, S. W. 1900– and W. GORDON EAST 1902– *The Spirit and Purpose of Geography* (1915). Two distinguished geographers trace the evolution of the science and suggest lines of future development. *Hillary $2.50.*

# 23. Anthropology and Sociology

**H. WENTWORTH ELDREDGE,** *Dartmouth College*

Anthropology, broadly speaking, is the comparative study of the beliefs and practices of all human societies, past and present. Its roots can be found in the reports written by explorers, missionaries, and traders who, after travels to little-known parts of the world, recorded the great differences they discovered between their own ways of life and those of other peoples. Ibn Batura's descriptions of the peoples of West Africa, India, and China, and Marco Polo's reports on Asia are among the earliest such records available to the modern reader. In the 15th and 16th centuries, especially after the discovery of the New World, the number of these reports increased. Most, however, reflect the biases of their writers, who tended to be critical of the behavior of other peoples when it differed radically from their own.

Anthropologists have since discovered that what may seem to us unusual practices or beliefs are really only alternative ways in which different people have tried to solve real problems and answer basic questions that face men everywhere: how to cure illness, insure a good harvest, placate supernatural spirits, and so on. It was the search for understanding of the great variety of human practices and beliefs that shaped anthropology into a genuine "science of man." Anthropologists' studies of many different societies have contributed hundreds of specimens for analysis and comparison, and controlled comparisons among them have demonstrated the character and universal nature of the problems man faces, as well as the variety of solutions different societies have evolved to meet them.

The early studies of the anthropologists were confined

for the most part to small, little-known peoples who lacked writing and had a simple technology; in recent years, however, anthropologists have begun to study larger and more complex societies. In this growing interest in modern nations it is possible to see anthropology and sociology drawing closer together.

In addition to its interest in the "designs for living" of various contemporary peoples, anthropology also includes the study of archaeology, which attempts to reconstruct the history of ancient societies by examining their material remains; linguistics, which studies the growth and structure of language; and physical anthropology, which is concerned with man's biological diversity and physical evolution. Recently, studies of human personality in the context of the cultures which shape it have become important. Applied anthropology, another new direction in the science, deals with problems encountered in attempts to change and improve the lives of people in underdeveloped areas, problems resulting from the introduction of new tools, techniques, and values which may conflict with the traditional adjustments of the society.

Sociology, which has grown to its present position among the social sciences from roots in social philosophy, social reform, and social reportage, differs from its forerunners in the assumptions upon which it rests and in its manner of assembling and handling the evidence, rather than in the kind of problems it deals with. Much current sociological writing is factual and mundane rather than intuitive and idealistic; but it has the virtue of showing more clearly how our own and other social institutions are actually constituted, how they relate to one another, and how they operate through time.

Sociologists have not yet reached any final decision about the boundaries and content of their subject, but most would agree that organized human behavior, especially in literate societies, is the focus of their study. Such behavior may be that of a juvenile gang in a big city slum, an extended family in a village of India, a community of crofters in a distressed area of Scotland, or an upper-income group in a metropolitan suburb.

The sociologist's concern is to describe accurately and fully the human interactions and interrelationships which bind groups such as these into effective wholes. Although all of the basic institutions which together make up the life of a specific society—that is, economic, political, religious, familial, educational, etc.—are studied by sociologists in terms of their human and cultural components, in actual practice many parts of this material are normally left to specialists in other social sciences; and the intensive field investigations of preliterate cultures is still regarded as the proper province of anthropologists. But the time may well be near when one unified behavioral science of man may take the place of the separate efforts of four or five isolated and traditionally competitive social sciences; many sociologists already take this wholistic point of view. The integration of sociology and anthropology, now well advanced toward a common goal in both theories and methods, may presage future developments on a broader front.

Meanwhile, sociology continues to focus most of its attention upon aspects of the society and culture of modern, urban-industrial peoples and their problems. If the most important new fact of the past half-century is, as Julian Huxley suggests, "that the human species, for the first time in its history, has begun to take stock of its position in the world," then sociology has an important role in this stock-taking. The growth in size and complexity of contemporary societies creates new problems and underlines the indispensable need for wider public understanding of them. Sociological analysis (increasingly empirical and statistical) of urbanism, crime, industrial relations, population growth, minority group problems, and family organization—to name a few areas of effort—has added greatly to our deeper knowledge of the increasing intricacies of modern life.

ARON, RAYMOND 1905– *The Century of Total War* (1954). The world revolution of our time viewed by the brilliant Sorbonne sociologist and commentator for the Paris newspaper *Figaro*. Doubleday $5, Bea.

BARBER, BERNARD 1918– *Science and the Social Order* (1952). A sociological investigation of the role of science in society today. *Free Press $5, Collr.*

———— *Social Stratification* (1957). An objective treatment of the form and function of social class. *Harcourt $6.95.*

BELL, NORMAN W. 1928– and EZRA F. VOGEL 1930– (eds.) *A Modern Introduction to the Family* (1960). Various authorities write lucidly and interestingly on various aspects of the family. *Free Press $7.50.*

BENEDICT, RUTH 1887–1948 *Patterns of Culture* (1934). Probably the most influential book of recent years about primitive societies, focusing on the theory that cultural values are relative, not absolute. Three primitive cultures are described and contrasted for the light they throw on our own society. Illuminating on the relation between culture and personality. *Houghton $4, Ment, SenEd.*

BLAU, PETER 1918– *Bureaucracy in Modern Society* (1956). Excellent short introduction to this important characteristic of the managerial revolution. *SS.*

BOAS *Primitive Art*. See "Fine Arts," page 195.

CHASE, STUART 1888– *The Proper Study of Minkind* (rev ed 1956). An authoritative and extremely readable discussion of the principal social sciences—anthropology, sociology, social psychology, economics, politics—and their interrelations. *Harper $4.50, CN.*

CHILDE *What Happened in History*. See "History," page 219.

CHINOY, ELY 1921– *Sociological Perspective* (1954). A brief survey of the salient problems in sociology. *SS.*

COON, CARLETON S. 1904– *Story of Man* (1954). A stimulating description of early man and his society, and one of the best reviews of the Old and the New Stone Ages. *Knopf $8.*

DAVIE, MAURICE R. 1893– *Negroes in American Society* (1949). Still the most comprehensive and authoritative survey of the status of American Negroes from colonial times to the present. *McGraw-Hill $7.50.*

DE GRAZIA, SEBASTIAN 1915– *Of Time, Work and Leisure* (1962). Some new insights into the problems of free time (perhaps leisure) in an automated world of seeming overabundance. *Twentieth Century Fund $6, Anch.*

DRIVER, HAROLD E. 1907– *Indians of North America* (1961). An authoritative, readable introduction to the past and present of the Indian. *Chicago $10.95.*

DURKHEIM, EMILE 1858–1917 *Suicide* (trans. 1951). The classical empirical study which has set a model for present sociological research. *Free Press $6.*

ELKIN, FREDERICK 1918– *The Child and Society* (1960). Clear explanation of the socialization process—that is, how society recruits its new members. *SS.*

*The Exploding Metropolis* (1958). Ed. by the staff of *Fortune*. On the border line between city planning and sociology, this is an up-to-date presentation. *Doubleday $3.95, Anch.*

## ANTHROPOLOGY AND SOCIOLOGY

GALBRAITH *The Affluent Society*. See "Economics," page 236.

GARN, STANLEY M. 1922– *Human Races* (1961). A compressed and understandable exposition of the whole business of race, written from a biological viewpoint by a physical anthropologist. *C. C. Thomas $5.50.*

GOLDSCHMIDT, WALTER 1913– *Man's Way* (1959). A deceptively simple, actually brilliant, combination of the best theory in both sociology and anthropology. *Holt $3.25, World $4.*

GREER, SCOTT 1922– *The Emerging City: Myth and Reality* (1962). The best of the recent books on metropolitan urban areas from a sociological point of view. *Free Press $5.75.*

HEILBRONER, ROBERT L. 1919– *The Future as History* (1959). A brilliant projection of social, political, and economic trends on the world scene today—a glimpse into "the world revolution of our time." *Harper $4, Ever.*

HEIZER, ROBERT F. 1915– (ed.) *Man's Discovery of His Past* (1942). Original reports of history-making archaeological discoveries that were turning points in the study of prehistoric man. *Spec.*

HIMES, JOSEPH S. 1908– *Social Planning in America* (1954). What has been done and what remains to be done in social planning. *SS.*

HOEBEL, E. A. 1906– *The Law of Primitive Man* (1954). An introduction to the methods of legal control in primitive societies. *Harvard $5.50.*

HOLLINGSHEAD, A. B. 1907– *Elmtown's Youth* (1949). An illuminating study of problems of adolescence in a Midwest community, with special attention to its social class structure. *Wiley $5.50, SciEd.*

HOMANS, GEORGE C. 1910– *The Human Group* (1950). Comparative study of the structure and function of small groups, which form the basic unit of all societies. *Harcourt $7.75.*

HOWELLS, WILLIAM W. 1908– *The Heathens* (1948). Primitive religions as they express the fundamental unity of human religious experience. *Doubleday $4, NHL.*

HUNTER, EDWARD 1902– *Brainwashing* (1956). On the borderline between psychology and sociology, this is one of the best analyses of Pavlovian conditioning applied brutally to remake personality. *Bookmailer $5, Pyr.*

HUNTER, FLOYD *Community Power Structure* (1953). An analysis of who actually makes decisions in American urban society. *North Carolina $5, Anch.*

KLUCKHOHN, CLYDE 1905–1960 *Mirror for Man* (1949). A wonderfully warm and informative introduction to cultural anthropology. *McGraw-Hill $5, McGH, Prem.*

_____ and D. C. LEIGHTON 1908– *The Navaho* (1946). Describes the total culture of a contemporary American Indian. *Harvard $5, Anch.*

LA FARGE, OLIVER 1901–1963 *Laughing Boy* (1929). A novel describing a Navaho's struggle to maintain the integrity of his culture. *Houghton $4, PB, SenEd.*

LEE, ALFRED McCLUNG 1906– and ELIZABETH BRIANT LEE 1908– (eds.) *Social Problems in America* (rev ed 1955). Comprehensive collection of readings and interpretative essays on the whole spectrum of social problems. *Holt $5.50.*

LERNER, MAX 1902– *America as a Civilization* (1957). This awesome tome is the most complete and readable analysis of our society and all phases of its culture. *Simon & Schuster $12, S&S.*

LEWIS *Children of Sánchez.* See "Latin America," page 61.

LINTON, RALPH 1893–1953 *The Tree of Culture* (1955). Encyclopedic synthesis of the development of man's culture in time and space. *Knopf $9.75, Vin.*

LIPSET, SEYMOUR MARTIN 1922– *Political Man* (1960). An excellent analysis of the social basis of politics, the borderline material between sociology and political science. *Doubleday $4.95, Anch.*

_____ and REINHARD BENDIX 1916– *Social Mobility in Industrial Society* (1959). A definitive study of movement up and down the American class structure. *California $6, Calif.*

LYND, ROBERT S. 1892– and HELEN M. LYND 1897– *Middletown* (1929) and *Middletown in Transition* (1937). Classic pioneer studies of culture patterns in a typical American city (Muncie, Ind.) before and during the depression. *Harv.*

MALINOWSKI, BRONISLAW 1884–1942 *Crime and Custom in Savage Society* (1926). A subtle use of socio-psychological insights applied to the preliterate peoples of the Trobriand Islands. *Humanities Press $4, Lita.*

MAYER, KURT B. 1916– *Class and Society* (1955). Excellent brief survey of the phenomenon of social class in modern society. *SS.*

MEAD, MARGARET 1901– *Sex and Temperament in Three Primitive Societies* (1935). A series of studies concerned with the cultural definition of sex roles in different primitive societies. *AE, Ment.*

_____ *Male and Female* (1949). Biosocial survey of the differences between the sexes by a famous American anthropologist. *Morrow $5, Ment.*

_____ (ed.) *Cultural Patterns and Technical Change* (1953). Case studies of Western impact on societies in underdeveloped areas. *Columbia $2.50, Ment.*

MEERLOO, JOOST A. M. 1903– *The Rape of the Mind* (1956). An evaluation of new techniques, both bureaucratic and psychological, for thought control. *World $5, UL.*

MERTON, ROBERT K. 1910– et al. (eds.) *Sociology Today* (1959). A complete and reliable survey of the problems and prospects of contemporary sociology. *Basic Books $7.50.*

MILLIKAN, MAX 1913– and DONALD L. M. BLACKMER 1929– (eds.) *The Emerging Nations* (1961). One of the best studies of the social, political, and economic problems facing underdeveloped nations and those who would help them. *Little $4.50.*

MILLS, C. WRIGHT 1916–1962 *White Collar* (1951). The new

middle class of the late industrial society sharply delineated. *Oxford $6.50, GB.*

———— *The Power Elite* (1956). Expansion of the provocative thesis that the United States is increasingly controlled (albeit only semiconsciously) by a small, interlocking group of big generals, big politicians, and big businessmen. *Oxford $6.50, GB.*

MOORE, WILBERT E. 1914– *Economy and Society* (1955). Explains the complicated interrelationships between economics and sociology. *SS.*

MUMFORD, LEWIS 1895– *The City in History* (1961). After some questionable beginnings in shady anthropological theorizing, this book emerges as a magnificent story of urban society from its beginnings to the present. *Harcourt $11.50.*

OLMSTED, MICHAEL S. 1923–1960 *The Small Group* (1959). A sound, readable survey of this increasingly important area of sociology and adjunct to the managerial revolution. *SS.*

PACKARD, VANCE 1914– *The Hidden Persuaders* (1957). Explains in layman's language how American public opinion today is manipulated, especially by specialists in motivational research. *McKay $5.75, PB.*

———— *The Status Seekers* (1959). Colorful, challenging summary of the shifting American class pattern. *McKay $5.50, PB.*

PARKINSON *Parkinson's Law.* See "Politics," page 231.

PETERSEN, WILLIAM 1912– (ed.) *American Social Patterns* (1956). Excellent examples of modern sociological monographs on interracial housing, bureaucracy, politics, and union democracy in modern America. *Anch.*

PIGGOTT, STUART 1910– (ed.) *The Dawn of Civilization* (1962). A gorgeously illustrated definitive treatment of prehistory. *McGraw-Hill $28.50.*

REDFIELD, ROBERT 1897–1958 *The Little Community* (1955). A noted anthropologist suggests various ways of looking at the culture of peoples in small, technologically simple societies. *Chicago $4, Phoen.*

RIESMAN, DAVID 1909– *Individualism Reconsidered* (1954). Stimulating essays on various facets of modern life. *Free Press $7.50.*

————, NATHAN GLAZER 1923–, and REUEL DENNEY 1913– *The Lonely Crowd* (1950). Provocative study of the changing social character of the American people—from "inner-directed" to "other-directed." *Yale $7.50, Yale.*

SAPIR, EDWARD 1884–1939 *Language* (1921). A classic and viable treatment of man's primary device for "culture-building"—its sounds, grammatical processes and concepts, kinds of structures, and changes in the course of history. *Harv.*

SIMPSON, GEORGE 1908– *Man in Society* (1954). Argues very well the need for the wholistic approach (integration of all the social sciences) to the study of human behavior. *SS.*

SIMPSON, GEORGE E. 1904– and J. MILTON YINGER 1916– *Racial and Cultural Minorities* (1958). A sound analysis of prejudice and discrimination, which unhappily play a large part in American life. *Harper $8.*

SPECTORSKY, A. C. 1910– *The Exurbanites* (1955). How upper-bracket intellectuals and executives live in the outer suburbs of New York, written with a journalistic flair. *Lippincott $4.95.*

STEIN, MAURICE R. 1926– *The Eclipse of Community* (1960). The development of *anomie* and alienation among the inhabitants of our great urban manheaps; extremely wide-ranging and sensitive. *Princeton $6.*

SUMNER, WILLIAM GRAHAM 1840–1910 *Folkways* (1907). Classic study in comparative sociology, showing how manners, morals, and customs vary according to time and place. *Ginn $10, Dov, Ment.*

SYKES, GRESHAM 1922– *Crime and Society* (1956). A modern analysis of criminal behavior and the muddled way we attempt to "reform" criminals. *SS.*

WHITE, LESLIE A. 1900– *The Science of Culture* (1949). A group of essays dealing with such diverse subjects as origins of the incest taboo, social evolution, the role of the individual in society, and the origins of culture. *Farrar, Straus $6, Ever.*

WHYTE, WILLIAM F. 1914– *Industry and Society* (1946). Articles dealing with characteristics and problems of human relations in industry. *McGraw-Hill o.p.*

———— *Street Corner Society* (rev ed 1955). Intimate study of adolescent gangs in city slums. *Chicago $6.*

WHYTE, WILLIAM H., JR. 1917– *The Organization Man* (1956). Expansion of the thesis that in modern, big-business America the individual, lost in huge bureaucracies, slides into the relaxed pattern of a "team member" incapable of developing independent personality. *Simon & Schuster $5, Anch.*

WIENER, NORBERT 1894– *The Human Use of Human Beings: Cybernetics and Society* (rev ed 1954). Presents a new approach to understanding society through the analysis of communications. *Houghton $3.50, Anch.*

WILLIAMS, ROBIN M., JR. 1914– *American Society* (2nd ed 1960). One of the most incisive sociological studies of our culture available, indicating the contradictions between ideas and practice. *Knopf $6.50.*

WOOD, ROBERT C. 1923– *Suburbia* (1959). An analysis of society and politics on the characteristic fringes of our great urban sprawls, expertly written. *Houghton $4.50, HM.*

WRIGHT, CHARLES R. 1927– *Mass Communication* (1959). An important characteristic of modern society analyzed from a sociological position. *SS.*

WRIGHT, G. ERNEST 1907– (ed.) *Biblical Archaeology* (abr ed 1962). Up-to-date appraisal of Biblical history in the light of recent discoveries in the Near East. *Wmin.*

WRONG, DENNIS H. 1923– *Population and Society* (2nd ed 1956). A definitive consideration of the population problem from a sociological viewpoint in small, well-written compass. *SS.*

# 24. Language

## NORMAN C. STAGEBERG, State College of Iowa

It is language that has given man his humanity. With language man makes a permanent record of the knowledge and wisdom he has garnered, enabling the race to accumulate and build upon the lore of the past. With language he maintains intercourse with his fellow beings, explaining, questioning, cajoling—listening, answering, weighing. Thus language is the *sine qua non* of man's communal and intellectual life, pervading every activity that distinguished him from the lower animals. What aspect of human life, then, can be more worthy of study, both as a phenomenon to be understood and a skill to be cultivated?

Language study branches out into many fields. Some of these, like communications theory, acoustic phonetics, and generative grammar, are highly technical and are readily comprehensible only to the specialist. But apart from such technical fields, there remain many areas of language study that may be explored with profit and enjoyment by the intelligent layman. It is these areas, by and large, that are dealt with in the books listed below.

There is richness and variety here. The decipherment of ancient unknown tongues is explained, in its fascinating detail, by Chadwick and Cleator. Questions of everyday usage are competently answered in two of the most reliable books on the subject, by Bryant and the Evanses. Three books are devoted to picturesque and surprising word-histories—by Weekley, Evans, and Greenough and Kittredge—and numerous others give such information along the way. A peek into the science of linguistics is afforded by Hughes and Nida. The influence of language upon human behavior is taken up by Chase, Payne, and

Whyte. The development of our own lively American tongue is recounted by Marckwardt, Mencken, and Pyles. Descriptions of two kinds of English off the beaten track are presented by Randolph and Cassidy. And so on.

In short, here is a bookshelf of agreeable reading that will pleasure the reader's palate and kindle his mind.

ANDERSON, WALLACE L. 1917– and NORMAN C. STAGEBERG 1905– (eds.) *Introductory Readings on Language* (1962). Selected readings in nontechnical language in such areas as the nature of language, word meanings and changes, logic, metaphor, semantics, dialects, structural grammar, and usage. *Holt $3.50, HRW.*

AYER *Language, Truth and Logic.* See "Philosophy," page 208.

BRADDOCK, RICHARD 1920– (ed.) *Introductory Readings on the English Language* (1962). Has different selections from Anderson (above) and includes material on lexicography, punctuation, spelling, style, and rhetoric. *Prentice-Hall $2.95.*

BROWN, ROGER 1925– *Words and Things* (1958). Linguistics and psychology come together here in the new field of "psycholinguistics." The author summarizes a good deal of research as he discusses such topics as meaning, reading, speech analysis, phonetic symbolism, metaphor, persuasion, and propaganda. *Free Press $6.75.*

BRYANT, MARGARET 1900– (ed.) *Current American Usage* (1962). An authoritative guide to American usage, alphabetically arranged, based on the linguistic atlas collections of data and over 900 research studies. Especially useful for moot matters upon which current textbooks give inadequate or misleading information. *Funk & Wagnalls $5.*

CARROLL, JOHN B. 1916– *The Study of Language* (1953). A concise survey of the fields of linguistics, followed by chapters on the relation of linguistics to psychology, the social sciences, philosophy, education, and communication engineering. Lucid and thought-provoking. *Harvard $4.75.*

CASSIDY, FREDERIC G. 1907– *Jamaica Talk* (1961). A description of Jamaican English, known as Jamaican Creole, touching upon pronunciation and grammar but emphasizing the vocabulary— by a scholar who has spent a decade preparing a historical dictionary of this language. *St Martin's $6.75.*

CHADWICK, JOHN 1920– *The Decipherment of Linear B* (1958). The exciting account of the decipherment of the Minoan-Mycenaean B script, which revealed a form of Greek used in Crete and in Greece about 1400 B.C. Shows the light which documents in this tongue throw on the life of the period. *Cambridge $3.75, Vin.*

CHASE, STUART 1888– *The Power of Words* (1954). A popular and highly simplified account of many topics in semantics and

## LANGUAGE

communication. Part II considers applications of concepts in semantics. *Harcourt $3.95.*

CLEATOR, P. E. 1908– **Lost Languages** (1959). The story of the decipherment of writings in lost languages—such as Egyptian, Persian, and Hittite—and what we learn from these writings about the people who produced them. *Day $4.50, Ment.*

DAVIES, HUGH SYKES 1909– **Grammar Without Tears** (1951). A pleasantly written little book on various kinds of grammar, particular grammatical problems that bother the layman, and the relationship of grammar and style. *Day o.p.*

DIRINGER, DAVID 1900– **Writing** (1962). The origins and early history of writing systems of the world, ancient and modern, by a world authority on the subject; well illustrated. *Praeger $6.95.*

ESTRICH, ROBERT M. 1906– and HANS SPERBER 1885– **Three Keys to Language** (1952). Word taboos, speech communities, language change, and style—presented with fresh illustrative material. Shows the relationship of language to cultural and political history, religion, sociology, and psychology. *Holt o.p.*

EVANS, BERGEN 1904– **Comfortable Words** (1962). A miscellany of agreeable thumbnail essays on words, phrases, and idioms, and their origins and uses, with occasional ventures into questions of usage. *Random House $5.95.*

——— and CORNELIA EVANS *A Dictionary of Contemporary American Usage* (1957). Gives wider coverage than Bryant (see above), including many word distinctions, grammatical definitions, and nuances of connotation, as well as points of usage. *Random House $5.95.*

GOAD, HAROLD 1878–1956 **Language in History.** (1958). Develops the thesis that language and culture are so interdependent that their survival or decline depends on the loyalty of the speech community to a common purpose. *Pen.*

GREENOUGH, J. B. 1833–1901 and G. L. KITTREDGE 1860–1941 **Words and Their Ways in English Speech** (1901). The classic work on etymology and word ways, although some examples are now dated. The treatment is sound, the style readable, the matter fascinating, and the contents well indexed. *Bea, Macm.*

HALL, EDWARD T. 1914– **The Silent Language** (1959). The interrelatedness of patterns in culture and language, and the differences in these patterns among various ethnic groups. Highly original and free from anthropological jargon. *Doubleday $3.95, Prem.*

HALL, ROBERT A., JR. 1911– **Linguistics and Your Language** (1960). Basic concepts of language and linguistics explained for everyman with clarity and vigor by a top-flight linguist. *Anch.*

HUGHES, JOHN P. 1920– **The Science of Language** (1962). For the layman a brief and intelligible introduction to contemporary language study. Includes fundamental concepts about language, the history of language study, languages of the world, and structural linguistics. *Random House $6.95.*

JESPERSEN, OTTO 1860–1943 *Growth and Structure of the English Language* (1905, 1955). Concise history of English through the Renaissance, with emphasis on the contributions of other tongues to English. *Macmillan $2.50, Anch.*

MARCKWARDT, ALBERT 1903– *American English* (1958). Brief history of the development of our language in the United States by the director of the *Linguistic Atlas of the North-Central States* project. Includes chapter on linguistic atlas findings. "Reads like a novel," reports one young university student. *Oxford $4.50, Ox.*

MENCKEN, HENRY L. 1880–1956 *The American Language* (abr ed) (1963). The 4th ed. plus two supplements, skillfully abridged, updated, and edited by Raven I. McDavid, Jr. A treasure-house of information written with verve and punch. *Knopf $12.95.*

MYERS, L. M. 1901– *Guide to American English* (1959). This book gives a brief coverage of American usage and grammar in an individual and entertaining way. It is characterized by good sense and adheres to no single school of grammar. *Prentice-Hall $4.95.*

NICHOLS, RALPH G. 1907– and LEONARD A. STEVENS *Are You Listening?* (1957). The tremendous importance of effective listening in today's life and how one can improve one's listening competence. An informed book based on research and experience. *McGraw-Hill $4.95.*

NIDA, EUGENE A. 1914– *Linguistic Interludes* (1947). In a series of professor-student dialogues, Nida explains in a simple way some basic linguistic processes and concepts. *Summer Institute of Linguistics o.p.*

PARTRIDGE *Shakespeare's Bawdy*. See "In Tudor England," page 82.

PAYNE, STANLEY L. 1911– *The Art of Asking Questions* (1951). Valuable lessons about the effects of word-choice and wording, learned through the framing of questions for opinion polls. *Princeton $4.50.*

POTTER, SIMEON 1898– *Our Language* (1950). A horseback sketch of the history of English, followed by chapters on word creation, etymology, usage, slang, personal and place names, British and American English, and the like. *Pen.*

PYLES, THOMAS 1905– *Words and Ways of American English* (1952). A scholarly and informal history of American English, written with grace and wit, and emphasizing vocabulary. *Random House $3.95.*

RANDOLPH, VANCE 1892– and GEORGE P. WILSON 1888– *Down in the Holler* (1953). Fascinating, and in spots hilarious, description of the language of the Ozarks. *Oklahoma $5.*

SAPIR *Language*. See "Anthropology and Sociology," page 249.

WEEKLEY, ERNEST 1865–1954 *The Romance of Words* (1912). A collection of word histories under captions like words and places, phonetic accidents, folk etymology, doublets, homonyms, and family names. *Dov.*

## LANGUAGE

**WHYTE, WILLIAM H., JR.** 1917– and the editors of *Fortune*
*Is Anybody Listening?* (1952). An informative, fascinating, highly
readable report on the role played in business by language,
symbols, myths, and status. *Simon & Schuster o.p.*

# 25. Psychology

PAUL C. OBLER, *Orange State College*

One of the most characteristic and influential accomplishments of the last half century of our scientific age is the development of a science of human behavior. What man knew about himself in his prescientific past he gleaned from introspection, random observation, and homely reasoning. Such knowledge he frequently projected—often with profundity—into his philosophy, arts, and religion. But only when theory could be checked against facts— systematized facts—could the scientific study of the mental activity and personality of man— a genuine psychology— be born. This genuine psychology builds upon physiology, and it extends its investigations into the borderlands of sociology, anthropology, politics, and even economics. Man is a physiological creature of sensation, perception, memories, thought, and emotions; but he is also a social being with habits of love and hate, work and play, creation and destruction, worship and art. Psychology's tremendous range of concern today has resulted in a bewildering variety of conflicting theories, specialized fields, and professional activities.

The literature of psychology is equally various and much of it is published in inexpensive paperbound editions. The newcomer needs to pick his way carefully among the genuine classics, the useful guides, the esoteric and statistics-laden monographs, and the oversimplified potboilers dispensing "psychology to the millions." The list of recommended books that follows is divided into four sections that cover the matter of psychology—with some overlappings, of course. The reader should begin by sampling books from each section in turn. Those in the first section will provide a general view of the subject, including its historical development and the contributions of its great pioneering figures, the founders of the early "schools." The general theories of the nature of man advanced by these schools—the Structuralists, Functionalists, Psychoanalysts, Behaviorists, and Gestaltists—are sampled in section two. Each school tends to be more interested in some problems than in others. Gestalt psychology, for instance, focuses on perception, while psychoanalysis is especially concerned with motivation. Contemporary psychologists are usually not rigid adherents of any one school; rather they are eclectics who use the theories and methods of a particular school because they are interested in certain problems.

The reader can thus begin to learn about modern psychology by seeing what psychologists are interested in and what they do with those interests. Sections three and four contain books about significant general and applied fields of psychological interest. That there is some overlap should not be disturbing; psychology is a fast-growing and dynamic enterprise. Often the procedures of its specialists will seem only remotely connected: what has an interest in glands as reacting mechanisms to do with the psychology of occupational adjustment or of rote learning? But if the reader will remember that psychology is by definition the science of human behavior, he will appreciate both its diversity of activities and its common theme. That theme is that nothing natural to man should be foreign to him; it is a modern application of the deceptively simple but profoundly difficult ancient admonition, "Know thyself."

## A. General Psychology

CROW, LESTER D. 1897– and ALICE CROW 1894– (eds.) *Readings in General Psychology* (1954). Almost 200 short selections provide a good broad introduction to the field, covering everything from the nature and scope of psychology to occupational adjustment. *B&N.*

DREVER, JAMES 1873–1950 *A Dictionary of Psychology* (1952).

An inexpensive collection of 4,500 generally excellent definitions. *Pen.*

DUSSETER, R. F. and J. HENDERSON *Introducing Psychology* (1962). Admittedly oversimplified in its handling of some concepts, this book written for teen-agers nevertheless provides a nontechnical, sympathetic introduction to the role of psychology in everyday life. *Pen.*

ENGLISH, HORACE B. 1892– and AVA C. ENGLISH *Comprehensive Dictionary of Psychological and Psychoanalytical Terms* (1958). A more detailed and comprehensive book than Drever (see above). *McKay $10.75.*

EYSENCK, H. J. 1916– *Uses and Abuses of Psychology* (7th ed 1962). Controversial in its evaluations but freighted with useful information on intelligence testing, psychotherapy, the roots of prejudice, abnormal behavior, and social attitudes. *Pen.*

HAHN, JOHN F. 1924– *An Introduction to Psychology* (1962). A concise, balanced, clearly written, intelligently organized general introduction. *CCG.*

HAVEMANN, ERNEST *The Age of Psychology* (1957). This little book, based on Havemann's articles on psychology, psychiatry, and psychoanalysis for *Life*, will be useful to anyone coming to the field completely fresh. *BC.*

ROBACK, A. A. 1890– *History of Psychology and Psychiatry* (1961). An encyclopedic compendium on the main psychological figures and schools from Aristotle to the present day. It tends, however, to include persons of minor importance and to limit the space devoted to major contributors. *Philosophical Library $7.50, Ctdl.*

# B. Psychological Theories

ADLER, KURT A. 1905– and DANICA DEUTSCH 1890– (eds.) *Essays in Individual Psychology* (1959). Some 50 psychiatrists and psychologists represent various contemporary applications of Alfred Adler's psychology, particularly his concepts of "inferiority feeling," "life style," and man's primarily social orientation. *Ever.*

FREUD, SIGMUND 1856–1939 *A General Introduction to Psychoanalysis* (1960). Freud's 28 introductory lectures should be the reader's first encounter with Freud. *Black, WSP.*

———— *A General Selection from the Works* (1957). Ed. by John Rickman. Groups his writings under convenient headings and moves from the earliest to the latest materials. *Tudor $5, Anch.*

HALL, CALVIN S. 1909– *A Primer of Freudian Psychology* (1954). This little book offers a lucid, nontechnical account of Freud's theories and is intended specifically for the beginning reader. *World $2.50, Ment.*

## PSYCHOLOGY

JAMES, WILLIAM 1842–1910 *Psychology: The Briefer Course* (1961). Ed. by Gordon Allport. Short of studying James' pioneer but long *Principles of Psychology*, the reader can get a good introduction through this book. *Collr, Torch.*

JONES *Life and Work of Sigmund Freud.* See "Biography," page 174.

JUNG, C. G. 1875–1961 *Modern Man in Search of a Soul* (1933). The basic introduction to Jung's analysis of the problems of contemporary psychological man. *Harcourt $5.75, Harv.*

KOHLER, WOLFGANG 1887– *Gestalt Psychology* (1947). The fundamental text of the Gestaltists and required reading for any serious student. *Black, Ment.*

MARCUSE, HERBERT 1898– *Eros and Civilization* (1956). Difficult, but immensely rewarding to anyone who wishes to explore the philosophical implications of Freudian theory. *Beacon $3.95, Vin.*

MASLOW, ABRAHAM H. 1908– *Toward a Psychology of Being* (1962). An exciting, wonderfully wise book presenting the new "third" force in psychological theory. Freudian psychology is based upon the neurotic personality; hence, it tends to identify health as safety. By using the "peak experiences" of psychologically healthy people as a foundation, the "third force"—drawing from the existentialists and from such people as Jung, Fromm, Horney, and Allport—evolves a scientifically based psychology in which growth and real self-actualization become possible. *IB.*

MAY, ROLLO 1909– (ed.) *Existential Psychology* (1961). Contends that no human being can be explained solely in terms of any of the usual psychological methodologies that focus on the *why* or *how* of a problem. *PP.*

MULLAHY, PATRICK 1912– *Oedipus: Myth and Complex* (1948). Analyzes the Sophocles play and gives a concise review of the development of psychoanalytic theory from the late 19th century to Horney, Sullivan, and Fromm. *Ever.*

NELSON, BENJAMIN 1911– (ed.) *Freud and the Twentieth Century* (1957). The pervasive influence of Freud on our ways of thinking and feeling are nowhere more convincingly demonstrated than in this centenary volume contributed to by social critics, theologians, and literary and art critics. *Peter Smith $3.50, Mer.*

PROGOFF, IRA *Jung's Psychology and Its Social Meaning* (1953). An excellently written study summarizing Jung's theories and interpreting their significance for the social sciences. *Ever.*

PUNER, HELEN WALKER *Freud: His Life and His Mind* (2nd ed 1961). A popular introduction to Freud by a writer who is more critical of his contributions than is Jones (see "Biography," page 174). *Dell.*

RANK, OTTO 1884–1939 *Beyond Psychology* (1941). Students of psychology who have a sophisticated interest in the social sciences as well will find fascinating this study that argues that the man-made supernatural world view, as projected in religion and reflected in the arts, gives meaning to the brute facts of biological and social existence. *Dov.*

WATSON, JOHN B. 1878–1958 *Behaviorism* (rev ed 1958). Watson's psychology bridges the distance between the study of animal behavior and the study of human behavior. This basic text is required reading for the advanced reader. *Chicago $5, Phoen.*

WAY, LEWIS *Adler's Place in Psychology* (1962). A fine general introduction to Adlerian psychology. *Collr.*

WELLS, HARRY K. 1911– *Ivan P. Pavlov* (1956). A sympathetic account of one of the fathers of contemporary psychology, whose studies on conditioned reflexes provided the basis for the development of brainwashing techniques. *International $3.50, NWP.*

# C. General Fields

BIRNEY, ROBERT C. 1925– and RICHARD C. TEEVAN 1919– (eds.) *Instinct* (1961). The selections, ranging from William James to recent proponents of instinct theory, provide a good cross-section of the primary literature of instinct. *IB.*

———— *Measuring Human Motivation* (1962). Essays on contemporary methods of measuring human motivation. *IB.*

CANDLAND, DOUGLAS K. 1934– (ed.) *Emotion: Bodily Change* (1962). A good set of selections introducing the reader to an enduring problem in psychology—what is emotion and how can it be measured? *IB.*

FARNHAM, MARYNIA F. 1899– *The Adolescent* (1951). Scholarly, up-to-date information on adolescent psychology written on a mature but nontechnical level. *Harper $4, Collr.*

FROMM, ERICH 1900– *Man for Himself* (1947). A leading current thinker argues persuasively for his own semi-Freudian interpretation of human nature. *Holt $3.75.*

GUTHRIE, EDWIN R. 1886–1959 *The Psychology of Human Conflict* (1938). A stimulating attempt to explain behavior in terms of a theory of associative learning encompassing all personality development; for advanced students only. *Peter Smith $4.25, Bea.*

HADFIELD, J. A. 1882– *Childhood and Adolescence* (1962). A well-written, college-level study of the subject. *Pen.*

HARRIS, T. L. 1910– and W. E. SCHWAHN 1916– (eds.) *Selected Readings on the Learning Process* (1961). Excellent essays by leading figures in the area; especially useful for teacher training. *Ox.*

HORNEY, KAREN 1885–1952 *Our Inner Conflicts* (1945). Sane, hopeful discussion of man's capacity and desire to be a decent human being and of the neuroses which arise from disturbed relationships. *Norton $4.50.*

KLEIN, MELANIE *The Psychoanalysis of Children* (1960). A report of pioneer work in child analysis, describing in detail the author's unique technique. *Hillary $5, Ever.*

LINTON, RALPH 1893–1953 *The Cultural Background of Personality* (1945). Later studies of culture and personality have been built on Linton's pioneer work. *Appl.*

McCARY, J. L. 1919– (ed.) *Psychology of Personality* (1959). Clear expositions of the six main approaches to personality now current. *Ever.*

RAPAPORT, DAVID 1911–1960 *Emotions and Memory* (3rd ed 1950). A solid work, integrating material from different languages and frames of reference, on the role of emotions in remembering and forgetting. *International Universities Press $4, SciEd.*

SCHNEIDER, DANIEL E. 1907– *The Psychoanalyst and the Artist* (1954). A useful antidote to the popular myth of the artist as a disturbed neurotic. *International Universities Press $4, Ment.*

STERN, KARL 1906– *The Third Revolution* (1954). Argues brilliantly and forcefully that the factual observations of psychoanalysis are compatible with religion, and that the great task of our age is the integration of the scientific and Christian ideas of man. *Harcourt $4, Im.*

SULLIVAN, HARRY STACK 1892–1949 *The Psychiatric Interview* (1954). Illuminating on what is involved. *Norton $6.50.*

VERNON, M. D. 1901– *The Psychology of Perception* (1962). A nontechnical outline of the psychological processes involved in our visual perception of things around us—shape, color, movement, space relationships. *Pen.*

WALLACE, ANTHONY F. D. 1923– *Culture and Personality* (1961). A book for initiated readers, explaining the culture-and-personality system and giving a thorough review and cogent critique of current work in this interesting field. *SA.*

WHITING, JOHN W. 1908– and IRVIN CHILD 1915– *Child Training and Personality* (1953). A provocative study of the extent to which and the ways in which the personality processes in individuals determine the integration of their culture. *Yale $5.50, Yale.*

# D. Applied Fields

ADAMS, JAMES F. 1927– *Problems in Counseling* (1962). Designed as a text for counselor training, the book discusses typical problems faced in educational, vocational, and personal counseling. *Macm.*

BROWN, J. A. C. 1911– *The Social Psychology of Industry* (1954). A lively account of challenging issues paramount in industrial relations. *Pen.*

KARN, HARRY W. 1907– and B. VON HALLER GILMER 1909–
(eds.) ***Readings in Industrial and Business Psychology*** (2nd ed 1962). A good selection covering organizational behavior, engineering psychology, communications, and the psychology of perception. *McGraw-Hill $6.95.*

MEARNS, HUGHES 1875– ***Creative Power, the Education of Youth in the Creative Arts*** (2nd rev ed 1958). Mearns' pioneer experiments in tapping the creative springs of children caused a minor revolution in the nation's schools. *Dov.*

PINTNER, RUDOLF 1884–1942 *et al.* ***Educational Psychology*** (5th ed 1956). Well-organized and concisely written book covering all aspects of educational psychology from the natural equipment for growth to the psychology of teaching. *B&N.*

# 26. Biological Sciences

## PAUL SHEPARD, Knox College

The scope of biology can be truly defined only in broad terms as the history of the earth and all its life—past, present, and future. Any definition of lesser scope becomes narrow and academic and fails utterly to convey the majestic sweep of the subject in time and space, embracing all that has made man what he is, and holding a foretaste of what he may yet become. For it has dawned upon scientists in recent years that neither man nor any other living creature may be studied or comprehended apart from the world in which he lives; that such restricted studies as the classification of plants and animals or descriptions of their anatomy and physiology (upon which the early biologists necessarily focused their attention) are but one small facet of a subject so many-sided, so rich in beauty and fascination, and so filled with significance that no informed reader can neglect it.

In the truest sense, there is no separate literature of biology or of any science. Knowledge of the facts of science is not the prerogative of a small number of men, isolated in their laboratories, but belongs to all men, for the realities of science are the realities of life itself. We cannot understand the problems that concern us in this, our particular moment of time, unless we first understand our environment and the forces that have made us what we are, physically and mentally.

Biology deals with the living creatures of the living earth. Pleasure in color, form, and movement, awareness of the amazing diversity of life, and the enjoyment of natural beauty are part of man's heritage as a living creature. Our first conscious acquaintance with the subject should come, if possible, through nature—in fields and forests and on the shore; secondarily, and by way of amplification and verification, we should then explore its laboratory aspects. Some of the most gifted and imaginative biologists have first approached their subject through the medium of sensory impression and emotional response. The most memorable writings—though they be addressed to the intellect—are rooted in man's emotional reaction to that life stream of which he is a part: the great naturalists such as Hudson and Thoreau have valid places in one's reading in biology.

As the frontiers of science expand, there is inevitably an increasing trend toward specialization, in which all the mental faculties of a man or group of men are brought to bear upon a single aspect of some problem. Thus, some biologists fix their attention upon certain groups or parts of organisms: mycology (funguses), virology (viruses), and neurology (nervous systems); and others upon biological structure or process: anatomy (internal parts), morphology (external form), and genetics (inheritance). But there is fortunately a counter tendency, which links different specialists together to work in cooperation. Oceanographic expeditions commonly include biologists of various kinds, chemists, physicists, geologists, and meteorologists —so diverse are the problems presented by one aspect of the earth's surface. Atomic physicists, by discovering that radioactive elements in fossils are minerals which disintegrate at a rate that can be determined, have provided biologists with a tool that has already revolutionized our concept of the age of the earth and permits a far more accurate approach than ever before to the problem of the evolution of man. Chemists and geneticists, by joining forces, are solving the riddle of the gene and the actual means by which it produces hereditary characteristics.

Only with the 20th century has biological thought been focused on ecology, or the relation of the living creature to its environment. Awareness of ecological relationships is—or should be—the basis of modern conservation programs, for it is useless to attempt to preserve a living species unless the kind of land or water it requires is also preserved. So delicately interwoven are the relationships that when we disturb one thread of the community fabric we alter it—perhaps imperceptibly, perhaps so drastically that destruction follows.

If we have been slow to develop the general concepts of ecology, we have been even more tardy in recognizing the facts of the ecology and conservation of man himself. At last awareness is growing that man, far from being the overlord of all creation, is himself part of nature, subject to the same cosmic forces that control all other life. Man's future welfare and probably even his survival depend upon his learning to live in harmony, rather than in combat, with these forces.

The books listed below reflect the richness and diversity of biology. Any one of them can lead to even wider vistas that the reader, according to his taste, may explore through still other books.

ADAMSON, JOY *Born Free* (1960). A delightful narrative of the rearing of Elsa, an African lion, showing the limits to which this animal can modify its behavior in a human environment. *Pantheon $4.95, Macf.*

ALLEN, DURWARD L. 1910– *Our Wildlife Legacy* (rev ed 1962). A clear, forceful account of wildlife as a natural resource and of the principles of conservation. *Funk & Wagnalls $6.50.*

ARDREY, ROBERT 1908– *African Genesis* (1961). A speculative history of the origin and development of man's social behavior, based on the study of other animals. *Atheneum $6.95, Delta.*

ASIMOV, ISAAC 1920– *The Wellsprings of Life* (1960). A popular summary of man's knowledge of the origin and development of life—of cell structure, biochemistry, regeneration, evolution, etc. *Abelard $3.75, Sig.*

ATKINSON, DONALD TAYLOR 1874–1959 *Magic, Myth, and Medicine* (1956). Clear, dramatic account of pioneering efforts in man's struggle to eliminate disease and prolong life. *Prem.*

BATES, MARSTON 1906– *The Forest and the Sea* (1960). Elementary but fascinating introduction to animal ecology. *Random House $3.95, Ment.*

BEEBE, WILLIAM 1877–1962 *High Jungle* (1949). The marvelously interwoven life of a tropical jungle, with its strangeness and beauty, re-created by a gifted naturalist. *Duell $6.*

BERRILL, NORMAN J. 1903– *Man's Emerging Mind* (1955). A fresh, thought-provoking discussion of man's development and evolution, with speculation on his future. *Dodd $4, AE, Prem.*

———— *You and the Universe* (1958). The nature of the universe and of life, and the interrelations between man and outer space. *Dodd $3.50, Prem.*

BUDDENBROCK, WOLFGANG VON 1884– *The Senses* (1958).

Detailed and illustrated description of the anatomy and function of the major sense organs. *Michigan $4.50, AAS*.

CARSON, RACHEL 1907– *The Sea Around Us.* See "Geography," page 240.

———— *Silent Spring* (1962). A controversial and influential study of the deleterious effects of insecticides, fallout, industrial poisons, etc., on the balance of nature. *Houghton $5, Crest*.

CHEESMAN, EVELYN 1881– *Insects* (1953). Insect habits, activities, and relationships described clearly and in attractive style. *Peter Smith $3.75, AE*.

CRISLER, LOIS *Arctic Wild* (1958). Written with beauty, honesty, and rare perception, this book is almost unique in its picture of one of the few true wildernesses remaining on earth. *Harper $4.95*.

DARLING, FRANK FRAZER 1903– *Wild Life in an African Territory* (1960). Narrative of a trip and a perceptive account of the ecology and threatened extinction of the large animals of Rhodesia. *Oxford $4*.

DARWIN, CHARLES 1809–1882 *The Origin of Species* (1859) and *The Descent of Man* (1871). The basic writings of Darwin now available in one volume. *MLG*.

———— *Voyage of the Beagle.* See "Biography," page 173.

DUNN, L. C. 1893– and THEODOSIUS DOBZHANSKY 1900– *Heredity, Race, and Society* (rev ed 1952). Group differences and how they arise; influences of heredity and environment on mankind. *Ment*.

EISELEY, LOREN C. 1907– *The Immense Journey* (1957). Exploration of evolutionary events important to the emergence of man and the natural world in which he developed. *Random House $3.50, Vin*.

HASKINS, CARYL P. 1908– *Of Societies and Men* (1951). Important scholarly discussion of the relationships between man the animal and man the "capstone of creation." *Comp*.

HUDSON, W. H. 1841–1922 *The Best of W. H. Hudson* (1949). Ed. by Odell Shepard. A sampling of the writings of a great naturalist, in whose words the world of biology comes to life. *Dutton $5*.

HUSSEY, RUSSELL C. 1888– *Historical Geology* (2nd ed 1947). Describes the changing shapes of continents and seas throughout geologic time, with account of the life characteristic of each period. *McGraw-Hill $7.50*.

HUXLEY, JULIAN 1887– *Man in the Modern World* (1948). Thirteen philosophic essays by a distinguished biologist on such topics as the uniqueness of man as an animal, climate and human history, eugenics and society. *Ment*.

HYLANDER, CLARENCE J. 1897– *The World of Plant Life* (2nd ed 1956). Readable, comprehensive, illustrated survey of plant life from the simplest to the most complex. *Macmillan $10.95*.

JONES, HAROLD SPENCER 1890–1960 *Life on Other Worlds* (1954). Pictures the universe in terms of modern astronomy and

# BIOLOGICAL SCIENCES

concludes that there are other worlds where conditions necessary for life may exist. *Ment.*

KRUTCH, JOSEPH WOOD 1893– **The Voice of the Desert** (1955). The extraordinary ways life meets the demands of the desert environment. The author's philosophic conclusions are significant for all life in all surroundings. *Sloane $3.75.*

LA BARRE, WESTON 1911– **The Human Animal** (1954). Speculative account of the primate and primitive origins of many biological and social traits commonly regarded as uniquely human. *Chicago $6.75, Phoen.*

LORENZ, KONRAD Z. 1903– **King Solomon's Ring** (1952). A delightful guide to understanding and keeping animals, mixed with original observations of social behavior. *Crowell $4.95, AE.*

MILNE, LORUS J. 1910– and MARJORIE J. MILNE 1914– **The Balance of Nature** (1960). Examples of interrelationships and chain reaction in nature, indicating how man's oversimplified "control" of nature may backfire. *Knopf $5.*

MOORE, RUTH 1908– **Man, Time, and Fossils** (rev ed 1961). Absorbing story of how the concepts of man's evolution have developed, from Lamarck and Darwin down to atomic-age methods of dating the past. *Knopf $6.95.*

MORGAN, ANN H. 1882– **Field Book of Ponds and Streams** (1930). A standard guide to fresh-water biology. *Putnam $5.*

———— **Field Book of Animals in Winter** (1939). Describes the adaptations to winter life made by a great variety of creatures. *Putnam $5.*

OSBORN, FAIRFIELD 1887– **Our Plundered Planet** (1948). Effectively presents the thesis that if man continues to prey on nature, nature will destroy him. *Little $3.75, Little.*

———— **The Limits of the Earth** (1953). A study of increasing populations set against the decline of the world's natural resources. *Little $3.75.*

PEATTIE, DONALD CULROSS 1898– **A Natural History of the Trees of Eastern and Central North America** (1950). By writing engagingly of the habits and characteristics of all the common trees, the author makes them more easily recognized and remembered. *Houghton $6.*

PORTMANN, ADOLF 1897– **Animals as Social Beings** (1961). A natural history of animal groups, particularly the instincts and learned behavior bringing about pair and herd formation. *Viking $6.*

RAYMOND, PERCY E. 1879–1952 **Prehistoric Life** (1950). Readable, well-illustrated survey of the forms of life that preceded man. Explains the role of environment in evolution. *Harvard $6.*

*Scientific American*, Editors of **Twentieth-Century Bestiary** (1955). Samples the curious and wonderful inventions of life: flight, navigation, parasitism, social organization. *S&S.*

———— **The Physics and Chemistry of Life** (1955). Current views on such topics as the origin of life, structure of the protein molecule, chemical basis of transmission of hereditary characteristics. *S&S.*

_____ *Plant Life* (1957). Good background reading, well illustrated, on the chemistry and genetics behind botany. *S&S*.

SEWELL, ELIZABETH 1919– ***The Orphic Voice*** (1960). An investigation of the relationship between biology and poetry, using the myth of Orpheus as the connecting link. *Yale $7.50*.

SINNOTT, EDMUND W. 1888– ***Biology of the Spirit*** (1955). An eminent biologist finds a basis for human aspirations and "the reality of the spirit of man" in the properties of protoplasm. *Comp*.

SNIVELY, WILLIAM DANIEL 1911– ***The Sea Within*** (1960). An introduction to many aspects of human physiology focused on the body fluids as the site of life processes and a heritage from the sea. *Lippincott $3.95*.

STORER, JOHN H. 1888– ***The Web of Life*** (1953). The balance of nature and the vital relation of living things to their environment, expressed clearly and simply for the layman. *Devin-Adair $3.50, Sig*.

TEALE, EDWIN WAY 1899– ***Adventures in Nature*** (1952). A delightful introduction to the literature of earth, sea, and sky, living things, and man's place in nature—through 150 selections from nature classics by Hudson, Thoreau, Muir, and others. *Dodd $5, AE*.

THOREAU ***Walden***. See "Biography," page 176.

VOGT, WILLIAM 1902– ***People! Challenge to Survival*** (1960). A summary of information on the exploding human population, indicating the possible world and human destruction it may bring. *Sloane $4.50, Macf*.

WORTH, C. BROOKE 1908– and ROBERT K. ENDERS 1899– ***The Nature of Living Things*** (1955). A lucid introductory account of the plant and animal life of the earth, with discussions of evolution, genetics, conservation, etc. *SigK*.

ZINSSER, HANS 1878–1940 ***Rats, Lice and History*** (1935). Absorbing story of the interrelations of insects, disease, and social evolution. *Little $6, Ban*.

For those who wish to observe nature at first hand, two excellent series of guide books are available: the ***Field Book Series*** (*Putnam $3.50 up*) and the ***Field Guide Series*** (*Houghton $4.50–4.95*).

# 27. Physical Sciences and Mathematics

PALMER W. TOWNSEND, *Air Reduction Company*

Fundamentally, the story of science—of its role in the biography of man—is the fascinating tale of the men and forces that have shaped our physical environment to meet our changing human needs. Both science and technology trace their roots to the earliest civilizations. The builders of Stonehenge, the pyramids, and the Incan temples had come a long way from the first man who picked up a stone and flung it at a charging beast.

By the 6th century B.C., freed from the dead weight of custom and ritual fear, and freshly motivated by mercantile needs for precision in weighing and counting and for better ways to manufacture and transport, the Ionian Greeks inaugurated a period of flourishing science and technology. But the Greek flair for hypothesizing far outstripped their skill at practical application, just as the Roman bias in favor of making things work stifled curiosity to know. By the Middle Ages, a return to a decentralized agrarian economy eliminated the need for technological progress. With the Renaissance, when science underwent a remarkable flowering, both merchants and scholars explored new roads, developed new orientations, and created new processes while they exchanged goods and ideas. From the 16th to the 20th centuries, science and technology have been vigorously impelled to discard the dead, inaccurate, or inadequate in their accumulated literature, and to rediscover and reapply old truths in dynamically new contexts.

In the Renaissance the scholar and scientist aspired to universal knowledge: da Vinci, a supreme artist, could contribute importantly to science as well. Today, the scientist is forced to aspire within a narrower range: he must specialize or work as a member of a team—even in academic laboratories. He must fight against technical obsolescence while struggling to unbury himself from avalanches of scientific writing.

Unhappily, modern science and technology offer mixed blessings. Automation raises living standards and increases leisure but also jeopardizes economic and social balances. Similarly, other solutions to our diverse technical problems create baffling social, political, even philosophical and religious disturbances. To understand the role of science and technology today, to use constructively its discoveries and inventions, and to project its ultimate effects, we need know its history and methods as well as keep abreast of its current accomplishments.

One thorough introduction to the subject is *A Guide to Science Reading* (Signet Science Library). The shorter, more selective list below is relatively free from technical jargon or difficult mathematics. The reader will find in these books accounts of scientific discoveries that often communicate the dramatic excitement of a first-rate "whodunit."

ANDRADE, EDWARD NEVILLE daCOSTA 1887– *An Approach to Modern Physics* (1956). Written primarily for readers with no extensive training in science and mathematics, this book explains simply the basic laws of nature and describes how scientists have arrived at them. *Peter Smith $3, Anch.*

BARNETT, LINCOLN 1909– *The Universe and Doctor Einstein* (rev ed 1957). Brilliant, relatively easy-to-grasp exposition of the quantum theory and relativity. *Sloane $3.50, Ment.*

BENADE, ARTHUR H. 1925– *Horns, Strings and Harmony* (1960). This unusual blending of science and art gives a clear and comprehensive account of both the scientific and esthetic nature of music. *Anch.*

BERNHARD, HUBERT J. 1916– *et al. New Handbook of the Heavens* (1954). Authoritative guide to the stars for the amateur. Explores and explains the universe of constellations, nebulae, plants, comets, the sun and earth. *McGraw-Hill $5.50, McGH, Sig.*

BITTER, FRANCIS 1902– *Magnets* (1959). An autobiography of a life dedicated to understanding magnets and the bewildering forces they exert. *Anch.*

BORN, MAX 1882– *The Restless Universe* (rev ed 1957). A Nobel Laureate guides the reader step by step through the maze of

## PHYSICAL SCIENCES AND MATHEMATICS

molecules, atoms, subatomic particles, and nuclear physics. Delightful illustrations in the form of flip-over "animated sequences." *Dov.*

BOYS, CHARLES V. 1855-1944 *Soap Bubbles and the Forces Which Mold Them* (3rd rev ed 1959). This classic, both good science and delightful reading, describes simple experiments anyone can do to bring him into direct contact with many of the basic forces of nature. *Anch, Dov.*

CERAM *Gods, Graves and Scholars.* See "History," page 218.

CHAPIN, HENRY and F. G. WALTON SMITH 1909- *The Ocean River* (1952). The story of the Gulf Stream and its influence on the climate and history of the Atlantic community. *Scribner $3.95, Scrib.*

CONANT, JAMES B. 1893- *Science and Common Sense* (1951). In a case-history analysis, the author reveals the scientist, not as a mere experimenter, but rather as the investigator of speculative ideas. *Yale $5, Yale.*

CURIE *Madame Curie.* See "Biography," page 173.

DAMPIER, WILLIAM C. 1867-1952 *A Shorter History of Science* (1957). An extremely satisfactory, concise history, with special emphasis on the relation of science to philosophy and religion. *Mer.*

DANTZIG, TOBIAS 1884-1956 *Number, The Language of Science* (4th ed rev 1954). Long considered one of the most successful presentations of mathematics to the layman, this book was described by Albert Einstein as "the most interesting book on the evolution of mathematics which has ever fallen into my hands." *Macmillan $6.50, Anch.*

FARRINGTON *Greek Science.* See "Greece," page 35.

FINCH, JAMES KIP 1883- *The Story of Engineering* (1960). Readable, well-illustrated history of the great builders from ancient times to the present, tracing the evolution of the various modern engineering disciplines. *Anch.*

FINK, DONALD G. 1911- and DAVID M. LUTYENS 1926- *The Physics of Television* (1960). A clear account of how men have learned to control electrons, photons, and electromagnetic waves to produce instantaneous moving pictures at great distances. *Anch.*

FRIEND, JOHN ALBERT NEWTON 1881- *Man and the Chemical Elements* (rev ed 1961). Absorbing narrative of the discovery and industrial applications of all the chemical elements. *Scribner $6.*

GAMOW, GEORGE 1904- *The Birth and Death of the Sun* (1941). A distinguished scientist who has few peers in interpreting science to the layman tells the story of stellar evolution and the anatomy of matter. *Viking $4.75, Ment.*

———— *Biography of the Earth* (rev ed 1959). The story of the earth—past, present, future. *Viking $4.95, Comp, Ment.*

———— *One, Two, Three . . . Infinity* (rev ed 1961). A splendid introduction to the facts and speculations of science. *Viking $5, Comp, Ment.*

## GOOD READING

    *The Creation of the Universe* (rev ed 1961). Explains the origin and evolution of the universe in layman's language. *Viking $4.50, Comp, Ment.*

    *Gravity* (1962). Relates the contributions of Galileo, Newton, Einstein, and others to our understanding of one of the greatest enigmas—the nature of gravity. *Anch.*

GARDNER, MARTIN 1914– *Fads and Fallacies in the Name of Science* (2nd ed 1957). The story of pseudo scientists, cults, and human gullibility fascinatingly recounted. *Bal, Dov.*

    (ed.) *Great Essays in Science* (1957). A brilliant collection of 31 varied essays, each solid in content and readable in style. *WSP.*

HURLEY, PATRICK M. 1912– *How Old Is the Earth?* (1959). Discussion of the origins and structure of the earth with particular emphasis on radioactivity—both as a powerful new geological tool and as a motive force for the shaping of the earth's surface. *Anch.*

JAFFE, BERNARD 1896– *Crucibles* (1962). The history of the advance of chemistry related to the lives of those who developed the science. *Prem.*

JEANS, JAMES 1877–1946 *The Universe Around Us* (4th ed 1944). Relegating mathematics to footnotes, this great astronomer relates physics, chemistry, and geology to astronomy. *Cambridge $4, CUP.*

    *The Growth of Physical Science* (2nd ed 1951). Compact, nontechnical history of the sciences from Babylon to nuclear fission. *Prem.*

JUNGK, ROBERT 1913– *Brighter Than a Thousand Suns* (1956). The fascinating story of the men who made the atom bomb. *Harcourt $5, BC.*

KRAMER, EDNA E. 1902– *The Main Stream of Mathematics* (1951). The fundamental concepts of mathematics explained for the layman and enlivened by many anecdotes about the great mathematicians. *Oxford $7.75, Prem.*

LESSING, LAWRENCE P. 1908– *Understanding Chemistry* (1959). Elementary account of laboratory discoveries in chemistry and of their relevance in everyone's life today. *Wiley $3.50, Sig.*

LEY, WILLY, 1906– *Satellites, Rockets and Outer Space* (rev ed 1962). An introduction to space flight for the layman, tracing rocket research from the earliest times to the present. *Sig.*

NEWMAN, JAMES R. 1907– (ed.) *The World of Mathematics* (1956). A 4-volume anthology of mathematical literature from the Greeks on, compiled for both the layman and the expert. *S&S.*

ORR, CLYDE, JR. 1921– *Between Earth and Space* (1959). Elementary discussion of the atmosphere as it affects man. *Macmillan $4.95, Collr.*

PEARSON, KARL 1857–1936 *The Grammar of Science* (1892). A classic interpretation of the scientific point of view. *Evman-h, Mer.*

## PHYSICAL SCIENCES AND MATHEMATICS 273

POINCARÉ, JULES HENRI 1854–1912 *Science and Method* (1910). Describes the basic methodology and psychology of scientific discovery; and analyzes the nature of experimentation, theory, and the human mind as they are applied to the acquisition of organized knowledge. *Dov.*

SANDFORT, JOHN F. 1911– *Heat Engines* (1962). Amusing and fascinating story of the history of the machines around which our lives are organized. Gives the reader an elementary understanding of the laws of thermodynamics, which govern the operation of the machines that power our industrial age. *Anch.*

SAWYER, WALTER WARWICK 1911– *Mathematician's Delight* (1943). The book dispels the fear of mathematics by presenting it as interesting mental exercise rather than as forbidding science. *Pen.*

———— *Prelude to Mathematics* (1955). The reader with only a confused recollection of elementary mathematics can understand this account of the more stimulating and surprising branches of mathematics. *Pen.*

SCHRODINGER, ERWIN 1887–1961 *Science, Theory and Man* (1957). Nine essays on man and the changing world, which serve to introduce the reader to the philosophical outlook of one of the founders of the new science. *Dov.*

*Scientific American*, Editors of  Many significant and handsomely illustrated articles published in *Scientific American* have been collected and reprinted under the following self-explanatory titles: *Atomic Power* (1956), *Automatic Control* (1956), *The New Astronomy* (1956), *Lives in Science* (1957), *The New Chemistry* (1957), *The Planet Earth* (1957), and *The Universe* (1957). *S&S.*

THIEL, RUDOLF 1899– *And There Was Light* (1957). The story of adventure and discovery in the world of astronomy, from ancient astrologers to modern astrophysicists. Knopf $6.95, *Ment.*

TITCHMARSH, EDWARD CHARLES 1899– *Mathematics for the General Reader* (1959). A relaxed account of the science of numbers from arithmetic and algebra on to the calculus. *Anch.*

VITRUVIUS *On Architecture*. See "Rome," page 41.

WHITEHEAD *Science and the Modern World*. See "Philosophy," page 210.

WIENER *The Human Use of Human Beings*. See "Anthropology and Sociology," page 250.

## Science Fiction

What is science fiction? According to Kingsley Amis, it is "that class of prose narrative that could not arise in the world we know, but which is hypothesized on the basis of some innovation in science or technology, or pseudo-science or pseudo-technology, whether human or extra-terrestrial in origin." As such, science fiction concerns developments in science or society that seem impossible at the time when they are described. Yet some of science fiction's predictions have been realized, like Jules Verne's rockets to the moon and submarines under the Arctic ice. In the tradition of Swift, Verne, and Wells, it is fascinating to examine the technical, social, and moral consequences of possible future developments of science and technology as they are envisioned by knowledgeable creative writers. The simple list of titles that follows is representative of a vast literature.

AMIS, KINGSLEY *New Maps of Hell: a Survey of Science Fiction.* Harcourt $3.95, Bal.

ASIMOV, ISAAC *The Caves of Steel.* Pyr.
 _____ *The End of Eternity.* Lance, Sig.
 _____ *The Martian Way.* Sig.

BRADBURY, RAY *The Golden Apples of the Sun.* Ban.
 _____ *The Martian Chronicles.* Doubleday $2.95, Ban.
 _____ (ed.) *Timeless Stories for Today and Tomorrow.* Ban.

CAPEK, KAREL *War with the Newts.* Ban.

CLARKE, ARTHUR C. *The City and the Stars.* Sig.
 _____ *The Deep Range.* Harcourt $3.95.
 _____ *The Sands of Mars.* Perm.

HEINLEIN, ROBERT A. *The Door into Summer.* Doubleday $2.95, Sig.
 _____ *The Menace from Earth.* Sig.

HOYLE, FRED *Black Cloud.* Harper $2.95, Sig.

STURGEON, THEODORE *Some of Your Blood.* Bal.

SWIFT *Gulliver's Travels.* See "The 18th Century," page 97.

VAN VOGT, A. E. *Destination: Universe!* Sig.

VERNE, JULES *From the Earth to the Moon.* Dov.
 _____ *Journey to the Center of the Earth.* Ace, Collr.
 _____ *20,000 Leagues Under the Sea.* Ban, Dolp.

WELLS, H. G. *The Invisible Man.* CoNC, WSP.
 _____ *The Stories of H. G. Wells.* Bal.
 _____ *The Time Machine.* Berk, Dolp.
 _____ *Three Prophetic Novels.* Dov.

# SPECIAL SECTION

# SPECIAL SECTION

## 28. Reference Books

**DONALD A. SEARS,** *Skidmore College*

Any book can be a reference book, for when we use a book to answer a specific question of fact or idea we are *referring* to it for our answer. *Good Reading,* for example, with its essays and annotated book lists, is a reference book to good reading: it answers questions about what is interesting and worthwhile to read in a large variety of fields. Another way to define a reference book is to say that it is one we dip into for a particular purpose and not one that we read clear through. We are not likely to read all of the *Encyclopaedia Britannica,* or *Who's Who,* or *Books in Print.* Each serves its purpose when we consult it; each is an example of a basic reference book.

Most of us have in our home a few reference books—a dictionary, a *World Almanac,* an atlas, a cookbook, or a garden encyclopedia. But few of us can afford to own all that we might wish to use. For most reference books we go to the reference collection of a library. And even a large library cannot have all the reference books in existence, but it will have a varied and useful collection.

The great advantage of a reference book is that it serves as a shortcut. By being familiar with reference tools we can get the answer we are seeking with little waste of time. We might have to look through several books on the Civil War before finding the exact date of the battle in which we are interested, but a dictionary of dates will yield the information in minutes. In so far as the library is the treasury of man's knowledge, reference books are the key to that treasury.

While more than 100 major titles are included in the following pages, they are only a small—yet representative—sampling of the great bibliographical and other reference guides that are available.

## A. Bibliographies and General Indexes

Nearly every library will have the *United States Catalog of Books in Print January 1, 1928*, the *Cumulative Book Index,* and the most recent *Books in Print.* These volumes bring reasonably up to date (with information about publisher, price, date, number of pages, etc.) the immense array of books published in this country. Information about a wanted book can usually be found under any of three or more entries: (1) author's name, (2) title of the book, and (3) subjects with which the book deals.

Libraries also have files of publications that analyze, usually under authors and subjects, the contents of magazines. Material on any subject can thus be found in files of hundreds of thousands of volumes of periodicals. Representative analyses are *Poole's Index, Readers' Guide, International Index,* and *P.A.I.S.* (Public Affairs Information Service). *The New York Times Index* (1913 to date) is issued semimonthly and may also serve indirectly as a guide to articles appearing in other newspapers. There are additional indexes for special and limited fields: art, bibliography, biography, business, education, music, technology, etc.

Abstracts are another kind of helpful analysis of the literature of a given subject: *Abstracts of English Studies, Biological Abstracts, Chemical Abstracts, Historical Abstracts,* and *Psychological Abstracts* are five of many such publications.

The *Essay and General Literature Index* (1900 to date), a subject analysis of thousands of miscellaneous books, gives citations of important articles that have appeared as parts of books. Almost any published short literary work can be found through special indexes: EDITH GRANGER's *Index to Poetry* (Columbia 4th ed 1953 $35), and its *Supplement, 1951–55* (Columbia 1957 $20); D. H. WEST & D. M. PEAKE's *Play Index* (Wilson 1953 $5), and in earlier allied publications by I. T. E. FIRKINS and HANNAH LOGASA and J. H. OTTEMILLER; D. E. COOK & I. S. MONRO's *Short Story Index* (Wilson 1953 $14), and its supplements covering the years 1950 through 1958; and M. E. SEARS' *Song Index* and *Supplement* (Wilson 1926 & 1934).

*Paperbound Books in Print,* first issued in the summer of 1955, is a monthly listing of new paperbound books and a three-times-per-year cumulative index to the growing array of inexpensive paperbound books (Bowker $16 per year).

Full and helpful lists of all sorts of reference books on every subject are LOUIS SHORES' *Basic Reference Sources* (American Library Assn. 1954 $6.25) and C. M. WINCHELL's *Guide to Reference*

***Books*** (A.L.A. 7th ed 1951 $10), with three ***Supplements*** for 1950 through 1958. Also useful is R. W. MURPHEY's ***How and Where To Look It Up*** (McGraw-Hill 1958 $15). Bibliographies have been cumulated annually since 1938 in ***Bibliographic Index.***

## B. Encyclopedias

Standard, frequently revised general encyclopedias with helpful index volumes are ***Encyclopedia Americana*** (30 vols), ***Encyclopaedia Britannica*** (24 vols), and ***Collier's Encyclopedia*** (24 vols). Each is kept up to date by annual yearbooks. Good single-volume works for an individual's desk are ***Columbia Encyclopedia*** (Columbia 1963 $49.50) and ***The Columbia-Viking Desk Encyclopedia*** (Viking 1960 $8.95).

## C. Fact Books

One of the small single volumes, each including an amazing collection of information, is a helpful companion near one's desk. Annually revised titles include ***Information Please Almanac*** (Publisher varies 1947 to date $1.35); ***World Almanac*** (N. Y. World-Telegram and Sun 1868 to date $1.35); and ***Statistical Abstract of the United States***, compiled by the U. S. Bureau of the Census (Govt. Ptg. Off. 1878 to date $3.75).

## D. Atlases

Of major scope is J. W. BARTHOLOMEW's ***The Times Atlas of the World*** (London Times 1955-59 5 vols $25 ea.). Good and not too cumbersome general volumes are ***Cosmopolitan Atlas*** (Rand McNally rev ed 1962 $14.95) and BARTHOLOMEW's ***Advanced Atlas of Modern Geography*** (McGraw-Hill 3rd ed 1956 $11.50). A specialized volume is W. R. SHEPHERD's ***Historical Atlas*** (Barnes & Noble 8th ed $15). Two useful paperbound atlases for the modest home library are E. D. ESPENSHADE's ***Regional Atlas*** (Rand McNally 2nd ed $2) and R. R. PALMER's ***Historical Atlas of the World*** (Rand McNally 75¢).

Allied to atlases are such books as ***The Columbia Lippincott***

*Gazetteer of the World* including *Supplement* (Columbia 1952 $65), *Webster's Geographical Dictionary* (Merriam rev ed 1960 $8.50), and W. G. MOORE's *Dictionary of Geography* (Penguin 95¢).

# E. Dictionaries

Outstanding comprehensive authorities are *The Oxford English Dictionary* (Oxford 1888–1933 13 vols); *New Standard Dictionary* (Funk & Wagnalls 1959 $40); and *Webster's New International Dictionary* (Merriam 3rd ed 1961 $47.50). Smaller works for an individual's desk include *The American College Dictionary* (Random House 1957 $5); *Standard College Dictionary* (Harcourt 1963 $5.50); *Webster's New World Dictionary* (World 1959 $5.75); and *Webster's Seventh New Collegiate Dictionary* (Merriam 1963 $5.75).

Other useful books in this category include H. W. FOWLER's *Dictionary of Modern English Usage* (Oxford 1937 $4.50); MARGARET NICHOLSON's *A Dictionary of American-English Usage Based on Fowler* (New American Library 75¢); L. V. BERREY & MELVIN VAN DEN BARK's *American Thesaurus of Slang* (Crowell 2nd ed 1960 $15); *Webster's Dictionary of Synonyms* (Merriam 1951 $6); and PETER ROGET's *Thesaurus of English Words and Phrases* (Evman-h, PB). Standard for etymologists is ERIC PARTRIDGE's *Origins* (Macmillan 1958 $16). There are also dictionaries for every major and most minor foreign languages.

# F. Literature

*Cassell's Encyclopaedia of World Literature* (Funk & Wagnalls 2 vols 1953 $25); the *Columbia Dictionary of Modern European Literature* (Columbia 1947 $10); PAUL HARVEY's *Oxford Companion to Classical Literature* (Oxford 2nd ed 1937 $4.50); and PAUL HARVEY & J. E. HESELTINE's *Oxford Companion to French Literature* (Oxford 1959 $12.50) are helpful in providing information about non-English books and authors.

*The Cambridge History of English Literature* (Macmillan 1949–53 reissue 15 vols $65) and *Literary History of the United States* (Macmillan rev ed in 1 vol 1953 $8.75) with *Bibliography* and *Supplement* (1962 $12.50) are the standard historical reference works. Still appearing is *The Oxford History of English Literature* (Oxford 12 vols 1945–).

General books, so miscellaneous and widely varied in the information they include as to be miniature encyclopedias, include, in addi-

REFERENCE BOOKS  281

tion to those already cited, others in the series of "Oxford Companions," all published by Oxford: PAUL HARVEY's *Oxford Companion to English Literature* (3rd ed 1946 $10); J. D. HART's *Oxford Companion to American Literature* (3rd ed 1956 $10); and PHYLLIS HARTNOLL's *Oxford Companion to the Theatre* (2nd ed 1957 $11.50). W. R. BENET's *The Reader's Encyclopedia* (Crowell 1955 $7.95) and *Brewer's Dictionary of Phrase and Fable* (Harper rev ed 1953 $5.95) are other useful volumes of this sort.

Who said it? Books of quotations will give the answer. Among a great many, the following five are particularly helpful: F. P. ADAMS' *FPA's Book of Quotations* (Funk & Wagnalls 1952 $5.95); JOHN BARTLETT's *Familiar Quotations* (Little 13th ed 1955 $10); H. L. MENCKEN's *New Dictionary of Quotations* Knopf 1942 $10); *The Oxford Dictionary of Quotations* (Oxford 2nd ed 1953 $10.50); and B. E. STEVENSON's *Home Book of Quotations* (Dodd 9th ed 1959 $25).

Poems may be located in anthologies, a particularly useful set of which is published by Oxford; an example is *The Oxford Book of Irish Verse* (1958 $5.75).

Critical opinion may be located through *Book Review Digest* (1905 to date).

## G. Biography

*Who's Who in America* (Marquis 1899 to date) is a biennial list of prominent living Americans. *Who's Who* (St Martin's 1849 to date) is an annual similar list, chiefly of Britishers. *International Who's Who* (Europa 1935 to date) and *Current Biography* (Wilson 1940 to date; annual vols $7 ea.)—a monthly (except August) publication, annually cumulated—give sketches of prominent people of various nationalities.

*Dictionary of American Biography* (Scribner new rev pop ed 22 vols incl. *Supplements* through 1940 and *Index* 1943–45 1958) contains authoritative biographies of Americans no longer living. *Dictionary of National Biography* (Oxford 1938 reprint incl. *Supplements* 27 vols) is the corresponding set for British lives. *New Century Cyclopedia of Names* (Appleton 3 vols 1954 $39.50) and *Webster's Biographical Dictionary* (Merriam 1943 $8.50) are widely inclusive but with brief, condensed entries.

Biographical reference books abound for nearly every area of human effort, from art to zoology. Here are a sample few concerning authors, all by S. J. KUNITZ & HOWARD HAYCRAFT: *American Authors, 1600–1900* (Wilson 1938 $6); *British Authors of the Nineteenth Century* (Wilson 1936 $5) and *Twentieth Century Authors* (Wilson 1942 $8.50) and its *First Supplement* (Wilson 1955 $8). *Biography Index* (Wilson 1947 to date)—annually cumulated from quarterly publications—locates biographical material in current books and periodicals.

# H. Art and Music

In the fine arts (except for music) many of the still standard reference books are old and out of print: for example, MICHAEL BRYAN's *Dictionary of Painters and Engravers* (1903–05 5 vols); J. D. CHAMPLIN's *Cyclopedia of Painters and Paintings* (1887 4 vols); and RUSSELL STURGIS' *Dictionary of Architecture* (1901–1902 3 vols). Recent smaller publications of this sort include B. S. MYERS' *Encyclopedia of Painting* (Crown 1955 $12.95); M. SEUPHOR's (pseudonym of F. HAZEN) *Dictionary of Abstract Painting* (Tudor 1957 $7.95); and HELEN GARDNER's *Art Through the Ages* (Harcourt 4th ed 1959 $9.50). Other recent good books in their respective fields are A. E. BURKE's *Architectural and Building Trades Dictionary* (Amer. Tech. Soc. 2nd ed 1955 $6.50); L. A. & H. B. BOGER's *Dictionary of Antiques and the Decorative Arts* (Scribner 1957 $13.95); and J. L. STOUTENBURGH's *Dictionary of Arts and Crafts* (Philosophical Library 1956 $6).

In music the standard monumental work is GEORGE GROVE's *Dictionary of Music and Musicians* including *Supplement* (St Martin's 5th ed 1954 9 vols). Less inclusive but useful general compendiums include WILLI APEL's *Harvard Dictionary of Music* (Harvard 1944 $9.50); W. S. PRATT's *New Encyclopedia of Music and Musicians* (Macmillan rev ed 1951 $12.50); P. A. SCHOLES' *Oxford Companion to Music* (Oxford 9th ed 1955 $25); and OSCAR THOMPSON & NICHOLAS SLONIMSKY's *International Cyclopedia of Music and Musicians* (Dodd 8th ed 1959 $25). For information about opera there is GUSTAV KOBBÉ's *Complete Opera Book* (Putnam rev ed 1954 $10). Contemporary music is well covered in three books by DAVID EWEN: *American Composers Today* (Wilson 1949 $4); *European Composers Today* (Wilson 1954 $4); and *Complete Book of Twentieth Century Music* (Prentice-Hall 2nd ed 1959 $7.50). Information about recordings will be found in a fourth book by DAVID EWEN: *Musical Masterworks* (Arco 2nd ed 1955 $3.95).

# I. Philosophy, Psychology, and Religion

In these fields the monumental standard works are both old: J. M. BALDWIN's *Dictionary of Philosophy and Psychology* (Peter Smith reprint ed 1946 3 vols in 4 $50) and JAMES HASTINGS' *Encyclopedia of Religion and Ethics* (Scribner 1908–26 13 vols). Briefer but more recent are D. D. RUNES' *The Dictionary of Philosophy*

(Littlefield 1956 $2.25) and J. O. URMSON's *The Concise Encyclopedia of Philosophy and Philosophers* (Hawthorn 1960 $15).

E. G. BORING'S *Harvard List of Books in Psychology* (Harvard 1955 with 1958 supplement $1.75) is a recent bibliography; and P. L. HARRIMAN's *Encyclopedia of Psychology* (Philosophical Library 1956 o.p.) traces contemporary trends and provides bibliographies. A useful small paperback is published by Penguin: *Dictionary of Psychology* ($1.25).

Old but standard for special areas of religion are *The Jewish Encyclopedia* (Funk & Wagnalls 1901–06 12 vols) and *The Catholic Encyclopedia* (16 vols plus supplements 1907–22; new edition in progress). *The New Schaff-Herzog Encyclopedia of Religious Knowledge* (Baker Book House 1951 13 vols) includes biography. Useful recent works include M. S. & J. L. MILLER's *Harper's Bible Dictionary* (Harper 7th ed 1962 $8.95) and *The Interpreter's Dictionary of The Bible* (Abingdon 4 vols 1962 $45).

## J. History

OSCAR HANDLIN and others have compiled a helpful bibliography of historical materials: *Harvard Guide to American History* (Harvard 1954 $10). The Everyman's Reference Library *Dictionary of Dates* (Dutton 1954 $4.25) is a useful compilation. W. L. LANGER's *Encyclopedia of World History* (Houghton rev ed 1952 $9) is a compact volume for the home desk. Limited to our own history, there is a similar range in scope and fullness in R. B. MORRIS' *Encyclopedia of American History* (Harper 1955 $8.95). Cambridge University Press has published reference histories: *Cambridge Ancient History* (1929–39 17 vols), *Cambridge Medieval History* (1911–36 8 vols), and *Cambridge Modern History* (1902–22 14 vols).

## K. Social Sciences

A no longer new but still authoritative and useful publication in these fields, first issued from 1930 to 1935 in 15 vols and reprinted as a "Popular edition" in 1948 in 8 vols, is E. R. A. SELIGMAN & ALVIN JOHNSON's *Encyclopedia of the Social Sciences* (Macmillan $110) and *Selections* from, compiled by RALPH B. SPENCE (Macmillan $8). The Wilson Company's *Business Periodicals Index* (1958 to present) is a subject index to business and trade periodicals.

For economics, there is H. S. SLOAN & A. J. ZURCHER's *Dictionary of Economics* (Barnes & Noble 4th ed rev 1960 $3.75). A useful series of annual volumes of statistics has been issued by the

National Industrial Conference Board: *Economic Almanac* (Crowell 1940 to date $5). For general coverage there are G. G. CHISHOLM's *Handbook of Commercial Geography* (Wiley 17th ed 1963); W. S. & E. S. WOYTINSKY's *World Population and Production* (20th Century Fund 1953 $12); and *Oxford Economic Atlas of the World* (Oxford 2nd ed 1959 $8). For information about our own country, *Historical Statistics of the United States, Colonial Times to 1957* is issued by the U. S. Bureau of the Census (Govt. Ptg. Off. 1960 $6).

For government or political science there is WALTER THEIMER's *Encyclopedia of Modern World Politics* (Rinehart 1950 o.p.); the annual *Yearbook of the United Nations* (United Nations 1947 to date $15); and, since 1927, the annual *Political Handbook of the World* (Harper $3.95). For information about state governments there has been issued since 1935 the biennial *Book of the States* (Chicago Council of State Governments $9); and, since 1934, for matters on the local level, the annual *Municipal Year Book* (Chicago International City Managers Assn. $10). E. S. SMITH & A. J. ZURCHER's *New Dictionary of American Politics* (Barnes & Noble rev ed 1955 $4.95) defines terms.

# L. Science

Representative works of general inclusiveness are *Van Nostrand's Scientific Encyclopedia* (Van Nostrand 3rd ed 1958 $30) and I. F. & W. D. HENDERSON's *Dictionary of Scientific Terms* (Van Nostrand 7th ed 1960 $12.50).

For astronomers there are E. A. BEET's *Guide to the Sky* (Cambridge 1950 $3), H. C. MACPHERSON's *Guide to the Stars* (Philosophical Library rev ed 1955 $2.75), and HAROLD S. JONES's *Space Encyclopedia* (Dutton rev ed 1959 $8.95).

Botanists will find useful B. D. JACKSON's *Glossary of Botanic Terms* (Hafner 4th ed 1949 $4.50); L. H. & E. Z. BAILEY's *Hortus Second* (Macmillan 1951 $13.50); and a dictionary, J. C. WILLIS' *Flowering Plants and Ferns* (Cambridge 6th ed 1931 $5.50).

In chemistry the encyclopedias and dictionaries range from such a monumental work as T. E. THORPE's *Dictionary of Applied Chemistry* (Wiley 4th ed 1937–56 12 vols) to C. T. KINGZETT's *Chemical Encyclopedia* (Van Nostrand 8th ed 1952 $18.50), and G. L. CLARK's *Encyclopedia of Chemistry* with 1958 *Supplement* (Reinhold 1958 $29.50), and HARRY BENNETT's *Concise Chemical and Technical Dictionary* (Chemical Pub. Co. 1947 $10). Annually revised is the *Handbook of Chemistry and Physics* (Chemical Rubber Co. 1914 to date $12).

For those seeking information about physical and mental health there is *Dorland's Illustrated Medical Dictionary* (Saunders 23rd ed 1957 $12.50) and L. E. HINSIE & R. J. CAMPBELL's *Psychiatric Dictionary* (Oxford 3rd ed 1960 $17.50).

For recent developments in science and technology there are the Wilson Company's *Applied Science & Technology Index* (1958 to date), a subject index to science and technology periodicals; C. W. & H. BESSERER's *Guide to the Space Age* (Prentice-Hall 1959 $7.95) and A. SPITZ & F. GAYNOR's *A Dictionary of Astronomy and Astronautics* (Littlefield 1959 $2.25).

Useful small paperbacks published by Penguin are *Dictionary of Biology* (95¢) and *Dictionary of Science* (95¢). New American Library publishes *A Guide to Science Reading* (60¢).

## M. Miscellaneous

In an attempt to hint at the availability over wide ranges of reference works, here is a miscellaneous selection of titles that have demonstrated their usefulness. (1) For the traveler: the annual *Official Hotel Red Book* (Amer. Hotel Assn. Directory Corp. 1886 to date $5). (2) For the sports enthusiast: F. G. MENKE's *Encyclopedia of Sports* (Barnes & Noble rev ed 1953 $12). (3) For the hobbyist and handyman: *How-To-Do-It Books: A Selective Guide* (Bowker 3rd ed 1963 $7.50). (4) For the editor and writer: *Manual of Style* (Chicago 11th ed 1949 $6). (5) For the job-seeker: GERTRUDE FORRESTER's *Occupational Literature* (Wilson 1958 $6.50). (6) For the socially perplexed: EMILY POST's *Etiquette* (Funk & Wagnalls 10th ed 1950 $5.95) or AMY VANDERBILT's *Complete Book of Etiquette* (Doubleday rev ed 1958 $5.50).

Librarians at schools, colleges, and universities and in public libraries are trained and experienced in aiding individuals to find their way about in the vast array of reference books. In nearly any library you will find a librarian whose obligation and pleasure it will be to help you find and consult the book you need.

# Author, Title, and Subject Index to the *Good Reading* Book Lists

*Abbey of Thélème,* 74
Abel, L., 169
*Abraham and Isaac,* 170
*Abraham Lincoln* (Sandburg), 175
*Abraham Lincoln* (Thomas), 176
*Absalom, Absalom!,* 142
*Abstracts of English Studies,* 278
*Acceptance World,* 129
*Accursed Kings,* 68
*Act One,* 174
Adam, L., 195
*Adam Bede,* 119
Adams, F. P., 281
Adams, H., 68, 172
Adams, J. F., 261
Adams, J. Q., 80
Adams, J. T., 224
Adamson, J., 265
Addison, J., 94
Adler, K. A., 258
*Adler's Place in Psychology,* 260
*Admiral of the Ocean Sea,* 75
*Adolescent, The,* 260
*Adolphe,* 104
*Advanced Atlas of Modern Geography,* 279
*Advancement of Learning,* 79
ADVENTURE, see BIOGRAPHY; GEOGRAPHY
*Adventures in Nature,* 268
*Adventures in the Skin Trade,* 153
*Adventures of Augie March,* 140
*Adventures of Huckleberry Finn,* 137
*Adventures of Tom Sawyer,* 137
*Advice to a Young Critic,* 183
*Aeneid,* 41
Aeschylus, 33
Aesop, 33
*Aesthetics and History in the Visual Arts,* 195
*Affair, The,* 129
*Affluent Society,* 236
AFRICA, 51 ff., 55
*African Genesis,* 265
*African Political Parties,* 56
*African Survey,* 55
*After the Seventh Day,* 240
*Against Nature,* 105
*Agamemnon,* 33
Agard, W. R., 35
*Age of Analysis,* 208
*Age of Belief,* 66
*Age of Chaucer,* 68
*Age of Chivalry,* 35
*Age of Elegance,* 221
*Age of Enlightenment,* 94
*Age of Enormity: Life and Writing in the Forties and Fifties,* 183
*Age of Fable,* 35
*Age of Faith,* 69
*Age of Ideology,* 206
*Age of Longing,* 112
*Age of Louis XIV,* 89
*Age of Psychology,* 258
*Age of Reason* (Paine), 96
*Age of Reason* (Sartre), 114
*Age of Reason Begins,* 89
*Age of Reason Reader, Portable,* 97
*Age of the Democratic Revolution,* 221

*Age of the Great Depression,* 225
*Age of the Reformation,* 220
Agee, J., 179
*Agony and the Ecstasy,* 176
Aiken, C., 159, 161
Akutagawa Ryunosuke, 48
Alarcón, P. A. de, 103
Albee, E., 167, 170
Albrecht-Carrié, R., 220
*Alcestis,* 33
Alcott, L. M., 134
*Aldine Library of Artists,* 195
Alegría, C., 59
Algren, N., 139
*Alice in Wonderland,* 119
Allen, D. L., 265
Allen, F. L., 224
Allen, G. W., 172
Allen, H. C., 220
*Almayer's Folly,* 119
*Ambassadors, The,* 136
*Ambassador's Report,* 46
*America as a Civilization,* 248
*America in Perspective,* 224
*American, The,* 136
*American Authors,* 281
*American Capitalism,* 236
*American Catholicism,* 214
*American College Dictionary,* 280
*American Commonwealth,* 230
*American Composers Today,* 282
*American Drama,* 166
*American Dream and the Zoo Story,* 167
*American English,* 254
*American Essays,* 179
AMERICAN HISTORY, 224 ff.
*American Judaism,* 214
*American Language,* 254
AMERICAN NOVELS, 131 ff.
*American Protestantism,* 214
*American Social Patterns,* 249
*American Society,* 250
*American Songbag,* 201
*American Thesaurus of Slang,* 280
*American Tragedy,* 141
Amis, K., 126, 274
*Anabasis,* 34
*Analects, The,* 47
*Anatomy of Melancholy,* 86
*Anatomy of Satire,* 181
*Anchor Anthology of Jacobean Drama,* 165
*Ancient Greeks,* 35
ANCIENT HISTORY, see GREECE; HISTORY; ROME
*Ancient Maya,* 62
*Ancient Myths,* 35
*And Quiet Flows the Don,* 114
*And There Was Light,* 273
Anderson, G. K., 68
Anderson, M., 80, 167
Anderson, P., 205
Anderson, S., 139
Anderson, W. L., 252
Anderson, W. R., 200
Anderson, Cmmdr. W. R., 240

Andrade, E. N. daC., 270
Andreyev, L., 110
*Animal Farm*, 128
*Animals as Social Beings*, 267
*Anna Karenina*, 106
*Another Country*, 140
Anouilh, J., 68, 167
*Anthology of English Drama Before Shakespeare*, 79
*Anthology of Mexican Poetry*, 60
*Anthology of Negro Poets in the U.S.A.*, 162
*Anthology of Russian Plays*, 165
ANTHROPOLOGY, 243 ff.
*Antigone*, 34
*Antiquary, The*, 98
Antonius, G., 52
Apel, W., 282
*Apes, Angels and Victorians*, 221
*Aphrodite*, 36
*Apocrypha*, 212
*Apologia pro Vita Sua*, 175
*Apology*, 34
*Applied Science & Technology Index*, 285
*Appointment in Samarra*, 144
*Approach to Greek Art*, 197
*Approach to Modern Physics*, 270
Apuleius, 39
*Arab Awakening*, 52
*Arab Unity*, 54
*Arabian Nights*, 52
*Arabic Literature*, 53
*Arabs, The* (Atiyah), 52
*Arabs in History*, 53
ARCHEOLOGY, see ANTHROPOLOGY; GREECE; HISTORY; RELIGION
*Architectural and Building Trades Dictionary*, 282
ARCHITECTURE, 198 ff.
*Architecture of Humanism*, 76
*Architecture of the 19th and 20th Centuries*, 198
*Architecture Through the Ages*, 198
Arciniegas, G., 60, 61, 240
*Arctic Wild*, 266
Ardrey, R., 265
*Are You Listening?*, 254
*Areopagitica*, 87
Aristophanes, 33
Aristotle, 33
*Armada, The*, 75
Armitage, A., 172
Arnold, M., 157
Aron, R., 245
*Arrowsmith*, 143
ART, see FINE ARTS
*Art and Architecture of China*, 45
*Art and Architecture of India*, 45
*Art and Architecture of Japan*, 45
*Art and Life in America*, 196
*Art and Scientific Thought*, 194
*Art Now*, 197
*Art of Asking Questions*, 254
*Art of Love*, 40
*Art of Making Dances*, 201
*Art of the East Library*, 195
*Art of the Play*, 166
*Art Through the Ages*, 196, 282
*Art Today*, 198
*Arts and the Man*, 194
*Arundel*, 98
Arvin, N., 173
*As I Lay Dying*, 142
*As You Like It*, 80

ASIA, see FAR EAST
*Asia's Lands and Peoples*, 241
Asimov, I., 265, 274
*Ask at the Unicorn*, 146
*Aspects of the Novel*, 181
*Assistant, The*, 144
*Assommoir, L'*, 106
ASTRONOMY, see PHYSICAL SCIENCES
*Astrophel and Stella*, 80
*At Lady Molly's*, 129
Atiyah, E., 52
Atkinson, D. T., 265
*Atlantic, The*, 187
ATLASES, 279
*Atomic Power*, 273
Aubrey, J., 85
*Aucassin and Nicolette, and Other Medieval Romances*, 66
Auden, W. H., 159, 161, 179, 199
Auerbach, E., 179
Augustine, St., 39
Austen, J., 118
*Authorized Version of the Bible*, 85
AUTOBIOGRAPHY, see BIOGRAPHY
*Automatic Control*, 273
Ayer, A. J., 208
Ayres, E., 240
*Aztecs, The*, 61
Azuela, M., 60

Babbitt, 143
Babel, I., 149
*Background of Modern Poetry*, 181
Bacon, F., 79
Bailey, L. H., 284
Bailey, T. A., 224
Bainton, R. H., 220
*Balance of Nature*, 267
Balanchine, G., 201
Baldwin, J., 140
Baldwin, J. M., 282
*Ballet*, 201
*Balthazar*, 126
*Balún-Canán*, 60
Balzac, H. de, 103
*Barabbas*, 112
Barber, B., 245
*Barber of Seville*, 94
*Barchester Towers*, 121
Barish, L., 213
Barnes, W. R., 230
*Barnes & Noble Art Series*, 195
Barnett, A. D., 47
Barnett, L., 270
Barr, A. H. Jr., 195
*Barren Ground*, 142
Barrow, R. H., 41
Barth, A., 230
Barth, J., 140
Bartholomew, J. W., 279
Bartlett, J., 281
Barzun, J., 199
Bascom, W., 240
Basham, A. L., 46
*Basic Jewish Beliefs*, 213
*Basic Reference Sources*, 278
Bate, W., 180
Bates, M., 240, 265
Bauer, M., 199
Beard, C. A., 224, 230
Beaumarchais, P. C. de, 94
Beaumont, F., 85
Beauvoir, S. de, 110
Becker, C. L., 97
Beckett, S., 110, 167, 170

Beebe, W., 265
Beegle, D. M., 214
Beerbohm, M., 126
Beet, E. A., 284
Beethoven, 201
Beggar's Opera, 95
Beginning and the End, 208
Behaviorism, 260
Bel-Ami, 105
Belgian Congo, 56
Bell, N. W., 246
Bellamy, E., 134
Bellow, S., 140
Ben Jonson of Westminster, 81
Benade, A. H., 270
Benchley, R. C., 180
Bendix, R., 248
Benedict, R., 246
Benét, S. V., 149, 159, 161
Benét, W. R., 281
Ben-Gurion, D., 52
Ben-Gurion, 54
Benjamin Franklin, 98
Bennett, A., 126
Bennett, H., 284
Bentley, E., 165, 169
Bentley, G. E., 166
*Beowulf*, 66, 161
Berdyaev, N., 208
Berenson, B., 74
Bergson, H., 208
Berkeley, G., 94, 206
*Berkshire Studies in European History*, 221
Berle, A. A., 235
*Berlin Diary*, 223
*Berlin Stories*, 127
*Berlioz and His Century*, 199
Bernhard, H. J., 270
Bernstein, M., 199
Berrey, L. V., 280
Berrill, N. J., 265
Besserer, C. W., 285
Bethers, R., 195
*Betrothed, The*, 105
Bettex, A., 240
*Between Earth and Space*, 272
*Between Man and Man*, 208
Beveridge, W. H., 235
*Beyond Psychology*, 259
*Beyond Sing the Woods*, 111
*Bhagavad-Gita*, 212
Biancolli, L., 199
*Bible, The*, 85, 212
*Bible and the Common Reader*, 214
*Bible Designed to Be Read as Living Literature*, 212
*Biblical Archaeology*, 250
*Bibliographical Index*, 279
Bierce, A., 149
*Big Money*, 141
*Biglow Papers*, 158
*Billy Budd*, 137
Binyon, L., 45
BIOGRAPHY, 171 ff.
*Biography Index*, 281
*Biography of the Earth*, 271
*Biological Abstracts*, 278
BIOLOGICAL SCIENCES, 263 ff.
*Biology of the Spirit*, 268
*Bird of Fire*, 70
*Birds*, 33
Birney, R. C., 260
*Birth and Death of the Sun*, 271
*Birth of China*, 47

*Birth of the Republic*, 98
Bitter, F., 270
*Black Boy*, 176
*Black Cloud*, 274
*Black Mother*, 55
Blackmer, D. L. M., 248
Blackmore, R. D., 118
Blake, W., 94
Blau, P., 246
*Bleak House*, 119
Bloch, M., 68
Blom, E., 182, 199
Boas, F., 195
Boccaccio, G., 66
Boeck, W., 195
Boethius, 39
Boger, L. A., 282
*Book of English Essays*, 179
*Book of English Poetry*, 156
*Book of the Play*, 166
*Book of the States*, 284
*Book Review Digest*, 281
*Books in Print*, 278
Boring, E. G., 283
Born, M., 270
*Born Free*, 265
*Bosses, The*, 60
Boswell, J., 94
BOTANY, see BIOLOGICAL SCIENCES
Botkin, B. A., 180
Bourjaily, V., 140
Bovill, E. W., 55
Bowen, C. D., 173
Bowen, E., 126
Bowers, C. G., 224
Bowers, F., 45, 48
Bowie, H., 195
Bowles, C., 46
Bowra, C. M., 35
Boyle, K., 140
Boyle, R., 86
*Boys, C. V.*, 271
Bradbury, R., 150, 274
Braddock, R., 252
Bradley, A. C., 81
Braine, J., 126
*Brainwashing*, 247
*Brave Men*, 226
*Brave New World*, 127
*Brave New World Revisited*, 231
*Bread and Wine*, 114
Brecht, B., 167
Bredvold, L. I., 88
*Brewer's Dictionary of Phrase and Fable*, 281
*Brideshead Revisited*, 129
*Brief Lives*, 85
*Brighter Than a Thousand Suns*, 272
*Brighton Rock*, 127
Brinnin, J. M., 156
Brinton, C. C., 97, 218, 222
*British Authors of the Nineteenth Century*, 281
*British Government*, 233
BRITISH NOVELS, 116 ff.
Brockway, W., 199
Brontë, C., 118
Brontë, E., 118
Brooks, C., 156
Brooks, V. W., 173, 180
*Brothers Karamazov*, 104
Brown, D. M., 46
Brown, H., 235
Brown, J. A. C., 261
Brown, L. A., 240

Brown, R., 252
Brown, W. N., 46
*Brown Decades*, 225
Browne, T., 86
Browning, E. B., 157
Browning, R., 157
Bruun, G., 222
Bryan, M., 282
Bryant, A., 221
Bryant, M., 252
Bryce, J., 230
Buber, M., 208
Buddenbrook, W. von, 265
*Buddenbrooks*, 112
Buddha, 213
*Buddhism*, 214
*Buddhism: Its Essence and Manifestations*, 45
Buell, R. L., 55
*Buffalo Bill and the Wild West*, 175
Bulfinch, T., 35
*Bulletin of the Atomic Scientists*, 187
*Bullivant and the Lambs*, 126
Bulwer-Lytton, E., 41
Bunce, W. K., 49
Bunyan, J., 86
Burckhardt, J., 75
*Bureaucracy in Modern Society*, 246
Burk, J. N., 200
Burke, A. E., 282
Burke, E., 94
Burks, A. W., 49
*Burl Ives Song Book*, 156
Burnet, J., 206
Burns, A. F., 235
Burns, J. M., 231
Burns, R., 94
Burrows, M., 52
Burton, R., 86
Bury, J. B., 35
*Business Periodicals Index*, 283
Buss, C. A., 50
Butler, S., 119
Butterfield, H., 97
*Butterfly, The*, 145
Butwell, R. A., 50
*Buyer's Market*, 129
Byron, G. G., 157
*Byzantine Painting*, 197
*Byzantium: Greatness and Decline*, 52

Cable, G. W., 134
*Caedmon Treasury of Modern Poets*, 162
Caesar, 39
*Caesar and Christ*, 41
Calder, R., 240
Calderón de la Barca, F. E., 61
Caldwell, E., 140, 150
*Call of the Wild*, 143
*Cambridge Ancient History*, 283
*Cambridge History of English Literature*, 280
*Cambridge Medieval History*, 283
*Cambridge Modern History*, 283
Campbell, R. J., 284
Camus, A., 111, 180
*Candide*, 97
Candland, D. K., 260
*Canterbury Tales*, 66, 162
Capek, K., 111, 274
*Capitalism, Socialism and Democracy*, 237
Capote, T., 140, 150

*Captain Cook's Voyages of Discovery*, 241
*Caravan*, 52
*Caribbean*, 61
Carlyle, T., 98
*Carmen*, 105
Carmer, C., 240
Carrier, W., 156
Carroll, J. B., 252
Carroll, L., 119
Carson, R., 240, 266
Cartmell, V. H., 166
Cary, J., 126
Casanova, G., 94
*Casanova's Chinese Restaurant*, 129
Caso, A., 61
*Cassell's Encyclopaedia of World Literature*, 280
Cassidy, F. G., 252
Cassirer, E., 98, 208
Castellanos, R., 60
Castiglione, B., 73
*Castle of Otranto*, 97
*Catch-22*, 143
*Catcher in the Rye*, 145
Cather, W., 88, 140
*Catholic Encyclopedia*, 283
Catullus, 39
*Caucasian Chalk Circle*, 167
*Causes of World War III*, 232
Cavert, S. M., 214
*Caves of Steel*, 274
Cellini, B., 73
*Century of Total War*, 245
Ceram, C. W., 218
Cerf, B. A., 166
Cervantes Saavedra, M. de, 73
Chadwick, J., 252
*Challenge*, 187
*Challenge of Scandinavia*, 223
*Challenge to America*, 237
*Chamber Music*, 201
Champlin, J. D., 282
*Changing Map of Asia*, 242
Chapin, H., 271
*Charlemagne*, 69
*Charles Dickens*, 174
*Charterhouse of Parma*, 106
Chase, M. E., 214
Chase, S., 246, 252
Chaucer, G., 66, 161
Cheesman, E., 266
Chekhov, A., 150, 167
*Chemical Abstracts*, 278
*Chemical Encyclopedia*, 284
CHEMISTRY, see PHYSICAL SCIENCES
Cheney, S., 169, 195
Chesterfield, Lord, 94
*Chief Elizabethan Dramatists*, 79
Child, I., 261
*Child and Society*, 246
*Child of the Century*, 174
*Child Training and Personality*, 261
Childe, V. G., 219
*Childhood and Adolescence*, 260
*Children Are Bored on Sunday*, 153
*Children of Sánchez*, 61
*Children's Hour*, 167
CHINA, 43 ff., 47
*Chinese Art*, 48
Chinoy, E., 246
Chisholm, G. G., 284
*Choephoroe*, 33
*Chronicles of America*, 224

*Chronicles of England, France, and Spain,* 67
*Chronicles of the House of Borgia,* 75
Churchill, W. S., 218, 222
Chute, M., 68, 81, 88
Ciardi, J., 156
Cicero, 40
*Cicero and the Roman Republic,* 41
*Citizen Hearst,* 176
*City and the Stars,* 274
*City in History,* 249
*City of God,* 39
*City of Man,* 199
*City of the Sun,* 74
*Civilization of Rome,* 41
*Civilization of the Renaissance in Italy,* 75
Clark, G. L., 284
Clark, J. M., 235
Clark, K. W., 195
Clarke, A. C., 274
*Class and Society,* 248
*Classic Theatre,* 166
*Classical Tradition,* 42
*Classics in Translation: Latin Literature,* 39
*Clea,* 126
Cleator, P. E., 253
Clemens, S. L., see Twain, M.
*Cleopatra,* 174
*Cloister and the Hearth,* 70
*Closing the Ring,* 223
*Clouds,* 33
Clough, S. B., 221
Clyde, P. H., 218
Cobban, A., 98
*Cocktail Party,* 170
Coffin, R. P. T., 161
Cohen, M. R., 208
Cole, A. C., 225
Cole, C. W., 221
Coleridge, S. T., 81, 157
Colette, 150
*Collier's Encyclopedia,* 279
Collins, W., 119
*Colonial American Writing,* 86
*Color of Darkness,* 152
*Columbia Dictionary of Modern European Literature,* 280
*Columbia Encyclopedia,* 279
*Columbia Lippincott Gazetteer of the World,* 279
*Columbia-Viking Desk Encyclopedia,* 279
*Comédie Humaine,* 103
*Comfortable Words,* 253
*Comic Tradition in America,* 182
*Coming of the Civil War,* 224
*Coming of the French Revolution,* 98
Commager, H. S., 224
*Commentaries* (Caesar), 39
Commins, S., 205
*Common Reader,* 185
*Common Sense,* 96
*Communist China and Asia,* 47
*Communist Manifesto,* 229
*Community Power Structure,* 247
*Compass History of Art Series,* 195
*Compleat Angler,* 88
*Complete Book of Etiquette,* 285
*Complete Book of Twentieth Century Music,* 282
*Complete Greek Drama,* 32
*Complete Greek Tragedies,* 32
*Complete Library of World Art,* 194
*Complete Opera Book,* 282
*Complete Roman Drama,* 39
*Complete Stories of the Great Ballets,* 201
*Composition in Pictures,* 195
*Comprehensive Dictionary of Psychological and Psychoanalytical Terms,* 258
Compton-Burnett, I., 126
Conant, J. B., 271
*Concerto, The,* 200
*Concise Chemical and Technical Dictionary,* 284
*Concise Encyclopedia of Philosophy and Philosophers,* 283
*Confessions* (Rousseau), 97
*Confessions* (St. Augustine), 39
*Confessions of an English Opium-Eater,* 173
*Confident Years,* 180
Confucius, 47
Congreve, W., 86
*Connecticut Yankee in King Arthur's Court,* 137
*Conquest by Man,* 241
*Conquest of Mexico,* 62
*Conquest of Peru,* 62
Conrad, J., 119, 126, 180
*Conscience of the Rich,* 129
*Consolation of Philosophy,* 39
Constant, B., 104
*Constitution and What It Means Today,* 230
*Constitution of the United States,* 94, 230
*Constitutions and Constitutional Trends Since World War II,* 230
*Contemporary Arab Politics,* 53
*Contemporary Philosophy,* 208
CONTINENTAL NOVELS, 101 ff.
*Conversation in Sicily,* 115
Conze, E., 45
Cook, D. E., 278
Cook, J., 241
Coon, C., 52, 246
Cooper, J. F., 134
Copland, A., 200
Coppard, A. E., 150
Corbett, P. E., 232
Corneille, P., 86
Corvo, F., 75
Corwin, E. S., 230
*Cosmopolitan Atlas,* 279
Coulton, G. G., 68
*Count of Monte Cristo,* 104
*Counterfeiters, The,* 111
*Courage to Be,* 210
*Course of American Democratic Thought,* 229
*Courtier, The,* 73
*Cousin Bette,* 103
Cousteau, J. Y., 241
Covarrubias, M., 61
*Cowboy Songs and Other Frontier Ballads,* 159
Cowden, R. W., 180
Cowell, F. R., 41
Cowley, M., 180
Craig, H., 81
Crane, B., 235
Crane, S., 135, 150
*Cranford,* 120
Craven, A. O., 224
Craven, T., 196

*Crazy Hunter*, 140
*Creation of Sculpture*, 197
*Creation of the Universe*, 272
*Creative Power*, 262
*Creative Process*, 194
Creekmore, H., 156
Creel, H. G., 47
Cressey, G. B., 47, 241
Crèvecoeur, St. J. de, 95
*Crime and Custom in Savage Society*, 248
*Crime and Punishment*, 104
*Crime and Society*, 250
*Crime of Sylvestre Bonnard*, 104
Crisler, L., 266
CRITICISM, 177 ff.
*Criticism*, 187
*Critique of Pure Reason*, 96
Cromer, E. B., 52
*Cross Currents in 17th Century English Literature*, 89
*Crosscurrents: Modern Techniques*, 180
Crossman, R. H. S., 229
Crow, J., 61
Crow, L. D., 257
*Crucibles*, 272
*Cruden's Complete Concordance to the Holy Scriptures*, 212
*Crusade in Europe*, 223
*Crusades, The* (Lamb), 69
*Cry, the Beloved Country*, 56
Cullen, C., 159
*Cultural Background of Personality*, 261
*Cultural Patterns and Technical Change*, 248
*Culture and Personality*, 261
*Culture of Cities*, 198
*Culture Worlds*, 242
Cummings, E. E., 159
*Cumulative Book Index*, 278
Cunha, E. da, 60
Cunliffe, M., 173
Curie, E., 173
*Current American Usage*, 252
*Current Biography*, 281
*Curtains*, 169
Curti, M. E., 225
*Cyclopedia of Painters and Paintings*, 282

*Damnation of Theron Ware*, 135
Dampier, W. C., 271
Dana, R. H., 173
DANCE, 201
*Dance Has Many Faces*, 202
*Dance to the Music of Time*, 129
*Dance to the Piper*, 201
D'Annunzio, G., 111
Dante Alighieri, 66
Dantzig, T., 271
Darkenwald, G. G., 242
*Darkness at Noon*, 112
Darling, F. F., 266
*Dartmouth Bible*, 212
Darwin, C., 173, 266
Davidson, B., 55
Davie, M. R., 246
Davies, H. S., 253
Da Vinci, Leonardo, 73
*Dawn of African History*, 56
*Dawn of Civilization*, 249
Dawson, C., 220

*Days of H. L. Mencken*, 174
*Dead Sea Scrolls*, 52
*Dead Souls*, 105
Dean, V. M., 45
*Death of a Salesman*, 170
*Death of the Heart*, 126
De Bary, W. T., 45
Debenham, F., 241
De Burgh, W. G., 41
*Decameron*, 66
*Decipherment of Linear B*, 252
*Declaration of Independence*, 94
*Decline and Fall of the Roman Empire*, 41
*Deep Range*, 274
*Defence of Poesy*, 80
*Definition of Tragedy*, 182
Defoe, D., 88, 95
De Forest, J. W., 135
De Grazia, S., 246
De La Mare, W., 150, 159
De Mille, A., 201
*Democracy in America*, 231
Demosthenes, 33
Denney, R., 249
De Quincey, T., 173
Descartes, R., 86
*Desert of Love*, 113
DESIGN, 198 ff.
*Design Fundamentals*, 199
*Desire Under the Elms*, 168
*Destination: Universe!*, 274
*Destiny of Fire*, 69
Deutsch, D., 258
*Development of English Drama*, 166
Dewey, J., 208
*Dialogues* (Plato), 34
*Dialogues Concerning Natural Religion*, 207
*Dialogues of the Dead*, 34
*Dialogues of the Gods*, 34
*Diana of the Crossways*, 120
*Diary* (Pepys), 88
*Diary of a Young Girl*, 173
Díaz del Castillo, B., 61
Dickens, C., 98, 119
Dickinson, E., 157, 162
Dickinson, G. L., 35
DICTIONARIES, 280
*Dictionary of Abstract Painting*, 282
*Dictionary of American Biography*, 281
*Dictionary of American-English Usage Based on Fowler*, 280
*Dictionary of Antiques and the Decorative Arts*, 282
*Dictionary of Applied Chemistry*, 284
*Dictionary of Architecture*, 282
*Dictionary of Arts and Crafts*, 282
*Dictionary of Astronomy and Astronautics*, 285
*Dictionary of Biology*, 285
*Dictionary of Contemporary American Usage*, 253
*Dictionary of Dates*, 283
*Dictionary of Economics*, 283
*Dictionary of Geography*, 280
*Dictionary of Modern English Usage*, 280
*Dictionary of Music and Musicians*, 282
*Dictionary of National Biography*, 281
*Dictionary of Painters and Engravers*, 282

*Dictionary of Philosophy*, 282
*Dictionary of Philosophy and Psychology*, 282
*Dictionary of Psychology*, 257, 283
*Dictionary of Science*, 285
*Dictionary of Scientific Terms*, 284
Diderot, D., 95
Diehl, C., 52
Dimock, M. E., 231
Dinesen, I., 150
Diogenes Laertius, 33
*Diplomacy in the Near and Middle East*, 53
*Diplomatic History of Europe Since the Congress of Vienna*, 220
*Diplomatic History of the American People*, 224
Diringer, D., 253
*Discourse on Method*, 86
*Discovering Poetry*, 180
*Discovery and Conquest of Mexico*, 61
*Discovery and Exploration*, 241
*Discovery of India*, 46
*Discovery of the World*, 240
*Divine Comedy*, 66
Dobzhansky, T., 266
*Doctor Faustus*, 80, 170
*Dr. Zhivago*, 113
*Documentary History of the United States*, 225
*Don Flows Home to the Sea*, 114
*Don Juan in Hell*, 170
*Don Quixote*, 73
*Doña Bárbara*, 60
*Doña Perfecta*, 105
Donleavy, J. P., 141
Donne, J., 79
*Door into Summer*, 274
*Dorland's Illustrated Medical Dictionary*, 284
Dos Passos, J., 141
Dostoevski, F., 104
Douglas, N., 126
*Down in the Holler*, 254
Downer, A. S., 166
DRAMA, 163 ff.
*Drama on Stage*, 166
*Dream of the Red Chamber*, 48
Dreiser, T., 141
Drever, J., 257
Drew, E., 180
Driver, H. E., 246
Druon, M., 68
Dryden, J., 86
*Dubliners*, 151
Du Bois, C., 50
Dudley, D. R., 41
Duerrenmatt, F., 111
Duffy, J., 55
Dumas, A., 89, 104
Dumas, F., 241
Dunn, L. C., 266
Durant, W., 35, 41, 69, 75, 89, 205
Durkheim, E., 246
Durrell, L., 126
Dusseter, R. F., 258
*Dyer's Hand*, 179

*Early English Ballads*, 162
*Early Greek Philosophy*, 206
East, W. G., 242
*East Asia: The Great Tradition*, 46
*East Asian History Today*, 50
*Eastern Christendom*, 215
Ebenstein, W., 229

*Eclipse of Community*, 250
*Eclogues*, 41
*Economic Almanac*, 284
*Economic and Social History of Medieval Europe*, 69
*Economic Geography*, 242
*Economic History of Europe*, 221
*Economic Institutions and Human Welfare*, 235
*Economic Interpretation of the Constitution of the United States*, 230
*Economic Issues of the 1960's*, 236
*Economic Report of the President*, 235
ECONOMICS, 234 ff.
*Economics: An Introductory Analysis*, 237
*Economics and Liberalism*, 238
*Economics of the World Today*, 238
*Economy and Society*, 249
*Economy, Liberty and the State*, 236
Edel, L., 173
Edman, I., 194, 205
*Education of Henry Adams*, 172
*Educational Psychology*, 262
*Egoist, The*, 120
*Egyptian, The*, 115
*Egypt's Liberation*, 54
*Eight Famous Elizabethan Plays*, 79
*Eight Great Comedies from Aristophanes to Shaw*, 166
*Eight Great Tragedies from Aeschylus to O'Neill*, 166
EIGHTEENTH CENTURY, 91 ff.
*Eighteenth Century Background*, 98
*Eighty-five Poems* (MacNeice), 160
Einstein, A., 200
Eiseley, L. C., 266
Eisenhower, D. D., 223
*Eleanor of Aquitaine and the Four Kings*, 69
*Elements of Geography*, 241
*Elements of Political Geography*, 242
Eliot, G., 75, 119
Eliot, T. S., 81, 159, 161, 170, 180
*Elizabeth and Essex*, 82
*Elizabeth the Queen*, 80, 167
*Elizabethan Lyrics and Shakespearean Sonnets*, 162
*Elizabethan Miniatures*, 82
*Elizabethan Reader, Portable*, 80
*Elizabethan Songbook*, 199
*Elizabethan Verse and Its Music*, 162
Elkin, F., 246
Elliott, G. P., 156
Ellis, J. T., 214
Ellison, R., 141
Ellman, R., 173
*Elmtown's Youth*, 247
*Elsie Venner*, 135
*Emergence of Modern America*, 225
*Emergence of Modern Turkey*, 53
*Emerging City*, 247
*Emerging Nations*, 248
Emerson, R. W., 157, 181
*Emile*, 96
*Emma*, 118
*Emotion: Bodily Changes*, 260
*Emotions and Memory*, 261
Empson, W., 181
*Empty Canvas*, 113
*Encyclopaedia Britannica*, 279
*Encyclopedia Americana*, 279
*Encyclopedia of American History*, 283

*Encyclopedia of Chemistry*, 284
*Encyclopedia of Modern World Politics*, 284
*Encyclopedia of Painting*, 282
*Encyclopedia of Psychology*, 283
*Encyclopedia of Religion and Ethics*, 282
*Encyclopedia of Sports*, 285
*Encyclopedia of the Social Sciences*, 283
*Encyclopedia of World History*, 283
ENCYCLOPEDIAS, 279
*End as a Man*, 147
*End of Eternity*, 274
*End of My Life*, 140
Enders, R. K., 268
*Endgame*, 167
*Enduring Art of Japan*, 49
*Energy Sources*, 240
Engels, F., 207, 229
ENGINEERING, see PHYSICAL SCIENCES
*England of Elizabeth*, 82
Engle, P., 156
English, H. B., 258
*English Democratic Ideas in the 17th Century*, 89
ENGLISH NOVELS, see BRITISH NOVELS
*English Philosophers from Bacon to Mill*, 206
*Enjoy, Enjoy!*, 181
*Enjoyment of Music*, 200
*Enneads, The*, 206
*Enquiry Concerning the Human Understanding*, 207
*Enriquillo*, 60
*Epic of America*, 224
*Epic of Latin American Literature*, 62
*Epitaph of a Small Winner*, 60
Erasmus, D., 74
*Erasmus of Rotterdam*, 76
*Erewhon*, 119
*Eros and Civilization*, 259
Espenshade, E. D., 279
*Essay and General Literature Index*, 278
*Essay Concerning Human Understanding*, 87
*Essay on Man* (Cassirer), 208
*Essay on the Principle of Population*, 96
ESSAYS, 177 ff.
*Essays in Biography*, 236
*Essays in Individual Psychology*, 258
*Essays of Elia*, 182
*Essays of Three Decades*, 182
*Essays on Elizabethan Drama*, 81
*Essential Left*, 229
Esslin, M., 169
*Esther Waters*, 120
Estrich, R. M., 253
*Ethan Frome*, 146
*Etiquette*, 285
*Eugénie Grandet*, 103
*Eumenides*, 33
Euripides, 33
*Europe and the French Imperium*, 222
*European and Comparative Government*, 232
*European Composers Today*, 282
EUROPEAN HISTORY, 219 ff.
EUROPEAN NOVELS, see CONTINENTAL NOVELS
*European Painting and Sculpture*, 197
Evans, B., 253

*Everyman*, 170
*Everyman's United Nations*, 232
Ewen, D., 200, 282
*Exile's Return*, 180
*Existential Psychology*, 259
*Existentialism from Dostoevsky to Sartre*, 208
*Expansion of Elizabethan England*, 82
*Experience and Nature*, 208
*Exploding Metropolis*, 246
*Exploring Poetry*, 156
*Exurbanites, The*, 250
Eysenck, H. J., 258

*F.P.A. Book of Quotations*, 281
*Fables* (Aesop), 33
*Fables* (La Fontaine), 87
*Face of North America*, 241
*Fads and Fallacies in the Name of Science*, 272
Fage, J. D., 55
*Failure of the "New Economics,"* 236
Fairbank, J. K., 46, 47
*Faith of the Roman Church*, 215
*Fall of the Spanish American Empire*, 62
*Familiar Quotations*, 281
*Family of Man*, 196
*Famous Chinese Short Stories*, 48, 150
*Famous Dancers*, 202
*Famous Utopias of the Renaissance*, 74
*Fanfare for Elizabeth*, 82
FAR EAST, 43 ff.
*Far East*, 218
*Far from the Madding Crowd*, 120
*Far Side of Paradise*, 174
Farb, P., 241
*Farewell to Arms*, 143
Farnham, M. F., 260
Farrell, J. T., 141, 150
Farrington, B., 35
*Fathers and Sons*, 106
Faulkner, R. N., 198
Faulkner, W., 141, 150
*Faust*, 157
Fay, S. B., 223
*Fear and Trembling*, 207
*Federalist Papers*, 95
Ferguson, W. K., 221
Fergusson, F., 169
*Feudal Society*, 68
FICTION, see NOVELS; SHORT STORY
*Field Book of Animals in Winter*, 267
*Field Book of Ponds and Streams*, 267
*Field Book Series*, 268
*Field Guide Series*, 268
Fielding, H., 95
*Fifteen Modern American Poets*, 156
*Fifty Centuries of Art*, 197
*Fifty Famous Artists*, 196
*Fifty Major Documents of the Twentieth Century*, 223
*Financier, The*, 141
Finch, J. K., 271
Finch, V. C., 241
FINE ARTS, 191 ff.
Fink, D. G., 271
Finley, M. I., 35
Firkins, I. T. E., 278
*First Night of Twelfth Night*, 81
*First Stage: A Chronicle of the Development of English Drama from Its Beginnings to the 1580's*, 170
Fisch, M., 205

Fischer, L., 46
Fisher, S. N., 52
Fisher, W. B., 241
Fitzgerald, F. S., 142, 150
*Five Approaches of Literary Criticism*, 183
*Five Great Philosophies of Life*, 209
*Flame of Islam*, 69
*Flame of Life*, 111
*Flaming Heart*, 197
Flanagan, G. A., 196
Flaubert, G., 104, 181
*Flaubert and Madame Bovary*, 175
*Flesh and Blood*, 113
Fletcher, J., 85
Flexner, J. T., 196
*Flies, The*, 60
*Flight from the Enchanter*, 128
Flornoy, B., 61
*Flowering of New England*, 180
*Flowering Plants and Ferns*, 284
*Folkways*, 250
*For 2¢ Plain*, 181
*Foreign Affairs*, 187
*Forest and the Sea*, 265
*Form and Function*, 198
*Form and Meaning in Drama*, 36
Forrester, G., 285
Forster, E. M., 126, 181
*Forsyte Saga*, 127
*Forty Days of Musa Dagh*, 115
*44 Irish Short Stories*, 150
*42nd Parallel*, 141
Foscue, E. J., 242
Fosdick, H. E., 213, 214
*Foundations of Modern Art*, 197
*Four Stages of Renaissance Style*, 76
*Four Verse Plays* (Anderson), 167
Fowler, H. W., 280
Fox, G., 86
France, A., 104, 111
Francis of Assisi, St., 67
*François Villon*, 69
Frank, A., 173
Frank, P., 209
*Frankenstein*, 121
Franklin, B., 95
*Franny and Zooey*, 145
Frazer, J. G., 35
Frederic, H., 135
*Freedom Reader*, 230
Freeman, D. S., 173, 225
Freeman, O. W., 241
*French Architecture*, 198
*French Revolution* (Carlyle), 98
*French Revolution* (Thompson), 222
*French Stories and Tales*, 150
Freud, S., 258
*Freud and the Twentieth Century*, 259
*Freud: His Life and His Mind*, 259
Friar, K., 156
Friend, J. A. N., 271
*Frogs*, 33
Froissart, J., 67
*From Here to Eternity*, 143
*From Homer to Joyce*, 36, 76
*From Lenin to Malenkov*, 223
*From the Earth to the Moon*, 274
Fromm, E., 260
*Frontier in American History*, 226
Frost, R., 159, 161
Fry, R. E., 194
Fuentes, C., 60
*Full Employment in a Free Society*, 235

*Functions and Policies of American Government*, 231
*Fundamental Principles of the Metaphysics of Morals*, 207
Fung Yu-lan, 47
*Future as History*, 247

Gabriel, R. H., 229
Galbraith, J. K., 236
Gallegos, R., 60
*Gallipoli*, 54
Galsworthy, J., 127
Galván, M. de J., 60
Gamow, G., 271
Gandhi, M. K., 46
*Gandhi*, 46
Gardner, H., 196, 282
Gardner, M., 272
*Gargantua*, 74
Garn, S. M., 247
Garnett, D., 127
Gaskell, E., 120
Gassner, J., 166, 169
*Gathering Storm*, 222
Gautier, T., 105
Gay, J., 95
Gaynor, F., 285
*General Introduction to Psychoanalysis*, 258
*General Theory of Employment, Interest and Money*, 237
*Geoffrey Chaucer of England*, 68
Geoffrey of Monmouth, 67
Geoffroy de Villehardouin, 67
GEOGRAPHY, 239 ff.
*Geography of Europe*, 241
*Geography of the Northlands*, 242
*Geography of the Pacific*, 241
GEOLOGY, see BIOLOGICAL SCIENCES; GEOGRAPHY; PHYSICAL SCIENCES
*George Washington, Man and Monument*, 173
*Georgics*, 41
*German Ideology*, 207
*Germinal*, 106
*Gestalt Psychology*, 259
*Getting and Spending*, 235
*Ghana*, 55
Ghiselin, B., 184
Gibb, H. A. R., 53
Gibbon, E., 41
Gide, A., 111
Giedion, S., 198
Gilmer, B. V., 262
Gilmore, M. P., 222
*Ginger Man*, 141
Ginsburg, N., 45
Giraudoux, J., 167
Gissing, G., 120
*Gladiators, The*, 42
Glasgow, E., 142
*Glass Menagerie*, 168
Glazer, N., 214, 249
Gloag, J., 198
*Glory That Was Greece*, 36
*Glossary of Botanic Terms*, 284
*Go Tell It on the Mountain*, 140
Goad, H., 253
*Goal of Economic Growth*, 237
*God That Failed*, 229
*God Was Born in Exile*, 42
*Gods and Men*, 220
*Gods, Graves, and Scholars*, 218
*Gods, Heroes, and Men of Ancient Greece*, 36

God's Little Acre, 140
God's Word into English, 214
Goethe, J. W. von, 95, 157
Gogol, N., 105
Gold, H., 142
Golden, H., 181
Golden Apples of the Sun, 150, 274
Golden Ass, 39
Golden Bough, 35
Golden Bowl, 136
Golden Land, 60
Golden Serpent, 59
Golden Trade of the Moors, 55
Golden Treasury, 156
Golden Warrior, 69
Goldin, J., 213
Golding, W., 127
Goldman, E. F., 231
Goldoni, C., 95
Goldschmidt, W., 247
Goldsmith, O., 95
Goliard Poets, 67
Gombrich, E. H. J., 194
Goncharov, I., 105
Gooch, G. P., 89
Good, D., 242
Good Companions, 129
Good Man Is Hard to Find, 152
Good Soldier: Schweik, 111
Good Woman of Setzuan, 167
Goodbye, Columbus, 153
Goodman, P., 181
Goodman, R., 166
Goodrich, M., 35
Gordimer, N., 55
Gorgias, 34
Gottmann, J., 241
Gourou, P., 241
Gover, R., 142
GOVERNMENT, see POLITICS
Government and Politics of Southeast Asia, 50
Government and Politics of the Middle East, 53
Government of Japan, 49
Grammar of Science, 272
Grammar Without Tears, 253
Grand Alliance, 222
Grand Mademoiselle, 89
Grandissimes, The, 134
Grandmothers, The, 146
Granger, E., 278
Grant, M., 42
Grant, U. S., 225
Granville-Barker, H., 81
Grapes of Wrath, 145
Grass Harp, 150
Graves, R., 35, 42, 181
Gravity, 272
Great American Poetry, 162
Great American Short Stories, 151
Great Ascent, 236
Great Britain and the United States, 220
Great Chain of Being, 209
Great English and American Essays, 179
Great English Short Stories, 151
Great Essays, 179
Great Essays in Science, 272
Great Expectations, 119
Great Gatsby, 142
Great German Short Novels and Stories, 151
Great Meadow, 145

Great Pianists, 201
Great Plains, 226
Great Poets of the English Language, 162
Great Political Thinkers, 229
Great Religions of the Modern World, 214
Great Russian Short Stories, 151
Great Voices of the Reformation, 213
GREECE, 29 ff.
Greek Anthology, 32
Greek Architecture, 36
Greek Civilization and Character, 36
Greek Experience, 35
Greek Historians, 32
Greek Literature in Translation, 32
Greek Mind, 35
Greek Myths, 35
Greek Philosophers, 36
Greek Poetry for Everyman, 32
Greek Reader, Portable, 32
Greek Science, 35
Greek Sculpture, 196
Greek Tragedy, 36
Greek View of Life, 35
Greek Way, 36
Greeks, The, 36
Greeks and Their Gods, 35
Green, H., 127
Green Continent, 60
Green Huntsman, 106
Green Mansions, 127
Greene, E. B., 225
Greene, G., 127
Greenough, J. B., 253
Greenough, H., 198
Greer, S., 247
Greg, W. W., 81
Grierson, H. J. C., 89
Grimm, H. J., 221
Grimmelshausen, H. J. C. von, 86
Gross, B. M., 213
Grosser, M. R., 196
Grout, D. J., 200
Grove, G., 282
Groves, C. P., 55
Growth and Structure of the English Language, 254
Growth of American Thought, 225
Growth of Physical Science, 272
Growth of Southern Nationalism, 224
Growth of the Soil, 111
Guide to American English, 254
Guide to Keynes, 236
Guide to Reference Books, 278
Guide to Science Reading, 285
Guide to the Sky, 284
Guide to the Space Age, 285
Guide to the Stars, 284
Guide to Western Architecture, 198
Guillaume, A., 214
Gulbranssen, T., 111
Gulliver's Travels, 97
Guthrie, E. R., 260
Guthrie, W. K. C., 35
Guy Mannering, 98

Hacker, L. M., 225
Hackett, F., 81
Hadas, M., 36
Hadfield, J. A., 260
Hadrian's Memoirs, 42
Hahn, J. F., 258
Hailey, W. M., 55
Haiti, The Black Republic, 62

Hakluyt, R., 79
Halecki, J. O. von, **218**
Hall, C. S., 258
Hall, D., 156
Hall, D. G. E., 50
Hall, E. T., 253
Hall, R. A., 253
Haller, W., 89
Hamilton, E., 36, 42
*Hamlet*, 80, 170
*Hamlet and Oedipus*, 82
Hamlin, T. F., 198
Hamsun, K., 111
*Handbook of Chemistry and Physics*, 284
*Handbook of Commercial Geography*, 284
*Handbook of Greek Literature*, 36
*Handful of Dust*, 129
Handlin, O., 283
Hansen, A. H., 236
Harari, M., 53
Harbage, A. B., **81**
Hardy, T., 120
Hare, F. K., 241
*Harper History of Painting*, 197
*Harper's Bible Dictionary*, 283
*Harper's Magazine*, 187
*Harper's Topical Concordance*, 212
Harriman, P. L., 283
Harris, T. L., 260
Harrison, G. B., 81, 156
Harrison, J., 36
Hart, J. D., 281
Hart, M., 174
Hartnoll, P., 281
*Harvard Dictionary of Music*, 282
*Harvard Guide to American History*, 283
*Harvard List of Books in Psychology*, 283
Harvey, P., 280, 281
Hasek, J., 111
Haskell, A., 201
Haskins, C. P., 266
Hastings, J., 282
Hauser, A., 196
Havemann, E., 258
Hawkes, J., 142
Hawthorne, N., 89, 135, **151**
Haycraft, H., 281
Hayek, F. A. von, 236
*Hazard of New Fortunes*, 136
Hazlitt, H., 236
Hazlitt, W., 181
*Hazlitt on Theatre*, 181
*Heart Is a Lonely Hunter*, 143
*Heart of Darkness*, 126
*Heart of Midlothian*, 98
*Heart of the Matter*, 127
*Heat Engines*, 273
*Heathens, The*, 247
*Heavenly City of the Eighteenth-Century Philosophers*, 97
*Heaven's My Destination*, 146
Hecht, B., 174
Heffner, R. D., 225
Hegel, G., 206
Heilbroner, R. L., 236, 247
Heilman, R. B., 81
Heine, H., 158
Heinlein, R. A., 274
Heizer, R. F., 247
Heller, J., 143
Hellman, L., 167

Héloïse and Abélard, 69
Hemingway, E., 143, 151
Henderson, H. G., 49
Henderson, I. F., 284
Henderson, J., 258
Henry, O., 151
Henry, R. S., 225
*Henry IV*, 70, 80
*Henry V*, 70, 80
*Henry VI*, 70
Henry James, 173
Hentoff, N., 201
*Hercules, My Shipmate*, 35
*Heredity, Race, and Society*, 266
*Herman Melville*, 173
Herodotus, 33
Herrick, R., 86
Herring, H. C., 61
Herrmann, P., 241
*Herself Surprised*, 126
Hersey, J., 223
Herskovits, M. J., 55
Heseltine, J. E., 280
Hesiod, 33
Hesse, H., 111
*Hidden Persuaders*, 249
*High Jungle*, 265
*High Tor*, 167
*High Wind in Jamaica*, 127
Highet, G., 42, 181
Hill, C. M., 214
Hill, R., 200
*Hills Beyond*, 153
Himes, J. S., 247
*Hinge of Fate*, 223
Hinsie, L. E., 284
*Hippolytus*, 33
Hirmer, M., 196
*Hiroshima*, 223
Hirschman, A. O., 236
*Historians of the Middle East*, 54
*Historical Abstracts*, 278
*Historical Atlas*, 279
*Historical Atlas of the World*, 279
*Historical Geology*, 266
*Historical Statistics of the United States*, 284
*Histories* (Polybius), 34
HISTORY, 216 ff.
*History* (Herodotus), 33
*History of Abyssinia*, 56
*History of American Life Series*, 225
*History of Christianity*, 215
*History of Civilization*, 218
*History of East Africa*, 56
*History of England* (Macaulay), 89
*History of England* (Trevelyan), 219
*History of France*, 219
*History of Greece*, 35
*History of Greek Literature*, 36
*History of Islam in West Africa*, 56
*History of Latin America*, 61
*History of Modern France*, 98
*History of Modern Philosophy*, 205
*History of Musical Instruments*, 200
*History of Persia*, 54
*History of Philosophy*, 205
*History of Poland*, 218
*History of Political Theory*, 229
*History of Popular Music in America*, 201
*History of Psychology and Psychiatry*, 258
*History of Rome*, 40
*History of Russia*, 222

History of Song, 201
History of the Arabs from the Earliest Times to the Present, 53
History of the Byzantine State, 54
History of the English-Speaking Peoples, 218
History of the Far East in Modern Times, 46
History of the Kings of Britain, 67
History of the Monroe Doctrine, 225
Hitchcock, H. R., 61, 198
Hitti, P. K., 53
Hobbes, T., 87
Hodeir, A., 200
Hodgkin, T. L., 56
Hoebel, E. A., 247
Hofer, W., 223
Hoffding, H., 205
Hole in the Bottom of the Sea, 240
Hollingshead, A. B., 247
Holmes, O. W., 135, 158
Holmes Reader, 230
Holt, P. M., 54, 56
Holy Bible, 212
Homans, G. C., 247
Home Book of Quotations, 281
Homecoming, 129
Homer, 33
Hoover, C. B., 236
Hoover, H. C., 225
Hopkins, G. M., 158
Horace, 40
Horia, V., 42
Horney, K., 260
Horns, Strings and Harmony, 270
Horse's Mouth, 126
Hortus Second, 284
Hotson, L., 81
House by the Medlar Tree, 106
House of Mirth, 146
House of the Seven Gables, 135
Housman, A. E., 158
How Old Is the Earth?, 272
How and Where To Look It Up, 279
How-To-Do-It Books, 285
Howard, J. T., 200
Howe, I., 158
Howells, W. D., 135
Howells, W. W., 247
Hoyle, F., 274
Huberman, L., 236
Hudson, G. F., 47
Hudson, W., 214
Hudson, W. H., 127, 266
Hudson, The, 240
Hudson Review, 187
Hughes, J. P., 253
Hughes, R., 127
Hugo, V., 69, 98, 105
Huizinga, J., 69
Human Animal, 267
Human Factor in Changing Africa, 56
Human Group, 247
Human Races, 247
Human Use of Human Beings, 250
Hume, D., 207
Humphrey, D., 201
Humphrey Clinker, 97
Humphreys, C., 214
Humphries, R., 156
Hunchback of Notre Dame, 69
Hunt, G. L., 213
Hunter, E., 247
Hunter, F., 247
Hunter, H. D., 238
Hunter, S., 196
Huntington, E., 241
Hurewitz, J. C., 53
Hurley, P. M., 272
Hurst, H. E., 242
Hussey, R. C., 266
Huxley, A., 127, 231
Huxley, J., 266
Huysmans, J. K., 105
Hyde, W. D., 209
Hylander, C. J., 266

I, Claudius, 42
Ibsen, H., 168
Idea of a Theatre, 169
Ideas and Men, 218
Ideas of the Great Economists, 238
Ides of March, 42
Idiot, The, 104
Iliad, 33
Illuminations, The, 158
Image and Idea, 183
Images of Truth, 184
Imitation of Christ, 68
Immense Journey, 266
Importance of Being Earnest, 170
Importance of Language, 209
In Dubious Battle, 145
In Praise of Folly, 74
In Praise of Love, 70
In the American Grain, 184
In the Cause of Peace, 223
In the Labyrinth, 114
In the Midst of Life, 149
Independence and After, 46
Independent Iraq, 53
Index to Poetry, 278
INDIA, 43 ff., 46
India and Pakistan, 233
Indian Art of Mexico and Central America, 61
Indian Political System, 46
Indians of North America, 246
Individualism Reconsidered, 249
Industry and Society, 250
Influence of Sea Power upon History, 1660–1783, 219
Information Please Almanac, 279
Informer, The, 128
Innocent Voyage, 127
Insects, 266
Instinct, 260
Intellectual Milieu of John Dryden, 88
International Cyclopedia of Music and Musicians, 282
International Index, 278
International Politics, 233
International Who's Who, 281
Interpreter's Dictionary of the Bible, 283
Introducing Psychology, 258
Introducing Shakespeare, 81
Introduction to Climate, 242
Introduction to Economic Science, 238
Introduction to Government, 233
Introduction to Haiku, 49
Introduction to Human Geography, 242
Introduction to Metaphysics, 208
Introduction to Modern Architecture, 199

*Introduction to Music,* 199
*Introduction to Psychology,* 258
*Introduction to Shakespeare* (Craig), 81
*Introduction to the Chinese Theatre,* 48
*Introduction to the History of West Africa,* 55
*Introductory Readings on Language,* 252
*Introductory Readings on the English Language,* 252
*Invisible Man* (Ellison), 141
*Invisible Man* (Wells), 274
Ionesco, E., 168
*Iron King,* 68
*Iron Men and Saints,* 69
*Irrepressible Conflict, 1850–1865,* 225
Irvine, W., 221
Irving, W., 151
*Is Anybody Listening?,* 255
Isaacs, J., 181
Isherwood, C., 127
*Islam,* 214
*Italian Painters of the Renaissance,* 74
*Ivan P. Pavlov,* 260
*Ivanhoe,* 70
Ives, B., 156

Jackson, B. D., 284
Jackson, S., 151
Jaeger, W., 36
Jaffe, B., 272
Jahn, J., 56
*Jamaica Talk,* 252
James, H., 136, 151
James, P. E., 242
James, W., 209, 214, 259
*James Family,* 174
*James Joyce,* 173
*Jane Eyre,* 118
JAPAN, 43 ff., 48
*Japan: A Physical, Cultural, and Regional Geography,* 49
*Japan, Past and Present,* 49
*Japanese Literature,* 49
*Japanese Literature, Anthology of,* 49
*Japanese Theatre,* 48
Jarrell, R., 182
Jarrett, H., 236
Jaspers, K., 209
*Jazz,* 200
*Jazz Makers,* 201
*Jean-Christophe,* 114
Jeans, J., 272
Jefferson, T., 96
*Jefferson,* 98
*Jemmy Button,* 61
Jespersen, O., 254
*Jew of Malta,* 80
*Jewish Encyclopedia,* 283
*John Adams and the American Revolution,* 173
*John Brown's Body,* 159
Johnson, A., 283
Johnson, E., 174
Johnson, M. C., 194
Johnson, S., 89, 96
Joinville, Jean de, 67
Jones, A. H. M., 56
Jones, C. F., 242
Jones, E., 82, 174
Jones, H. S., 266, 284

Jones, J., 143
Jonson, B., 79
*Joseph Andrews,* 95
*Joseph Tetralogy,* 112
*Journal of the Plague Year,* 88
*Journey to Greatness,* 200
*Journey to the Center of the Earth,* 274
Joyce, J., 128, 151
*Jude the Obscure,* 120
*Judgment Day,* 141
Jung, C. G., 259
Jungk, R., 272
*Jungle, The,* 145
*Jung's Psychology and Its Social Meaning,* 259
*Juno and the Paycock,* 168, 170
Jurji, E. J., 214
*Justine,* 126
Juvenal, 40

Kafka, F., 112, 151
Kahin, G. M., 45, 50
Kant, I., 96, 207
Kapek, K., see Capek, K.
Karn, H. W., 262
Kaufmann, E. Jr., 198
Kazantzakis, N., 112
Keats, J., 158, 182
Keene, D., 49
Kelly, A., 69
*Kenilworth,* 82
Kennan, G. F., 232
Kennedy, J. F., 174
*Kenyon Review,* 187
Kerouac, J., 143
Key, V. O., 231
Keynes, J. M., 236
Khadduri, M., 53
*Kidnapped,* 121
Kierkegaard, S., 207
Kimble, G. H. T., 242
*Kim,* 128
*Kindly Ones,* 129
*King and the Queen,* 114
*King James (Authorized) Version of The Bible,* 85
*King Lear,* 80
*King Leopold's Congo,* 56
*King Solomon's Ring,* 267
*Kingdom of Jordan,* 54
Kingsley, C., 120
Kingzett, C. T., 284
Kipling, R., 128, 151
Kirk, G. E., 53
Kitto, H. D. F., 36
Kittredge, G. L., 253
Klein, M., 260
Kluckhohn, C., 247
Kniffen, F. B., 242
*Knights,* 33
Knoles, G. H., 218
Kobbé, G., 282
Koestler, A., 42, 112
Kogon, E., 223
Kohler, W., 259
Kohn, H., 231
*Koran, The,* 53
Kramer, E. E., 272
*Krapp's Last Tape and Other Dramatic Pieces,* 167
*Kreutzer Sonata,* 106
*Kristin Lavransdatter,* 70
Krokover, R., 202
Kronenberger, L., 179

Krutch, J. W., 182, 267
Kunitz, S. J., 281
Kyd, T., 79

La Barre, W., 267
Laborde, E. D., 241
*Labyrinth of Solitude*, 62
*Lady Chatterley's Lover*, 128
*Lady into Fox*, 127
La Farge, O., 247
Lafayette, Madame de, 87
La Fontaine, J. de, 87
Lagerkvist, P., 112
Lagerlöf, S., 112
Lamb, C., 182
Lamb, H., 69, 75
Lampedusa, G. di, 112
Lamprecht, S. P., 205
*Land of the 500 Million*, 47
*Landmarks for Beginners in Philosophy*, 205
Lang, P. H., 200
Langer, W. L., 283
Langland, W., 67
LANGUAGE, 251 ff.
*Language*, 249
*Language in History*, 253
*Language, Truth and Logic*, 208
Lanier, S., 158
*Laokoon*, 96
Lardner, R., 151
*Lark, The*, 68
Larkin, O. W., 196
La Rochefoucauld, Duc de, 87
Lasswell, H. D., 231
*Last Days of Pompeii*, 41
*Late George Apley*, 144
*Late Mattia Pascal*, 113
LATIN AMERICA, 57 ff.
*Latin America* (James), 242
*Latin America* (Thomas), 222
*Latin American Architecture Since 1945*, 61
*Latin American Politics and Government*, 232
*Latin Poetry in Verse Translation*, 39
Latourette, K. S., 215
*Laughing Boy*, 247
Lavedan, P., 198
*Law of Primitive Man*, 247
Lawrence, A. W., 36
Lawrence, D. H., 128, 151, 182
Lawrence, T. E., 53
*Lawrence of Arabia*, 175
*Laws, The*, 34
*Leaves of Grass*, 159, 162
Lebon, H. G., 242
Le Corbusier, 194
*Lectures on Shakespeare*, 81
Lee, A. M., 248
*Lee's Generals*, 225
Le Febvre, G., 98
Leff, G., 69
*Legacy of Greece*, 36
*Legacy of the Ancient World*, 41
*Legends of Charlemagne*, 35
*Legislative Struggle*, 213
Leibniz, G. W. von, 87
Leighton, D. C., 247
Leithauser, J. G., 242
Lenczowski, G., 53
Lenin, V. I., 229
*Leonardo da Vinci*, 196
*Leopard, The*, 112
Lerner, M., 248

Lessing, G. E., 96
Lessing, L. P., 272
LETTERS, 177 ff.
*Letters from an American Farmer*, 95
*Letters from Joseph Conrad*, 180
*Letters of James Agee to Father Flye*, 179
*Letters to His Son* (Chesterfield), 94
*Leviathan*, 87
Levin, H., 82
Lewis, A. O., Jr., 183
Lewis, B., 53
Lewis, D. B. W., 69
Lewis, O., 61
Lewis, S., 143
Lewis, W. H., 89
Ley, W., 272
*Liberia*, 55
*Library of Great Painters*, 194
Lie, T., 223
*Lie Down in Darkness*, 146
Lieuwen, E., 62
*Life and Labor in the Old South*, 225
*Life and Times of A. Vespucci*, 240
*Life and Work of Sigmund Freud*, 174
*Life and Works of Beethoven*, 200
*Life in Mexico*, 61
*Life in Shakespeare's England*, 79
*Life of Abraham Lincoln*, 174
*Life of Billy Yank*, 226
*Life of Greece*, 35
*Life of Jesus*, 42
*Life of Johnny Reb*, 226
*Life of Michelangelo*, 75
*Life of Nelson*, 175
*Life of Samuel Johnson*, 94
*Life of William Shakespeare*, 80
*Life on Other Worlds*, 266
*Light and the Dark*, 129
*Light in August*, 142
*Lime Twig*, 142
*Limits of the Earth*, 267
Lin Yutang, 48, 205
Lincoln, A., 182
Lindsay, A. D., 229
Lindsay, V., 159, 161
*Linguistic Interludes*, 254
LINGUISTICS, see LANGUAGE
*Linguistics and Your Language*, 253
Linscott, R. N., 205
Linton, R., 248, 261
Lipset, S. M., 248
*Literary Critics*, 184
*Literary Essays*, 183
*Literary History of the United States*, 280
*Literary Opinion in America*, 185
*Literary Situation*, 180
*Literature and Psychology*, 182
*Literature of the Anglo-Saxons*, 68
*Little Community*, 249
*Little Flowers*, 67
*Little Foxes*, 167
*Little Novels of Sicily*, 153
*Little Treasury of World Poetry*, 156
*Little Women*, 134
*Lives* (Plutarch), 34
*Lives* (Walton), 88
*Lives in Science*, 273
*Lives of Eminent Philosophers*, 33
*Lives of the Painters*, 74
*Lives of the Poets*, 89
*Living Japan*, 49
*Living Stage*, 169
*Living Talmud*, 213

Livingstone, R. W., 36
Livy, 40
Locke, J., 87
Loesser, A., 200
Logasa, H., 278
*Lolita*, 144
Lomax, A., 159, 200
Lomax, J. A., 159
London, J., 143, 152
*London Journal*, 94
*Loneliness of the Long-Distance Runner*, 129
*Lonely Crowd*, 249
*Lonely Passion of Judith Hearne*, 144
*Long Stories* (Mann), 152
*Longest Journey*, 126
Longfellow, H. W., 158
*Look Homeward, Angel*, 147
*Looking Backward*, 134
*Loom of History*, 54
Lorant, S., 174
Lorca, F. G., 168
*Lord Jim*, 126
*Lord of the Flies*, 127
Lorenz, K. Z., 267
*Lorna Doone*, 118
*Lost Cities of Africa*, 55
*Lost Languages*, 253
*Lottery, The*, 151
Louys, P., 36
Lovejoy, A. O., 209
*Loving*, 127
Lowell, J. R., 158
Lowenthal, R., 47
*Loyalty of Free Men*, 230
Lucas, F. L., 182
Lucas, H. S., 75
Lucian, 34
*Lucien Leuwen*, 106
*Lucky Jim*, 126
Lucretius, 40
Ludwig, E., 174
Lullies, R., 196
*Lust for Life*, 197
Lutyens, D. M., 271
Lynd, R. S., 248
Lynn, K. S., 182
Lyons, J., 200
*Lysistrata*, 33

Macaulay, T. B., 89
*Macbeth*, 80, 170
McCary, J. L., 261
McCullers, C., 143
MacDonald, A. F., 232
MacFarquhar, R., 47
MacGowan, K., 169
Machado de Assis, J. M., 60
Machiavelli, N., 74, 182
Machlis, J., 200
MacKendrick, P. L., 42
McKinney, H. D., 200
MacLeish, A., 160
MacNeice, L., 160
Macpherson, H. C., 284
*McTeague*, 137
*Madame Bovary*, 104
*Madame Curie*, 173
Madariaga, S. de, 62
*Mademoiselle de Maupin*, 105
*Madwoman of Chaillot*, 167
MAGAZINES, 186 ff.
*Maggie: A Girl of the Streets*, 135
*Magic Barrel*, 152
*Magic in the Web*, 81

*Magic Mountain*, 112
*Magic, Myth, and Medicine*, 265
*Magnets*, 270
Mahan, A. T., 219
Mailer, N., 143
*Main Stream of Mathematics*, 272
*Main Street*, 143
*Mainsprings of Civilization*, 241
*Major Governments of Asia*, 45
*Makers of Contemporary Architecture*, 198
*Making of an American*, 175
*Making of Economic Society*, 236
*Making of Europe*, 220
*Making of the Modern Mind*, 219
Malamud, B., 144, 152
*Malcolm*, 144
*Male and Female*, 248
Malinowski, B., 248
Malory, T., 67
Malraux, A., 112
Malthus, T. R., 96
*Man and the Chemical Elements*, 271
*Man for Himself*, 260
*Man from Nazareth*, 214
*Man in Society*, 249
*Man in the Modern World*, 266
*Man of the Renaissance*, 76
*Man, Time, and Fossils*, 267
*Man Who Invented Sin*, 152
*Man Who Was Not With It*, 142
*Man with the Golden Arm*, 139
Manach, J., 60
*Mandarins, The*, 110
Mandel, O., 182
Mandeville, J., 67
Mann, T., 112, 152, 182
*Manon Lescaut*, 96
Mansfield, K., 152
*Manual of Style*, 285
*Many Mexicos*, 222
Manzoni, A., 105
Mao Tse-tung, 48
*Marble Faun*, 135
Marckwardt, A., 254
Marcus Aurelius Antoninus, 40
Marcuse, H., 259
*Marius the Epicurean*, 42
Marke, J. J., 230
Marlowe, C., 79
Marquand, J. P., 144
*Marriage of Figaro*, 94
Marshall, A., 237
*Martí, Apostle of Freedom*, 60
*Martian Chronicles*, 274
*Martian Way*, 274
Martin du Gard, R., 113
Martindale, C. C., 215
Marvell, A., 87
Marx, K., 207, 229
*Mary of Scotland*, 80, 167
Masefield, J., 160
Maslow, A. H., 259
*Mass Communication*, 250
*Master of Ballantrae*, 121
*Masterpieces of the Spanish Golden Age*, 87
*Masters, The*, 129
*Masters of Modern Art*, 195

*Masters of the Drama*, 169
*Masters of World Architecture*, 198
*Mathematician's Delight*, 273
MATHEMATICS, 269 ff.
*Mathematics for the General Reader*, 273
Matthews, G., 56
Matthews, G. T., 75
Matthiessen, F. O., 156, 174
Mattingly, G., 75
Maugham, W. S., 128, 152, 174, 182
Maupassant, G. de, 105, 152
Mauriac, F., 113
*Maxims* (La Rochefoucauld), 87
May, R., 259
Mayer, K. B., 248
*Mayor of Casterbridge*, 120
Mead, M., 248
*Meaning in the Visual Arts*, 75
Means, G. C., 235
Mearns, H., 262
*Measure of Man*, 182
*Measuring Human Motivation*, 260
*Medea*, 33
*Mediaeval Culture*, 70
*Mediaeval Mind*, 70
*Mediaeval Society*, 69
*Medici, The* (Schevill), 220
*Medici, The* (Young), 76
*Medieval Cities*, 220
*Medieval Feudalism*, 220
MEDIEVAL HISTORY, 219
*Medieval Latin Lyrics*, 67
*Medieval Latin Poetry*, 67
MEDIEVAL LITERATURE, see MIDDLE AGES
*Medieval Panorama*, 68
*Medieval People*, 69
*Medieval Philosophers, Selections from*, 67
*Medieval Reader, Portable*, 67
*Medieval Thought from St. Augustine to Ockham*, 69
*Meditations*, 40
*Meek Heritage*, 114
Meerloo, J. A. M., 248
Mehdi, H. T., 54
*Melanctha*, 145
Melnitz, W., 169
Melville, H., 136, 152
*Memento Mori*, 129
*Memoirs* (Casanova), 94
*Memoirs* (Hoover), 225
*Memoirs* (Truman), 176
*Memoirs of the Crusades*, 67
*Men of Good Will*, 114
*Men of Music*, 199
*Men, Women, and Pianos*, 200
*Menace from Earth*, 274
Mencken, H. L., 174, 182, 254, 281
Menke, F. G., 285
*Mentor-UNESCO Art Series*, 195
Meredith, G., 120
Merezhkovsky, D., 75
Mérimée, P., 105
Merton, R. K., 248
Merton, T., 174
*Metamorphoses*, 40
*Metaphysics of Morals*, 96
*Metatheatre: A New View of Dramatic Form*, 169
*Metropolis: 1985*, 238
*Mexican Painting in Our Time*, 62
*Mexico Today*, 61
*Midcentury*, 141

*Mid-Century American Poets*, 156
MIDDLE AGES, 63 ff.
MIDDLE EAST, 51 ff.
*Middle East*, 52
*Middle East: A Physical, Social, and Regional Geography*, 241
*Middle East in World Affairs*, 53
*Middlemarch*, 120
*Middletown*, 248
*Middletown in Transition*, 248
*Midsummer Night's Dream*, 80
Mill, J. S., 174, 207
*Mill on the Floss*, 119
Millay, E. St. V., 160
Miller, A., 168, 170
Miller, H., 144
Miller, M. S., 283
Miller, P., 98
Millikan, M., 248
Mills, C. W., 232, 248
Milne, L. J., 267
Milton, J., 87
*Mimesis*, 179
*Mirror for Man*, 247
*Misanthrope, Le*, 87
*Misérables, Les*, 105
*Miss Lonelyhearts*, 146
*Miss Ravenel's Conversion from Secession to Loyalty*, 135
*Mister Jelly Roll*, 200
Mistral, G., 60
*Mixed Company*, 153
Mizener, A., 174
*Moby Dick*, 136
*Modern American Painting and Sculpture*, 196
*Modern American Poetry, Modern British Poetry*, 156
*Modern Art in the Making*, 196
*Modern Corporation and Private Property*, 235
*Modern Democratic State*, 229
*Modern Egypt*, 52
*Modern Fiction Studies*, 187
*Modern French Painters*, 197
*Modern Germany*, 219
*Modern History of the Sudan*, 56
*Modern Instance*, 135
*Modern Introduction to the Family*, 246
*Modern Japanese Literature*, 49
*Modern Literary Criticism*, 181
*Modern Man in Search of a Soul*, 259
*Modern Music*, 200
*Modern Poetry*, 156
*Modern Reader's Bible*, 212
*Modern Reader's Guide to the Bible*, 215
*Modern Science and Its Philosophy*, 209
*Modern Theatre*, 165
*Modes of Thought*, 210
*Modulor, The*, 194
*Mohammedanism*, 53
Molière, 87
*Moll Flanders*, 95
*Molloy*, 110
Monro, I. S., 278
Monroe, E., 56
*Mont Saint-Michel and Chartres*, 68
Montaigne, M. de, 74
*Monuments of Early English Drama*, 170
*Moon and Sixpence*, 128
*Moonstone, The*, 119

Moore, B., 144
Moore, G., 69, 120
Moore, G. E., 209
Moore, M., 160
Moore, R., 267
Moore, W. E., 249
Moore, W. G., 280
Moorehead, A., 54
Moravia, A., 113
More, T., 80
*More Light on the Dead Sea Scrolls*, 52
Morgan, A. H., 267
Morgan, C. H., 75
Morgan, E. S., 98
Morgan, K. W., 46
Morgenthau, H. J., 232
Morison, S. E., 75
Morley, S. G., 62
Morris, R. B., 283
*Morte d'Arthur*, 67
Morton, F., 174
Mosca, G., 229
Mosse, G. L., 221
Motley, J. L., 75
*Mountolive*, 126
*Mourning Becomes Electra*, 168
Mozart, W. A., 182
*Mozart's Letters*, 182, 199
Muhammad at Mecca, 54
Muhammad at Medina, 54
Muir, J., 202
Mullahy, P., 259
Muller, H. J., 54
Mumford, L., 198, 225, 249
*Municipal Year Book*, 284
Munro, H. H., see Saki
*Muntu*, 56
Muntz, H., 69
Murasaki, S., 49
*Murder in the Cathedral*, 170
Murdoch, I., 128
Murphey, R. W., 279
MUSIC, 199 ff.
*Music in American Life*, 199
*Music in History*, 200
*Music in Western Civilization*, 200
*Music Through the Ages*, 199
*Musical Masterworks*, 282
*Mute Stones Speak*, 42
*My Ántonia*, 140
*My Mother's House*, 150
Myers, B. S., 62, 196, 282
Myers, L. M., 254
Myrdal, G., 237
*Mysticism*, 215
*Mysticism and Logic*, 209
*Myth of Sisyphus and Other Essays*, 180
*Myth of the Negro Past*, 55
*Mythology* (Bulfinch), 35
*Mythology* (Hamilton), 36
*Myths and Symbols in Indian Art and Civilization*, 47

Nabokov, V., 144
*Naked and the Dead*, 143
*Naked Masks*, 168
*Nana*, 106
Nash, O., 160, 161
Nashe, T., 80
Nasser, G. A., 54
*Nasser's New Egypt*, 54
*Nation, The*, 187
*Nationalism in Colonial Africa*, 56
*Nationalism, Its Meaning and History*, 231
*Nationalist Movement*, 46
*Native Problem in Africa*, 55
*Native Son*, 147
NATURAL HISTORY, see BIOLOGICAL SCIENCES
*Natural History of the Trees of Eastern and Central North America*, 267
*Nature of Living Things*, 268
*Nature of the Non-Western World*, 45
*Nausea*, 114
*Nautilus 90 North*, 240
*Navaho, The*, 247
*Negroes in American Society*, 246
Nehru, J., 46, 175
Nelson, B., 259
Nerval, G. de, 105
Neumann, R. G., 232
Nevins, A., 225
*New Astronomy*, 273
*New Atlantis*, 74
*New Borzoi Book of Ballets*, 202
*New Century Cyclopedia of Names*, 281
*New Chemistry*, 273
*New Dictionary of American Politics*, 284
*New Dictionary of Quotations*, 281
*New Encyclopedia of Music and Musicians*, 282
*New England: Indian Summer*, 180
*New England Mind*, 98
*New English Bible*, 212
*New Grub Street*, 120
*New Handbook of the Heavens*, 270
*New Maps of Hell: a Survey of Science Fiction*, 274
*New Men*, 129
*New Poems by American Poets*, 156
*New Poets of England and America*, 156
*New Republic*, 187
*New Schaff-Herzog Encyclopedia of Religious Knowledge*, 283
*New Standard Dictionary*, 280
*New York Times Index*, 278
*New Yorker*, 188
*Newcomes, The*, 121
Newman, E. S., 230
Newman, J. H., 175
Newman, J. R., 272
Newman, W. S., 200
*News and Rumor in Renaissance Europe*, 75
Newton, E., 197
Newton, I., 87
Nexø, M. A., 113
*Next Hundred Years*, 235
Nichols, J. H., 215
Nichols, R. G., 254
Nicholson, M., 280
Nicoll, A., 169
*Nicomachean Ethics*, 33
Nida, E. A., 254
Nietzsche, F., 207
*Nigger of the Narcissus*, 119
*Nile, The*, 242
*Nine Stories* (Salinger), 153
*1984*, 128
*1919*, 141
*Ninety-three*, 98
Njal Saga, 67
*No Exit and Three Other Plays*, 168

No Single Thing Abides, 162
Nock, A. J., 98
Noon Wine, 144
Norris, F., 137
Northwest Passage, 98
Nose, The, 105
Noss, J. B., 215
Nostromo, 126
Notebooks (Da Vinci), 73
Notes from the Underground, 104
NOVELS, 101 ff.
Nude, The, 195
Number, The Language of Science, 271
Nurkse, R., 237
Nussbaum, F. L., 222
Nutting, A., 175

Oblomov, 105
O'Casey, S., 168, 170
Occupational Literature, 285
Ocean River, 271
O'Connor, Flannery, 144, 152
O'Connor, Frank, 152
Octopus, The, 137
Odes (Pindar), 34
Odets, C., 168
Odyssey, 34
Odyssey: A Modern Sequel, 112
Oedipus: Myth and Complex, 259
Oedipus Rex, 34, 170
Of Human Bondage, 128
Of Lions, Chained, 54
Of Societies and Men, 266
Of Time, Work and Leisure, 246
O'Faolain, S., 152
Official Hotel Red Book, 285
O'Flaherty, L., 128
O'Hara, J., 144, 152
Oil and State in the Middle East, 53
Old Goriot, 103
Old Mortality (Porter), 144
Old Mortality (Scott), 89
Old Regime and the French Revolution, 98
Old Wives' Tale, 126
Oldenbourg, Z., 69
Oldsey, B. S., 183
Oliver, R., 56
Oliver Twist, 119
Oliver Wiswell, 98
Olmsted, M. S., 249
Omar Khayyam, 54
Omoo, 136
On Architecture, 41
On Liberty, 207
On the Laws of Japanese Painting, 195
On the Nature of Things, 40
On the Road, 143
On the Road to Christian Unity, 214
On the Truth of the Catholic Faith, 68
On These I Stand, 159
One Hundred Dollar Misunderstanding, 142
100 Selected Poems (Cummings), 159
One, Two, Three . . . Infinity, 271
O'Neill, E., 168
Onís, H. de, 60
Only in America, 181
Only Yesterday, 224
Opera Reader, 199
Orations (Demosthenes), 33
Ordeal of Mark Twain, 173

Ordeal of Richard Feverel, 120
Oregon Trail, 175
Oresteia, 33
Organization Man, 250
ORIENT, SEE FAR EAST
Origin of Species, 266
Origins, 280
Origins of Modern Science, 97
Origins of the World War, 223
Orlando, 130
Orphic Voice, 268
Orr, C., Jr., 272
Ortega y Gasset, J., 229
Orwell, G., 128, 183
Osborn, F., 267
Ostrogorsky, G., 54
Othello, 80
Other Voices, Other Rooms, 140
Ottemiller, J. H., 278
Our American Music, 200
Our Inner Conflicts, 260
Our Language, 254
Our New Music, 200
Our Philosophical Traditions, 205
Our Plundered Planet, 267
Our Town, 168
Our Wildlife Legacy, 265
Out of My Life and Thought, 175
Outline of European Architecture, 199
Ovid, 40
Overcoat, The, 105
Owl in the Attic, 184
Oxford Addresses on Poetry, 181
Oxford Book of American Verse, 156
Oxford Book of Irish Verse, 281
Oxford Book of Seventeenth Century Verse, 88
Oxford Companion to American Literature, 281
Oxford Companion to Classical Literature, 280
Oxford Companion to English Literature, 281
Oxford Companion to French Literature, 280
Oxford Companion to Music, 282
Oxford Companion to the Theatre, 281
Oxford Dictionary of Quotations, 281
Oxford Economic Atlas of the World, 284
Oxford English Dictionary, 280
Oxford History of English Literature, 280
Ozenfant, A., 197

Packard, V., 249
Paideia, 36
Paine, R. T., 45
Paine, T., 96
Painter, S., 69
Painter's Eye, 196
PAINTING, 194 ff.
Painting in the Far East, 45
Pale Horse, Pale Rider, 144
Palgrave, F., 156
Palgrave's Golden Treasury, 162
Palmer, N. D., 46
Palmer, R. R., 221, 279
Pamela, 96
Pamphlets on American Writers, 183
Panofsky, E., 75
Pantagruel, 74
Paperbound Books in Print, 278
Parables for the Theatre, 167

*Paradise Lost*, 87
Parker, D., 152, 160
Parkes, H. B., 220
Parkinson, C. N., 231
*Parkinson's Law and Other Studies in Administration*, 231
Parkman, F., 175
Partridge, E., 82, 280
Pascal, B., 88
*Passage to India*, 127
Pasternak, B., 113
Patai, R., 54
Pater, W., 42, 75
Paton, A., 56
*Pattern of Asia*, 45
*Patterns of Culture*, 246
Payne, R., 48
Payne, S. L., 254
Paz, O., 60, 62
Peake, D. M., 278
Pearson, K., 272
Peattie, D. C., 267
*Pedro Páramo*, 61
Pegis, A. C., 213
Pei, M., 69
Peirce, C. S., 209
*Pelican Guide to English Literature*, 68
*Pelican History of Art*, 45, 194
*Pelle, the Conqueror*, 113
*Peloponnesian Wars*, 34
Peltason, J. W., 231
*Pendennis*, 121
*Penguin Island*, 111
*Pensées*, 88
*People! Challenge to Survival*, 268
*People, Yes*, 161
Pepys, S., 88
Pérez Galdós, B., 105
PERIODICALS, see MAGAZINES
Perkins, D., 225
*Personal History of Henry VIII*, 81
*Personal Memoirs of U. S. Grant*, 225
*Perspectives on Conservation*, 236
*Peter the Great and the Emergence of Russia*, 54
Petersen, W., 249
Petrarch, 67
Petronius, 40
Pevsner, N., 199
Peyser, E., 199
*Phaedo*, 34
*Phaidon Press Books*, 195
Phelps, E. S., 237
Phillips, U. B., 225
*Philosophical Writings* (Peirce), 209
*Philosophies of India*, 47
PHILOSOPHY, 203 ff.
*Philosophy* (Spinoza), 88
*Philosophy in America from the Puritans to James*, 205
*Philosophy of Administration*, 231
*Philosophy of History*, 206
*Philosophy of the Enlightenment*, 98
PHOTOGRAPHY, 194 ff.
PHYSICAL SCIENCES, 269 ff.
*Physics and Chemistry of Life*, 267
*Physics of Television*, 271
*Picasso*, 195
*Pickwick Papers*, 119
*Picture History of Photography*, 197
*Picture of Dorian Gray*, 121
*Piece of My Mind*, 184
*Piers Plowman*, 67
*Pigeon Feathers*, 153

Piggott, S., 249
*Pilgrim's Progress*, 86
Pindar, 34
Pinson, K. S., 219
Pintner, R., 262
*Pioneers, The*, 134
Pirandello, L., 113, 168
Pirenne, H., 69, 220
*Plague, The*, 111
*Planet Earth*, 273
*Plant Life*, 268
*Planting of Christianity in Africa*, 55
Plato, 34
Plautus, 40
*Play, The: A Critical Anthology*, 165
*Play Index*, 278
*Playboy of the Western World*, 170
PLAYS, see DRAMA
*Playwright as Thinker*, 169
*Pleasure Dome*, 161
*Pleasures of Music*, 199
*Pledge, The*, 111
Plotinus, 34, 206
*Plough and the Stars*, 168
Plutarch, 34
*Pocket Book of Verse*, 157
*Pocket History of American Painting*, 196
*Pocket Library of Great Art*, 195
Poe, E. A., 152, 158
*Poems from the Greek Anthology*, 32
POETRY, 154 ff.
*Poetry and the Age*, 182
*Poetry of the New England Renaissance*, 157
Poincaré, J. H., 273
*Point Counter Point*, 127
*Points of My Compass*, 184
*Points of View*, 182
*Poisoned Crown*, 68
*Political Handbook of the World*, 284
*Political Man*, 248
POLITICS, 227 ff.
*Politics*, 33
*Politics Among Nations*, 232
*Politics, Parties, and Pressure Groups*, 231
*Politics: Who Gets What, When, How?*, 231
Pollack, P., 197
Polo, M., 67
Polybius, 34
*Poole's Index*, 278
*Poor White*, 139
Pope, A., 96
*Popol Vuh*, 61
*Population and Society*, 250
Porter, K. A., 144, 152
Porter, W. S., see Henry, O.
Portmann, A., 267
*Portrait of a Lady*, 136
*Portrait of the Artist as a Young Man*, 128
*Portraits in Miniature and Other Essays*, 184
*Portuguese Africa*, 55
Post, E., 285
Potter, S., 254
Pound, E., 160
Powell, A., 129
Power, E., 69
*Power Elite*, 249
*Power of Words*, 252
*Practical Criticism*, 183
*Pragmatism*, 209

*Prairie, The*, 135
Pratt, W. S., 282
Praz, M., 197
*Precious Bane*, 129
*Prefaces to Criticism*, 180
*Prefaces to Shakespeare*, 81
*Prehistoric Life*, 267
PRE-HISTORY, see ANTHROPOLOGY; GREECE; HISTORY; RELIGION
*Prejudices: A Selection*, 182
*Prelude to Mathematics*, 273
Prescott, W. H., 62
*President: Office and Powers*, 230
Prévost, A., 96
*Pride and Prejudice*, 118
Priestley, J. B., 129
*Primer for Playgoers*, 169
*Primer for Protestants*, 215
*Primer of Freudian Psychology*, 258
*Primer of Modern Art*, 195
*Primitive Art* (Adam), 195
*Primitive Art* (Boas), 195
PRIMITIVE ARTS, see ANTHROPOLOGY; FINE ARTS; GREECE
*Prince, The*, 74
*Princess of Cleves*, 87
*Principia*, 87
*Principles of Economics*, 237
Pritchett, V. S., 152
*Problems in Counseling*, 261
*Problems of Capital Formation in Underdeveloped Countries*, 237
*Problems of Philosophy*, 209
*Professor's House*, 141
*Profiles in Courage*, 174
Progoff, I., 259
*Prolegomena to Any Future Metaphysics*, 207
*Prolegomena to the Study of the Greek Religion*, 36
*Proper Study of Mankind*, 246
Proust, M., 113
*Psychiatric Dictionary*, 284
*Psychiatric Interview*, 261
*Psychoanalysis of Children*, 260
*Psychoanalyst and the Artist*, 261
*Psychological Abstracts*, 278
PSYCHOLOGY, 256 ff.
*Psychology of Human Conflict*, 260
*Psychology of Perception*, 261
*Psychology of Personality*, 261
*Psychology: The Briefer Course*, 259
*Public Affairs Information Service*, 278
*Public Wants and Private Needs*, 237
*Pudd'nhead Wilson*, 137
Puner, H. W., 259
Purdy, J., 144, 152
Pyle, E., 226
Pyles, T., 254

*Quarry, The*, 111
*Queen Victoria*, 176
*Quentin Durward*, 70
*Question of Hamlet*, 82
*Question of Upbringing*, 129

*R. V. R.: The Life and Times of Rembrandt*, 90
*Rabbit, Run*, 146
*Rabble in Arms*, 98
Rabelais, F., 74
*Racial and Cultural Minorities*, 249
Racine, J., 86
Rahv, P., 183

*Rainbow, The*, 128
*Rameau's Nephew*, 95
Randall, J. H., 219
Randolph, V., 254
Rank, O., 259
Ransom, J. C., 160
Rapaport, D., 261
*Rape of the Mind*, 248
*Rashomon*, 48
*Rats, Lice and History*, 268
Rauch, B., 223
Raymond, P. E., 267
Read, H., 183, 197
Reade, C., 70
*Reader's Encyclopedia*, 281
*Readers' Guide*, 278
*Reading Modern Poetry*, 156
*Readings in General Psychology*, 257
*Readings in Industrial and Business Psychology*, 262
*Readings in Western Civilization*, 218
*Realities of American Foreign Policy*, 232
*Reason and Existenz*, 209
*Reason and Nature*, 208
*Rebellion in the Backlands*, 60
*Rebirth and Destiny of Israel*, 52
*Reconstruction in Philosophy*, 208
RECORDS, see DRAMA; POETRY
*Red and the Black*, 106
*Red Badge of Courage*, 135
Redfield, R., 249
*Redgauntlet*, 98
REFERENCE BOOKS, 277 ff.
*Reflections on the Revolution in France*, 94
*Reformation, The*, 221
*Reformation Era, 1500–1650*, 221
*Regional Atlas*, 279
*Regional Geography of Anglo-America*, 242
Reischauer, E. O., 46, 49
*Religio Medici*, 86
RELIGION, 211 ff.
*Religion and the Rise of Capitalism*, 89
*Religion of the Hindus*, 46
*Religions in Japan*, 49
*Religious Aspect of Philosophy*, 209
Remarque, E. M., 114
*Remembrance of Things Past*, 113
RENAISSANCE, 71 ff.
*Renaissance, The* (Durant), 75
*Renaissance, The* (Ferguson), 221
*Renaissance, The* (Pater), 75
*Renaissance and the Reformation*, 75
*Renaissance: Its Nature and Origins*, 222
*Renaissance Philosophy of Man*, 76
*Renaissance Reader, Portable*, 74
Renan, E., 42
*Rendezvous with Destiny*, 231
*Reprieve*, 114
*Republic, The*, 34
*Restless Atmosphere*, 241
*Restless Universe*, 270
*Return of the Native*, 120
*Revolt of the Angels*, 111
*Revolt of the Masses*, 229
*Revolutionary Generation, 1763–1790*, 225
*Rhymes and Verses*, 159
Riasanovsky, N. V., 222
Rice, D. T., 197
*Rich Lands and Poor*, 237

*Richard II*, 70
*Richard III*, 70
Richards, I. A., 183
Richards, J. M., 199
Richardson, S., 96
Rienow, R., 233
Riesman, D., 249
*Rights of Man*, 96
Riis, J. A., 175
Rimbaud, J. A., 158
*Rinehart Book of Verse*, 157
*Rise and Fall of the Third Reich*, 223
*Rise of American Civilization*, 224
*Rise of Modern Europe*, 222
*Rise of Puritanism*, 89
*Rise of Silas Lapham*, 135
*Rise of the Dutch Republic*, 75
*Rise of the Spanish American Empire*, 62
Ritchie, A. C., 197
*Rivals, The*, 97
*Rivers of America*, 226, 240
*Road to Serfdom*, 236
*Rob Roy*, 98
Robach, A. A., 258
Robb, D. M., 197
Robbe-Grillet, A., 114
*Robert E. Lee*, 173
Roberts, E. M., 145
Roberts, K., 98
Robinson, E. A., 160
*Robinson Crusoe*, 95
Rockefeller Brothers Fund, 237
*Roderick Random*, 97
Rodman, S., 62
Roeder, R., 76
Roget, P., 280
Rolland, R., 114
Romains, J., 114
*Roman Mind at Work*, 42
*Roman Readings*, 39
*Roman Way*, 42
*Romance of Leonardo da Vinci*, 75
*Romance of Tristan and Iseult*, 67
*Romance of Words*, 254
*Romans, The*, 41
ROME, 37 ff.
*Rome in the Augustan Age*, 42
*Romeo and Juliet*, 80
Romier, L., 219
*Rommel, the Desert Fox*, 55
*Romola*, 75
*Room at the Top*, 126
Roosevelt, E., 175
*Roosevelt and Hopkins*, 175
*Roosevelt from Munich to Pearl Harbor*, 223
Rose, H. J., 36
Rosenfeld, I., 183
Rosenthal, M. L., 156
Ross, A. M., 237
Roth, P., 153
*Rothschilds, The*, 174
Rouse, W. H. D., 36
Rousseau, J. J., 96
Rowell, H. T., 42
Rowland, B., 45
Rowse, A. L., 82
*Royal Succession*, 68
Royce, J., 209
*Rubáiyát*, 54
Rulfo, J., 61
*Ruling Class*, 229
Rumaker, M., 145
Runes, D. D., 282

Ruskin, J., 183
Russell, B., 209
Russell, R. J., 242
*Russian Reader, Portable*, 113
*Russia's Soviet Economy*, 237

Sabartes, J., 195
Sabine, G. H., 229
Sachs, C., 200, 202
*Sailor, Sense of Humour, and Other Stories*, 152
*Saint Joan*, 70
St. John, R., 54
Saki, 153
Salinger, J. D., 145, 153
*Same Door*, 153
Samuelson, P. A., 237
Sandburg, C., 160, 161, 175, 201
*Sandburg Reads Sandburg*, 161
Sandfort, J. F., 273
*Sands of Mars*, 274
Sansom, G. B., 219
Santayana, G., 209
Sapir, E., 249
Sartre, J. P., 114, 168, 183
*Satanstoe*, 135
*Satellites, Rockets and Outer Space*, 272
*Satires* (Juvenal), 40
*Saturday Night and Sunday Morning*, 129
*Saturday Review*, 188
*Satyricon*, 40
Sawyer, W. W., 273
Sayegh, F. A., 54
*Scarlet Letter*, 89
Scarlott, C. A., 240
*Sceptical Chymist*, 86
Schevill, F., 220
Schneider, D. E., 261
Schneider, H. W., 205
Schnitzler, A., 114
Scholes, P. A., 282
Schonberg, H. C., 201
*School for Scandal*, 97
Schopenhauer, A., 207
Schrodinger, E., 273
Schuman, F., 233
Schumpeter, J. A., 237
Schwahn, W. E., 260
Schwartz, H., 237
Schweitzer, A., 175
*Science and Common Sense*, 271
*Science and Method*, 273
*Science and the Modern World*, 210
*Science and the Social Order*, 245
SCIENCE FICTION, 273 f.
*Science of Culture*, 250
*Science of Language*, 253
*Science Ponders Religion*, 215
*Science, Theory and Man*, 273
*Scientific American*, 188
*Scientific American*, Eds. of, 267, 273
Scott, A. C., 48
Scott, G., 76
Scott, R. G., 199
Scott, Walter, 70, 82, 89, 98
Scott, Wilbur, 183
*Scrolls from the Dead Sea*, 55
SCULPTURE, 194 ff.
*Sculpture of the 20th Century*, 197
*Sea Around Us*, 240
*Sea Within*, 268
Sears, M. E., 278
*Second Shepherd's Play*, 170

Second World War, 222
Secret History of the American Revolution, 226
Selected Readings on the Learning Process, 260
Seligman, E. R. A., 283
Sell, H. B., 175
Sellery, G. C., 222
Seltman, C. T., 197
Sender, R., 114
Seneca, 40
Sense and Sensibility, 118
Senses, The, 265
Sesame and Lilies, 183
Seton-Watson, H., 223
Seuphor, M., 282
Seven Gothic Tales, 150
Seven Pillars of Wisdom, 53
Seven Storey Mountain, 174
Seven Types of Ambiguity, 181
Seven Who Were Hanged, 110
SEVENTEENTH CENTURY, 83 ff.
Seventeenth Century Background, 90
Seventh of October, 114
Severed Head, 128
Sévigné, M. de, 88
Sewall, R. B., 183
Sewanee Review, 188
Sewell, E., 268
Sex and Temperament in Three Primitive Societies, 248
Shadow of a Gunman, 168
Shadows on the Rock, 88
Shakespeare, W., 70, 80, 162, 170
Shakespeare, A Survey, 81
Shakespeare and the Nature of Man, 82
Shakespeare First Folio, 81
Shakespeare of London, 81
Shakespeare Without Tears, 82
Shakespearean Tragedy, 81
Shakespeare's Audience, 81
Shakespeare's Bawdy, 82
Shakespeare's England, 82
Shakespeare's Globe Playhouse, 82
Shakespeare's Imagery and What It Tells Us, 82
Shapiro, N., 201
Shapley, H., 215
Shaw, G. B., 70, 168, 170, 183
Shaw, I., 153
She Stoops to Conquer, 96
Shelley, M. W., 121
Shelley, P. B., 158
Shepherd, W. R., 279
Sheridan, R. B., 97
Sherwood, R. E., 175
Ship of Fools, 144
Shirer, W. L., 223
Shock of Recognition, 184
Sholokhov, M., 114
Shores, L., 278
Short History of Chinese Philosophy, 47
Short History of India and Pakistan, 47
Short History of Music, 200
Short History of Opera, 200
Short History of the Middle East, 53
SHORT STORY, 148 ff.
Short Story Index, 278
Shorter History of Science, 271
Shropshire Lad, 158
Sickness Unto Death, 207
Sickman, L., 45

Siddhartha, 111
Sidney, P., 80
Silas Marner, 120
Silent Don, 114
Silent Language, 253
Silent Spring, 266
Silent World, 241
Sillanpää, F. E., 114
Sillitoe, A., 129
Silone, I., 114
Silver Treasury of Light Verse, 157
Simplicissimus, 86
Simpson, G., 249
Simpson, G. E., 249
Simpson, L. B., 222
Sinclair, U., 145
Sinnott, E. W., 268
Sino-Soviet Dispute, 47
Sister Carrie, 141
Sitwell, E., 82
Six Feet of the Country, 55
Six Restoration Plays, 166
Sixteen Sonnets (Shakespeare), 162
Sketch Book, 151
Skin of Our Teeth, 168
Skira Art Books, 195
Slade, R. M., 56
Sloan, H. S., 283
Slonimsky, N., 282
Small Group, 249
Smith, A., 97
Smith, A. J., 156
Smith, E. S., 284
Smith, F. G. W., 271
Smith, I., 82
Smollett, T., 97
Snively, W. D., 268
Snow, C. P., 129
Snyder, L. L., 223
Snyder, R. K., 218
Soap Bubbles and the Forces Which Mold Them, 271
Social Contract, 90
Social Forces in Southeast Asia, 50
Social History of Art, 196
Social Mobility in Industrial Society, 248
Social Planning in America, 247
Social Problems in America, 248
Social Psychology of Industry, 261
Social Stratification, 246
Sociological Perspective, 246
SOCIOLOGY, 243 ff.
Sociology Today, 248
Solitary Singer, 172
Some Main Problems of Philosophy, 209
Some of Your Blood, 274
Some Prefer Nettles, 49
Song Index, 278
Sonnets (Millay), 160
Sonnets (Shakespeare), 80
Sonnets and Songs (Petrarch), 67
Sonnets from the Portuguese, 157
Sons and Lovers, 128
Soper, A., 45
Sophocles, 34, 170
Sorell, W., 202
Sorrows of Young Werther, 95
Sot-Weed Factor, 140
Soule, G., 238
Sound and the Fury, 141
Sources of Chinese Tradition, 45
Sources of Indian Tradition, 45

*Sources of the Japanese Tradition*, 45
SOUTH AMERICA, see LATIN AMERICA
*South Wind*, 126
SOUTHEAST ASIA, 50
*Southeast Asia and the World Today*, 50
*Southeast Asia Today—and Tomorrow*, 50
Southey, R., 175
*Soviet Union Today*, 233
*Space Encyclopedia*, 284
*Space, Time, and Architecture*, 198
Spaeth, S., 201
*Spanish Stories and Tales*, 153
*Spanish Tragedy*, 79
Spark, M., 129
Spate, O. H. K., 242
Speare, M. E., 157
*Spectator, The*, 94
Spectorsky, A. C., 250
Spence, H., 215
Spence, R. B., 283
Spencer, T., 82
Spender, S., 160
Spenser, E., 80
Sperber, H., 253
Spinoza, B., 88
*Spirit and Purpose of Geography*, 242
Spitz, A., 285
*Splendid Century*, 89
*Sportsman's Sketches*, 106
Spurgeon, C. F. E., 82
Stafford, J., 153
Stageberg, N. C., 252
*Standard College Dictionary*, 280
*State and Revolution*, 229
*Statistical Abstract of the United States*, 279
*Status Seekers*, 249
Stebbing, L. S., 209
Steegmüller, F., 89, 175
Steele, R., 94
Steele, W. D., 153
Steffens, L., 175
Stein, G., 145
Stein, M. R., 250
Steinbeck, J., 145, 153
Stendhal, 106
Stephenson, C., 220
*Steppenwolf*, 111
Stern, K., 261
Sterne, L., 97
Stevens, D. W., 201
Stevens, L. A., 254
Stevens, W., 160
Stevenson, B. E., 281
Stevenson, R. L., 121, 183
*Sticks and Stones*, 198
Stobart, J. C., 36
*Stoic, The*, 141
*Stoic and Epicurean Philosophers*, 206
Stone, I., 176, 197
Storer, J. H., 268
*Story of America's Religions*, 215
*Story of Art*, 194
*Story of Engineering*, 271
*Story of Gösta Berling*, 112
*Story of Man*, 246
*Story of Maps*, 240
*Story of Philosophy*, 205
*Story of Religion in America*, 215
*Story of the Confederacy*, 225
*Story Poems*, 157
Stotz, C. L., 242

Stout, H. M., 233
Stoutenburgh, J. L., 282
Stowe, H. B., 137
Strachey, L., 82, 176, 184
*Strange Case of Dr. Jekyll and Mr. Hyde*, 121
*Strange Interlude*, 168
*Stranger, The*, 111
*Strangers and Brothers*, 129
*Strangled Queen*, 68
*Strategy of Economic Development*, 236
*Street Corner Society*, 250
Strindberg, A., 168
*Structure of Literature*, 181
Struppeck, J., 197
*Studs Lonigan*, 141
*Study of History*, 219
*Study of International Law*, 232
*Study of Language*, 252
Sturgeon, T., 274
Sturgis, R., 282
Styron, W., 146
Subercaseaux, B., 61
*Subtreasury of American Humor*, 184
*Suburbia*, 250
*Suicide*, 246
*Suleiman the Magnificent*, 75
Sullivan, H. S., 261
Sullivan, J. W. N., 201
*Summing Up*, 174
Sumner, B. H., 54
Sumner, W. G., 250
*Sun Also Rises*, 143
Suzuki, D. T., 209
Swallow, A., 157
Swanberg, W. A., 176
*Swann's Way*, 113
Sweet, W. W., 215
Swift, J., 97
Swinburne, A. C., 158
*Swords of Anjou*, 69
Sykes, G., 250
Sykes, P. M., 54
*Sylvie*, 105
*Symphony, The*, 200
*Symposium*, 34
Synge, J. M., 170
Sypher, W., 76

*Table Talk*, 181
Tacitus, 41
Tagore, R., 47
*Tale of Genji*, 49
*Tale of Two Cities*, 98
*Tales from a Troubled Land*, 56
*Tales of Good and Evil*, 105
*Tamburlaine*, 80
Tanizaki, J., 49
Tawney, R. H., 89
Taylor, F. H., 197
Taylor, H. O., 70
Taylor, O. H., 238
*Teachings of the Compassionate Buddha*, 213
Teale, E. W., 268
Teevan, R. C., 260
*Telegraph, The*, 106
*Temper of Western Europe*, 222
*Tempest, The*, 80
*Ten Greek Plays in Contemporary Translations*, 32
*Ten Little Novels*, 114
*Ten Makers of Modern Protestant Thought*, 213

Tender Is the Night, 142
Tennyson, A., 158
Tenth Muse, 183
Terence, 41
Tess of the d'Urbervilles, 120
Thackeray, W. M., 121
Theatre, The, 169
Theatre in the East, 45
Theatre of the Absurd, 169
Theban Plays, 34
Theimer, W., 284
Their Finest Hour, 222
Theogony, 33
Theory and Practice of Hell, 223
Theory of Literature, 184
Theory of the Leisure Class, 238
Therefore Be Bold, 142
Thesaurus of English Words and Phrases, 280
Thiel, R., 273
Thielen, T. T., 215
Thinking to Some Purpose, 209
Third Revolution, 261
This I Remember, 175
Thomas à Kempis, 68
Thomas Aquinas, St., 68
Thomas, A. B., 222
Thomas, B. P., 176
Thomas, D., 153, 160, 161, 170
Thomas, N., 146
Thompson, J. M., 222
Thompson, O., 282
Thoreau, H. D., 176
Thorpe, T. E., 284
Three-Cornered Hat, 103
Three Dialogues Between Hylas and Philonous, 206
Three Keys to Language, 253
Three Lives, 145
Three Musketeers, 89
Three Prophetic Novels, 274
Three Who Made a Revolution, 224
Through the Looking-Glass, 119
Thucydides, 34
Thurber, J., 184
Thurber Country, 184
Tillich, P., 210
Time, 188
Time and the Wind, 61
Time Machine, 274
Time of Hope, 129
Time of Indifference, 113
Time of Man, 145
Time Regained, 113
Timeless Stories for Today and Tomorrow, 274
Times Atlas of the World, 279
Times of Melville and Whitman, 180
Tinker, H., 233
Titan, The, 141
Titchmarsh, E. C., 273
To Be a Pilgrim, 126
To the Finland Station, 230
To the Lighthouse, 130
Tocqueville, A. de, 98, 231
Tolstoi, Leo, 106
Tom Jones, 95
Tono-Bungay, 130
Torres-Rioseco, A., 62
Toward a Psychology of Being, 259
Toward Freedom, 175
Toynbee, A. J., 36, 219
Trade Union Wage Policy, 237
Tragic Era, 224
Tragic Sense of Life, 210

Translations from the Chinese, 48
TRAVEL, see GEOGRAPHY
Travels (Mandeville), 67
Travels (Polo), 67
Treasure Island, 121
Treasury of American Folklore, 180
Treasury of Art Masterpieces, 196
Treasury of the Theatre, 166
Treasury of the World's Great Letters, 184
Treatise Concerning the Principles of Human Knowledge, 94
Tree of Culture, 248
Trevelyan, G. M., 219
Trewartha, G. T., 49, 242
Trial, The, 112
Trial and Error, 54
Trimingham, J. S., 56
Tristram Shandy, 97
Triumph and Tragedy, 223
Triumph of American Capitalism, 225
Triumph of Science and Reason, 222
Troilus and Criseyde, 66
Trojan Women, 33
Trollope, A., 121
Tropic of Cancer, 144
Tropical World, 241
Troubled Sleep, 114
Truman, H. S., 176
Tsao Hsueh-chin, 48
TUDOR ENGLAND, 77 ff.
Tunnard, C., 199
Turgenev, I., 106
Turn of the Screw, 136
Turner, F. J., 226
Twain, M., 137, 153
Twelfth Night, 80
Twentieth Century Authors, 281
Twentieth-Century Bestiary, 267
Twentieth Century Views Series, 184
24 Favorite One-Act Plays, 166
20,000 Leagues Under the Sea, 274
Two Cheers for Democracy, 181
Two Gentle Men, 88
Two Treatises of Civil Government, 87
Two Years Before the Mast, 173
Tynan, K., 169
Typee, 136

U.S.A., 141
Ulrich, H., 201
Ulysses, 128
Unamuno, M. de, 210
Uncle Tom's Cabin, 137
Under Milk Wood, 170
Underdogs, The, 60
Underhill, E., 215
Understand and Enjoy Modern Art, 196
Understanding Chemistry, 272
Understanding Music, 200
Understanding Poetry, 156
Undset, S., 70
Unfortunate Traveller, 80
United States and China, 47
United States and India and Pakistan, 46
United States and Japan, 49
United States Authors Series, 184
United States Catalog, 278
Universe, The, 273
Universe and Doctor Einstein, 270
Universe Around Us, 272
Updike, J., 146, 153

Untermeyer, L., 156, 157
*Up From Slavery*, 176
*Upanishads*, 47
Urmson, J. O., 283
*Uses and Abuses of Psychology*, 258
*Utilitarianism*, 207
*Utopia*, 74, 80

Valency, M., 70
Van Den Bark, M., 280
Vanderbilt, A., 285
Van Doren, C., 98, 226
*Vanity Fair*, 121
Van Loon, H. W., 90
*Van Nostrand's Scientific Encyclopedia*, 284
Van Valkenburg, S., 242
Van Vogt, A. E., 274
*Varieties of Religious Experience*, 214
Vasari, G., 74
Veblen, T., 238
*Vein of Iron*, 142
Venezuela, 62
Verdun, 114
Verga, G., 106, 153
Vergil, 41
Verissimo, E., 61
Verne, J., 274
Vernon, M. D., 261
Vernon, R., 238
*Vicar of Wakefield*, 95
*Victim, The*, 140
*Victorian England*, 222
*Viking Book of Aphorisms*, 179
Villon, F., 68
Vinacke, H. M., 46
*Violent Bear It Away*, 144
*Virginia Quarterly Review*, 188
*Virginibus Puerisque*, 183
*Vision and Design*, 184
*Vision of Tragedy*, 183
*Visions and Revisions in Modern American Literary Criticism*, 183
Vitruvius Pollio, 41
Vittorini, E,, 115
Vogel, E. F., 246
Vogt, W., 268
*Voice of the Desert*, 267
*Volpone*, 79
Voltaire, 97, 207
Vossler, K., 70
*Voyage of the Beagle*, 173
*Voyages* (Hakluyt), 79

Waddell, H., 67, 70
*Waiting for Godot*, 167, 170
*Walden*, 176
Waley, A., 48
Wallace, A. F. D., 261
Wallbank, T. W., 47
Walley, H. R., 166
Walpole, H., 97
Waltari, M., 115
Walton, I., 88
*Wandering Scholars*, 70
*Waning of the Middle Ages*, 69
*War and Peace*, 106
*War Premeditated—1939*, 223
*War with the Newts*, 111, 274
*Warden, The*, 121
Ware, N. J., 238
Warner, L., 49
Warner, R., 36
Warren, A., 184
Warren, R. P., 146, 156

Washington, B. T., 176
*Waste Land and Other Poems*, 159
Watson, G., 184
Watson, J. B., 260
Watt, W. M., 54
Watts, H. H., 215
Waugh, E., 129
*Waverley*, 98
Way, L., 260
*Way and Its Power*, 48
*Way of All Flesh*, 119
*Wealth and Welfare*, 238
*Wealth of Nations*, 97
Weatherford, W. D., Jr., 238
*Web of Life*, 268
Webb, M., 129
Webb, W. P., 226
Weber, J. S., 36, 76
Webster, M., 82
*Webster's Biographical Dictionary*, 281
*Webster's Dictionary of Synonyms*, 280
*Webster's Geographical Dictionary*, 280
*Webster's New International Dictionary*, 280
*Webster's New World Dictionary*, 280
*Webster's Seventh New Collegiate Dictionary*, 280
Wecter, D., 225
Weekley, E., 254
Weinstock, H., 199
Weizmann, C., 54
Wellek, R., 184
Wells, H. G., 130, 274
Wells, H. K., 260
*Wellsprings of Life*, 265
Welty, E., 153
Werfel, F., 115
Wescott, G., 146, 184
*Wesley Clair Mitchell*, 235
West, D. H., 278
West, N., 146
*Western World and Japan*, 219
*Westward Ho!*, 120
Weybright, V., 175
Wharton, E., 146
*What Happened in History*, 219
*What Is an Ecumenical Council?*, 215
*What Is Literature?*, 183
*What Is Modern Interior Design?*, 198
*What Is Modern Painting?*, 195
*What to Listen For In Music*, 200
Wheelock, K., 54
*Where the Air Is Clear*, 60
*Where Winter Never Comes*, 240
Whicher, G. F., 67, 157
White, C. L., 242
White, E. B., 184
White, H., 70
White, K. S., 184
White, L. A., 250
*White Collar*, 48
*White Pony*, 48
*White Umbrella*, 46
Whitehead, A. N., 210
Whiting, J. W., 261
Whiting, K. R., 233
Whitman, W., 159, 162
Whittier, J. G., 159
*Who's Afraid of Virginia Woolf?*, 167, 170
*Who's Who* (British), 281
*Who's Who in America*, 281

Whyte, W. F., 250
Whyte, W. H., Jr., 250, 255
Wiener, N., 250
Wilcox, C., 238
*Wild Life in an African Territory*, 266
Wilde, O., 121, 159, 170, 184
Wilder, T., 42, 146, 168
Wilenski, R. H., 197
Wiley, B. I., 226
*Wilhelm Meister's Apprenticeship*, 95
Willetts, W., 48
Willey, B., 90, 98
Williams, O., 157
Williams, R. M., Jr., 250
Williams, T., 168
Williams, W. C., 184
Willingham, C., 147
Willis, J. C., 284
Wilson, E., 55, 184, 230
Wilson, G. P., 254
Winchell, C. M., 278
Windelband, W., 205
*Winesburg, Ohio*, 139
*Wings of the Dove*, 136
Winter, C., 82
*Winter's Tale*, 80
*Winterset*, 167
*Wisdom of Catholicism*, 213
*Wisdom of China and India*, 205
Wolfe, B. D., 224
Wolfe, T., 147, 153
*Wonder That Was India*, 46
*Wonderful World of Dance*, 201
Wood, R. C., 250
Wooldridge, S. W., 242
Woolf, V., 130, 185
*Words and Their Ways in English Speech*, 253
*Words and Things*, 252
*Words and Ways of American English*, 254
Wordsworth, W., 159, 162
*Works and Days*, 33
*World Almanac*, 279
*World Drama*, 169
*World History of the Dance*, 202
*World of Copernicus*, 172
*World of Humanism*, 222
*World of Mathematics*, 272
*World of Odysseus*, 35
*World of Plant Life*, 266

*World of Rome*, 42
*World of the Inca*, 61
*World of the Thibaults*, 113
*World of Washington Irving*, 180
*World Population and Production*, 284
*Worldly Philosophers*, 236
*Worlds Beyond the Horizon*, 242
*World's Great Religious Poetry*, 214
*World's Great Thinkers*, 205
Worth, C. B., 268
Woytinsky, W. S., 284
Wright, C. R., 250
Wright, E. A., 169
Wright, F. L., 199
Wright, G. E., 250
Wright, R., 147, 176
*Writer and His Craft*, 180
*Writing*, 253
*Writings and Buildings*, 199
Wrong, Dennis H., 250
*Wuthering Heights*, 118
Wylie, E., 160

Xenophon, 34

*Yale Review*, 188
*Yankee from Olympus*, 173
*Yearbook of the United Nations*, 284
Yeats, W. B., 160
Yinger, J. M., 249
*You and the Universe*, 265
Young, D., 55
Young, G. F., 76
Young, G. M., 222
*Young Lonigan*, 141
*Young Manhood of Studs Lonigan*, 141
Yourcenar, M., 42

Zabel, M. D., 185
*Zen Buddhism*, 209
Zernov, N., 215
Zimmer, H., 47
Zinsser, H., 268
Zola, E., 106
ZOOLOGY, see BIOLOGICAL SCIENCES
*Zuleika Dobson*, 126
Zurcher, A. J., 230, 283, 284
Zweig, S., 76